Responses Since the Original
Publication of *Victims No Longer*

FROM PROFESSIONALS AND SURVIVOR ORGANIZATIONS

"Accessible, moving, and validating, *Victims No Longer* is a beacon of hope for sexually abused men and their loved ones. Tracking the difficulties boys and men have acknowledging and healing from sexual victimization, Mike Lew's pioneering book has inspired thousands of male survivors of sexual child abuse to face their traumatic past with courage, knowing they are not alone."
>—Richard Gartner, Ph.D., author of *Betrayed as Boys*

"Mike Lew sheds a bright light on the darkness of sexual abuse. With compassion, insight, and deep respect, he conveys essential aspects of the process of healing. . . . Over the years this book has become a touchstone of guidance, hope, and understanding that helps therapists, survivors, and their loved ones develop a common language for healing."
>—Ernesto Mujica, Ph.D.

"Fifteen years ago when *Victims No Longer* was first published, I thought of it as the Bible for Male Survivors of Childhood Sexual Abuse. His book has always been an inspiration to me. It sits on my desk as a reference guide for both myself and my clients."
>—Vicki Polin, M.A., ATR, LCPC, Director and Founder,
>   The Awareness Center

"*Victims No Longer* is the first book I recommend to new clients who are dealing with sexual abuse, and I have repeatedly heard from them how this book must have been written just for them. *VNL* facilitates great insights, and leads to survivors being able to empower themselves to regain control over their lives and stop the victimization cycle."
>—Howard Fradkin, Ph.D., Male Survivor Retreat Chairperson

"*Victims No Longer* is *the* definitive book on men who were abused. I refer other professionals to the book and make it required reading for my clients seeking recovery from their abuse."
>—Joe Amico, M. Div., CAS, CSAC President, National
>   Association for Lesbian and Gay Addiction Professionals

"*Victims No Longer* is *the* classic work for male survivors and their loved ones. It breaks the isolation, shame, and sense of uniqueness that most male survivors struggle with. It is on my recommended reading list for sexual abusers as well, to help them understand the long-term effects of sexual abuse."

—Ken Singer, LCSW, Executive Director, NJ Association for the Treatment of Sexual Abusers

"I witnessed perhaps the most moving testimony to the power of Mike Lew's book when I gave it to a young male student who had determined to return home to confront his mother, who had been his abuser in childhood. The young man literally carried the book with him and never let go of it for three days. It represented for him a truthful and wise presence he needed to hold on to if he were to survive."

—John McDargh, Associate Professor, Religion and Psychology, Boston College

"As an Episcopal priest, I have done considerable counseling over the years with survivors of sexual abuse, particularly clergy abuse. I read the original *Victims No Longer* when it first appeared and found it a wise, compassionate, and very useful resource. I depend upon Mike Lew's insights in my daily work and have benefited greatly from his firm and gentle approach to the sorrowful, complex, and soul-damaging aftermath of abuse. This updated version is timely and much-needed."

—The Reverend Anne C. Fowler, Rector, St. John's Episcopal Church, MA

"Mike Lew has done the impossible by improving on *Victims No Longer*. The second edition continues to be *the* bible in the treatment of male survivors of sexual abuse."

—Jill A. Kuhn, Ph.D., editor of *In Cabin Six: An Anthology of Poetry by Male Survivors of Sexual Abuse*

"The reissuing of this revised and updated edition of Mike's book underscores the lesson of this important work, timely in its origin and current in its perspective: regarding relational integrity, everybody is equally accountable to everyone."

—Roman Paur, Ph.D., Executive Director, Faith Community Learning Resource

"I've probably read this book twenty or thirty times since I bought it. . . . This should be one of the first books you read. [It] mixes male survivors' stories and chapters full of good advice."

—from Men Surviving Web site

"Mike's warmth . . . allowed me to experience feelings and learn new things about myself, as though I was having my own private therapy session across the Atlantic Ocean. As a therapist I can assist men's recovery in many ways, but they also have to do some work of their own. Asking clients to read *Victims No Longer* has brought about dramatic transformations. Mike Lew leads us through our trauma gently and sensitively, allowing us to confront our abuse and take back so much of what we had lost."

—Ian Warwick, Survivors (Sheffield)

"A salvation. . . . Its bright fire of hope lights the way for men to . . . become whole. Miraculously, in just one volume, Mike Lew tackles a taboo, oft-ignored subject and simultaneously starts men on the road to healing."

—Joe Kelly, author of *Dads and Daughters*

"*Victims No Longer* continues to provide male survivors with an awakening that they are not alone, and offers them a sense of belonging, understanding, and a realization that they can move on from being a victim to a survivor."

—Steve Bevan, Survivors Swindon

FROM SURVIVORS

"*Victims No Longer* was recommended to me by my therapist, and it has been a lifesaver. . . . I know I'm not alone, though I always thought I was."

"*Victims No Longer* has given me many tears, memories and pain. It has also given me hope, some understanding and thought."

"What a frightening, yet liberating experience to be reading [*Victims No Longer*]. It's the first thing that's ever helped truly break through the Iron Curtain of loneliness surrounding my abuse."

"*Victims No Longer* . . . helped me through a suicidal depression that at times felt hopeless. Thank you for your remarkable book."

"*Victims No Longer* is just the most wonderful resource. I can't thank you enough for sharing your expertise and compiling those inspirational personal stories from other survivors. Your words have given me such comfort and hope. I really treasure the work you do."

"*Victims No Longer* has challenged me to allow more growth and healing in my own life. . . . Thank you for the freedom you have bestowed upon the many men in the world who never knew they can talk about this issue."

"I was given *Victims No Longer* by a friend in AA who is also a survivor. Your book 'rocked my world' . . . quite literally!"

"A very well-written and a powerful book. . . . I found many of the survivors' personal stories very moving, and I can empathise with all of them. . . . I thank you for your words, which have given me much hope and comfort for the future."

"*Victims No Longer* helped me more than any other resource I've found on the subject."

"Your contribution to my life already, through your book, has changed me forever."

"*Victims No Longer* has been so central to me, so very personal and close."

"*Victims No Longer* has changed my life."

"This is just a breakthrough for me. Your book is earthshaking to me."

"The reading and rereading of your book was pivotal in helping me to make sense and understand something that is beyond my comprehension. [I] just wanted to make you aware of that and how helpful your book has been in my healing."

"I am a recovered incest survivor. I purchased your book three years ago and it has helped me a great deal in my healing process."

FROM PARTNERS, FAMILY, AND FRIENDS OF SURVIVORS
"As I read *Victims No Longer,* it touched me deeply. I was given much insight into the male perspective of childhood abuse, and the stories shared by the male survivors in the book brought me to tears many times. This gave me more understanding of my husband's mostly unspoken pain and anger, and the impact that being sexually abused in childhood has had on our marriage."

"A godsend . . . a miracle."

"A great help to those seeking resources that would help their efforts on behalf of the survivor. From all the books I have read I realize the great importance of the information that is contained therein."

VICTIMS
NO
LONGER

VICTIMS NO LONGER

The Classic Guide for Men Recovering from
Sexual Child Abuse

SECOND EDITION

MIKE LEW

HARPER

NEW YORK · LONDON · TORONTO · SYDNEY

HARPER

The names that have been changed are those on the survivors' statements, as noted in the text.

Grateful acknowledgment is made for permission to reprint:

"The Hatred of Innocence" by Richard Hoffman. Copyright © 1998 by Richard Hoffman. Reprinted by permission of the author.

Selected excerpts from *The Prince of Tides* by Pat Conroy. Copyright © 1986 by Pat Conroy. Reprinted by permission of Houghton Mifflin Company.

Selection from *The Survivor's Suite* by Keith Jarrett. Copyright © 1977 by Keith Jarrett. Reprinted by permission of ECM Records.

HarperCollins books may be purchased for educational, business, or sales promotional use. For information please write: Special Markets Department, HarperCollins Publishers Inc., 10 East 53rd Street, New York, NY 10022.

A previous edition was published by Perennial Library in 1990.

First Quill edition published 2004.

Designed by Joseph Rutt

Library of Congress Cataloging-in-Publication Data

Lew, Mike.
     Victims no longer : the classic guide for men recovering from sexual child abuse / by Mike Lew.—2nd ed., rev. and updated Quill ed.
          p. cm.
     "This revised edition contains new content, Focuses, and Statements"—Introd.
     Includes index.
     ISBN 0-06-053026-X
     1. Adult child sexual abuse victims—Psychology. 2. Incest victims—Psychology.
3. Boys—Abuse of—Psychological aspects. 4. Male sexual abuse victims—Psychology.
5. Self-help techniques. 6. Adult child sexual abuse victims—United States—Psychology. I. Title.

HV6570.2.L48 2004
362.79'4—dc22   2003062225

13 14 15 NMSG/RRD 20 19 18 17 16 15

To my colleagues who care,
To the memory of abuse victims who were overcome by the struggle,
And to all survivors as they recover and flourish,
I dedicate this book with respect and admiration.

CONTENTS

ACKNOWLEDGMENTS

It is impossible to give adequate thanks to the many individuals who provided me with information, help, advice, encouragement, solace, and understanding during the writing of (and revisions to) *Victims No Longer*. The book would not exist without them. I am grateful for the part that each has played in my life.

I must begin by acknowledging the loss of five heroes who died since the original publication of *Victims No Longer:*

Ian Bennett of Christchurch, a founder and shining spirit of the male survivor movement in New Zealand.

Tom Economus, founder and driving force of The Linkup organization for survivors of clergy abuse.

Fay Honey Knopp, founder of the Safer Society Program and Press, crusader, mentor, and force of nature.

Peter Salgo, lawyer, social worker, guardian and protector of children.

Dan Sexton, creator of the Survivors of Childhood Abuse Program and stalwart of the National Child Abuse Hotline.

The world is diminished by their deaths, as it was enriched by their lives. I am awed by their contributions, spirit, and courage. They, and others who devoted their lives to healing humanity, left the world better than they found it. I honor them. I miss them.

I have been fortunate in having had more than my share of outstanding teachers, mentors, and friends. The late Professor Carol Fisher of Syracuse University demonstrated that it is possible to push students to the limits of their intellectual and critical capacities without loss of kindness, humanity, or humor. Professor H. Daniel Smith, of the same institution, shared unstintingly his love of learning and openness to the great traditions of Eastern and Western cultures. The late Dr. Margaret Mead continually challenged, frustrated, confused, frightened, bullied, teased, and encouraged me to be more than I believed I was—and kept on demonstrating that popularizing a subject leads to wider availability of information. The late Dr. Colin M. Turnbull expressed his deep love of humankind in all its diversity—in the beauty of his writing and the generosity with which he encouraged a young graduate student. Professor Joan Phillips Gordon took a chance on me, and kept taking chances on "nontraditional" students and teachers. And my friend and colleague Professor Shalom Endleman, for more years than seems possible, steadfastly helped me navigate academic and professional shoals. I shall always be grateful to all of them.

Friendships are measured by the ability to applaud your friends' victories, celebrate their joys, and remain steadfast through hard times. By this yardstick, I have been extremely fortunate in having friends and colleagues who stayed the course during dark times, and never failed to provide light when it was most needed.

It is no longer possible to separate friend from colleague. Knowing them all has enriched my life. Many thanks, in many diverse ways, to: Jim Acosta, Kathi Aguero, Sam Allen, Ayal Armon, Jon Arterton, Jeanne Axler, Bob Balfour, Chris Balfour, Euan Bear, Terry Bednall, Steve Bevan, Lenore Blake, Ron Blake, Sandra Bloom, Mario Bourgeois, Brian Brock, Rebecca Bruyn, Craig Campbell, Hervé Canals, Ken Clearwater, Nina Corwin, Mary Susan Convery, John Crowe, Cynthia Crowner, Richard Curen, Laura Davis, Ed DeVos, Lisa Diaz, David Donovan, Susan Freireich, Seth Frohman, Charles Fuller, Richard Gartner, Ed Gebhart, Mark Gianino, Doug Goldschmidt, Ellen Greenhouse, Jim Hickey, Ellen Highfield, Alastair Hilton, Rafi Hoch, Richard Hoffman,

Jim Hopper, Claire Hurst, Brenda Ioris, John Jamieson, Geneviève Joublin, Joel Kasow, Libby Keller, Colin Knox, Polly Kornblith, Felix Kramer, Bob Lamm, Carol Lamm, Chuck Latovich, Rochelle Lefkowitz, Barbara Lerner, Hank Lerner, Injy Lew, Jason Lew, Janet Lewis, Peggy Marengo, Randy Marinez, John McDargh, Ricky McQuillan, Patrick Meyer, Peter Milne, Marcie Mitler, Naoko Miyaji, Robin Moulds, Ernesto Mujica, Linda Naef, Paul Nagano, Alexis Neophytides, Andreas Neophytides, Peggy Pahl, Roberta Pasternack, Helen Percy, Nash Perkins, Mikele Rauch, Peggy Rauch, Rose Rauch, Sol Rauch, John Reine, Avi Rose, Cindy Rosenbaum, Kathy Samon, David Savitz, Judy Schechtman, Andrea Simon, Ken Singer, Jim Sliker, Seymour Slive, Fred Small, Alison Smith, Joan Sokoloff, Martin Sokoloff, Andrea Soler, Larry Spindel, Lynn Thornton, Les Wall, Ian Warwick, Helene Wong, and Dan Zupan.

Particular thanks to Thom Harrigan, Steve Klarer, and Zoya Slive for the many hours they devoted to reading the manuscript in its roughest form and providing me with careful, thoughtful comments—liberally interspersed with hugs. For similar help and support with the revisions, I thank Anne Fowler, Thom Harrigan (again and always), and Richard Hoffman. You didn't make it easier, but it is infinitely better because of you. The same goes for my computer mavens, John Hallum and Steve Klarer.

My literary agent, Charlotte Raymond, has been steadfast in her enthusiasm for this project. Thanks for putting up with me and for coming up with the wonderful cover photo.

Thanks, too, to Peter Nevraumont for suggesting the writing of this book, and to my original publishers, Peter Nevraumont and Ann Perrini, for their gentleness and patience while guiding a fledgling writer in the right direction—and their optimism when I was most discouraged. I have benefited from the skills of the other editors who worked on various incarnations of this book—Janet Goldstein, Peternelle van Arsdale, and my current editor, Christine Walsh.

Special thanks to my loving "mob" in Western Australia and the Northern Territory: "The Perth Four": psychologists Jonathan Kester and Anna Wright, art therapist Elissa Livingstone Kester, and social worker Prem Tej Sacha—activists all; the amazing Maria De Ionno and Tony Franklin in Darwin; and Ken Hampton in Alice Springs. Your efforts were heroic.

To my New Zealand "mates," and my dedicated friends and colleagues in the U.K. You know who you are—I hope you know how much I value you.

I thank my parents, May and Gerson Lew, who, well into their nineties, continue to rise to the occasion—and the rest of my sprawling extended family (especially the little ones).

Thanks to all the past and present members of the "Soup Group," for years of wisdom, support, and sanity.

I apologize to anyone I may have inadvertently omitted from this list. All of you enrich my life. You are responsible for the success of this book; its shortcomings are my responsibility alone.

T.W.—through the years—in hard times and good times—my thanks and my love.

Finally, my thanks to my clients and to survivors everywhere who continue to teach me about life, love, and recovery.

PREFACE TO THE SECOND EDITION

I recently spent a month in Australia, conducting workshops for male survivors and trainings for professionals in diverse parts of that amazing country. I returned to the United States exhausted, jet-lagged, exhilarated, impressed, saddened, enriched, deeply moved, and very encouraged. During my first weeks back I thought of little else, and even my dreams were filled with images of events of that month—especially of the many impressive people I had the privilege of meeting during this all-too-brief adventure.

There are two reasons for writing about Australia in this new preface. First, my mind is filled with things Australian, and—at least for the moment—there's not room for much else. Second, in many ways the situation in "OZ" parallels the growth of the male survivor recovery movement in the United States, Canada, United Kingdom, Ireland, New Zealand, and elsewhere.

Throughout the world one can find many examples of how severely children are harmed. (On July 30, 2002, *ABC Evening News* reported the rape of a nine-month-old baby in South Africa. It included the statistic that, in that country, a child is raped every eight minutes. The South African doctor interviewed for this report attributed much of the problem to a widely held belief that sex with a three- to five-year-old child will cure HIV/AIDS.)

Fortunately, there are also abundant manifestations of courage, strength, and healing. The situation in Australia is neither typical nor extreme. Issues raised in this book are not unique to the United States or the English-speaking world. I am using Australia as an example of how, although sociocultural attitudes about masculinity, sexual child abuse, and recovery differ throughout the world, there is great overlap and some aspects appear to be universal.

A series of fortuitous events led to my spending September 2002 in parts of Australia I hadn't visited before—Western Australia and the Northern Territory. In Perth, Western Australia, we offered an evening talk open to the public, a two-day training for professionals who work with men, a daylong recovery workshop for male survivors, and, for the first time anywhere, a daylong workshop called "Training the Trainers" for professionals interested in offering workshops and groups for male survivors of sexual child abuse. In Darwin, Northern Territory, there were also workshops, trainings, and a public talk. And the organizers even managed to pull off a two-day training in the town of Alice Springs in Central Australia (population ca. 25,000).

As a result of these events, many seeds have been planted. It looks like there will be further exciting adventures in OZ. More on these later.

I arrived in an Australia that was dealing with recent revelations of widespread sexual child abuse by clergy of several denominations (and cover-ups of violations by high-ranking church officials), similar to the environment I had just left in the United States. Each day newspapers, television, and radio carried stories of accusations of child abuse by Roman Catholic and Anglican priests and nuns, Jehovah's Witnesses, and others. Reports of generations of clergy sexual abuse of Aboriginal children were added to the other atrocities and injuries committed by the dominant culture against indigenous communities. Most of these stories closely replicate the disclosures of recent years in the Northern Hemisphere.

Similar to the situation in other countries, there is great cause for concern, but also reason for hope and optimism.

On the negative side, one still finds denial and minimization of the scope and severity of sexual abuse of children—and lack of understanding of boyhood victimization:

> The *bloke* culture of Australian *machismo* keeps many boys and men silent about abuse they have suffered.

Churches and other institutions continue to abdicate responsibility for harm committed by their representatives—often attacking rather than supporting victims, survivors, and their allies. (For example, despite active outreach and offers of group discounts for their staff, one Catholic diocese refused even to authorize distribution to its parishes of information about the trainings and workshops.)

Hurtful stereotypes about male survivors occasionally appear in the media, and homophobia continues to cloud the issues and impede recovery.

An Australian psychologist told me of a high incidence of anal gonorrhea in boys and girls admitted to his local hospital.

Notwithstanding these outrages and horrors, there is reason for hope. Despite all the discouragement and misinformation about boyhood victimization:

The male survivor events and resources that are evolving from them generated significant media interest. Five radio interviews—three local and two national (including one on the all-Aboriginal CAAMA network)—and three newspaper articles increased public awareness and supplied male survivors with information about resources.

A number of organizations have been created to provide resources and support to survivors in general and to male survivors specifically. Not only are some men's organizations addressing the concerns of survivors, many groups that traditionally provided services only to women are now starting to offer similar resources to men. (Among those who participated in my trainings were staff members of Sexual Assault Centres and Domestic Violence Programs.)

Those who attended the professional trainings included not only therapists and counselors but prison personnel, probation officers, police, medical doctors, nurses, occupational and physical therapists, clergy, lawyers, workers in homeless shelters and youth centres, teachers and students.

Men who participated in the recovery workshops came from a range of age, race, ethnicity, and background. They included doctors, lawyers, psychologists, counselors, mining engineers, farmers, bikers, occupational therapists, businessmen, and students. They all displayed impressive courage, commitment, and caring.

In Alice Springs, the Salvation Army gave us the use of their meeting hall for the trainings in exchange for allowing two of their staff to attend.

The organizers of the events in Perth are already planning further workshops and trainings, next time to include a residential weekend recovery workshop for male survivors.

Professionals in Perth and Darwin are now offering groups for male survivors.

Support and networking groups for people who work with male survivors have been started in all three locations—with at least two meeting in Perth.

Organizers of the trainings in Darwin and Alice Springs are talking of next year's trainings being expanded from two days to three.

Some Aboriginal health services and other organizations are producing culturally sensitive informational publications about sexual abuse and recovery—and are looking for the best ways to fund recovery resources.

As I said earlier, seeds were sown. Although there wasn't time to expand the scope of the trainings and workshops this year, new interest has been expressed for 2003 and 2004 by people in the states of South Australia, New South Wales, and Queensland.

Most exciting of all, we are working with members of Aboriginal groups to create culturally relevant trainings to help indigenous people work with child victims and adult survivors within their own communities.

Individuals are speaking up and taking power on many levels. On this trip I met male survivors who stood up to abusers, protected younger siblings, and took perpetrators to court. I heard from men who changed careers, locations, and relationships to better reflect their recovered sense of self and possibility. I heard people's thoughtful, caring statements about themselves, their loved ones, other survivors, and the world. Here are some examples:

- The male survivor workshop in Perth was held on September 10th. During the lunch break we all gathered at an Italian restaurant, seated at one long table. The conversation, of course, turned to the horrors of September 11th of the previous year, and then to the Australians' fears that the saber-rattling of the Bush administration would lead to large-scale war. One of the men, a mining engineer, turned to me and said softly, "I hope Americans find a safe way to grieve." I felt understood, cared about, and challenged.

- An Aboriginal woman who participated in the Darwin trainings said that this was the first time she hadn't fallen asleep during a training session. When one of her coworkers observed that the colleague had never known her to ask questions or make a comment in a professional setting, she replied that this was the first time she "felt equal enough."

- Minh Lam, a young Vietnamese-born Australian reporter who interviewed me for an article in the *Western Australian* newspaper, asked many insightful questions about male survivor issues, concluding the interview with a question I'd never been asked in quite this way. He asked me, "What do you get out of it?" With that phrasing, he shifted the usual emphasis of the question ("Isn't it overwhelming work?" "Don't you get depressed?" "How can you stand it?"), and invited me to talk about the joys of doing this work—especially the strength, courage, and creativity of survivors and their allies.

- A medical doctor, a general practitioner, told me that part of the reason he attended the trainings was in the hope that he would receive information to help him open a dialogue with a male survivor relative—and finally be able to offer him support in his recovery.

• The ever-impressive Maria De Ionno, a self-described "Italian grand-mother," when I asked her why she put so much effort into organizing these events—which were unlikely to break even financially—said, "It's not enough just to work. I guess I always need a cause."

• Ken Hampton, the Alice Springs organizer I mentioned earlier, is Aboriginal, a forty-year-old father of five, counselor, survivor, activist, and a member of Australia's Stolen Generations. In keeping with government policy, he was taken from his mother at birth and raised by a German family. ("By the 1930s assimilation was policy. Children were to be taken away from their parents so they could be forced to adopt non-indigenous culture. They were forbidden to speak indigenous languages and separated from their families and heritage. Aboriginal spokespeople say that community service workers continue to take children away from Aboriginal parents even today, often without consulting the community." [*Northern Territory News,* Darwin, September 17, 2002, pp. 20–21.] This official policy—and its results—are poignantly portrayed in the Australian film *Rabbit Proof Fence.*)

Despite these and other abuses he suffered, Ken survived and thrived. He told me that when he first saw *Victims No Longer* he was destitute, but knew he had to have the book—so he stole it. Seeing where that theft has led him makes it the finest crime I can imagine. He is not only reaching out to Aboriginal survivors as a counselor but is actively involved in organizing services for his *mob* (slang for "group" or "people"). Further, he is using his painfully gained insights to help hone his skills and create a bridge between his indigenous people and white Australian society.

Ken is a loving, attentive father, and I value the time I got to spend with him, his partner, Yvette, and their three sons, Yarran, Murrandah, and Amos. I was moved to tears when Ken told me, "If not for your book, my three *littlies* [Aussie slang for "children"] wouldn't have a bloody father." I can think of no finer appreciation, nor any better reason for having written this book.

When I told Ken that I believe he has the potential to become an important leader of his people (a sentiment shared by others who have met him), he responded with characteristic modesty, "But

I'm just one bloke." I replied, "So were Gandhi and Martin Luther King." The possibility is there. One individual can change the world. Ken is one of many brave, caring, powerful, charismatic survivors throughout the world, dedicated to changing the ways we interact with one another and treat our children.

These were just some of the many examples of reasons to be optimistic about the future of recovery in Australia. They are repeated in many forms—again and again—in every country. I'm encouraged. With people this powerful and thoughtful, everywhere, committed to understanding, healing, and creating a healthier world, how can things fail to improve?

My sense of hope and encouragement isn't limited to Australia:

• In New Zealand I met a grandfather (a butcher by trade) whose life mission is raising public awareness of male survivor issues and creating resources for healing.

• I've met male survivors in active recovery who are Native Americans, Canadian First Nations People, Maoris, Australian Aborigines, Hassidic Jews, Muslims, Buddhists, Hindus, Protestants, Catholics, Atheists, Caucasians, Latinos, Africans and African-Americans, South Asians, Norwegians, and many more.

• I've spoken with individuals and groups, survivors and professionals who are creating brilliant, innovative resources for male survivors in Canada, England, Australia, Japan, and especially New Zealand.

When I was a boy my goal in life was to meet everyone in the world. At the time it seemed to be a perfectly reasonable dream. When I realized that it couldn't happen—and even if it were possible, the quality of the relationships wouldn't be very deep—I was severely disappointed. But my life has seen that dream realized in a more profoundly satisfying form than I could have hoped. I am fortunate to have a job that involves frequent travel; everywhere I go I meet amazing people—interesting, creative, courageous, and brilliant. It's pretty close to my boyhood dream.

Most of the questions I am asked by survivors—and by their allies—

boil down to one question: Is recovery possible? Nothing I have experienced in the past fifteen years has changed my mind about the answer. Is recovery possible? Absolutely. How do I know? I have the evidence. Every day I encounter men and women who are actively and successfully engaged in recovery from the effects of sexual child abuse. They are from all over the world and all backgrounds, ages, and stations of life. Yes, recovery is real and it matters. *You matter.* It is still a long, difficult, and often painful process, but it is possible and the results justify the struggle. The pain diminishes and the survivor moves from surviving to thriving.

Another question I am frequently asked is, "What do you mean by recovery?" It has taken me a while to answer that one. I had been depending on other people's definitions of recovery until I developed one that worked for me (just as you must come to one that makes sense for you). Mine is simple. For me, it is about freedom. *Recovery is the freedom to make choices in your life that aren't determined by the abuse.* The specific choices will be different for each of you; the freedom to choose is your birthright.

Once again, I thank you for confirming my basic optimism about the nature of human beings. We must keep reaching for one another's humanity—and for our own.

INTRODUCTION TO THE SECOND EDITION

At first, I didn't get it. Why were my editors, agent, and others insisting that this revised edition of *Victims No Longer* requires a new introduction? After all, I reasoned, most people who pick up this book will be doing so for the first time, and will need the same introduction to the material as past readers. Survivors who are new to recovery struggle with massive levels of fear, shame, and confusion. They (perhaps *you*) are looking for information, resources, and answers. But they are also in need of something more important—something they may not even know they are seeking: reassurance, encouragement, and respect. The introduction is a logical place to try to find it. The same is true for people who are in relationships with male survivors; they need to know that there will be an end to the pain—that life can and will get better—for their loved ones and for themselves.

If you are a reader who is well along in your healing and are returning to this book to see how it speaks to you now, I'm sure you wouldn't mind a little encouragement and reassurance as well. It never hurts to receive confirmation that you're doing well. In addition to reassurance, however, you are probably interested in learning how things have developed since you first began your recovery process. You may be interested in reading about recent changes in thinking about male recovery. You may want to locate resources that weren't previously available to you. And you may be looking for guidelines about the next step in your continuing recovery. I hope this introduction, and the material that follows it, will help you accomplish those goals.

If you have a professional interest in this subject, or just want to learn more about male survivors—or if you aren't quite sure about why you chose to read this book—I welcome your interest and hope that what you find in these pages will increase your understanding and empathy.

Although encouragement about the reality of recovery seemed to me to be enough, those who advocated for a completely new introduction argued for more. They said that there have been many changes over the past fifteen years. The introduction, they suggested, should outline the current issues concerning sexual child abuse and recovery for male survivors. In that context, they asked me to write about changes in the climate of discussion about sexual abuse of boys and men, the wider acceptance of the reality of male victimization, the global scope of the problem, the backlash that survivors have endured, the increasing numbers of men stepping forward to acknowledge and resolve their boyhood traumas, and to discuss the ongoing effects of sexual child abuse, the shame and fear felt by victims and survivors, and the issue of sexual abuse by clergy.

I argued that, while these are all important topics, it would be unrealistic to attempt to present them adequately in an introduction. They are all addressed in the body of the book. If they could be distilled into a sentence or two, there would be no need for a whole book—an article would be sufficient.

It took me a while to appreciate that both views are correct, and to agree to write a fresh introduction that incorporates necessary bits of the original into the new material.

Rereading the original introduction led me to agree that a new one is necessary. Things are indeed different now from fifteen years ago. The original introduction traced my initial search for information that would help me understand some of my clients, and how that search led to my writing the first book for male survivors. It was written in a social and therapeutic environment that had barely begun to address sexual victimization of girls and recovery for female survivors. It was a time of widespread resistance to acknowledging the sexual victimization of boys and men—let alone the existence of female perpetrators. I wrote of the almost total lack of resources for male survivors during the late 1980s, and the parallel absence of accurate clinical information for professionals.

We still face significant obstacles to preventing sexual child abuse and meeting the recovery needs of survivors and their allies, but there is no doubt that we have made significant progress. One would have to have been living in a cave to be unaware of the reality of sexual child abuse and even of the sexual victimization of boys. The old introduction offers historical perspective but doesn't reflect where we are today. I'm considering posting parts of the original introduction on my Web site to provide reassurance during discouraging moments. It might contradict feelings of hopelessness that things will ever improve. To see what I mean, take a look at an old copy of this book.

When I reread this book in preparation for revising it, it came as a relief that most of the material it contains is still relevant (it meant that I had less work to do). Relief was quickly followed by sadness that most of it is still relevant after fifteen years (there is so much work left to do). I'm gratified that so many survivors continue to find *Victims No Longer* helpful with their recovery, and profoundly disappointed that there remains such great need for this information.

Although this is a brand-new introduction, there are three important items from the first edition preface that need to be included here:

1. Please do not attempt to read this book in one sitting. There is too much powerful content. Take your time, read it slowly, bit by bit, so that you don't get overwhelmed. You may find it better not to read the book at night, or when you are alone. It helps to have someone (therapist, friend, partner, another survivor) with whom you can talk about it.

2. I have been criticized for not including information for survivors who are also abusers. I wrote this book for *nonoffending* male survivors, reflecting my area of experience. I have not worked extensively with perpetrators, and must leave the topic of offender-survivors to the experts. This does not mean that I believe these individuals don't need and deserve attention. (Just as the fact that I don't work with children doesn't mean that children don't merit help—simply that I don't have much professional experience with them.) I am appreciative of the letters I receive from survivors who are also perpetrators, including several who found *Victims No Longer* personally helpful. I wish them every success in their recovery from abusing and from having been

abused, and I continue to believe that no one can recover from abuse while abusing another person.

3. In the first edition of *Victims No Longer* I invited readers to write or call me with their reactions, and I replied to every letter and returned all phone messages. However, I underestimated the volume of response to the book and overestimated my ability to handle it. I still invite your letters and e-mail messages. I will read them all and learn from them, but I am not able to provide a personal reply to each. I will continue to be available to come to your local area for survivor workshops, professional trainings, and public talks whenever people have the interest, energy, and resources to organize them. To make arrangements, contact:

    The Next Step Counseling and Training
    PO Box 1146, Jamaica Plain, MA 02130, USA
    Phone: (617) 277-7172
    E-mail: nextstep.counseling@verizon.net
    Web site: www.victimsnolonger.org

    The Web site includes periodic updates of resources for survivors and professionals, links to other helpful sites, a long bibliography, a calendar of upcoming events, and an occasional column where I write about various matters that I hope you will find helpful or interesting.

A lot has improved, and sometimes we take these improvements for granted as we concentrate on all that is still needed. More than fifteen years ago I was one of three therapists who met in Cambridge, Massachusetts, to talk about abuse and recovery—and to try to locate and share the meager information that was available. At this writing, our "Soup Group" is much larger and still meeting monthly. Many such groups are now meeting throughout the United States and abroad. There has been a parallel growth of resources for survivors. In fact, there is so much more information and support available that a time traveler from only ten years ago would be amazed.

But this book wasn't written for those who have successfully negotiated their difficult journey of healing. I wrote *Victims No Longer* as a handbook of recovery for men who experienced boyhood incest or other sexual child abuse—and for the people who care about them. My initial goals haven't changed:

> To provide as much information as possible to as many people as possible about a subject that is still ignored as often as possible

> To present a framework within which male survivors can explore and share their experiences

> To reassure readers that they can recover from the effects of sexual child abuse

> To promote discussion about the nature of recovery

> To share experiences (mine and others') of what has been helpful to men in their recovery

> To provide specific resources to male survivors, the professionals who work with them, and the people who love them

> To invite the reader to join with other men in a shared odyssey of recovery.

The first time I used the term "odyssey" to describe the recovery process, my editor, Peter Nevraumont, responded, "I think this word is a key one . . . the word has many pertinent, positive connotations. Odyssey meaning voyage of discovery of a problem that has been hidden and discovery by the victims that they are not alone. Odyssey meaning heroic journey *in* (to the psyche) requires as much if not more bravery than a journey *out* (to the external unknown). Odyssey meaning journey of considerable length; the odyssey you are proposing is not like a trip to the corner for a quart of milk. The odyssey you are proposing requires strength of character, curiosity, a sense of adventure, and a willingness to stick with it. Odyssey is an accurate metaphor for what you have set out to accomplish in your book."

During the years since Peter wrote those words, I have learned a great deal from survivors in recovery. Nothing I've learned, however, has diminished my belief in the difficulty and importance of this heroic undertaking. Neither has it lessened my respect for the courageous men who embark upon this odyssey. Indeed, my admiration for all survivors (and those who stand with them) has only increased with time.

This journey is not easy or simple. You may begin with no more than a faint idea of what you hope to accomplish, and not the least clue as to how to go about it. Eventually, your work gathers momentum, and at times you feel that you have no life apart from recovery. When not specifically engaged in therapy, you find yourself thinking about abuse recovery, talking about it, meeting other survivors, and listening to their experiences. For a while, everything you hear, see, read, or do is viewed through a very specific lens—awareness of abuse and recovery. Every conversation seems to turn to the topic of sexual abuse; those that don't focus on these issues may seem irrelevant to you.

You experience periods of confusion; at other times you feel totally overwhelmed. You find yourself wondering how you dared to take on such a painful effort, and whether you will ever "get it right."

But recovery is not only about difficulty and frustration. At times your recovery will seem to have acquired an exhilarating momentum of its own. You begin to understand the connections between what was done to you as a child and the difficulties you have been facing since. You develop fresh insight into your relationships, and change some of your self-defeating behaviors. Each new piece of information, insight, and interaction provides another helpful piece of the puzzle—eventually creating a coherent, informative picture. Despite periods of dejection and hopelessness, you experience occasions of elation—when you know you are on the right track.

In the course of your voyage of discovery—as in a classical odyssey—you will traverse a varied landscape, encountering "monsters" and "heroes." As you make contact with other survivors and allies, and tell them about your life, you hear stories of startling power: histories of physical violence, neglect, emotional and sexual abuse that may leave you crying, shaking—or numb. Your emotions will be "all over the map." You are moved by the courage, intelligence, and creativity with which survivors (like you and your loved ones) negotiate their lives: The children who were forced to create their own explanations of irrational, abusive situations—who figured out how to survive in the absence of accurate information, support, encouragement, and love. And the adult survivors—often feeling as though they were clinging to a cliff edge by their fingernails—hanging on to their intuitive understanding that healthy humans treat one another with respect, thoughtfulness, and cooperation—hanging on to the hope of someday experiencing that kind of relationship. Like me, you will be impressed by survivors' success in pulling together the pieces of their lives. The more you hear their stories, the greater your respect for them grows— and eventually you come to understand that you are equally impressive and deserving of the same respect.

I don't expect you to believe all of what I am saying, but if you continue with your recovery, I have no doubt that you will come to agree with most of it. Try it. Do your own work, trust your judgment, and see for yourself. Your life can and *will* improve. Much of what is contained in this book reflects my admiration for what male survivors have accomplished; the responses I receive from readers validate this perspective.

This book isn't for everyone. I aimed to create a resource for male survivors and the people involved with them. It is not a work of scholarly research. It quotes few statistics and contains no footnotes. Others have produced academic treatises on boyhood sexual trauma. (Readers interested in technical, academic, or statistically oriented material can refer to the expanded bibliography on my Web site.)

I tried to present information in "plain English" so that it would be accessible to the widest possible readership. Given the vast scope of the subject matter, I had to be selective about what was included. *Victims No Longer* doesn't contain everything that can be known about abuse and recovery. We are learning more all the time. The material presented in this book will continue to be written and rewritten by many individuals with many different perspectives—survivors and allies, professionals and non-professionals—as our understanding grows.

The following pages contain much of what I have found to be true about sexual child abuse and recovery. There is a great deal of information and a great many suggestions. I hope the information is helpful and the suggestions are practical, but you must make that determination yourself. What is in this book is neither law nor gospel. Please select what is useful to you and ignore the rest. It is clear to me that different pieces of information speak to survivors at different points in their recovery. The information in this book comes from a wide variety of sources. It provides a rich banquet. I encourage you to consume it slowly, not moving on to another course before you are ready.

As a therapist, my primary interest is recovery. For this reason, I don't waste time arguing about (or trying to prove) the existence of the sexual abuse of boys. It happens. This book addresses the effects of that abuse and ways to recover from them. In every chapter, you will find words of encouragement and suggestions for recovery.

Some themes receive special emphasis. Among these are issues concerning *trust, isolation, shame,* and *intimacy.* They are given specific attention because understanding them is crucial to survivors.

While I have tried to be as accurate as possible, *Victims No Longer* necessarily reflects my personal philosophies and biases. This is not a neutral book; I hope it is not dispassionate. I am passionately committed to the prevention of, and recovery from, sexual child abuse. I have no patience with child abusers or apologists for child abuse. I believe that there is a great deal wrong with a society that allows individuals to profit at the expense of children. I believe we have a long way to go to create a world where child abuse is unknown and unthinkable—and I believe we can accomplish it.

There are other ways that this book isn't for everyone. Some people remain in deep denial about the existence of boyhood sexual abuse. They will interpret this book as fiction or exaggeration. It is neither. There are individuals and groups who resist what this book has to say because acceptance would necessitate change—involving loss of their power and privilege. Choosing to remain comfortably ignorant of the pain and suffering one causes (or condones) constitutes another form of abuse.

Abusive childhoods isolate victims in a number of ways. Some survivors never learned to read, or cannot sustain a long-enough attention span. Others are so mired in hopelessness that they can't believe that anything will do any good, or they have been so badly hurt in boyhood that they need treatment far beyond the scope of a "self-help" book. And there are some for whom the information is still too immediate or painful to approach.

But you have picked up this book. You're looking for something, and a part of you—however small—knows that things aren't completely hopeless. By reading about the experiences and feelings commonly shared by male survivors, you may recognize your own situation. If so, you will find yourself in good company on the road to recovery.

The following chapters present information in several different ways. When writing about theory or general matters, I often use the somewhat neutral third person. However, when relating personal experience or the specifics of recovery, I attempt to speak directly to "you," the reader. I sometimes repeat or rephrase material I consider particularly important, or when it fits into several contexts. Denial and fear surrounding abuse-related issues are so powerful that some information needs to be repeated many times before it is heard.

I try to use pronouns in a conscious way throughout the text. Because this book is about male survivors, I tend to employ the masculine pronouns when referring to survivors. To avoid both sexist assumptions and overdependence on unwieldy phrases like "he or she" and "him/herself," I alternate masculine and feminine pronouns when referring to therapists, partners, family members, friends—and perpetrators. Beyond these intentional idiosyncrasies (and despite the expert help of friends, colleagues and editors), stylistic difficulties reflect the limitations of the author.

Within chapters there are special sections I call **"Focuses."** A Focus is set apart from the main text because it deserves special emphasis, bears repeating, or speaks to a specific experience or group. They vary in length from a paragraph to about a page; their content relates to the chapters in which they are found.

Focus

Victims No Longer: On the Use of the Terms "Victim" and "Survivor"

There are difficulties involved in the use of either of these words when talking about adults recovering from sexual child abuse.

The dictionary definition of "victim" ("one who suffers through no fault of his own; one who is made to suffer by persons or forces beyond his control") is an accurate description of the reality of childhood sexual abuse. But the word also suggests an emotional image of hopelessness and helplessness.

While this may have been true at the time of the original abuse, it is by no means reflective of your present situation. Regardless of how you feel about yourself, or how severely abuse has wounded you, you are a strong, creative individual. You had the ability to survive to this point, and now you have the ability and the resources to recover. That doesn't sound like a victim, does it? Therefore, in this book I shall try to use "victim" only when referring to the condition of the child at the time of the actual abuse.

There are similar limitations with the term "survivor," which evokes pictures of people clinging to flotsam while their ship sinks, or hanging by their fingernails from a cliff edge. While this might be an accurate description of the *feelings* of the person who was sexually abused, it neglects the reality that *survival isn't enough*.

Survival means enduring until something better comes along. Recovery involves learning to live a satisfying life—to *thrive* instead of merely survive. But, for now, "survivor" is the best word we have, and I use it until something better comes along. (Some people have suggested Adults Molested As Children [AMAC], but that feels even more passive to me than "survivor.") In this book, "survivor" refers to an adult who was sexually abused as a child. But we must always be aware that survival is a *temporary* state, one that will be replaced by something better.

Placed between some chapters are personal accounts, or **"Statements,"** by adult male survivors relating their own experiences. I provided only the most general guidelines to the men who wrote these Statements. For most, I suggested they include some combination of: (a) something about themselves; (b) something about what was done to them; (c) something about the effects; (d) something they have found useful in recovery; (e) anything they would like to say to other male survivors (who might not know anyone with whom they can talk). These statements are anonymous, identified only by the approximate ages of the authors. Names have been changed to protect each individual's privacy. Editing was kept to a minimum.

As you will see, Statements vary in scope and presentation, ranging in tone from coolly detached to highly emotional, in length from a few paragraphs to several pages. I once saw a television interview with a Hollywood filmmaker (whose name I have unfortunately forgotten, as I'd like to give him credit). When asked about the difference between a "story" and a "plot," he replied that an example of a plot would be, "A man died and then his wife died." An example of a story is, "A man died and then his wife died of a broken heart." The survivors' Statements provide the stories that impart life and intimacy to this book. I am extremely grateful to the men who shared their experiences, ideas, and feelings so courageously and powerfully.

This revised edition contains new content, Focuses, and Statements. There is a new chapter about clergy abuse, rewritten and updated sections on groups and workshops, and some new material about therapeutic techniques and the "backlash." The Resources sections include an updated bibliography and list of support organizations worldwide. This edition has four new Focus sections, and three additional Statements by male survivors.

Victims No Longer means a lot to me. Writing it challenged me, taught me, and changed me profoundly. Responses to it have been humbling and moving. I have high hopes for this book:

That it validates and honors the accomplishments of readers who are well along in their recovery

That it helps those who care about male survivors to understand, appreciate, and support them in their recovery

That, if you are new to healing the wounds of your childhood, you derive guidance and reassurance from its contents.

I offer you this book in a spirit of growth and healing. I hope you will find it a worthwhile companion on your own odyssey of recovery.

—M.L.

Part One

ABOUT ABUSE

1

SEXUAL CHILD ABUSE: MYTHS AND REALITIES

And those that create out of the holocaust
of their own inheritance anything more than a convenient
self-made tomb shall be known as "Survivors."
—Keith Jarrett, THE SURVIVOR'S SUITE

Child abuse. The term has entered our vocabulary with an eerie everyday familiarity. It is an enemy we can all rally against. Good people everywhere unite in condemnation of the few evil, sick individuals who abuse children. We talk confidently about the need to protect our children from these weird, trench-coated strangers who lurk about schoolyards with molestation on their minds. We create programs that teach kids not to accept rides or candy from strangers. We assume we know what child abuse is.

At the same time we create an image of the perfect family. Television shows and movies portray wise, caring fathers and loving, nurturing mothers imparting decent values to their children in an atmosphere of trust and openness. When problems arise, Dad has a fatherly talk with Sonny and gently guides him to the path of reason. Mom sits on the edge of Sis's bed and talks about her own childhood, dispensing motherly wisdom liberally laced with hugs. Or the family sits down together at the dining room table to solve the little problems of childhood through easy communication and folksy stories. We create a fantasy of family life whose problems can be solved within the episode, and then we believe our own creation. We assume that we know what family life is.

WHAT IS ABUSE?

If you have decided to read this book, it is likely that your own experience was dramatically different from this ideal. If you were abused as a child, your memories of family life present another picture. Dad's "fatherly talk" was anything but reasonable, and his guidance far from gentle. Mom's own childhood memories may have been of violence and sexual abuse. And mealtimes were occasions to be endured or avoided. You may remember absent, unavailable or nonprotective parents—unable to help you because they couldn't help themselves. A family evening at home might have included screaming fights, bouts of drunkenness, episodes of physical violence, cowering children hiding in fear, nightmares, tears, confusion, stony silences, unreasonable blame, ridicule, repeated beatings, missed meals, helplessness, attempts to protect a parent or sibling . . . or sexual abuse. Your memories may include not being believed and having no source of protection. You may have little or no detailed memory of your childhood, positive or negative, and wonder why you can't recall those happy times—those "golden childhood years." Some of you pretended it was otherwise, imagining your family as happy, wise, healthy, and harmonious. In this way you attempted to protect yourself from the abuse, holding on to the fantasies as long and as tightly as you could manage until reality forced its way into the picture. You may still find yourself tempted to rewrite your family history to bring it more in line with the way you wish it had been.

As a society and as individuals, the images of family life we've created are pleasant and comforting. It is no wonder we cling to them so fiercely—we defend them against the intrusion of a harsher reality. Even when we are in the midst of an abusive situation, it is often easier to pretend it is otherwise. In fact, your fantasy of an ideal family may have been the only refuge available to you as a child. Realizing this makes it easier to understand a child's insistence—in the face of blatant evidence of abuse—that nothing is wrong. In my clinical practice I have heard many people tell heartrending stories of brutality and violence, only to have them react with surprise when I refer to their childhood as abusive. This begins to make sense only when we combine misinformation about the nature of child abuse with the mythology of perfect family life.

"The Family" is a sacred construct in most cultures. Politicians are elected on the basis of their commitment to Family Values. Educators and clergy decry the "erosion of Family Life." No one is willing to risk violating the sanctity of The Family. Along with the value placed on the family, Americans cherish the concepts of Privacy and Independence.

"A man's home is his castle." Within this castle, the king and queen rule absolutely. Few people are willing to make suggestions as to how children should be raised, let alone interfere with their treatment. It is seen as solely the parents' responsibility. This combination of cultural values leaves parents (who may themselves be products of abusive childhoods) isolated when dealing with the stresses of family life. It creates an environment wherein children (and wives) are seen as property. "Ownership" confers license to treat a child as one wishes.

Our respect for independence and diversity provides leeway for a wide range of parental behavior. The importance we ascribe to individual and family privacy allows some harmful and shocking behavior to go unnoticed (and extremes of abuse to go unreported). Only recently has the need to protect children from abusive parents begun to be recognized. But change is slow and tentative. Interference with the family by child protective agencies is viewed with suspicion.

The reality is that abuse exists. It is real and it is common. It takes many forms, some blatant and others subtler. The spectrum of child abuse ranges from neglect to physical violence. It includes torture, beatings, verbal and psychological maltreatment, child pornography, and sexual abuse (ranging from seductive behavior to rape). Abuse of children is seldom limited to one of these manifestations. Abuse appears in varying combinations, duration, and intensity. All forms have devastating, long-term effects on the child.

In the face of absolute parental authority, a child loses all "adult" rights—to privacy, independence, and even control over his or her body. We continue to maintain the fiction that abusive behavior by those closest to the child is less severe than that which is perpetrated by strangers. Without a doubt, the reverse is true.

Kids are remarkably resilient. With proper support, consistent love, and encouragement, they recover from even the most severe hurts of childhood. When, however, the very individuals who should be crucial to the healing process commit the injuries, where can the child turn? The safety of the world is destroyed and the child is isolated in the abuse. When the perpetrator is a family member, the entire family—even those who are unaware of the abuse—is affected. The relationships between the abused child, the perpetrator, and the other family members become sources of anxiety and confusion.

I have not attempted to provide an exact description of "the abusive family" for two reasons. First, because there is no precise profile of the environment where incest and other forms of child abuse are found. While we can discuss cultural values and social climates that provide a fertile environment for abuse, we can't describe the abusive family with the same precision with which we present the fictional ideal "perfect family."

A second reason for not attempting to spell out the profile of the abusive family is the tendency of survivors to self-eliminate. It is natural to want precise answers and an exact framework within which to work. You may be saying to yourself, "If only he would give me a description of the abusive family, then I could decide whether my situation fits the picture." What a relief to be able to say for certain that it wasn't really abusive—or that your situation wasn't too bad because you didn't experience number seven on a list of characteristics of the abusive family—but such self-exclusion wouldn't be helpful.

If you are a survivor of sexual child abuse, you've spent more than enough time feeling different, excluded, and isolated. Let us include you as we explore a range of possibilities. Let's assume that you are welcome here; whether you have clear and exact memories of years of sexual abuse or only picked up the book because "it might be interesting"—whether your family was chaotic or "seemed so normal"—this book is for you. You have a right to read it, have feelings about it, and use it in any way that helps you take charge of your life.

Focus

Current Effects

Men who participated in a weekend recovery workshop for male and female survivors compiled the following list. The items it contains are in response to the question, "In what ways does childhood sexual abuse continue to affect your adult life?" Not all responses apply to every survivor. I have presented them all, without editing, as the participants listed them.

• Nightmares (intense; violent)

• Fear that everyone is a potential attacker

- Shame

- Anger

- Guilt

- Fear of expressing anger/difficulties in starting to get angry

- Need to be in control

- Need to pretend that I am not in control (helplessness)

- Fear of being seen/fear of exposure/agoraphobia

- Running from people

- Fear of intimacy/running away from intimacy

- "Avoidism"

- Pain and memories of physical pain

- Flashbacks

- Not being able to "think straight"

- Difficulties in communicating

- Intruding thoughts

- Compulsive eating/not eating/dieting/bingeing/purging/etc.

- Self-abuse

- Wanting to die

- Sexual acting out

- Feeling asexual

- Sexual dysfunction

- Feelings of unreality/detachment

- Image of myself as a failure

- Need to be completely competent at all times

- Feeling that "It's my fault."

- Self-doubt/feeling that I'm not good enough

- Jealousy

- Envy

- Feeling inadequate

- Wishing I were someone else

- Inability to receive comfort/nurturing

- Feeling ashamed when I'm complimented

- Low self-esteem

- Keeping unnecessary secrets

- Being "walled in"

- Finding it hard to connect with other people

- Isolation

- Difficulty in expressing vulnerability, being heard, and cared about

- Feeling that "If they know me, they'll reject me."

- Escaping into addictions

- Frozen emotions

- Fear of other people's ulterior motives

- Fear that people will use me

- Inability to say "No."

- Lack of ability to recognize the truth

- Confusion about roles/identity/sexuality

- Ambivalence about wanting to be taken care of

- Fear of authority

- Fear of rules

- Fear of women

- Fear of men

- Fear of speaking out

- Inability to relax

- Disconnection from feelings

- Feeling stuck

- Linking abuse with love

- Forgetting/amnesia about parts of childhood

- Depression

- "Out of body" experiences

- Poor choices of partners

The equation doesn't have to be exact. I invite you to use this book as a context or guide for exploring experiences from your own childhood. As we look at many aspects of abuse, survival, and recovery, take what is helpful to you and leave the rest. As we talk of abusive/dysfunctional/chaotic families, recognize that differences are variations, not reasons for discounting your own experience. You have had hurtful childhood experiences within your family or by other adults who should have protected you. This book is offered as a resource to use in healing those injuries.

How can we justify permitting family members to engage in hurtful behavior that would never be tolerated from strangers? Only by isolating parents in the name of independence, and maintaining a view of the child as property—devoid of feelings and the right to physical or emotional autonomy. Although I have said this before, it is so important that it bears repeating here: Seeing children as property is where the problem starts and is crucial to the whole question of abuse.

There are many theoretical perspectives brought to the question of what constitutes abusive behavior. Personally, I'm not terribly interested in arriving at an exact definition of abuse. I'm more concerned with recovery. As a clinical psychotherapist, I look at the effects of abuse. In the course of working with many survivors, I came to recognize frequent adult manifestations of sexual child abuse. If you come to me with memories, feelings, and/or problems that may have resulted from abuse, my responsibility is to help you to explore and understand how that childhood trauma hurt you and how it continues to affect your adult life. But understanding alone is not enough. The wounds of boyhood sexual abuse must be healed so you can move on to enjoyment of a full and satisfying adult life. I know that recovery is possible. I have seen it happen for survivor after survivor. It isn't quick and it isn't easy, but it is real.

As with my therapy practice and workshops, the purpose of this book is not to analyze or to come up with the definitive theory of abuse, but to talk about effects of sexual child abuse and how to recover from it. Addressing the question of what constitutes abusive behavior toward children, I can sum up my feelings briefly. I believe that children have a right to care and protection. This right is absolute. When anyone who is in a position of greater power—strength, authority, or experience—violates that right in any way, the behavior is abusive. There is no valid justification for the abuse of children. Abuse is never deserved, nor is the child ever responsible. It is only when we recognize as a living reality that children require protection from all forms of abuse—when we incorporate this recognition into the depths of our beings and reflect it throughout our social institutions—will we become a truly healthy society.

DEFINING INCEST

Incest is a particular manifestation of sexual child abuse. The traditional definition of incest is sexual activity between blood relatives. The degree of closeness necessary to constitute an incestuous union has been variously defined by different societies. In all cultures I am aware of, sexual activity between parent and child and between siblings is viewed as incestuous and is prohibited.

The definition of incest I use in my clinical practice (and in this book) is more inclusive. It is shared in large measure by therapists who work with issues of sexual abuse and by support organizations of incest survivors. *Incest is a violation of a position of trust, power, and protection.* Sex between blood relatives is one part of this larger, more inclusive view of incest.

Incest differs from other forms of sexual abuse in that *the perpetrator is assumed to stand in a protective (parental) role to the victim.* The very person the child should be able to turn to for care, comfort, and understanding violates that trust by sexualizing the relationship. For this to be a traumatic experience, it is not necessary that the "parenting" figure be a family member. Children naturally trust adults who are closest to them—until there is reason not to. Sexual exploitation by *any* older caretaker is, by this definition, incestuous because it destroys that natural trust. This is true whether the perpetrator is a relative by blood or marriage, parent, stepparent, older sibling, neighbor, family friend, teacher, member of the clergy, therapist, physician, baby-sitter, camp counselor, or any other caretaker. In all instances the results are similar. The child's world becomes unsafe—confusing and frightening. To survive, the child must make sense of his/her situation.

By focusing on this aspect of boyhood victimization, I have no desire to minimize the results of other types of sexual abuse. No matter who the abuser is, relative or stranger, the effects of sexual abuse on a child are always serious. One of the aims of this book, however, is to look at some of the specific consequences when the perpetrator is someone close to the child—and why these wounds are especially deep and difficult to heal.

The difference between sexual attack by a stranger and sexual attack by a family member (or other adult known by and close to the child) must be seen in context. We are taught from earliest childhood that family and friends are to be trusted. We are warned about the danger of trusting strangers. Home is equated with safety. The message is clear and widely reinforced.

I watched a program of animated cartoons made in the 1940s and 1950s. The themes of these cartoons were surprisingly similar. A youngster (human or animal) strayed from the protection of home and family. In the course of his explorations, he found himself in danger (from the forces of nature or evildoers), only to be rescued at the last minute. The rescuer was usually the youngster's mother, although sometimes the father, both parents, another relative, or family pet played a part. The message conveyed to a child viewing the film is strong and unequivocal: Safety is with the family. Obey the rules. Do what your parents tell you. Stay with what is familiar.

Similarly, in the classic children's film *The Wizard of Oz*, Dorothy returns to the safety of her parental figures, Auntie Em and Uncle Henry, by repeating the phrase "There's no place like home." The enchantments and delights of the outside world are fraught with danger. Protection is found only in the familiar.

Sexual attack by a stranger therefore carries different weight than attack by someone known to the child. We are somewhat more prepared for external dangers. Except in a very general way, the child victim never trusted the stranger in the first place. It is logical for a child who has been attacked by a stranger to turn to family for support, understanding, and nurturing—to begin healing in safety. If it is necessary to retreat from the world into the protection of loved ones, he can do so. The family comforts, encourages, protects, and eventually guides the child back to the larger world. It teaches him to better protect himself and determine a reasonable level of trust.

But what if Mommy or Daddy (or Uncle Henry or Auntie Em) is the attacker? Who does the child trust? Where does he turn for understanding and protection? The closer the relationship of the victim to the perpetrator, the more certain is the loss of trust. This statement refers not simply to a biological relationship but to the emotional connection between the two. The more closely the child victim is tied to the abuser, the more the issue of trust comes into play. The victim of incestuous abuse has to deal not only with the results of a physical act, but the devastation of his ability to trust. If he cannot trust those closest to him, how can it be safe to trust anyone? The ability to trust (and to rebuild after its destruction) is a key issue for survivors. As such, it is a central theme of this book.

SEXUAL CHILD ABUSE IN CONTEXT

"What sort of monster would sexually abuse a little child?"
"Isn't it awful that depraved incestuous families still exist!"
"How widespread is it really?"
"I can't imagine anyone we know doing such a thing."
"That sort of thing only happens among _____."
(Fill in your favorite stereotype.)

"What do you actually mean by sexual abuse?"
"But they seemed like such nice people."
"How could I not have known?"

All these quotes represent the type of questions I am frequently asked. They reflect a general assumption about the nature of sexual child abuse, stemming from widespread ignorance and the difficulty of looking directly at an upsetting subject. Rather than accept a painful and over-whelming reality, people tend to view the sexual abuse of boys as though it were either some extremely rare manifestation of individual pathology or another of the distasteful heathen customs of exotic savages. In their desire to avoid unpleasant realities, human beings resort to doubting, denying, or distancing themselves from ugly truths.

We prefer to believe that "It can't happen here," maintaining our denial at a great cost: the repeated isolation and damage inflicted on millions of young people—yes, millions. Even if we take the more commonly accepted figures about sexual child abuse (about one in three girls and one in ten boys are victims of sexual abuse) and assume that they have been inflated tenfold, we are still talking about millions of children. And it isn't likely that these figures are exaggerated. In fact, current evidence points to a strong possibility that they represent significant underestimation. We are talking about millions of victims, and millions of perpetrators. Who are they? Where are they found? It doesn't take much calculation to realize that we aren't just looking at a few "savages" and "lunatics." The savage and lunatic populations aren't that large, and would be exhausted long before we accounted for those millions of victims and abusers. And we are not look-ing at an isolated phenomenon peculiar to a particular ethnic group, sec-tion of the country, or time in history.

Anthropologists and historians discovered that prohibition of incest existed in all known societies and at all times of history. Psychiatrists, psy-chologists, cultural anthropologists, and others propounded many theo-ries to account for the universality of the incest taboo. Some arguments are biological. (Incest had to be prohibited to prevent genetic defects resulting from inbreeding.) Others are economic (stressing the need to encourage breeding outside the family to broaden the base of power and wealth); sociological (solidifying a society through the widest possible network of connections, interactions and relationships); or psychological. (In *Totem and Taboo,* Sigmund Freud used cross-cultural data in his attempt to explain the prehistoric origins of this phenomenon.)

All these theories have adherents and detractors. They all have plausible aspects and flaws. There is no generally agreed-upon definitive explanation of the origin of the incest taboo. Volumes have been written on the subject, and scholars still disagree. It isn't the purpose of this book to examine various theories of the origin of incest and the development of its prohibition. If readers wish to pursue those topics, they will find ample resources for their research. This book seeks to explore more immediate issues—the nature of sexual child abuse, the ways it affects people who have been victimized, and means of recovery from these injuries. For our purposes, it is sufficient to acknowledge the universality of the incest taboo and the logical conclusions to be drawn from this acknowledgment: *There is no need to prohibit something that doesn't exist.* In short, there are incest taboos everywhere because every culture recognizes the need to protect children from incestuous abuse. The universal taboo against incest reflects the universality of the *act* of incest. That the incest taboo (at least in our culture) has been massively ineffective in protecting children from sexual abuse is evidence that we must take stronger measures. It shows that we have severe social problems that need to be identified, explored, and rectified. It is another reason for my writing this book.

In addition to being found everywhere in the world and throughout history, incestuous child abuse is not limited to one particular segment of society. Despite our tendency to distance ourselves from unpleasant realities, incest is not something done by "them." It exists in "the nicest of families," among the wealthy, the poor, and the middle class. It is found in two-parent, single-parent, step-, foster, and extended families. It occurs in religious and nonreligious, white- and blue-collar, northern and southern, farm- and apartment-dwelling families. In fact, incest appears to cut across all racial, religious, ethnic, age, class, geographical, and rural/urban/suburban lines. It is done to people just like you. And for many reading this book, it was done to you.

If you are a male survivor, the essential thing to know is that there are many other men who were victimized. The exact numbers don't matter. Whatever they are, they are vast. And knowing of the existence of even one other survivor helps you break through the isolation. There are factors that are infinitely more important to understanding abuse and recovery than numbers and categories.

Focus
Rethinking the Language of Abuse

It is well known that our ideas and values are expressed in the language we employ. We are less willing to accept that the words we use influence our perceptions and behavior. Richard Hoffman makes a strong case for thinking about the language we use when talking about abuse and abusers—and for changing our words to reflect reality.

This article appeared in The Boston Globe, *November 23, 1998. It is reprinted here by permission of the author.*

THE HATRED OF INNOCENCE
by Richard Hoffman

My ten-year-old daughter brought us the news. She told of a little boy across town who had been kidnapped, raped, and killed. She insisted I turn on the TV to find out more. I hesitated, wanting to protect her, as if protecting her from the truth were the same as protecting her from evil. I turned on the news.

Mostly I was concerned for my daughter's feelings. But as a parent, my heart also ached for the parents of this boy whose name we did not yet know. And as a man who was raped at age ten by a coach who, before he was stopped, went on to devastate the lives of hundreds of children, I felt an old rage surface again. Soon we would learn that the boy's name was Jeffrey Curley.

Because of my own history, I have been trying to understand the enormity of this evil for a long time now. I have come to few conclusions except that we have to begin with a different set of terms if we are to avoid the same fear, helplessness, and despair that have incapacitated us so far and continued to place children at risk. I believe we have been misled by the language we use, by the way we talk about those who would harm our children. Our words are important. Words are how we think. We talk of them as "sick." We use names that accept their denial and distortion. We become tangled in language that does not reflect reality, but hides it until, over and over, child after child, it is too late.

Let's begin by refusing to use the word *"pedophile."* The word comes from Greek and means, literally, "one who loves children." What an Orwellian inversion! To use this word to describe those who violate children, and in many instances kill to silence them, is to help the wolf into his wooly disguise.

The term pedophile is more than a poor word choice, however; a pseudo-medical term, it asks us to see such evil as arising from disease or illness, evil in its effect, perhaps, but no more intentional than other natural misfortunes like diabetes, say, or muscular dystrophy. This makes the violation of children a part of the natural order and the perpetrator one who cannot help himself.

In place of the term pedophile, then, let me offer an alternative: *pedoscele,* from Latin *"scelus,"* meaning "evil deed." Try it. Ped-o-skeel: one who does evil to children. And let's stop calling them "sex offenders," as if their crimes had anything to do with sex. (Perhaps Jeffrey Dahmer was a "food offender.") As the poet Linda McCarriston once pointed out, "Saying 'the man had sex with the child' is like saying, 'The man had dinner with the pork chop.' "

The rape of a child is a violent act of contempt, not an expression of sexuality or affection. Pedosceles want us to believe otherwise. This is why they talk of "love" between men and boys. All too often we fall for it. For example, in a newscast about the man who had devastated the childhoods of several generations in my hometown, including mine, a TV commentator said that the defendant had "admitted that he is overly fond of young boys." (The word "pedophile" is there, in the shadows.) At that pre-trial hearing, one boy said the man had threatened to cut off his genitals if he told. Another boy testified that the man threatened to shoot his little brother. Overly fond indeed.

A couple of years ago a pedoscele named Thomas Hamilton massacred a kindergarten class in Dunblane, Scotland. He had been driven, unwelcome, from one community to another for decades, but police were not able to find parents unashamed to take a case to court. Instead, he was shooed along, referred to as a "misfit," and became, each time, the next community's problem. The subsequent slaughter, like the murder of Jeffrey Curley, unmasks the real nature of this type of child abuse. At its core is a hatred of that naiveté and vulnerability we call innocence. Men like Thomas Hamilton, or Jesse Timmendequas who killed Megan Kanka, or the murderers of Jeffrey Curley, cannot stand that quality and must defile it. Failing that, they must kill the child who represents it.

While we're at it, let's retire the word "molest." On a family vacation recently, we took a day trip to a bird sanctuary where the signs read: Do Not Molest the Birds. Look it up. It means to bother. Bother? Excuse me, sir, you're bothering my child.

Even speaking informally we communicate mostly ignorance, discomfort, and confusion. I have heard the word diddle used to describe (and dismiss) the violation of children, as in "He likes to diddle little boys." It is a word that seems made to order, silly sounding, sniggering, naughty. Diddling, fondling, fooling around—great foggy euphemisms into which real children like Jeffrey Curley vanish.

We need to create safety for our children. But the first step in doing so is to see reality clearly. Using language that reflects the real nature of the crimes committed against children, maybe we can figure out, at long last, how to protect them from people who—make no mistake about it—hate them for being what they are: young, trusting, and innocent.

PATTERNS OF ABUSIVE BEHAVIOR

All behavior, including sexual child abuse, exists within a social and cultural context. We must examine this framework to further our understanding of the most fertile environment for establishment and development of abusive patterns. We must also look at family attitudes, patterns of behavior, and other dysfunctional aspects of intrafamily interaction that allow (and encourage) the sexual abuse of children.

Many researchers and clinicians believe that the relative severity of the effects of sexual child abuse is directly related to the age of the victim, severity of any physical violence involved, chronic nature of the abuse, closeness of the relationship between perpetrator and victim, sex of the child, whether the perpetrator was the same sex as the victim, and/or the way it was explained to (and perceived by) the child. I have no doubt that further research on these and other factors will guide us in our understanding of the nature of abuse and recovery. I hope we will continue to explore these factors without losing sight of the fact that *all* abuse of children is harmful, severe, and wrong. Our goals in examining different manifestations of abuse should be to increase our understanding of prevention of all sexual abuse and to facilitate recovery for *all* survivors.

I am reluctant to place much emphasis on exploring differences between the effects of various kinds of sexual child abuse. I have three reasons for my hesitancy:

First is the lack of hard evidence. While extensive research is being done on sexual child abuse, our knowledge of this topic is still limited. In the case of male children, we have only the sketchiest data on the frequency of sexual abuse. We can hazard some educated guesses, but we still have much to learn about differences between a single (acute), isolated abusive incident and prolonged (chronic) patterns of sexual exploitation. We don't have a firm understanding of what it is like to have been subjected to one abuser or more than one; to seduction or violent attack; to penetration, fondling, or sexual innuendo. We are limited in our understanding of the differences among men abused in infancy, early, middle, or late childhood, or adolescence. We don't know whether there are significant differences when members of the abusive families are also alcoholic, violent, drug-addicted, or severely mentally ill. We have much to learn about what, if any, unique problems arise when there are several victims of sexual abuse in a family rather than one. As you can see, we have a long way to go. These and other questions will occupy the research efforts of behavioral scientists for some time. Preliminary findings provide us with information that sheds light on the nature of boyhood sexual trauma and the recovery process. No doubt research will continue to increase our understanding of how to heal the wounds.

The second reason for my hesitancy to emphasize differences is that doing so can interfere with the recovery process. The experience of abuse is an isolating one. The perpetrator must isolate his/her victim from possible sources of protection within the family. The perpetrator may also be successful in keeping the family unit separated from nonfamily members. A first step of recovery depends on breaking down isolation in any way possible. Continued recovery requires sustained effort to overcome the effects of years of isolation. The first time a survivor hears someone else say, "That happened to me, too" or "I've always felt like that," his life changes. Listening to someone else tell of experiences and feelings that mirror his own contradicts a lifetime of being certain that no one will ever be able to understand. It is far more important to recognize similarities than differences. Many of the distinctions we cling to as important are, in reality, arbitrary and trifling. Through recognition of commonalities, connections are born, and the progress of recovery continues.

My third reason for hesitating to focus on differences is that the basic effect of sexual child abuse is damage to the ability to trust. Loss of trust is common to survivors, regardless of the specific forms that the abuse took.

Having expressed my reasons for believing that we shouldn't dwell on the differences, I'll briefly mention a few dysfunctional patterns frequently found in incestuous families—and offer some speculation about severity of effects. (**Remember:** If your experience doesn't exactly fit these patterns, it does not mean that you weren't abused or that your abuse was less serious than someone else's. We aren't attempting to set up a hierarchy of sexual abuse victims. You deserve full attention, consideration, and support in dealing with what was done to you, regardless of the details of anyone else's experience.)

Many, but by no means all, incest survivors come from families where there were multiple patterns of abuse or dysfunction. I have known individual clients and group members whose parents (and/or other close adults) were alcoholics, drug addicts, compulsive overeaters, child beaters, wife batterers, suicidal, severely depressed, paranoiac, manic-depressive, criminals, and/or were themselves survivors of abuse. These other dysfunctions may even serve to help keep the abuse from being discovered. If anyone perceives that the victimized child is troubled, it can be explained as the result of having a drunken father (or a crazy mother, etc.).

But sexual trauma is certainly not limited to multi-abusive environments. I have spoken with many survivors whose families appear to an outside observer as models of respectability: stable, financially secure, sober, clean, and reverent. Since, for abuse to be possible, secrecy must be maintained, what better camouflage than a model family? (And what better means of keeping the victim confused?) It is massively harmful for a child to be the keeper of the one painful secret in a "wholesome" family. He will often keep the secret in an attempt to protect the stability of the family.

As with female survivors, many men report family situations where one or both parents were absent or otherwise unavailable for significant periods. Whether these absences were caused by chronic physical illness, mental hospitalization, job requirements, imprisonment, death, or other factors, the child may have spent considerable time in foster care, with other relatives or family friends, in institutions, or in the care of an abusive parent, sibling, stepparent, or other parent surrogate. This situation left the child vulnerable to victimization by the other parent or another adult.

The very unavailability of the absent parent to fulfill her (sometimes his) "conjugal duties" has been used as an excuse for the sexual exploitation of children. In these instances, the victimized child is forced into the role of replacing the absent parent and taking responsibility for assuming the "duties" of a spouse: companionship, housekeeping, child rearing— and sex. The absence is not necessarily physical. Sexual and emotional rejection by a mate has caused both male and female children to be served up as substitutes. A patriarchal society fosters the idea—sometimes reinforced by law—that a husband has the "right" to receive sexual satisfaction. Many male perpetrators use their wives' unavailability to rationalize and justify abusive behavior. Once again, we are looking at frequent, but not inevitable, patterns of abusive families.

Sexual child abuse also occurs in families where the parents report that they sustain an active (sometimes mutually satisfactory) sex life. This may seem contradictory unless we remember that we are not talking about normal adult consensual sexual activity, but *abuse* of children that takes a sexual form. A society that treats any class of citizens as property—whether they are black, poor, disabled, women, or children—creates a social framework that is geared to perpetuating patterns of violence and sexual abuse. It is a cultural context that breeds incestuous families. Only by changing our attitudes toward the rights of all individuals can we eliminate incestuous abuse. This must be a long-range goal of all caring people. In the meantime, we must seek to protect all children from further abuse and support all adult survivors in their recovery. You have been isolated by the abuse for too long; now is the time to overturn the effects of isolation. The path of recovery may be long, but it doesn't have to be lonely. You are not alone.

Speaking with hundreds of therapists and thousands of survivors led me to one inescapable conclusion: The most striking feature about sexual child abuse is the *similarity* of its effects on adult survivors. True, there are differences of specific situations and how individuals are affected by abuse. There might be other factors that we haven't yet recognized. We will have more answers someday. For now, these matters are speculative. We know that the effects of sexual child abuse result from violation of what should be a loving, protective relationship. When this was done to a child, the hurts are profound. When they begin to share their stories, talk about and express their feelings, survivors—male or female, heterosexual or gay—recognize each other as brothers and sisters.

Commonalities provide a basis for understanding, sharing, and connecting. They are a foundation for figuring out how to approach recovery. In light of these tremendous similarities, differences no longer seem terribly significant. Themes that appear in later chapters will probably strike some uncomfortably familiar chords for the very reason that they reflect experiences shared by many survivors. They include:

• Issues of masculinity, gender, and sexuality in the context of abuse

• Feelings: how we learn to hide and deny them, and how to regain our ability to feel and express emotions in a healthy way

• Themes of loss of childhood and other losses

• Isolation and loneliness

• Coping strategies that have helped survivors get through their abusive childhoods, and how to change these childhood strategies when they turn into adult problems

• Aspects of recovery—overcoming fear and mistrust to move on with the specifics of healing your life.

The next three chapters focus on what it means to be a man in the context of sexual child abuse. Their purpose is not to create divisions between men and women, and certainly not to imply that abuse of boys is more or less serious than that of girls. To rid society of abuse, we must understand all its aspects. We must explore our attitudes toward men as victims, seeing how they differ from ways we view women. We must examine how we perceive sexuality and feelings to understand the effects of abuse and provide us with clues for recovery.

Keith's Statement

Speaking directly to his fellow survivors—his "brothers in suffering and in courage"—Keith, a thirty-seven-year-old survivor, writes of struggle and hope.

I would be dead today if there were not people who thought that incest, sexual abuse, and violence against children was a crime. I promised myself that whatever else I wrote for this book, that statement would be the first thing I wrote. I write today to you, my brothers in suffering and in courage, so that you can know that another feels as you do. I want to give you courage to feel what you know to be true—that a crime of violence was committed against you, an innocent. And I write for myself, too, because for hope to be real, it must be felt like a friend who touches us with a kind and gentle hand. If my words give you hope, they give you courage. The courage of knowing that not every human being is a beast who will hurt you, or a coward who will betray you. The courage of knowing that there are other human beings who understand just how much courage it takes for you to hold on to your dreams of love and being understood and accepted. And, yes, the courage in your dreams of wanting to love, understand, and accept those who truly love you. Perhaps finally, the courage to act against your suffering—to win for all of us another life filled with innocence, gentleness, and courage. That is, a human life.

Incest is the story of silence. The silence of the innocent, of the vulnerable, of the trusting, of the sensitive, of the sweet, of the human. That silence alone thunders condemnation of the weak, sick, pathetic, cruel, and vicious individuals who destroy the expression of innocence, vulnerability, trust, sensitivity, sweetness, and humanity in another human being. This remains true even if our abusers were not the totally depraved individuals that some of our number suffered under. Even if there was some love in the hearts of our abusers, insofar as they abused us, they were not expressing love, but the disintegration and degradation of their humanity.

There is a violence in every betrayal of trust. That violence is at the core of the incest experience. Incest is not only a reprehensible crime of violence against the person of a child, but also a crime against the future of that child. There are three crimes in incest. The actual torture and/or using and/or neglect of the child is one. Denying that child an environment in which to express his childish love is the second. The last is denying that child a future based on the good things in life and the highest level of human achievement founded on the secure development of a human being. I was that child.

Like many survivors of abuse who have protected themselves by consciously forgetting, I struggle daily to turn my images of extreme sexual and physical violence directed against me—as well as my overpowering feelings of having been seductively overwhelmed—into memories. I have very clear images that are disassociated from the emotions I felt at the time they were happening, as well as very strong physical sensations that are disassociated from the events that engendered them.

I utterly reject the actions of those who forced me to drink at the trough of human experience, wanting humiliation to mark me forever so that they would never have to answer for or explain their actions. Instead, they saw in my suffering and confusion an easy way out of their guilt, or even a justification of their violence and cowardice.

Today I am not silent. Today I write with rage that speaks in a human voice about all the things that were forced on me and all the things that were denied me. To my question, who gave my abusers the right to make me suffer the way I did, I answer back that human beings have only the right to love each other and to care for each other.

I was abused by my mother. It is still frightening to me to say that, but today I can say it. Tomorrow, within the context of loving men and women who share my struggle against the violence of our childhood, I will be able to feel it.

Why is it that the community of survivors is so important? If we had lived lives of joy in childhood (which is our birthright), we would not even think of asking. We would know that the ultimate joy in human life is to share the love and the experience of life with other humans.

What we longed for—to be touched, loved, nurtured, supported, understood, accepted, noticed, and appreciated, an innate human longing that speaks before words, is felt before feelings and is known before knowledge—was used against us, or given as reason for our punishment by those who could not live with the reality of their own humanity and sought to purge themselves of their feelings of guilt, or shame, or horror, or fear, or cruelty by blaming us for their feelings or desires. They acted cruelly and blamed us for their actions. To cover up their crimes, they made us participate in them. To make themselves seem less frightened and more powerful, they made us call it love. Is it any wonder, with these humans as teachers, we have all looked for a way to be human all alone?

We have all gone as far as we could, for as long as we could and as deeply as we dared, alone. If you have picked up this book, you know that you can never run far enough to make you happy.

You have run—always with one eye toward the love of others—
wishing to stop, to rest, to finally and deeply and simply and
completely trust another, and so win back your trust in yourself.
For who understands a call that is not echoed back? The joy in life
is in fitting our song in the chorus of life.

It is only our abusers who value our silence and isolation. "If
you are silent, you are not real," they say. "And if you talk I/we will
make sure no one recognizes your words as human because you
are crazy, ugly, stupid, dirty, stubborn, bad, selfish, weak, lying,
unlovable, and unbelievable."

But we survivors—part of the chorus of humanity—answer
back, "We believe *you,* not them. We believe you before you feel
the outrage of what was done to you, before you know for certain
and forever that *what* was/is a crime, before we have met, because
you are ourselves and your story is our story."

And so it begins. I speak to your hands that hold this book, to
your eyes that read these words, and to your heart that jumps—
ever so slightly, cautiously—or perhaps even leaps at the sound of
my love, which is a call to battle. And your hands respond, feeling
that this book feels good in your hands. Your eyes respond, going
back to that one sentence in this piece that didn't filter through
your brain, but leapt directly to your heart. And your heart
responds; your tired, weary heart, sick of all the violations, silences,
denials, betrayal, and cowardice. Your heart has loved life so much
you have never completely given up your hope that there might be
human beings who would love you for the whole truth of who you
are, and where you have been, and not hurt you or deny you
because of it. Your heart has stood ready to forgive humanity as a
whole despite what some among its number have done to you, if
only someone would step forward and tell the truth.

On this day, at this moment, on this page, in this book, I am
that person. And I say to you: You *are* innocent. If you are holding
this book in your hands; if you have allowed your heart to express
the boundless courage that beats within it and the hopes you have
refused to let die, then you already have within you all that is
required to carry this struggle through to the end.

Ours is not an easy struggle, taking place as it does at the most fundamental levels of human character. But remember this: If you have been abused, you are already engaged in the struggle.

The core of our being was not destroyed by our abuse, but the lengths we had to go to survive left us very vulnerable to life. To act in the world takes an innocence based on trust. The more completely we avoid fighting the battle to find the human beings we can trust and so begin to learn to trust our own judgments, feelings, and thoughts to make sense of the world, the more completely our abusers will have robbed us of our innocence and the more guilty we will feel and act in a world that seems confusing, impenetrable, and frightening.

What you lack is help, and help is something you can get. If we do not reach, however, the kind of help that allows us to connect our experience to that of humanity as a whole and not just the particular perversion of it expressed in the actions of our abusers, we suffer tremendous losses in the real attempts we make to connect with the good things in life. We have no way of using the best we humans have come up with to dispel our ignorance, calm our fears, soften our pain.

Life does not remain static. Some losses and some mistakes cannot be undone and the continued defeat of our hopes over time takes a toll that for some of us leads to death. There are those among our number who did not get the help that would have allowed them the support and understanding to act in such a way as to get the love they needed and so to experience hope in the only way it can be experienced: to have something real—really ours—now, here, right now, today and tomorrow.

I know what I'm talking about because I was almost one of those human beings. My denial of the effects of incest/ sexual/physical violence in my life cost me the love of a woman I really loved, a family (her daughter), and a move into what was going to be a deeper level of adulthood. I could not protect the gains I had managed to make in life despite my incest history. I could not make the move I wanted to make to win for myself a deeper level of satisfaction in life, without looking incest squarely in the face. I bargained with time to face that fear and lost a deeply crucial and inexpressibly dear set of relationships and hopes, as my lover and friend lost her faith in me (in combination with whatever pulls there were in her own history and the development of her own life in relation to mine).

One year ago, in the immediate aftermath of the breakup, I did make a move to Boston to join a group I had heard about for male survivors of incest. It was do that or die by ending my life. I hope this book helps you to decide to get the help you need to really go after incest and get it out of your life completely. There is no compromise with an enemy who has no pity. Take your time; find the ways to proceed with kindness and safety for yourself, but do it. It is an illusion to think that once we begin there will be no turning back, because there was no turning back from the day our abuse began. Our only choice is to live in fear or to live with courage.

We were not the lucky ones, but because of our experiences and our integrity in the face of them—which is the deepest form of self-knowledge—we bring a special tenderness, a special gentleness, a special courage, and a special joy to the realm of human experience. If we take up this battle with courage and truth and follow it to the end, we bring that joy not only to others but also to ourselves. We have something true to say about human love. No human could ask for more.

I used to dream of the day when I would not feel shame in my heart at the fact that I existed. I used to dream of the day when my shame at being a human with human needs that seemed so "awful" would be dispelled by the love of others and my love for the life that flowed through me. I have always lived and died with my heart. I have always longed to be a man who would live and die with the truth of that heart. Today, I am becoming that man. Tomorrow, I hope to join you on the other side of our current struggle, where your voice and tender story of love and hope sound like the sweet protecting embrace and call to action that I hope my voice sounds to you.

I also promised myself that the last sentence I wrote would read: "And this goes for all the women, too."

Part Two

ABOUT MEN

2

MESSAGES ABOUT MASCULINITY

If you have been put in your place long enough,
you begin to act like the place.
—Randall Jarrell

The tone I use on my son will be the tone he uses on himself.
—a male survivor

Every life experience exists within a cultural context. The way we respond to the sexual abuse of children is the direct result of how we define sexual abuse and what we think about children. By the same token, our society's response to the sexual abuse of boys and the aftermath of that abuse reflects how we define maleness. Not only does our perception of men (and of victimization) set a context for abuse, it provides a backdrop for our perception of the male survivor. To understand the context in which abuse, survival, healing, and recovery take place, we must examine a number of our cultural beliefs. We need to look at the nature of our ideas about abuse, victims and perpetrators, children, and women. And we must be aware of what we think being a man is all about. Examining the messages we receive about being male lets us see how gender stereotypes affect the recovery process.

SEEING THROUGH STEREOTYPES

Some years ago, Ellen Greenhouse, Ph.D., and I cotaught a college course called "Sex Roles and Sexuality." One of our assignments had the students choose a mass-circulation magazine or watch three hours of television. They were to ignore the content of the articles or programs, instead focusing their attention on the commercial advertisements. They were investigating what the media were telling them about how to be a man or a woman. With very few exceptions, the messages showed little variation, regardless of the nature of the publication, time slot, or type of program. That the media were presenting us with consistent messages about masculinity and femininity came as no revelation to the students. Neither were they surprised by the themes, which offered traditional stereotypes of male and female temperaments, interests, and roles.

What came as a shock were the frequency and persistence of the communication. Many of the students realized they had no idea of the extent to which they were subjected to this indoctrination. Students who chose to expand their investigation found the same messages in other advertising media: billboards, radio, newspapers, direct mail, and so on. But these messages are not limited to the advertising industry. They abound in the content of films, literature, textbooks, theater, song lyrics, music videos, fashion, and children's toys, games, and stories. Everywhere we turn we are learning about what we "should" do to be acceptably male or female.

The training begins at birth, supplied unconsciously by parents and other adults who were themselves raised according to similar standards. Studies have shown that male and female babies are held differently, treated differently, and given differing degrees of attention. Words of appreciation and admiration for infants of different sexes are as different as blue and pink baby blankets. Even parents who strive diligently to purge their children's environment of gender-stereotype limitations cannot keep them insulated from the outside world. Other adults and peers will offer rewards for "gender-appropriate" behavior and punishments for the reverse. All but the most unusual of schools further reinforce these ideals: To gain acceptance and approval, children learn what is expected of them. They are quick to figure out how they can fit in, and equally astute in their understanding of the ways they can't "measure up." Continual frustration of a child's striving for belonging can lead to resentment, hopelessness, or even vengeful behavior. The child who feels "different" most often feels inferior and isolated as well. No matter how persistently parents strive to rid themselves of these conventions, they rarely have complete success.

If our ideas of appropriate maleness (and femaleness) are ever questioned, it is only in the most superficial manner, since we are seldom aware of how deeply we have internalized these cultural stereotypes. Just as a fish, having known nothing else, can have no perspective on water, it is the rare individual who is able to step outside of cultural conditioning. Since these cultural ideals are reinforced everywhere we turn, we are most likely to accept them as "natural" and universal, rather than see them as what they are—one expression of human possibilities. Instead of opening ourselves to the virtually unlimited potential and flexibility of which human beings are capable, we concentrate our energies on trying to live up to an ideal. The fact that ideals are absolutes (and therefore never completely attainable) leaves us open to feelings of frustration and inadequacy. Nonetheless, we continue in the hope that if we only could get ourselves to look, act, or feel differently (better), we would be okay (perfect). These negative self-judgments are reinforced every time we look outside ourselves for confirmation of our self-worth. Once we accept that we fail to meet the standard of masculinity (or femininity), we carry a sense of inferiority into most areas of life. Men have spent their lives trying to "prove" their masculinity, or have succumbed to the feeling that because they aren't "all man," they aren't men at all.

If you have any doubt about what I'm referring to, try this experiment yourself. Pretend you are a Martian trying to learn about Americans. Pick up a copy of the first magazine you come across at a newsstand, supermarket checkout line, or waiting room. Watch an hour of prime-time television, another of daytime shows ("women's programming"), and a third of sports offerings ("men's programs"). If you're ready for a real shock, check out some Saturday-morning cartoons ("children's programs"). Listen for the words used to describe men and those that refer to women. (The differences are equally apparent for boys and girls.) Look at posture and body positioning. Who appears to be dominant more often? Who is portrayed as being "in control"? What possessions do men (or women) appear to have? What careers? And in what frequency? Even the background music in commercials may be different if the advertisers are trying to sell a "male-oriented" product. It won't be long before you have a pretty good idea of "what it means to be a man." Multiply these messages by literally thousands of times a day, every day, in a multitude of forms, and you can appreciate their power—and the difficulty involved in recognizing, understanding, and contradicting them.

Another experiment can be done alone or with friends. Come up with a list of adjectives such as strong, pretty, silly, competent, mechanical, passive, dizzy, dominant, seductive, athletic, nurturing. Ask people to list their first response to each word as masculine or feminine. Even individuals who know that none of these adjectives is limited to either gender will have a hard time denying that they have internalized some feelings about them. The most "ardent feminist" or most "liberated male" was also raised in a sexist society that unquestioningly accepted stereotypic views of masculinity and femininity.

To free ourselves from the limitations of these stereotypes, we have to be aware of their existence and recognize their negative effects. This calls for work and attention. Automatic judgments about masculinity and femininity are everywhere. Even our supposedly neutral, judgment-free reference books display cultural biases. A look at a major thesaurus reveals the following synonyms for the word "feminine": delicate, tender, docile, submissive, effete, sissyish, and faggy. For "womanly," listings include: mature, soft, ladylike, refined, sympathetic, tender, and motherly. Turning to synonyms for "masculine," we come across macho, robust, muscular, athletic, strong, vigorous, lusty, energetic, powerful, potent, brave, fearless, unafraid, hairy, and butch. The entry for "manly" yields two-fisted, he-mannish, hairy-chested, mighty, broad-shouldered, red-blooded, rugged, intrepid, audacious, daring, tough, unflinching, ready for anything, honorable, decent, and ballsy. The message is clear. What is expected of one sex is denied to the other. A woman cannot be "masculine"; no true man displays "womanly" attributes. To be a woman one must be passive, soft, nurturing . . . and weak. Men, in turn, must not evidence these "softer emotions." They must be strong, devoid of fear, unflinching, and capable ("ready for anything"). Any lapse into doubt, confusion, tenderness, or emotion is perceived as weakness—a female characteristic.

Reference works don't create cultural attitudes, they *reflect* them. Perhaps there really is a "rule book" for being a man—it just isn't called that. And it isn't written down in one place; these "rules" are found everywhere. You only need to listen to our speech patterns to understand the restrictions these distinctions place on us.

In the process of becoming men, little boys watch, listen, and learn. They mimic the postures, gestures, speech, and behavior of adult males. They are exposed to the values, ideals, and norms of their culture, neighborhood, and family. They are punished for behavior that is considered unacceptable and reinforced for desirable responses. Some cultures are more flexible about the range of permissible behavior and less punitive when the rules are broken. But every society has ideas about what constitutes masculinity and femininity. To keep their cultural viewpoints intact, each group limits individual expression of diversity. The traditional American (northern and western European) view of men as physically strong, powerful, dominant, controlled, independent, self-reliant, and successful, while it may make for a good movie action figure, has serious limitations in the lives of real men.

Restricting the range of permissible behavior and emotions compromises a man's creativity and ability to respond flexibly to life situations. (How this creates problems for abuse survivors will be addressed later.) Moreover, for the man (or boy) whose temperament is incompatible with that image, life can be hell. He may be teased, ridiculed, shunned, or even brutalized. It may be difficult for him to achieve credibility in social, educational, and professional environments. He may be rejected by his family as a source of embarrassment. Faced with pressure to conform, he may continually strive to meet society's expectations of a man, exhausting his energies and denying his essential nature in order to gain acceptance. Failing to develop into the male ideal, some men pretend to be what they are not, turning themselves into a parody of traditional machismo. Others give up the attempt, rejecting themselves because of their perceived failure as men.

The specifics don't much matter. However it manifests, the traditional view of the "ideal" man leaves every man isolated. Forced to depend only on himself (for fear of seeming less than a man) cooperation becomes a virtual impossibility. Vulnerability, seen as weakness, is equally impossible. What remain are isolation and pretense. The difficulty of a restricted view of what it means to be male (or female) is that we are confined to limited resources. Women are kept from realization of the stronger, lustier, more reckless, and "tougher" aspects of their natures. Men, in turn, do not have access to their tender, emotional, nurturing, and sympathetic qualities. And everyone loses—in deference to a competition that sets men against men, women against women, and the sexes against each other.

We have to stop being concerned with determining the "right" way to be a man. There is ample room for diversity of interests, personalities, temperaments, and capabilities for women and men. Most disturbing is the inevitable result of an attitude that limits human diversity. We have accepted a collective mind-set that limits our range of choice. Curtailing freedom of expression of our variety weakens us as people, creating a climate that enables us to accept and justify victimization of anyone who is different. It isn't wrong for you to be a certain way. Freedom means the right to be who you are, whether or not you are compatible with an acceptable image—without fear of ridicule or rejection.

Rigid adherence to a particular view of masculinity not only increases the incidence of victimization, but severely inhibits prospects for recovery. It does so by equating "different" with "wrong." If we view diversity as bad, it is only a small step to sanctioning the punishment, rejection, or abuse of those who look or act "unacceptably." We stand a far better chance of becoming healthy (individually and collectively) when we come to appreciate who we are and applaud our human diversity.

Intolerance inhibits the full expression of our humanness. Allowing others their differences (and celebrating their uniqueness) opens the door to self-acceptance and self-appreciation. As will be seen, self-appreciation is a cornerstone of recovery.

Focus

Our Debt to the Women's Movement

It is important to say a few words about feminism and the "women's movement." Feminists have received a great deal of criticism based on misunderstanding their aims and ideas.

I believe that men recovering from boyhood sexual abuse have no greater ally than the feminist movement. By exploding the traditional view of what it means to be a woman (or a man), feminists opened greater possibilities of realizing our full potential as human beings than ever existed before. They challenged the inevitability of a patriarchal system that accepts the exploitation of smaller and physically weaker individuals. They explored ways of interrelating through cooperation and mutual respect, rather than seeing violence and competition as the only means of resolving differences. They attempted to change our attitudes and behavior toward children. And, to an amazing extent, they succeeded.

Change is slow and difficult. Power and privilege don't yield easily. But, more and more, our laws, social behavior, institutions, and ways of interacting reflect new awareness of possibilities. There is no doubt that the active work of the feminist movement forced our society to recognize the existence of childhood sexual victimization. Feminists continue to resist and contradict the forces that seek to deny the realities of abuse, sweep them under the rug, or minimize their effects.

People are skilled at ignoring what they don't want to deal with. To effect a change of attitude and behavior, a climate must be created that recognizes the need for change and encourages correction of problems. Change has to occur in context.

Judith Herman, M.D. (author of *Trauma and Recovery*), referred to the need for "a movement" to insure that information about trauma doesn't have to be "rediscovered" every hundred years. Without a movement to remind and reinforce, the best research data are ignored. Society at large (including mental health professionals) finds it less stressful to look the other way.

Proponents of feminist theory and action haven't permitted this ostrichlike denial. They continue to insist that we deal with the realities of many important life issues, including child abuse. They forced recognition of these issues in the face of resistance and misunderstanding. It is no accident that only recently has the sexual abuse of boys and girls become a topic of widespread public discussion. Years of struggle by feminists set the stage.

Adult male survivors are among the beneficiaries of the work of the feminist movement. We must ignore stereotypes we have heard about "women's libbers"; these stereotypes arise out of fear—and the fear comes from ignorance of the facts. The fact is that feminists have improved life for all of us. By helping us realize our potential as humans, they have touched every woman, man, and child.

When we can really look at what these changes mean to us, we will be well on our way to creating a world where abusive behavior is unthinkable. That will be the ideal climate for recov-

ery from past hurts, and safe nurturing of all children. We are
still a long way from realizing these goals, but we would be a lot
further from them if not for the work of feminists. Indeed, it is no
exaggeration to say that the women's movement is enabling us
to become "real men."

MEN AS VICTIMS

Looking at what happens to a man when he is victimized, we have to be
careful to set up no artificial distinctions between abuse of boys and girls.
The effects of abuse are equally profound whether the victim is male or
female; they are also generally similar. It is likely that a greater number of
variations can be attributed to individual personality characteristics than
to differences between the nature of men and women. As I discussed,
there are differences in the ways that we raise male and female children,
based on how our culture views the sexes. It is reasonable to assume that
since we have different ideas about the nature, temperament, and capabilities of men and women—our different expectations of boys and girls are
reflected in how we raise them—we will also have somewhat different
ideas about male and female victims of sexual abuse.

Male survivors are not immune from viewing themselves through the
lens of culturally determined male stereotypes. You are likely to have
some different perceptions and expectations of yourself than if you were
a female survivor in similar circumstances. Recognizing that these gener-
alizations do not apply to all men or all women, this chapter looks at particular emphases and perspectives regarding men as victims.

Human babies, male and female, are born with equal capacity for
feeling and expressing the full range of human emotion. Shortly after
birth, however, adults begin the process of teaching children the ways of
their culture. Much of this training is unconscious, the adults not even
realizing they are teaching the child (by their words and behavior) what is
considered appropriate to their group. Part of this training (anthropologists call it enculturation) includes learning the different ways men and
women are supposed to behave. All societies differentiate between
behaviors and roles they consider "male" and those they consider

"female." Specific definitions of masculine and feminine, however, vary tremendously from culture to culture. Behavior and personality traits considered masculine in one society would be thought of as feminine in another and as gender neutral in yet another.

The culture and personality school of anthropology investigates ways in which being raised in a particular cultural tradition influences a person's adult personality structure. The work of these psychological anthropologists provides us with ample evidence that human beings are infinitely adaptable—capable of a great range of behavior, personality characteristics, and emotional styles. Each society develops its beliefs and behavior from a vast spectrum of possibilities. However, members of a particular society are usually unaware that their ideas about masculinity/femininity are choices. We assume that the system by which we view the world is the only logical and normal way (and, by extension, any other way is strange and illogical). This limited vision (anthropologists call it ethnocentrism) fails to recognize that our ideas about ourselves are not "natural," but *learned*. We must, therefore, look at what our own culture teaches us about gender.

In no area of life is the difference between our expectations of men and women more obvious than in sexuality. The male is expected to be the confident, knowledgeable, experienced, aggressive, dominant sexual partner. Women, in turn, are supposed to remain passive, "virginal," tentative, and submissive. Men are to be the seducers, arousers, and controllers, while women are passively swept away by passion. In sex (as in ballroom dancing) men have been expected to lead and women to follow. A woman who freely enjoys sex is viewed with some suspicion, particularly when she initiates it. The traditional ideal is that women remain virgins until marriage, whereas men should have prior experience. Young men "sow their wild oats," while young women are said to "go wrong."

That these notions are the result of self-deluded male fantasies, with little basis in fact, hasn't prevented them from showing remarkable persistence in male-female relationships. (Even the "female" fantasies found in romance novels and "love comics" reinforce the idea that men are romantic seducers, and women are initiated into sex by the more powerful, controlling males.) On the surface it would appear to be a system where men benefit and women are oppressed; however, in reality no one benefits from a sexist structure. When a society limits individual diversity, everyone loses. Setting arbitrary distinctions between the sexes inhibits development and expression of individual talents. None of us can freely explore our potential. This is true for both sexes; men as well as women fall victim to the rigidities of sexism.

In one rather odd way, these distinctions between what we expect of men and women have added to the difficulties of male survivors. Since women are expected to be passive, weaker, powerless beings, there is room for sympathy when they are victimized. Again, this does not mean that female victims have an easier time of it. (On the contrary, the very acceptance of victimization of women perpetuates abuse and inhibits their recovery.) But there is a particular focus of the problem faced only by men. It arises from our culture providing no room for a man as victim. Men are simply not supposed to be victimized. A "real man" is expected to be able to protect himself in any situation. He is also supposed to be able to solve any problem and recover from any setback. When he experiences victimization, our culture expects him to be able to "deal with it like a man." Unfortunately, "dealing with it like a man" usually translates as avenging the hurt (preferably violently) and then forgetting about it— moving on. When he cannot—or is unwilling to—resort to this mode of problem solving, he is called a coward and scorned as unmanly. As much as we are aware of the lack of logic in this sort of macho thinking, it is the rare individual who hasn't unconsciously internalized these attitudes to some degree. A male survivor may know that violent revenge would be a dangerous response to his situation, but still feel like a weakling for not resorting to it. Men are also supposed to be in control of their feelings at all times. The survivor's ongoing feelings of confusion, frustration, anger, and fear can become further evidence of his failings as a man.

Since men "are not supposed to be victims," abuse (and particularly sexual abuse) becomes a process of demasculinizing (or emasculation). If men aren't to be victims (the equation reads), then victims aren't men. The victimized male wonders and worries about what the abuse has turned him into. Believing he is no longer an adequate man, he may see himself as a child, a woman, gay, or less than human—an irreparably damaged freak. (This perspective is not limited to European-American cultures. *Ningen Shikkaku,* the autobiographical novel by the important Japanese writer Osamu Dazai [1909–1948], recounts in the first person the devastating effects of boyhood trauma. The title of the English translation of this powerful but unremittingly bleak work is *No Longer Human* [New Directions Paperback, 1973].)

Some survivors resort to broad parodies of "acceptably masculine" behavior to counteract this self-perception. Men in my recovery groups have talked of the lengths to which they have gone to prove their masculinity, including daredevil activities, sexual promiscuity, violent behavior, lawbreaking, military exploits, and the like. Others report having "given up," accepting repeated victimization as inevitable. Frequently, a male survivor feels he must conceal the fact that he was abused, for fear that he will be rejected, disdained, or exposed to ridicule. Having internalized the view of victims as less than men, he is certain that others would view him in the same way. The lack of available information about sexual abuse of male children leads him to imagine that he must face his difficulties alone and few if any other men share his situation. (Many men who have attempted to receive help have had their problems discounted, ignored, or treated insensitively. This treatment serves as confirmation that they should not be considered worthy of respect as men.)

Seeing himself as less than a man, the survivor may view such "male" attributes and accomplishments as strength, power, and success as beyond his reach. Success seems an impossible dream; the most he thinks he can hope for is survival by conscientiously (and exhaustingly) keeping up appearances. His only success, he believes, lies in keeping others from discovering the true extent of his shortcomings. As long as his act isn't exposed, he can get by. He lives in continual anxiety, certain that exposure is only a matter of time. He discounts any success he achieves as temporary at best—since it is based on deception. Similarly, he devalues his strength and power because he alone knows how weak and defenseless he feels. Whether his strengths, power, and success are physical, financial, professional, romantic, sexual, emotional, athletic, academic, intellectual, or social, he finds cause to write them off. No picture of reality is able to penetrate his wall of self-negation.

Alternatively, the male survivor might exert himself beyond all reason to prove himself a man. Feeling that he must conceal his shortcomings through worldly success, he strives for (and often achieves) wealth, recognition, and power. But even massively impressive attainments leave him feeling uncertain. There is always the possibility of discovery and humiliation. He fears that if anyone truly found out who he is (a fraud) and what he is (a victim of abuse), all his accomplishments would mean nothing. The no-win situation appears again. If he achieves success through traditional education and hard work, he feels the system has worked despite his personal inadequacies. If he forges his own path to success, he views it as a fluke, and feels he never could have made it the way most (normal) people do. Whichever path he takes, the male survivor is certain that his knowledge, skill, strength, courage, personality, and aptitude are different from (and inferior to) those of other people.

The male survivor didn't receive the same information as other children. Not having been issued the "rule book" about how to survive and prosper, he may spend his life figuring out how to achieve success, power, and strength. Obsessed with hiding his faults and pretending to be normal, he is unable to appreciate (or even notice) his actual successes and strengths. If he does recognize that he has made it, he still can't let down his guard. He must strenuously protect what he has built. Taking time for rest and enjoyment would cause him to be overtaken, displaced, and revealed as a failure. However the world views him, he knows the "truth." He is a victim; his only hope is in striving to keep that information hidden for as long as he can. It is exhausting to maintain his image and keep people from seeing his "true" self. If anyone gets intimate with him, there is danger that they will see through the act. The survivor feels he must either sustain an illusion with anybody who gets close to him, or keep everyone at a distance so they won't see that he is a fraud.

The price of his "deception" is exhaustion and isolation. He never stops to consider another possibility—that his accomplishments and attributes are genuine. He is so busy worrying about being "found out" that it never occurs to him that other people might admire him *despite* his act, rather than because of it. He is so certain he is unacceptable that the idea of someone liking him for himself is alien beyond consideration. People who like him are either fools or are being fooled. A major challenge of recovery for most survivors is rebuilding their self-esteem to the point where they begin to see in themselves what others see, and recognize that those perceptions are accurate. As they accomplish this, they move toward liking themselves as much as others like them.

Another difficulty faced by the male survivor arises from confusion between power and abuse. The progression of this confusion is as follows: As a child, he had the experience of powerful adults abusing their power. In fact, the perpetrator may have also been his primary role model. Because of this, he is likely to draw the conclusion that to be a man he must be abusive. It isn't necessary for *every* powerful adult to behave abusively—one such experience can easily be generalized. The old saying "Once bitten, twice shy" operates most efficiently when the child was "bitten" by someone who meant so much to him. This logical misconception that confuses masculinity with abusiveness can play itself out in various ways. The survivor may set himself up as:

1 / **A perpetrator.** He feels that he must achieve power to avoid further victimization. In a world divided into victims and perpetrators, abuse can be interpreted as power. The only way of masculinizing (empowering) himself seems to be by turning someone else into a victim. As terrible as it feels to be an abuser, it feels like his only chance to leave the role of the victim. He never wants to play the victim again. I have no doubt that this is much of the reason many child abusers are found to have been abused themselves.

2 / **A victim.** Once again, the survivor feels that the only options open to men are the roles of victim or perpetrator. Knowing how he felt as a victim, he is determined never to victimize another human being. So he resigns himself to remaining a victim. Since power is abusive, he reasons, the way to avoid being an abuser is to remain powerless. The role of victim has become familiar to him, and he carries it into all his adult interactions, expecting to be (and often being) taken advantage of. In each revictimization he finds confirmation of the inevitability of his position.

3 / **A protector.** Feeling that children are in constant danger from adults, many male survivors deal with their fear of being abused by taking on the role of protector. On a very basic level they may be attempting to give others the protection they needed as children (or still want for themselves). They may see their role of protector as the only way to achieve nonabusive closeness to other people. Our culture assigns the role of nurturer and caretaker to women. Men, too, have a need to be nurturing. They can sometimes meet this need by taking on the role of protector in human service professions, or by following "nontraditional" male pursuits, such as

nursing or day-care work. My first men's recovery group consisted of six adult male survivors. Five of them were human service professionals; all of them dealt professionally with people in emotional crisis. I believe it is no accident that there are great numbers of survivors (male as well as female) in the helping professions. Some survivors remain victims, others become perpetrators, and many become protectors.

I have called the belief that men have to be abusive a "logical misconception." I mean that abused children have limited perspective on the world, based on having received incorrect and incomplete information. I often refer to sexual abuse of children as *lying* to them. Lies taught by abuse include misinformation about the nature of power, control, intimacy, sex, love—and what it means to be a man or a woman. If you are a survivor, then you have been lied to. These untruths were instilled forcefully over a long period of time.

Focus

Why Did I Wait This Long?

Try not to punish yourself for not having dealt with the abuse sooner. There are many excellent reasons why you didn't do it until now:

1 / *The abuse was still too fresh.* You needed time and distance to regain your equilibrium and gain enough perspective to begin your recovery work.

2 / *You hadn't defined it as abuse.* It takes time and correct information to undo lies. What might be obvious to an outsider is not necessarily apparent to someone in the midst of a situation.

3 / *You were still caught by the ways that the perpetrator got you to keep silent.* It is difficult to question what we learned as children.

4 / *You were afraid.* Although the abusive situation is over, it can still *feel* dangerous. Even a dead perpetrator's presence can be felt strongly.

5 / *The time and place weren't right.* Not everyone is ready to hear about abuse. You were right to wait until you found a safe and supportive environment for recovery.

6 / *You didn't know you had options.* Women have only recently begun to work on recovery. This is an even newer area for men.

7 / *You were feeling too weak, battered, and hopeless to take action for yourself.* Or you felt like such a terrible person that you didn't feel deserving of anything better.

8 / *There was too much else going on.* When you are dealing with daily crises and a basic struggle for survival, there are few resources and little energy left for anything else. You had to get your life under better control in the present before tackling the past.

This list could go on, but I hope you get the point. *Forget about self-blame. You couldn't have done what you are doing one minute sooner.* The time wasn't right, and for whatever reasons, you weren't ready. Punishing yourself about it isn't realistic. Neither will it decrease your recovery time. If anything, it will get in the way of your progress. There are solid reasons why most survivors don't begin to deal with these issues until they are in their thirties, forties, or fifties. Men in their teens and twenties usually are still too locked in denial and confusion to take much action on their recovery. If you started this work in your teens, you're off to a good start. But don't worry if you didn't. People start their recovery in different ways and at different points in their lives. We have no choice but to work in the present. The future is promising. *You are exactly where you "should" be in your recovery process.*

As a survivor you will find that a significant aspect of your recovery consists of learning to identify ways you have been lied to. You must come to recognize what you were taught about masculinity, power, and abuse—and what was wrong with that information. You must deal with your feelings about having been lied to, and the time you lost because you believed the lies. You must grieve lost opportunities and failed relationships. You must express hopelessness about ever achieving a balanced life, confusion about whether you will be able to pick up the pieces, and fear about trying alternatives. And you will probably need to express further outrage at the lies and anger at the liars.

All these endeavors will help you (as they have helped other survivors) understand what was done to you, clear your thinking, and allow you to explore some different perspectives on human nature. Having had your trust so severely shattered, it isn't easy for you to accept new possibilities. You must move slowly, testing every person and every new idea.

To effect recovery, adult survivors must come to believe that recovery is possible for them. No one can accomplish this feat on faith alone. As an adult survivor, you have to know that what you are doing makes sense. You must test your perceptions against your own experiences and those of other people, including other survivors. All this constitutes the process of recovery. It is a means of building a solid foundation of understanding, good judgment, experience, and some trust. With this as a base, adult survivors set out to build self-esteem, positive relationships, and a satisfying life.

Recovery is difficult, but exciting. You are not alone in what you are doing. As you proceed with your own recovery, you will be able to make use of the support, experience, knowledge, and understanding of many allies: male and female, survivors, professionals, and friends. Yes, recovery involves hard work and pain, but there are rewards and pleasures along the way. You will also experience wonder, renewed energy, and the delight of discovery. Every time the dark curtains part—even for an instant—to reveal the reality that awaits you on the other side of the struggle, you will know why you are doing this work. You will have a vision of recovery. The world can never be again quite as bleak. You will come to know safety, belonging, and welcome. Recovery also involves lightness and joy.

3

MEN AND FEELINGS

If fire could be contained in ice, that's how I get angry.
—David, a male survivor of abuse

*Strange to say, if you do not stamp yourself with the words exhilarated
or terrified, those two things feel the same in a body.*
—Barbara Kingsolver,
THE POISONWOOD BIBLE

We have all felt the effects of stereotypes about men and emotions. When
we have feelings that are "inappropriate" to our gender, we are apt to
worry about whether we are masculine/feminine enough. We may pretend to feelings we don't actually have, dramatizing "correct" emotional
expression (or lack of expression) in a parody of how we think we should
act. These limitations make us suspicious of our own feelings; we see
them as having to be kept under rigid control, so we aren't perceived as
weak, cowardly, or "overemotional." We are turned into emotional "one-
note songs" (angry men whose reaction to any difficulty is to rage, bluster, and bully; women who burst into tears at any frustration) or, worse,
adults who are incapable of recognizing that they *have* feelings, let alone
expressing them.

"Real men don't cry." When you think about this statement, it is as silly
as saying "Real women don't laugh" or "Real dogs don't bark." Yet this line
has been repeated so often that many of us accept it unquestioningly—
much to our detriment. We have heard this kind of mistaken notion so
many times that both men and women have been fooled into believing:

• Men can't cry.

• Men shouldn't feel any emotion.

• There are "male feelings" and "female feelings."

• Feelings are weak or unhealthy.

• Emotional expression is juvenile.

• Adults outgrow their need to cry.

• Women have free access to their feelings and men do not.

• Logic is masculine and feelings are feminine.

• Feelings get in the way of thinking.

• Expressing your feelings means you are out of control.

Most of the male survivors I know have spent a great deal of frustrating time trying to *think* their way out of their feelings. It is an exercise in frustration because the trauma of sexual child abuse doesn't yield to reason or logic alone. Trauma isn't just a "mistake" brought about by "illogical thinking." Perpetrators of sexual child abuse aren't simply behaving illogically, they are harming children deeply. It is not illogical to hurt a child: it is wrong. Harming a child in this way wounds him emotionally. These injuries are inflicted by people who themselves have emotional problems. You can't "reason" with abusive behavior and you can't "think" the hurts away. Abuse is a highly emotionally charged situation. To understand it and heal its scars requires the "logic of emotions." Until you understand and work through your history of abuse on an emotional as well as a logical level, it will continue to interfere with your enjoyment of life. This chapter looks at the myths and realities of our attitudes toward our feelings. It explains why we must change our ideas about emotions in order to successfully recover from sexual abuse.

Buying into conventional ideas about emotions without examining where they are incorrect places you at a tremendous disadvantage in your recovery from abuse. Looking at the reality of emotions enables you to reject misinformation and get on with the business of healing.

As I noted earlier, each society teaches its children (consciously and unconsciously) the traits and behaviors it considers appropriate to males or females. The expression of emotions is subjected to the same determinants as any other aspect of behavior. Therefore, we must look at what our own culture teaches us about gender and feelings in order to understand the relation of men to their emotions.

It would be easy to conclude that, in our culture, women are allowed to feel and men aren't. But that would be an oversimplification. Both men and women face limits on their expression of emotions, but in different ways. It is considered inappropriate for either men or women to express their full range of feelings freely. Women are given permission to experience those feelings that we tend to label as feminine (grief, fear, embarrassment). They are therefore allowed more freedom to express these emotions by crying, trembling, blushing, and giggling—activities generally considered to be a display of weakness in a man. Since it is considered less seemly for women to feel the more masculine ("stronger") emotions (anger, hearty excitement, powerful joy), they consequently receive more discouragement from expressing rage or full-throated laughter.

Learning acceptable male and female emotions begins early. Adults are quicker to shame young boys for being "crybabies." In fact, the form that the shaming takes often compares them to girls—the ultimate insult. Boys learn to repress certain emotions to avoid the stigma of appearing weak and feminine. Little girls are not unaware that they are considered inferior. Yet members of "the weaker sex" are punished more frequently when they assert their anger. A little girl who is strong and self-confident is criticized for being a "tomboy." The message is clear. There are ways male and female children are supposed to behave—there are appropriate and inappropriate emotions for each sex—and woe unto the child who expresses the wrong kind of behavior or feelings.

Sanctions continue even more strongly into adolescence and adulthood, reinforced by pressure from peers. Social institutions and role models evolve to reinforce our image of the stoic, strong, sometimes angry, logical, and insensitive (sensitivity being suspect as a feminine virtue) male and the emotional (sometimes hysterical), illogical, weaker female. Although some of these ideas are changing, changes come slowly.

For the individual who was raised in an incestuous family, especially one that is also violent (or otherwise dysfunctional), the problem of feelings is further complicated. In such a family, emotional expression is associated with abuse. Feelings build until they burst out in a torrent of anger, leading to verbal, physical, and/or sexual abuse. To respond emotionally to these assaults only makes matters worse. Crying, trembling, or even laughter is likely to provoke renewed attacks. One man recounted that he had been severely beaten as a child because his mother had overheard him laughing from the next room. She assumed he was laughing at her, and he didn't have time to tell her that he had been reading a comic book. His voice was flat when he told me, "It probably wouldn't have mattered anyway. I was always getting it for something."

A boy's crying or trembling is even more likely to provoke a violent response. The behavior is considered weak and unmasculine, and becomes justification for the adult's brutality. Many of my clients talk about learning to control their tears and fears to avoid triggering renewed physical or sexual attacks. One said, "My father told me, 'Stand up straight and stop that cringing. You look like a whipped dog.' Then he whipped me." The phrase "Stop crying or I'll give you something to cry about" is familiar to most children, although children don't cry without reason. Once again, the abused boy is receiving a message: Keep your feelings in check and try to prevent other people from expressing theirs; feelings can only hurt you. The boy is learning to hide, deny, and control his emotions and help others do the same. By the time he reaches adulthood, the technique has been mastered. Learning to thaw this emotional ice jam is a difficult process, but one that is essential to recovery.

An abused child will often pick up an additional message about feelings. His perception of the world is that there are only two kinds of people, abusers and victims. It is clear to him where the power lies; only the abuser is permitted to express anger. The child is not allowed to express his angry feelings. Any angry response by the child can provoke further abuse. Anger is an emotion reserved for those in power. This leads the abused child to equate anger with power. (He has also witnessed that crying and trembling are perceived as weaknesses and lead to victimization.) He draws the logical conclusion that to be powerful, he must be angry. If only the powerful are allowed to be angry, he reasons, only the angry can be powerful. Since anger is allowed only to men, the prohibition against his own angry feelings serves to further diminish his sense of masculinity. In an attempt to counteract feelings of vulnerability and impaired masculinity, the adult male survivor can end up feeling that his only protection lies in intimidating the world with a theatrical display of anger. This works, with varying degrees of success, in keeping potential abusers at bay. Unfortunately, it also keeps everyone else away, leaving the survivor angry . . . and isolated. This dramatization of anger seldom represents a pure emotion. It is more likely to be a protective mask, hiding what lies behind it (usually fear or sorrow).

"True" anger is a powerful and "juicy" emotion. It takes the form of righteous indignation in the face of abuse and other injustices. I have not seen it expressed nearly as often as the other, "theatrical" variety. It only seems to present itself after a great deal of other recovery work has been done. But, when it is present, it is impressive, and everyone who sees it recognizes it as genuine. When a survivor reaches a point of feeling and expressing this form of anger, he feels alive and powerful, perhaps for the first time in his life. There are many emotional steps to be taken to reach that point. There will be tears, trembling, and even laughter. It may also be necessary for the survivor to engage in the other, more theatrical display of anger—especially if he has never before had permission to do so. This will be helpful as a path to the underlying fear and sorrow.

When I refer to the dramatization of anger, I don't mean to imply that it is a consciously contrived act. The survivor may or may not know that his anger is a show of bravado. He simply feels that he has no choice. It is too dangerous to risk letting go of his "protective" display of anger.

Feelings are a source of great confusion to the male survivor. He is afraid to have them (because they would lead to loss of control or reveal his weaknesses) and he is afraid of not having them (because that would be evidence that he is a numb, barren, incomplete person). No wonder it is a difficult and frightening topic. Chapter 8 concerns ways that survivors numb their feelings. For now, it is important just to say that recovery of feelings is a major part of the healing process.

It is difficult to unlearn misinformation we were taught as children. The adult male survivor must explore what feelings are really about. He must slowly come to accept that he is capable of emotions (yes, the entire range of human feelings), that it is all right to feel and even express his feelings. He must understand the difference between appropriate and inappropriate expression of emotions, and how feelings can be sources of healing rather than adjuncts to abuse.

It is a tremendous breakthrough when the male survivor begins to talk about his feelings more and more openly. Initially, it may happen in therapy or in a group. Although the ultimate goal is to be able to do it with family and/or friends, it may be too much to expect in the early stage of recovery. The safety isn't there; neither, perhaps, are the friends.

Laura Davis, author of *Allies in Healing,* tells how, in the early stages of her recovery, she was completely obsessed with the process—and only another survivor could have had the interest to listen as much as she needed to talk about it. The survivor may need to talk about feelings in individual therapy or in a recovery group to bring himself to the point of making friends he can talk with. As important as this talking is, it is even more exciting (though terrifying) when the survivor discovers the safety to actually *acknowledge, feel,* and *share* his feelings. No one ever died of feelings, but a life devoid of emotions is a form of living death.

How is recovery of the ability and permission to feel accomplished? My best answer is, "Slowly and patiently." It took a long time to learn to deny your emotions; it will take a while to recover them. The process is a natural one. You haven't lost your ability to feel—that is an innate part of being human. It has been hidden away. It needs to be found, dusted off, and brought into the open. You don't even have to search. It happens of its own accord as you establish sufficient safety. When you are encouraged and offered aware, nonjudgmental caring, the feelings will present themselves.

At first, as you begin to shed a few tears, shake a little, let yourself laugh out loud, or even permit yourself to get a little angry, you are likely to be frightened. It will feel as though you are completely out of control, and it will feel dangerous. But reality is quite the opposite. You will cry until you no longer need to, having worked through a piece of your grief; shake until the fear is gone; laugh and tremble your way through the embarrassment and shame; rage through your anger; and yawn away the physical tensions and body memories of abuse. (**Note:** Survivors are often amazed that they find themselves experiencing wave after wave of yawning—one yawn following the last uncontrollably. They wonder whether they are being rude or if they are tired or bored. Feeling impolite, they will apologize for yawning, or try to hide or stifle their yawns. But yawning is to be encouraged. There is evidence that this type of yawning is a way that the body releases muscular tension and works its way through the physical aspect of abuse. Since part of the hurt was installed physically, healing must also have a physical component. Yawning is one aspect of the physical part of emotional recovery. Humans are the only animals that try to stifle yawning. I suggest that you do not attempt to control your yawns. Let them roll and experience how much better you feel afterward.)

In the right environment, all expressions of emotion are therapeutic.

The problem is that we confuse the *healing* of our hurts with the injuries themselves. Crying is not grief; it is a way of *getting over* your grief. Trembling isn't the same as fear. Rather, it is part of letting go of fear. In the same manner, embarrassed laughter, yawning, raging, and even rapid, excited talking are parts of the healing process that get mistaken for symptoms of the problem.

While not every setting is appropriate for expressing feelings (it may not be a great idea to yawn a lot when talking to your boss, to shake your way through a job interview, or to burst into tears at a dinner party), it is important to find settings that are safe enough to let you relearn how to feel, and—through your feelings—heal. This is why much of the early part of your healing may need to be done in the company of other survivors. Later, you will focus part of your energy integrating your gains into the everyday world.

Don't worry that it is hard at first. Your ability to feel and express emotions will improve with experience. The first tear running down your cheek can feel as powerful as Niagara Falls. Don't worry about duration and intensity. There will be times of intense feeling and expression of emotions—and periods of calm. You won't cry, shake, laugh, yawn, or rage forever. You won't even need to talk about it forever. But it *will* take some time. Janet Yassen, a Boston-area social worker who leads groups for female survivors, talks of the necessity of at least "fifteen hundred hours of crying" to get over the hurts. Now, you don't have to set your watch for the countdown. This is not a precise measure. Rather, it is a statement of recognition that: (a) It's okay to cry; (b) Crying is a valuable and necessary aspect of recovery; (c) Recovery is an ongoing process that takes a long time. Don't allow other people to pressure you to "get over it" or to stop crying and "making such a fuss." They don't understand; their impatience is *their* problem. And don't pressure yourself, either. Cry as long as you need to. Everyone has a different timetable; your recovery will take as long as it takes.

Finally, try not to berate yourself for not having done this sooner, or to feel that the task is hopeless. You couldn't have done it a minute earlier. You simply weren't ready. You now have the determination, hope, and resources. As you come to accept the reality of a safe, welcoming environment for your healing, the emotions will begin to appear. Each time someone listens to you with awareness and interest, the walls will come down a little more. It will feel sudden and magical, but you've actually been working toward it for a long time. Everything else you did in your life led you to this moment. Now is the time you have. Can you let yourself feel the excitement?

Martin's Statement

Martin, fifty-three, gave me this statement in the form of a poem at the end of a weekend male survivors' workshop. I have found no clearer example of the healing power of emotions.

Seeing Men Cry
Another clamp unclamps around my heart.
I never saw my father cry, though I
heard once that he had once and it was like
a great story out of mythology.
This event, my father's crying, my mind
has seen a thousand times: He chased my brother
the older disobedient other
one, 13 miles from our farm to our house
a high-speed car chase, my father behind
trying to catch up but never able to.
And when he finally reached the house
and came indoors, he sat on the couch
looked at my always astonished mother, said
"Well, whose side are you going to take this time?"
and wept, holding his wide graying head
in his hands. My mother told me about
this when I was 12. I could barely
believe my ears. Me, I cried all the time.
Always had. I had plenty to cry about
though it made me weak in my own eyes, not
a man (true, I wasn't a man, but a boy)
and this image of my father's weeping

the prospect of it, was like . . . like what?
An ancient mystery—Olympian
a temple in a desert, a shimmering
mirage, a not quite graspable reason
to live, ever powerful, ever looming
something like God. Seeing men cry, I'm
rattled. Another clamp unclamps my heart.

4

SEXUALITY, HOMOPHOBIA, AND SHAME

I feel like an alien.
—survivors everywhere

Male survivors often deal with confusion about their sexuality. Since the abuse was committed sexually, it is frequently mistakenly seen as an act of sexual passion instead of what it really is—an aggressive, destructive violation of another human being. Survivors who were sexually abused by other men question what this experience means about their sexuality. (**Note:** Since the great majority of reported cases of sexual child abuse—of both boys and girls—involve male perpetrators, most of the attention of this chapter will be on men who [as boys] were sexually abused by men. This is not meant to deny the reality or minimize the severity of the many cases of boys abused by female perpetrators. See the Focus later in this chapter for a discussion of issues specific to male survivors of abuse by women.)

Male survivors, regardless of their sexual orientation, face questions about their sexuality. Although the specific form of these questions varies slightly, their essence is the same whether the survivor is heterosexual, gay, bisexual, "asexual," undecided, or confused. Many survivors have moved among these categories in search of answers. The essential question is, "What did the abuse do to my sexuality?" Heterosexual survivors wonder whether a "victim" can ever function successfully as a sexual partner to a woman—"Am I man enough?" This concern can lead to sexual "performance anxiety" or promiscuous behavior in an attempt to "prove his manhood." The anxiety may be acted out through fear and avoidance of gays (lest the survivor himself be identified as gay) or by more active, sometimes violent, expressions of homophobia. For most of the men, the question also involves whether being sexually victimized by a man *causes* homosexuality. The tone of the question for heterosexual men is, "Does this *mean* I'm gay?" For gay men, it more often takes the form, "Is this *why* I'm gay?" or "Did this happen to me *because* I'm gay?" (struggling with reinforcement of the stereotype of gays as victims). These are difficult questions, and it would be wrong to attempt to solve them with easy answers.

A great deal of research and theorizing has been done about the "causes" of homosexuality. Some investigators begin with a bias for or against homosexuality. Others look for origins in an attempt to find a "cure." It is not within the scope of this book to propound a theory of the genesis of sexual orientation, gay or heterosexual. There is extensive psychological, biochemical, sociological, anthropological, philosophical, medical, and religious literature on the subject—all of it inconclusive. We don't know what "causes" homosexuality (or, for that matter, heterosexuality). We do know that apparently, throughout history and in all cultures, approximately 10 percent of the population was (and is) sexually oriented toward their own gender. This figure appears to be consistent whether or not the individuals were sexually abused as children. We don't have adequate figures about adult male survivors. There are too many difficulties that stand in the way of obtaining them:

- Sexual abuse of male children is only beginning to be accepted as a reality.

- Many men will not accept or disclose their sexuality.

- Many men will not disclose or recognize their history of abuse.

- There is no universal agreement as to what constitutes a particular sexual orientation—there are many possibilities and shades of gray.

- There is disagreement as to what constitutes sexual abuse.

- There is no way of determining a direct correlation between abuse and the establishment of sexual orientation.

We know that both heterosexual and gay men are survivors of boyhood sexual abuse. Abuse is probably not the *cause* of sexual orientation, but it almost always leads the survivor to have *confused feelings* about his sexuality. Survivors worry about sexual feelings of any sort, so that any feeling of attraction toward someone of the same sex can cause great anxiety. It feels like a setup for further abuse. Since all feelings of intimacy are likely to be sexualized, just to *like* another man can feel like a sexual act. Virtually all the gay men in my recovery groups report that they have tried to trace their homosexuality to the abuse. Most have (sometimes reluctantly) concluded that they experienced attraction to other males prior to having been abused.

Another question asked is, "Did this happen to me *because* I'm gay?" The assumption that homosexuals will be victimized and that such victimization is permissible leads us to deal with a much deeper issue, that of *homophobia*. Homophobia is variously defined as:

• Hatred of gays

• Fear of gays

• Fear of contagion (fear of becoming gay)

• Fear that people will think you are gay

• Dislike and denial of your own homosexuality (known as "internalized homophobia").

Whatever its definition, adult gay men and lesbians face rejection, discrimination, ridicule, stereotyping, and even violence based on their sexual orientation. A homophobic culture does not limit its fear and hatred to adults; the oppressive behavior is extended to children. Adults, gay or straight, speak of the tortures they were subjected to as effeminate "sissy boys" or tough little "tomboys." The sickness of homophobia hasn't been confined to ridicule and beatings of children who don't conform to acceptable behavioral norms. Weak, effeminate, or gay children (yes, researchers believe that sexual orientation is established well before puberty) have suffered sexual abuse simply because of who they are. It is also possible that an incident of sexual abuse could activate awareness of a sexual orientation that might otherwise have manifested itself later on in a less traumatic fashion.

Some other male survivors feel completely unable to define themselves as sexual beings. Any sexuality has become so associated with abuse that to be sexual means to define oneself as abuser or victim. Male survivors may present themselves as asexual or simply confused about their sexuality. Whether or not they see themselves as sexual beings, it is unlikely they will feel sexually desirable. Low self-esteem (coupled with fear of further abuse) doesn't allow them to feel attractive. When the topics of self-esteem and sexuality come up in recovery groups, male survivors are amazed to discover the understanding and support available to them.

Another issue that causes major difficulties for male survivors is the fear of becoming an abuser. There is a popular mythology that men who have been sexually abused inevitably become abusers themselves. This has been called the "Bite of the Vampire Theory." This belief springs from studies that have found that most child abusers were themselves abused as children. While this is so, the reverse does not follow. In fact, many men who were abused as children dedicate their lives to protecting others from abuse. It is no accident that so many survivors enter careers in human services. They provide what they needed to receive as children. Some individuals, of course, become both protector and abuser, as is evidenced by stories of sexual abuse in day care, teaching, by scoutmasters, clergy, and in therapy. But it is not inevitable. Many men join recovery groups because they have (or are about to) become fathers and are determined to end the cycle of abuse—so their children will not have to go through what they have experienced. Feeling like potential abusers, male survivors often fear and avoid any affectionate contact with their own or other children. This is a loss to everyone. A recovery group provides a forum for distinguishing between fears or feelings, and behavior. Group members support one another in sorting out myth from reality, and in figuring out how to allow themselves to be loving, caring, nonabusive men.

It is impossible to understand the effects of abuse without considering shame. Adult survivors of sexual abuse live their lives in the face of massive shame. As was stated previously, "men are not supposed to be victims." If they have been victimized (even if it was done to them as infants), they conclude that they are failures as men. Survivors face shame that they "allowed themselves" to be demeaned, demasculinized, and weakened. If any part of the abuse felt good (see Focus: What If I Enjoyed It?, p. 142), they see it as further confirmation of their shortcomings—they have failed as human beings and as men.

Since our culture has institutionalized sexism as well as homophobia, to be less than a man is seen as feminization. The heterosexual survivor, clearly not a woman, worries about whether he is that even more shameful being—a feminized man, a homosexual. Gay men as well internalize our culture's homophobia. Raised in a society that teaches them that it is shameful to be gay, they must work extremely hard to overcome negative messages and build self-esteem. This task is made considerably more difficult when they bear the added burden of shameful feelings arising from sexual victimization. At its worst, internalized homophobia causes gay men to wrongly blame themselves (or their gayness) for their having been abused. This ultimate form of blaming the victim (the victim blaming himself) says that just by being who he is—gay, weak, needy, or otherwise flawed—he brought the abuse on himself. It is important for such individuals to learn about homophobia and rebuild their damaged self-esteem so responsibility for abuse can be laid where it belongs.

Sexual abuse of children forges a connection between sex and shame. For a survivor, heterosexual or gay, any sexual activity with a man or woman (or even a sexual reference) can restimulate shameful feelings. Sex has been so strongly associated with victimization (and therefore with shame) that it takes great effort to break the connection. Homophobia adds another link to the chain and makes the task of regaining self-esteem even more complicated. Separating sexuality from shame is a major goal of recovery.

Focus
When the Abuser Is a Woman

A boy faces a particular form of confusion and isolation when he is sexually abused by a woman. Sexual activity between older women and young boys is rarely treated as abusive. It may be ignored, discounted, or disbelieved. Men (even boys) are supposed to be the sexual aggressors, strong enough to protect themselves against unwanted attention from members of the "weaker sex." What is ignored in these cases is that there is more involved than physical strength, and sexual abuse is not limited to sexual intercourse.

The boy is probably aware of cultural attitudes toward sex between women and boys. In many instances it is romanticized, seen as "scoring" or initiation into manhood. (The French are particularly fond of romanticizing this type of intergenerational sex in their literature and films.) A boy who talks about having been sexually abused by a woman is often greeted by disbelief, denial, trivializing, and romanticizing of his story by police, doctors, therapists, media, and the general public. Faced with a society that seems to be celebrating his pain, the child victim is unlikely to risk talking about it. He may try to redefine the experience to fit in with other people's perceptions, even to the point of bragging or joking about it. He knows that no one will understand what he is feeling, so he might as well just try to fit in.

Society's blindness to this aspect of abuse places him in a powerful double bind. If any part of the experience felt good or was arousing, then it wasn't abusive. If he didn't enjoy it, he must be a homosexual. Once again we see the result of confusing sex with sexual abuse. It is shameful for a man to admit to not enjoying any form of sex with a woman. The victim, then, is faced with the expectation that he should enjoy his victimization. (This has parallels with romanticizing the rape of women.)

Not knowing how to cope with his confusion, he may push it into the recesses of his mind, losing all conscious memory of the event until years later. It is my impression that male survivors are more likely to repress memories of abuse by women than by men. It is not uncommon that previously forgotten or partially occluded traumatic memories reappear in the safety of a recovery group. Memories of female perpetrators seem to be more resistant to recovery; when they do come up, they appear to be more devastating and emotionally draining.

Men have entered with clear memories of male perpetrators and, during the course of the group, recovered additional memories of abuse by a woman. One male survivor, who had gone to his father's bed to escape his mother's, had never consciously thought of the sexual activity with his mother as abusive. Another man, during a group meeting, blurted out, "Oh, my God, my mother, too!" His anguish and dismay were apparent to everyone in the room. This type of discovery is not that unusual once sufficient safety has been provided.

I can't speak to whether the situation is greatly different for women survivors, but I believe it is likely that the effects and implications of abuse by a woman take on a particular emphasis for men. Being victimized by a woman appears to produce an added level of shame; men are more likely to blame themselves or discount it as not really being abuse.

This is especially true when the perpetrator is the survivor's mother. It may be due to a cultural stereotype that says that mothers are to be trusted more than fathers. Mothers occupy a special, sacred place in any culture. For many people, it is unthinkable that a mother would not be a nurturing, protective, loving figure. Even children who have experienced extreme physical, emotional, and sexual abuse by their mothers may find themselves protecting their tormentors through pretense and self-blame.

Outsiders commonly dismiss a child's report of abuse by his mother as fantasy or exaggeration. If we are to deal with abuse effectively, we must create a climate that recognizes all sexual abuse for what it is. Sexual child abuse is harmful regardless of the gender of the perpetrator or of the victim.

A frequent result of the sexuality–shame connection is sexual dysfunction, a problem that is found among both male and female survivors. Some type of sexual dysfunction is so common among male survivors that if a client enters treatment for sexual dysfunction of any sort, I ask about childhood sexual abuse and keep alert for signs of abuse in his history. The survivor's problem may take any number of specific forms (e.g., inability to achieve or maintain an erection, premature ejaculation, inability to ejaculate, fear of specific sexual acts, sexual obsessions and fetishes, compulsive masturbation, inability to separate sex from humiliation, shame, pain, or physical injury). Whatever form it takes, I am convinced that the source of the problem lies in childhood sexual trauma.

The devastation of trust that occurred when he was abused as a child turns adult sexual activity into an encounter fraught with anxiety.

The problem of sexual dysfunction is one that generates feelings of depression and hopelessness for many male survivors. They despair of ever being able to "get over their problem" and lead a "normal" sex life. But the situation is far from hopeless. If you get at the root of a problem, the symptoms tend to lessen and eventually disappear. I have seen survivor after survivor overcome sexual dysfunction during the natural course of recovery. It doesn't happen magically or overnight, but as they move through their shame, as they continue to rebuild trust and self-esteem, and as they forge healthy friendships and intimacies, their sexual problems begin to diminish. (Yes, even yours! You are not a unique, hopeless case.) Much to their amazement and delight (usually tinged with a little nervousness and mistrust) they find themselves moving into a healthy sexuality.

The only reasonable way to begin to release yourself from shame that results from connecting abuse and sexuality is to recognize that we are not dealing with an issue of sexual attraction or sexual orientation. *The issue is abuse!* Repeat it to yourself as often as you can. Write it on your bathroom mirror. Post it on your bulletin board. Have friends remind you. Be clear about it. The issue is not sexuality; it is abuse. It always was. It doesn't matter whether you are gay, straight, bisexual, all of the above, or none of the above. You were sexually abused. You didn't bring it on yourself, no matter what kind of child you were or what you did. It got confused with sexuality because the abuse wasn't limited to physical violence or emotional exploitation. It also had a sexual component. But the real issue for the male survivor (as for the female) isn't sexual orientation. We are really looking at trust, intimacy, and self-esteem. As these elements are explored, understood, and strengthened in healthy, encouraging, nonabusive relationships, the issues of sexuality will become clearer and more comfortable. You will be happier with who you are, and you will develop a new perspective on your sexuality. Sexuality is one facet of a total (and worthwhile) person. Shame will increasingly yield to self-acceptance and self-appreciation.

ABOUT ABUSERS

Since this is a book for and about survivors of boyhood sexual trauma, and because I don't work with abusers, I have been reluctant to devote much time and attention to writing about perpetrators. But it is relevant to this chapter to say a few words about sexual abusers in the context of sexuality. When a man sexually abuses a boy, it is often incorrectly seen as a homosexual act. Once again, this is a mistake. We are not talking about sex, but about *sexual child abuse.* (As I once heard someone say, "If you hit someone over the head with a frying pan, you wouldn't call it cooking.") An adult male who abuses a little girl is not engaging in heterosexual behavior; he is sexually abusing a little girl. The same is true when the victim is a little boy. The issues—anger, hostility, control, and power—are the same; the effects are equally harmful. The question, then, is not one of homosexuality or heterosexuality, but of sexual child abuse and its results.

Just as a young male victim of sexual abuse is not necessarily—nor will he inevitably become—gay, the male perpetrator is not necessarily homosexual. In fact, all available statistics indicate that the reverse is true. The vast majority of perpetrators of sexual abuse of boys (as well as of girls) are heterosexual men. Most of them would be shocked and surprised to even be considered homosexual. Pedophilia (sexual attraction to children) can focus on the same sex, opposite sex, or be indiscriminate. The attraction is to children, not to men or women. Same-sex child abuse is only seen as a homosexual act when we deny the reality that sexual child abuse is not about sex, but about abuse and power. (We have begun to accept that adult rape is about violence and power rather than about sex. We must make the same distinction regarding sexual abuse of children.)

The perpetrator, *male or female,* is a sexual abuser of children. It makes no difference whether the children he (or she) abuses are male or female. It doesn't matter whether or not the abuser relates sexually to other adults as a heterosexual or a homosexual. Worrying about sexuality only confuses the issue and misses the point; we're dealing with adults harming children. When we are ready to accept this reality—and stop treating it as anything other than sexual child abuse—we will be able to begin to create a society where children are afforded the protection and nurturing they deserve.

Robert's Statement

Robert, a twenty-eight-year-old survivor, tells of the echoes of incest in his adult relationships—and the challenge of learning to love himself.

I am a survivor of an incestuous family. It hurts to say that because I still want to believe, at twenty-eight years old, that my parents' myth of their perfect family is true. It is not true. It has never been true. My family was far from perfect. I hesitate to even call it good. It has been very difficult to realize the pain that I carry within myself. I have not wanted to look at how much I hurt and how much that pain has influenced my whole life.

I started writing this with a question, "Where do I begin?" It is very difficult to know where to begin to explain the depth of the fear and the pain that I still carry when it is so all-encompassing in my life. It is hard for people who are not incest survivors to realize and to understand just how much it forms the core of my whole way of looking at life. Each and every minute of my life is full of fear and mistrust. I am always afraid that someone is going to abuse me.

My mother was my emotional and sexual abuser. My father abused me with physical beatings and emotional absence. They played me off of one another. My mother literally took my food away from me to give it to my father. She also sent me to him for "disciplining" when I behaved poorly (which meant, from her perspective, that I refused to take care of her). My father could not deal with my mother's emotional instability and her great needs. She often talked of committing suicide. He couldn't deal with her. Early on he recognized that somehow I "got along with and understood" my mother.

He periodically sent me into the bathroom, where she would be screaming and wailing, and expected me to calm her down and "take care of her." It got to the point where she so much counted on me to assuage her painful feelings that she began to have her outbursts in my bedroom. She would then get into my bed and wait for me to come into my room to make her feel better. I still

remember the smell and the feel of her in my bed, and it repulses
me. My father seemed to appreciate the whole arrangement. He
escaped dealing with her anger and anguish and great depression
by making me do it. She more and more appreciated my attention
to the point that she wanted all of it. She didn't want me to date.
She told me to watch out for girls because they only had sex on
their minds.

My girlfriend/romance relationships have been difficult from
the beginning. The moment I first start feeling attraction or
excitement over a female companion I start getting nauseous. I
have vomited my way through every relationship I have ever had
that was at all interesting to me. I have finally realized some of the
cause of that intensity. My whole system has been rebelling against
the intrusion of another relationship on my own well-being. My
relationships with my parents have made the impression on me
that being in a relationship means being dangerously close to
death. Because of the beatings from my father, I have been afraid
of men, thinking that they are all violent. Because of the sexual
and emotional abuse from my mother, I have been constantly
afraid of women, thinking that they all want to use and abuse me.
This has left me feeling that all relationships result in me being
hurt. I have tended all my life to have few friends and to spend a
lot of time alone and avoiding people.

I am working hard this time at taking care of myself. It is a
difficult process to learn. I always wanted someone to take care of
me, but since no one ever would, I felt as though I must not be
worth taking care of. I am now struggling to learn that I am
valuable. This includes doing therapy in group and in individual
forms, feeding myself good meals regularly, and trying to
recognize how I feel about people and situations and then acting
according to my feelings rather than the feelings of others.

I am trying to learn to love myself. It is really hard to love
myself when the things I have been shown about loving are so
abusive. Even now, when I am more than two thousand miles
away from my family, I can feel their abuse of me. Even when I
don't talk with them, or see them, or hear from them, my sense of

self is so low that I carry on my own abuse. It is hard not to be self-abusive when abuse is most of what I have ever known. I need to learn not to be so hard on myself before I will ever be comfortable with the intimacy of being in a relationship with someone else. I desire to be close to someone, to trust someone, and really to love someone so much. I want to show someone the love that I have, that it is a pleasure—not an obligation; that it is beautiful and free—not oppressive and demanding. I am working on feeling positive about myself in ways that feel good to me. I need to feel good about myself before I can really feel good about someone else. Hopefully the day will not be too long in coming when I will feel strong and healthy about myself rather than unhealthy and abused. I have to believe in that hope.

Part Three

ABOUT SURVIVAL AND AFTEREFFECTS

5

LOSS OF CHILDHOOD

I grew up hating his guts because I was always afraid in his house and because it's difficult to forgive anyone who has robbed you of your childhood.
—Pat Conroy, PRINCE OF TIDES

"Loss" feels like a very imprecise word to use when we are talking about the childhood of an abuse survivor. How can you lose something you never had to begin with? Can a childhood be lost if it was never allowed to exist?

We have created a mythology about childhood. "The best years of your life" are supposed to be carefree and happy, protected from the harsh realities of adult life. These fantasies are reinforced by movies, literature, and television shows that idealize family life and the childhood years. Any departure from that image is treated as an aberration, the exception that tests the rule. The trials of childhood are minimized and seen as temporary. They are tempests that will subside with the advent of adulthood. (No one seems to see any contradiction between viewing childhood as a carefree time and expecting that adulthood will solve all its problems.)

Reality is quite different. Even the best childhood is no picnic. There is a whole universe to be made sense of. Children are continually exposed to confusing and conflicting messages. They are faced with information that is beyond their level of understanding—not the least of which is the incomprehensible behavior of those most peculiar alien beings: grownups. The world is not tailored to their size or level of ability. They must endure rules that make no sense to them, often imposed without explanation or clarification. Every adult appears to have the right to criticize or discipline them "for their own good." Any attempt to resist, disagree, or even understand may be punished as "backtalk," insolence, or rudeness. They are unlikely to be consulted in any meaningful way even about those decisions that affect them personally; their problems are ignored, trivialized, or discounted. Children may be seen as cute, amusing, or entertaining, but are seldom taken seriously. They may be loved and cared for, but it is unusual for them to be respected by adults.

It is small wonder that children aren't impressed by grown-ups who rhapsodize about the joys of youth. They have evidence to the contrary. They chalk it up as one more unfathomable grown-up behavior. No, it's not all it's cracked up to be—and I'm talking about a "good" childhood. I'm talking about a relatively stable family, where the children are afforded love, caring, and protection. Even children raised in a benign environment face difficulties that test their strength and resilience. As we think about these issues, it becomes clear that even the luckiest of children have a hard time.

But, as we have seen, few if any families approximate the ideal. The happy, loving, financially secure, nuclear family—the traditional image (of hardworking, sober, strict-but-fair father; mother as nurturing, attentive, wise, pretty homemaker; two healthy children; dog and cat; neat, clean home with protected yard)—may not be a complete myth, but it is certainly not the norm. Only a tiny minority of families fulfills that picture. Increasingly, pressures are added to family life by economic, social, and political realities. In more and more families both parents must work to provide an adequate living standard—or choose to work to realize their potential as human beings.

A huge number of single parents don't have the luxury of choosing not to be working parents. While their families may be quite happy and well adjusted, the children as well as the adults face added pressures. Children in poor or single-parent families may be forced to take on adult responsibilities earlier than in the "traditional" family. They may become more serious and self-sufficient at an earlier age. Although not necessarily a bad thing, it departs from our popular image of the carefree child.

Many other children are born into less fortunate circumstances. Not all children are wanted; not all adults are willing or able to care for them. People have children by accident, in response to family pressure, and for a variety of other questionable reasons. Indeed, having a baby may be easier than preventing the birth of an unwanted child. There are fewer requirements for parenthood than for driving a car or catching a fish. Children are born into alcoholic, drug-addicted, violent, and otherwise dysfunctional families. Babies are born to addicts, psychotics, children, and people who hate them—and children are exposed to adults who sexually abuse them.

If a "normal" family presents difficulties, it is far more difficult to survive an actively abusive childhood. You may, in fact, still be experiencing some of the reactions of the abused child. That you are now an adult—and the original abuse is far behind you—does not mean that you feel safe, secure, or adult. The hurts of your abusive childhood have ripples; you will feel the loss of childhood long after childhood's end. Adult survivors report feelings and behaviors that are the direct results of their childhood losses.

What pieces of childhood does the sexually abused child actually lose? How are these losses manifested in the survivor's adult life? Unfortunately, the list is extensive:

1 / **Loss of memory of childhood.** Sexual child abuse is extremely difficult to endure. One way of dealing with the pain is to put what is happening out of mind. If a child has to deny or forget what is being done to him to survive an abusive situation, he may find, as an adult, that he has literally lost his childhood. A great many survivors have little or no memory of childhood. In fact, this method of dealing with childhood trauma is so common that when clients tell me they have no recollection of whole pieces of their childhood, I am alert to the possibility of some sort of abuse. When childhood memories begin to be recovered, it is usually clear why they were forgotten. People tend to remember the good things. We have a tendency to glorify the past. One of my clients cried when he recalled that his only positive childhood memories were of when he was alone. These were the only times he could be sure that no one would hurt him. Protection, then, was only found in isolation.

2 / **Loss of healthy social contact.** When a little child feels that his only safety is in isolation, it seriously impairs his ability to respond to others. Protecting himself from abusers by keeping to himself, he misses out on the possibility of positive, healthy social interaction—with peers or adults. The perpetrator often reinforces his

isolation. As a way of keeping the abuse secret the abuser may, usually successfully, attempt to isolate the child from other people. The child may play an active role in maintaining this isolation, trying to protect the family secret. As an adult he may continue to feel isolated, no matter how many people care about him. He feels he must maintain protective barriers and put on an act for other people. Only when he is alone can he let down his guard and allow himself to feel. And the way he feels at those times is not good or safe; it is lonely, different, and sad.

3 / **Loss of opportunity to play.** If you were to ask people what children do with their time, the most frequent answer would probably be "Play." This is not true for many abused children. True play is interactive; it requires playmates. This can be extremely difficult for the abused child. He cannot relax or trust others enough to enjoy playing. Easy, active, spontaneous playfulness feels too much like loss of control. And loss of control, in his experience, only leads to hurt. He is reluctant to move too close to others, and he knows that life (survival) is serious business. His seriousness and reticence interfere with his ability to make friends. There is another reason why participation in relaxed playfulness can be so hard; it puts the reality of his situation into sharp contrast. It may be easier to endure an abusive childhood if you can believe that it is normal. Experiencing the contrast between playfulness and abusiveness can be too painful. The loss of opportunity to play leads to difficulties in adulthood. The adult survivor may experience stiffness and tension when he is in a playful situation. Many survivors tell me they "don't know how to relax." Vacations, weekends, and social situations become occasions of discomfort and anxiety. They see themselves (and may be seen by others) as stiff and somber.

4 / **Loss of opportunity to learn.** Childhood play is more than frivolous enjoyment. In every society children learn through play. Childhood games incorporate cultural values. In the course of their games, children learn to understand and take charge of their environment. They learn communication, cooperation, competition, problem solving, coordination, motor skills, creativity, "age-appropriate" and "gender-appropriate" behavior, and they share

information. "Child's play" is a major part of learning. Through their games children help one another to figure out what the world is all about. By playing at being adults, children learn to become adults. The abused child, however, must make sense of the world by himself. He has learned that people lie, and it is dangerous to trust anything but his own direct experience. And his experience has been isolation and pain. He has lost the opportunity to learn in the company of his peers, and this causes problems for the adult survivor. Filtered through the lens of abuse, the survivor's picture of the world is clouded. Having been robbed of the opportunity to learn as other children do, the adult survivor feels naive, stupid, and socially inept. He feels he must always play catch-up with people who have learned to negotiate the world successfully.

5 / **Loss of control over one's body.** Childhood is a time when individuals learn to differentiate between what is theirs and what belongs to others. The most intimate aspect of oneself is one's body. Sexual abuse violates a child's sense of himself in the most basic way. Someone else takes control of his body against his will. He feels he has neither the right to his body nor the ability to protect himself from attack. The childhood loss of control over his body that robbed him of other protective abilities has its adult aftermath. He may go through life being revictimized—taken advantage of in any number of ways. Not expecting anything but abuse, he looks for—and finds—confirmation that the world is an unsafe place. Despite his adult strength, size, and agility, the survivor feels small, weak, and helpless. When he looks in the mirror, he sees a puny (or fat), cringing, ugly, weak child. Despite all evidence to the contrary, he accepted the lies that abuse teaches. It is important to remember that all abuse involves lies. Children are being lied to about themselves, about love, and about the nature of human caring. They are being taught that there is no safety in the world, and they have no right to control their own bodies. Loss of control of their bodies leads to control being a central issue of their adult lives. They can become inflexible, controlling, and suspicious—or helpless and indecisive. How can they be

expected to be trusting as adults when their natural desire to trust
was so badly betrayed?

6 / **Loss of normal, loving, nurturing environment.** It's been said
before, but it can't be repeated enough: Every child deserves to be
loved. Every child needs to be cherished and nurtured. Childhood
should be a time when a child learns that he is good, she is lovable, he is wanted, she is welcome, and information, understanding, and protection are available from loving adults. Child abuse
prevents all this. Any genuine loving and nurturing that may be
available to the child is diminished, belied, and negated by the
abuse. Perhaps the greatest loss in an abusive childhood is loss of
safety in the world. It leads the survivor to have tremendous difficulty in developing healthy adult intimacy, a feeling of belonging,
and a strong sense of his own value. Not having been valued as a
child makes it extremely hard to create positive adult self-esteem.

7 / **Other losses.** This list could go on and on, as we recount how
the loss of many aspects of a normal childhood—family, identity,
certainty, and so on—leads to further losses in adult life. The boy
victim endures loss of control, safety, playfulness, trust, calm, self-
confidence, self-esteem, sexual maturation, intimacy, comfort, and
security. As an adult, he must deal with the fallout from these
losses and perversions of childhood. No doubt you can add to this
list from losses you have experienced. It may be difficult for you
to imagine that life can be any other way. But we will explore roads
out of the abuse. The way is difficult, but far from impossible—
and the rewards are worth the struggle.

Previously in this chapter, I equated child abuse with lying to a child
about the nature of love, safety, and caring. When these lies are so powerfully instilled and reinforced, it is extremely difficult to unlearn them and
make room for the truth. Victimized children experience the *perversion of
childhood.* They lose *every child's right to a normal childhood*—loving, protective,
and nurturing. In fact, the abusive childhood hasn't been lost at all. It
remains with the survivor every minute of his adult life.

The effects of loss and perversion of childhood manifest in many different ways. To understand how childhood losses affect the adult survivor,

we must look at what actually happens to a child when he is faced with sexual abuse. That he cannot trust his environment to be safe prohibits him from feeling comfortable or secure in any situation. The need to take care of himself and be ever vigilant turns him into a serious, watchful person, unable to display the playfulness of other children. He may be suspicious and remote, having few friends. This is a direct consequence of the confusion and isolation that results from abuse. He has reason to be distrustful; his innate trusting nature has been taken advantage of. Indeed, he may reject overtures of friendship from other children and adults, fearful of what might lurk behind the friendly gestures and kind words.

Experiencing violence and abuse, he may learn only this distorted mode of relating to others. Rejected by other children for his aggressive behavior, the abused child will often act out to get attention. Alternatively, he may withdraw further into isolation.

A child may also latch on to a friend's family. In doing so, he is attempting to compensate for his loss of childhood and family by finding a substitute. This creative attempt to change his situation can be a lifeline for the abused child. Unfortunately, it is usually only partially successful. Unable to tell them why he is reluctant to go home, he will remain within this protective family until he has overstayed his welcome and is forced to return to his abusive home. The contrast between the two families can be painful and confusing.

At worst, he may feel that the only person he can get close to is the one who is abusing him—and the only possible intimacy is sexual. Faced with the apparent choice between isolation and abuse, he may allow himself to be revictimized in order to be close to *someone.* He may refuse to acknowledge the reality of the abuse, because the perpetrator is the only person he has been able (or allowed) to get close to. One of my clients, who was sexually violated by a camp counselor when he was a child, vigorously defends the counselor and the experience. This client came from a home that was physically violent, verbally and emotionally abusive. That the counselor "only had sex with" him, and didn't beat, berate, or scream at him, made the abuse feel like a caring, tender act. To relinquish this image of "tenderness" would have left my client bereft of any positive childhood memories. He discounts the coercive and seductive nature of the abuse by saying that afterward he looked for a repeat of the contact. He has yet to understand that children seek tenderness and closeness, and will put up with a great deal in order to obtain it. His low self-esteem does not yet permit him to recognize that all children (including him) deserve caring and protection that is nonsexual and nonabusive. The counselor took advantage of this child's needs, and another child bought into a lie about sexual child abuse.

The abused child has no opportunity to learn to establish reasonable protective boundaries. Not having experienced safety, he cannot distinguish dangerous people and situations. He may throw himself into wildly perilous circumstances or, at the other extreme, refrain from daring any level of risk.

He may learn the trick of seeming to disappear without leaving the room: The good, quiet child may be trying to escape notice for fear of attracting abusive attention. Alternatively, an abused child may go to tremendous lengths to obtain approval, notice, and recognition. He is attempting to "learn the rules" so that he can survive and be accepted. Bright, clever, and funny, no one would ever suspect the tremendous secret burden that he carries every waking moment.

When I spoke of this secret burden to one male survivor, he wrote to me:

"Secret burden": Isn't the main thing that is lost . . . the freedom (innocence) not to have to concern himself with sexuality in its adult mode? He loses the opportunity to emerge into a full sexual being at a "normal" pace. The victim of sexual abuse is unceremoniously snatched out of childhood innocence into the world of adult sexuality—which the victim is not ready or prepared for—and worse yet, into the world of thoughtless & dysfunctional adult sexuality. This creates a "schizophrenic" situation for the young boy. In one part of his life he is brutally thrust into the world of adult sexuality at its worst. On the other hand he continues in his regular life relating to his peers and their collective coming into sexual awareness and function. These two worlds are set apart from one another. His relationship with the adult is secret and the adult does not want to hear about the boy's sexual life with others the child's age. In fact the adult doesn't want to relate to the child except as an object of sexual gratification. The boy, of course, finds it impossible to carry the abusive situation back into his childhood life—it is not something he can share—he has been frightened into secrecy by the abuser. Even if the boy is aware of another child being abused by the perpetrator, there is very little sharing of information between the two children. Shame and a lack of real understanding of what is happening prevent communication. And with friends who are not being abused (as far as he knows) there is no forum for sharing this secret imposed on him by the adult world. "The Secret Burden."

The abused child may become a superior student, star athlete, class clown, or popular comrade in his attempt to deal with his hurt. But the sense of shame and failure never really goes away. Loss of childhood? It certainly is. But, contrary to popular wisdom, the losses don't disappear with the end of childhood. The effects are felt well into the adult years.

When you first become aware of what you have lost through having been subjected to an abusive childhood, you may react with a sense of hopelessness. You feel you have been cheated, robbed of any hope of attaining a satisfying life. Because of the abuse, you feel you have lost your chance at happiness. Take heart. While it is true that you have been cheated, your recognition of this fact puts you on the road to recovery. What has been lost can be found, but first you have to know what you are looking for. You can't create a happy childhood for yourself; to pretend you had an idyllic childhood would be denial of what really happened. And denial doesn't allow you to let go of the pain. Neither can you find as an adult the love you needed as a child. However immature you may feel, you are no longer a child.

It will be important to seek the caring you need as an adult. It isn't fair that you didn't get the love you needed and deserved as a child, but it would be far less fair to allow that fact to keep you from ever getting your adult needs met. You may need to express feelings of sadness and anger at what was lost (or, perhaps more accurately, stolen from you). But this anger and sadness are recognition that you deserved better treatment. They are signs of self-esteem—hopeful signs. After all, if you felt completely hopeless about your chance for recovery, you wouldn't be reading this book. Childhood, once lost, cannot be recovered. As hard as it may be to accept, it is the truth. As one survivor put it, "There is no way to go back and have a *Leave It to Beaver* childhood. That was ruined by a thoughtless, selfish adult." But even though what was lost cannot be recovered, *there is recovery from the effects of the loss.*

Focus

Frequent Issues and Problems Faced by Survivors of Sexual Child Abuse

Not every survivor experiences all of these. Sadly, this list is far from exhaustive, but includes many of the problems most commonly reported by male survivors:

- *Anxiety* and/or confusion; panic attacks; fears and phobias

- *Depression*—often including suicidal thoughts or attempts

- *Low self-esteem*—a feeling of being flawed or bad

- *Shame and guilt*—over acts of commission and/or omission

- *Inability to trust* themselves or others

- *Fear of feelings*—a need to control feelings and behavior (their own and others'); compulsive caretaking

- *Nightmares* and *flashbacks*—intensely arousing recollections

- *Insomnia*—and other sleep disorders

- *Amnesia*—memory loss, forgetting large pieces of childhood

- *Violence*—or fear of violence

- *Discomfort with being touched*

- *Compulsive sexual activity*

- *Sexual dysfunction*

- *Hypervigilance*—extreme startle response

- *Social alienation*—feeling isolated and alone

- *Inability to sustain intimacy* in relationships and/or entering abusive relationships and being revictimized

- *Overachievement and/or underachievement/underemployment*—feeling like an impostor professionally

- As adults, becoming *abusers* and/or *protectors*

- As adults, becoming *victims* of further abuse

- Having *split* or *multiple personalities*—or feeling as though they do

- *Substance abuse*—drugs, alcohol, and so on

- *Eating disorders*

- Other *addictive* or *compulsive behaviors*

- Unrealistic and *negative body image*—feeling distant from their own bodies

- Feeling like a *frightened child*

- Hyperconsciousness of *body and appearance*

As part of your recovery, it will be important to return to your childhood—not to make it right, but to understand what really happened and what was your actual role. You will, in essence, be getting to know and befriend a little boy—yourself as a child. You've been carrying him inside you your entire adult life. And you haven't ever really understood him. Self-understanding is one of the missing parts of your childhood. The person who abused you stole it from you. He lied to you when he told you that you were bad. She perverted your need for human love and physical nurture. He confused you about who you are. So you lost perspective on the child within you. You owe that child a lot, you know. If not for his courage and survival skills, you wouldn't be here. He deserves your reassurance.

As you come to understand this little boy, you will redefine him in the light of truth. You will understand completely and explain to him that *he was always good.* What *was done* to him was bad. He always did the best he could, trying to figure out what was going on. But he was faced with situations that no kid should have to handle. As an adult, you can see the lie for what it is, and expose it. In doing so, you won't recapture what you lost as a child, but you will put the losses into perspective—and stop beating yourself up about your childhood. You can actually talk to that little child within you, and reassure him of a world beyond the abuse, and that he will live to partake of it. After all, who knows that better than you? You are living proof of his survival.

By getting to know this special little kid—learning about his courage, intelligence, insight, and goodness—you rediscover those qualities in yourself. You are, of course, related to him. As you build your self-esteem, you recover your ability to relax and even to play. Returning to your childhood is not just a journey into pain. At best, it is an assertion of power and pride.

Changes are not accomplished without struggle. Returning your attention to the abuses of your childhood may evoke a sense of hopelessness. (And while you remain in a state of hopelessness, there is little chance you will be anything but helpless to effect positive change in your life.) But the hopelessness is temporary. As you continue to work on your recovery, you will move out of the despair. At that point a welter of feelings will arise, including sadness, fear, and anger. Don't be discouraged; you are not going to remain stuck in these emotions. Uncomfortable as they may be, having these feelings is another hopeful sign. Recognizing losses and acknowledging them are the first steps in emerging from hopelessness. The process is accompanied by strong feelings.

As you acknowledge your losses, you begin to mourn them. Through the grief process, you will recognize ways you were lied to and ripped off. This recognition that you were completely the victim and never the perpetrator will bring up your outrage—righteous indignation at what was done to you. Directing your anger toward the perpetrator, rather than against yourself, leads to determination. You become determined to recover. Abuse will no longer run your life. You will stand up to abuse by taking charge of your life in a satisfying way. Instead of sitting in pain, you will evoke and experience it *in order to move through it*. You are recovering from abuse, and your recovery is the ultimate overturning of the lie.

Recovery doesn't involve regaining the specifics of what you have lost, but the essence. Recovery is taking charge of your life in a satisfying, adult way. It means feeling positive about yourself and creating mutually satisfying relationships. It includes feeling your strength, intelligence, and creativity. And it involves helping the world regain something we have all lost—unwavering commitment on the part of all human beings to provide children with a healthy childhood. Recovery means understanding the past and using your awareness to create a brighter future. All of these are well within your power; you are already on your way.

Philip's Statement

This story is eloquent testimony to the power of the human spirit. Although his statement is wrenchingly difficult to read it commands respect and admiration. Philip is forty-four years old.

Hello.

Although I'm a proper Bostonian and of the strata of Cabots who spoke only to Lowells and the Lowells who spoke only to God, my family spoke to everyone, yet rarely said anything at all.

My name is Philip. It's not the one I'm using now. I actually have several choices (Edward, George, Bruce), indicative, I suppose, of the initial marital unrest and inability to agree on the part of my parents. In my forty-fifth year, I am a war baby who has only recently begun to fight. But, perhaps I'm getting ahead of myself. I offer this brief autobiographical sketch. I'll consider it a success if it has engendered an empathetic response, caused utter disbelief, or pointed out the perversity, perseverance, and humor of the human spirit. Please feel free to hiss, boo, and applaud. I've always played to the balcony (anything closer and they'd see it was all sham).

Curtain:

Born to a twenty-five-year-old woman and a sixteen-year-old man, I was an unwelcome "circumstance" of a romance on the rebound and the yearnings of a neo–Don Juan. An unlikelier pair would have been hard to come by: my mother from genteel—if recently tarnished—Brahmin stock; and my father, at best, considered a "bead-rattling" French Canadian.

I was three when I met my father for the first time. He had returned home from the war. He was a member of the Merchant

Marine (the U.S. Navy felt he was too unstable for their ranks). At the time, we were living in my grandparents' town house on the Hill (it being the end of war and [there being] an acute housing shortage). My initial and ongoing recollections of that time are of a liberal, intellectual, and libertine philosophy coupled with a need to put a good face on everything, no matter what the cost. It wasn't until years later that I realized that the "cost" was often myself.

Mother had to get married. Although I had surmised this by the age of thirteen, she did not confirm it until two months before her death. From the beginning I was *something* special to her, something she had sacrificed for and something for which she had great expectations . . . regretfully not just in the area of accomplishment, but also in an intense intimacy and ongoing symbiotic relationship which survived until her death. From the time my father arrived home from the war it was understood that she and I suffered his presence, tolerated his rudeness, and paid the price of "legitimacy" by giving lip service to the myth of good marriage and solid family.

For the first three years I was spoiled rotten. The household consisted of doting maternal grandparents, a great-aunt, a second cousin (who for some unspoken reason could not return home), my mother, a housekeeper/cook, a butler, a series of maids fired weekly by my grandfather as "incompetents," and myself. Initially, I shared my mother's room. From age two until my father returned, I shared her bed. Upon his return I was given a cot in the same room until a room on another floor could be found.

My parents hardly knew each other. Tension was quite high and often accompanied by violent arguments and equally violent lovemaking. I became "psychogenically" deaf from age three to four and a half. Coincidental with the return of my hearing was the relocation of my bedroom.

My father never really fit in. He was uneducated, performed menial labor, spoke broken English, and was a total illiterate (remains so to this day, only recently having been diagnosed as dyslexic). He was the product of a broken home, a fair amount of early deprivation, and a disastrous adolescence. It seems he had few choices. Forced to participate in the Civil Conservation Corps or go to jail for assault and battery and later charged with involuntary manslaughter, he joined the Merchant Marine rather than serve a two-year jail sentence. At age sixteen he married my mother under the threat of rape charges.

Mother was hardly a saint herself. She was grossly obese, a rebel, and a social misfit throughout her childhood and adolescence. She was the fifth child born to a mother who was forty-three years old and a father who was fifty-seven. Needless to say she was a mistake; her next oldest sibling was fifteen years her senior. Early on, she learned the facile skills of jolliness and denial. Her diaries lead me to believe she was the recipient of unwanted affection and anger from her father, who was frustrated by his wife's youth and vitality as he approached old age. Mother attended but never graduated from high school, finishing school, and college. She finally got a doctorate in clinical psychology in 1968. Although a brilliant woman with a host of close friends, she suffered from chronic low self-esteem and depression.

My brother was born when I was five. We shared a room until I was eight, when I finally inherited my second cousin's now-deserted bedroom. Throughout this period my father had many jobs from which he was either fired or which he left. He had an explosive and violent temper which, coupled with a good measure of paranoia, made him nearly unemployable. I am sure that remaining dependent upon my grandparents must have been terribly stressful. There was absolutely no way he could ever hope to duplicate the lifestyle of my mother's family.

I was six years old when I received my first real beating from my father. Every Sunday morning he would read the funny papers to my brother and me. Being illiterate, he made up the stories according to the pictures. I had just started to learn to read. I corrected him. It cost me a split lip, three stitches, and four years of remedial reading classes. I was sent to a child psychiatrist who, in all his wisdom, decided that it was "tense" at home and recommended that we all share a glass of wine together before dinner.

My mother and father had been bitterly fighting and in

marriage counseling for over a year by the time I was nine. In April of that year my mother confronted my father with various marital infidelities (grandfather had hired a private detective in order to gain some control over my father after having received a bill from the family physician for treatment of my father's V.D.). His "wings were clipped," she would no longer make love to him, and his comings and goings were closely watched. Given that my father was already paranoid, this new turn of events made life nearly untenable. The tension was extremely high.

It was the habit of the house that when my father came home from work my mother would retire for a nap and my brother and I would play with my father from five until half past six, at which time my mother would sit with us while my brother and I ate supper. My father bathed and changed for dinner with the adults at seven. During the play periods we would often roughhouse. Once my father's wings had been clipped, this time took on a whole new aspect. My father became increasingly more attentive to me. Within less than a month (my brother was away overnight at a friend's), my father, while roughhousing, pulled my sweatshirt back over my head, pinning my arms behind me, pulled down my jeans, forced me on my stomach, put some "3 In One" oil on his penis and (I still don't know what word to use here) Fucked me, Raped me, Screwed me, Buggered me, Made Love to me. It hurt awfully bad. As I began to scream he threatened to kill me. When I could no longer control whether I screamed or not, he forced my head to the side and bit down hard on my lower lip, breaking the skin. When he was finished, he insisted I fellate him to clean him up. At supper my mother put a Band-Aid on the lower lip. (I'd like to think it was a slip, referring to parts of my body as if they weren't mine; it's not, I've been doing it for years.) She reprimanded my father and me for playing too hard. The routine was quickly established. Within a week I had (what do you call it when it's repeated?) been with him twice more.

I ended up in the hospital with a high fever. Initially, the doctors thought it might be polio (it was during the period of the epidemic). After careful examination, however, they repaired a tear in my large intestine and, with antibiotics, the peritonitis cleared. No one ever asked me what had happened, or how. Just recently, I requested copies of the records. All that is listed is high fever and anal repair.

Upon my return home, he resumed his assaults as before. I grew to anticipate how and when they would come. If he could not get to me, he would become verbally and physically abusive to my mother and brother, eventually escalating the level of violence until he was throwing things and slapping us around. I became quite accomplished at getting my mother out of the way quickly, of convincing my brother that he and I should play with Dad separately, and always me first. If lucky, I could get away with fellating him; if unlucky, I submitted to anal intercourse. It's funny how quickly I learned "not to be there," to numb out. I could, within three or four minutes, shut off my mind and go on "automatic." It wasn't till much later in my life that I lost control of this ability and became increasingly "not there." I would come around, usually in a great panic, trying to piece together what I had missed. For a time, however, it served me well, thank God.

By the time I was eleven, my father was becoming quite disturbed and had been psychiatrically hospitalized twice for paranoia. It was not uncommon when accompanying him in the car to the local store for him to become quite paranoid, be convinced someone was following him, and end up in New York City as an avoidance technique. It was on one of these trips that my father and I ended up in New York late on a Friday. He had calmed down enough to realize that he was no longer in danger and decided we should eat in the Village. It was here I first acted as a decoy for my father. I was told to ask a young man standing on the street to come join my younger brother and me in the car. He did and ended up fellating father. Between the age of eleven and thirteen, this happened six additional times.

At age thirteen, I came home from school one day and found mother packing our bags. She said she'd had enough. Mother had discovered that father was having an affair with the marriage counselor. He had taped an individual session during which he and the counselor had made love. He played this the night before at the dinner table for all of us to hear. Dad had demanded his marital prerogative, asked her to perform an "unnatural act," and she had refused. He'd threatened to kill her and that was the final straw. For the first time in my life, I realized that, maybe, I wasn't crazy. I was inwardly thrilled to be leaving. (It is only recently, as I look back, that I have become bitter when realizing that only when it came to her welfare did my mother take action.) She had known of my father's assaults on me. When I was in the hospital, they had come to visit. She had gone out for ice cream and, upon her return, had interrupted my father in the process of forcing me to fellate him. I could never get her to talk about any aspect of this incident. Well, we did leave and moved into the summer house. I soon became my mother's keeper.

The town we moved to was a small, exclusive seaside community of the overprivileged, old-monied, politically conservative. It was promiscuous and two-faced in all other respects. Children went to boarding schools. There were ski trips and island trips and the New York Yacht Club cruise.

Mother was ill prepared to be the breadwinner. Having committed the unpardonable sin of divorcing her husband, she was promptly cut off from all financial and emotional support. We were quickly flat broke, literally dependent upon "the kindness of strangers." Mother drank heavily for the next two years, often coming home either loaded or with a perfect stranger (perhaps I should say a not-so-perfect stranger). This was one of the most difficult and desperate times for me. I thought I had finally escaped and instead I found I had inherited an entirely new and complex set of problems.

I was a quick study. I'd already learned to give whatever it took to get by. Mother increasingly turned to me as confidant, seeking approval and emotional support. Her new friends included me as her chaperone/escort. At age fifteen I was driving the car without a license, drinking at parties, restaurants, and bars. The illegality of it was never an issue. To this day I am amazed at how easily I made the transition from son to gigolo and how easily my role was accepted. I was treated as an equal by her friends and my mother alike. People often assumed we were brother and sister or that mother had again taken a young lover (I wish this were an exaggeration, but it is not!). For the first time my grades at school suffered, and I began to have marked fluctuations in weight (gaining and losing fifty pounds regularly; dieting, bingeing and purging episodically).

I took complete charge of running the household: shopping, cooking, cleaning, and when not acting as a chaperone, baby-sitting. I quickly learned how to put off bill collectors, juggle three checkbooks, forge signatures, and write excuses for school with authority and bravado. The only function I did not perform was that of lover. I believe mother was keenly aware of the danger that would have been for me (and I do remain thankful for that small favor). The manner in which she avoided it, however, was nearly as devastating. She had a series of indiscreet love affairs, at times insisting that I witness various forms of her lovemaking as I drove her and her beau home. Thankfully this stopped at fellatio. I only dared complain once and was told I was too conservative, a stick-in-the-mud. To prove the point she promptly tried to seduce the delivery man in my presence. I never challenged her again. In retaliation, I slept with my mother's best friend and lost my heterosexual virginity at age fifteen.

I grew to cherish the turmoil, the difference between my peers and myself. I had entrée into an adult world that was far beyond anything they could even anticipate. I had only one friend during this entire time. He was also gay and living a similar lifestyle, being brought up by his grandparents. We often shared stories and (I like to believe) provided a safety valve for one another. I learned early on to keep my mouth shut. My mother and her friends would say I was the essence of discretion (at times, however, I felt like the invisible man). Included in this lesson was the discovery of the force of my willpower, that I could accomplish nearly anything. All I really had to do was figure out what someone wanted (and, if possible, why) and then play to it. I successfully maintained (I still do) two, if not three or four,

separate lifestyles. I was at that time (still am) inwardly quite
confused because all realities became viable. At any given moment
I had to remember and maintain several facades. I think this was
near the acme of my ability to totally divorce myself from feelings.
(To this day I'm often not sure what I'm feeling, whether or not
I've manufactured a called-for response.)

In late adolescence I went to three different prep schools
(only two were boarding schools; mother wanted me home nights
and weekends to attend to household and chaperone duties).
Changing schools so regularly allowed me to be whoever I wanted
without fear of someone knowing my past. I discovered
amphetamine for weight control and quickly found it helped
support an increasingly diverse/disparate lifestyle. My first real
stint away from home was freshman year in college. I chose (over
objections of all aunts and uncles) to attend an extremely liberal,
small college in upstate Vermont. Drugs, dope, sex, and academic
freedom. Sophomore year I began the round of Ivy League
colleges. My uncles, in combination with my ability to gain
scholarships, convinced me to transfer. I did so yearly for the next
three years. I always maintained a 4.0 average and was given full
credit from school to school. As I've said, I was a quick study.
When brains didn't work, influence and my persuasion did. I
decided I wanted to become a social worker and chose a graduate
school in the Midwest (miles from the safe and sane Northeast) in
a large urban city. I wanted to work with disadvantaged youth, but
was instead placed in the Welfare Department at the time of the
steel strikes and massive layoffs at the automotive plants. Needless
to say it was nearly disaster. For the first time in my life I barely
scraped by (barely living up to my academic record of achievement
and totally unable to adjust). I bowed to family pressure and the
recollection of being broke as a teenager and applied and was
accepted to medical school, graduating in 1968 with one residency
in surgery and another in psychiatry. I couldn't stand the
arrogance of the surgeon, and I was increasingly seeking answers
to what had gone wrong with my life. I was chronically depressed,
sexually promiscuous, pan-sexually so, drug abusive, and in

general a great success. Rewards were no longer keeping up with gains. I, however, was still convinced that if I could just get it right, everything would be okay.

I married the year I graduated from medical school. I was absolutely terrified that if I didn't do it soon, I'd be lost. Someone would surely find out about me: my gayness, my fakery, my vulnerabilities. My mother graduated the same year with a doctorate in psychology and was entertaining fantasies about forming a joint practice with me. I needed to put as much distance between us as possible. I married a woman who had done volunteer work with my mother, was introduced to me by my mother, and was the first woman I dated of whom my mother approved. Julia was a fine Midwestern (read unsophisticated/ naive) young woman from a Waspy family. A child of the sixties, Julia had made one small "sad" mistake by getting herself pregnant out of wedlock and had borne a child. (Ignore the echoes of my mother's marriage—I was too scared to care.) The father of the child was a man with whom I had slept and continued to sleep until my marriage to Julia.

All was not gloom. Although I was a gay man, afraid of my own shadow, I was also a graduate of medical school and an adoptive father to a beautiful redheaded little girl named Susan. It didn't dawn on me that I was also father to a dependent wife who was just as scared as I was—she eventually became a little sister to me. Susan, however, was something I did right. Perhaps in my entire life, she was the only person I loved without guilt and trusted absolutely and wholeheartedly. For me she was a child of choice, without blame on my part. I do not want to overly romanticize this period. I was just starting out and Julia was going full-time to pharmaceutical school. I assumed total responsibility for running the household as well as making a living. I often felt like I was living a rerun of my late teens.

Susan inherited the best of both worlds: her mother's solid Midwestern honesty and openness, coupled with a good dose of New England sophistication/cynicism and an appreciation for the finer and absurd things of life. High points were sitting at

breakfast on Sunday on Newbury Street watching the parade and
acting wicked as we rated all who passed by. Susan and I spoke the
language of Best Friend/Uncle and Daughter. (Susan had always
known her real father.) She made me so very proud, providing me
with a touchstone that often deflated my balloon and laughing
with me as the air ran out and I began to wrinkle with age. Once
Susan was in college, Julia and I parted good and committed
friends (not without rancor, but certainly without a bang). After
all, we had always pretended to be mature adults; we were too
proud to be otherwise at divorce.

Susan died in the summer of 1982 in an automobile accident
in France. Julia had joined her there at the end of the summer,
intending to spend August with her. I had recently switched jobs
and could not get the time to join them. They had squabbled and
Julia returned early. I located Julia and, between the two of us, we
literally forced her onto an already fully booked plane bound for
France. It was the only time in my entire relationship to Julia that
she was single-minded and assertive. A day later, seventy-eight
hours after the accident, I received a call at work from Julia. (Julia
and I had always agreed that extraordinary means were not to be
used to prolong life when life was no longer viable.) She and the
doctor were in Susan's room. While I sat at my desk at work, with
the help of the nurse, Julia put the receiver to Susan's ear and the
three of us sang her a lullaby as the doctor shut down the life-
support system.

In the mid-seventies I took a male lover for the first time. He
was a nice formerly married man with two school-aged children. For
me this was my first monogamous relationship and my first gay one
of any significance. Bob was Italian—volatile, warm, outrageous, and
confrontative. He was also promiscuous and a true tramp. I wonder
if I didn't go from being figuratively married to my mother to being
married to my father. I cherished the turmoil. Bob was one of the
first gay men to be diagnosed with AIDS in the Greater Boston area.
My medical training had given me enough warning to steer clear of
sexual liaison with Bob once it became clear that multiple sexual
partners might be a cause of the (then new) disease. (To date I

remain seronegative.) Bob became increasingly ill and despondent until one god-awful Monday morning in April. While we were speeding to Boston for chemotherapy, he, in great despair, turned the car into a granite wall at about eighty-five miles per hour. I was thrown clear, he died.

My next three years were spent in plastic surgery and physical therapy. I got to choose a totally new look. Such a mixed blessing. I suppose if I had known who I was, it would have been an easier adjustment. I was depressed and, in a real sense, at times totally unable to care for myself emotionally and physically. My mother came to the "rescue," moving in with me and going about the motions of caring. Now in her sixties, she had lived life, if not in the fast lane (she used to say her soul was in the clouds, but her mind was in the gutter), at least recklessly. It has been costly physically. She was quite obese, smoked four packs of cigarettes a day, had numerous dependent friends and patients. Her emphysema required daily suctioning, nearly constant oxygen, and often functional immobility. She moved a cot into my room so that I could monitor her breathing. (After forty years I was again sharing a room with my mother.) Within six months I was feeling well enough to want some privacy. I rented her an apartment and sent her traveling at my expense for several months (not an inexpensive proposition when medical supplies must be arranged everywhere she went). She returned to my house on Labor Day, informing one and all of her wonderful time, poured herself a Manhattan and went to bed. She died early the next morning dashing to the toilet.

During the spring prior to Mother's death, encouraged by her admission of my illegitimacy, I endeavored to confront her about Father's abuse (one final time) in order to gain some insight into why it wasn't stopped and why it had gone on so long before we left. Her response was woefully inadequate (or perhaps I was seeking the impossible) and yet terribly accurate. With emotional resignation in her voice and tears in her eyes, she said, "Ya had to be there to appreciate just how bad it was."

"But! Ma! I was there! I do know."

She replied, "I thought you did, I know you did. We shared that, didn't we? I have often felt I made a mess of things, ya know. Oh my goodness, perhaps you should now talk with your father."

Fairly soon after mother died, I wrote to my father, requesting a meeting and outlining a protocol for the meeting. I left it that I would be calling him in two weeks, once he had had a chance to think it over. Within twenty-four hours of his receiving the letter, I got a phone call from him saying he was on the Cape. I agreed to meet at a local restaurant within the hour. Already I had given in and broken the outlined protocol I had hoped to follow.

When I arrived at the restaurant, there was no sign of him or his car. I tried to cool my heels leaning on the hood of my VW Beetle. I was "not too scared," just absolutely terrified. I was becoming keyed up and, in a real sense, beginning to "numb out." After about half an hour he pulled up. I was not prepared for the man who stepped out of the new Caddy Seville wearing a red sportscoat, gray flannel slacks, gray silk shirt, and an ascot and leading two golden cocker spaniels on a tangled leash. (I was to find out later that he had named them Nanette and Louisa after his present wife and my mother.) He walked directly in front of me without recognizing me (I'd had so much plastic surgery, he didn't know me right off). When I realized what had happened, I called out to him and was immediately launched into a frenzy of broken French/English and tears. He rushed to his car to get his camera and insisted that a passerby take a picture of us together. He was laughing, crying, and quite out of control. I became outwardly more and more reserved, while inwardly overwhelmed and frightened.

I had hoped to find a table in the back of the restaurant but had to scratch the idea as a busload of tourists headed in for breakfast, increasing the likelihood that his emotionality would draw attention to us. I thought the two of us might sit in my car, however, I'm six feet two and my father is six feet four, so I agreed to sit with him in his car. I had again broken my own protocol about being alone with him.

Once in the car, he said he understood that I might have

questions. He offered that he had questioned his paternity from the very beginning. Without being able to get a word in edgewise, I sat there trying to re-form my questions. Suddenly he automatically locked the doors of the car, raised the armrest dividing our seat, and while starting to fondle my leg, unzipped his fly. Grabbing the back of my neck and twisting it sharply downward toward him, he said he thought I called because I wanted to get together again to do it. While yelling, "No, not on your fucking life," I struggled to sit up, only to have the side of my head banged solidly against the steering wheel. As I yelled, he forced my open mouth down on the steering wheel, burying its rim so far back in my mouth my lower and upper back teeth on both sides were smashed. I pushed my way out of the car, swallowing blood. I ran for my car, locked myself in, and drove home. I tried to pull myself together and found myself slipping in and out of "being there." I reached my psychiatrist and set up an appointment that morning. By the time I arrived I was quite suicidal, damning myself for my poor judgment, convinced that somehow I had led my father on and caused it all to happen again like when I was nine. My psychiatrist was reassuring. He assured me that, at age thirty-nine, I had survived far worse and he was sure I would go on. He could only give me fifteen minutes. At the dental service, they removed several pieces and made an appointment for me the next day. I never went back to that psychiatrist and have yet to have the broken stubs in the back of my mouth repaired. One year later I had my neck rebuilt for the second time in my life. I can now "look straight ahead," barely able to turn to the right or left. I have a partial hearing loss in my right ear. I've switched jobs four times since, finally removing myself from clinical practice, taking the time (who's kidding who?), needing the time to finally address the question of *me*.

I entered therapy for the eighth time. Having had one somewhat successful attempt at coming to grips with aspects of my problem, I decided to address some of the incest issues. Approximately a year before, I had met a young therapist associated with the AIDS Action Committee for which I was also a volunteer. We had had one nasty run-in, and he had successfully stood up to my rather arrogant and offhanded manner of dismissing him. I was impressed. Within a year, he was running two advertisements in the local gay newspaper. One group was for gay men in their forties, who wished to explore issues of middle age and relationships. The other group was for survivors of incest. Of course, I was interested in the group dealing with incest and not the least bit interested in the middle-aged men's group. I therefore interviewed him and questioned him and watched him closely for an additional six months, then approached him about the middle-aged men's group. At that point, I decided to be honest and talk about the incest issues. I was struck by his lack of preconceived notions, or at least the care taken not to put them forth, thus freeing me from having to pander to them and accommodate them. My second major concern was the fact that I was an M.D. and he was a master's-level clinician. The concern was twofold: Would he be threatened by me and could he be trusted with the issues of confidentiality? Of course, ultimately therapy involved relationships, transference, countertransference, all the therapeutic garbage that came with the two of us being clinicians—wildly clouded by the incest issue of trust.

Two years later, I've taken a lover (also an abused male and child of alcoholic parents). It isn't the least bit easy for either of us. Trust is hard to come by, intimacy something as alien as living on the sun, and sex something to hope for as my lover is seropositive. My ex-wife is again pregnant and I've been diagnosed with Hodgkin's disease.

I ask myself, are there echoes? Thankfully, yes, and depending upon my mood I cherish them and call them memories and file them under wisdom; or alternately run agitatedly from ghosts, too scared to say "help," feeling too unworthy to trust responses.

I used to think, "live a day at a time." Progress means now planning two weeks ahead, with fantasies for the future. I still suffer from TUD (The Unknown Dread)—but then, who doesn't?

6

SURVIVAL STRATEGIES: A NEW PERSPECTIVE

We do not see the world as it is, we see the world as we are.
—the Talmud

"Do you know what I mean?" This would appear to be a matter-of-fact, straightforward question. In the course of everyday conversation, people check to make certain their listeners understand them. For many, this line becomes a figure of speech, a conversational mannerism, in a class with "Y'know?" "See?" or the Canadian "Eh?" It is a simple way to affirm the connection between speaker and listener, and may mean no more than "Are you still listening?" The speaker is probably unaware that he or she is using the phrase.

As I worked with survivors of abuse, I found myself increasingly aware of this question and others like it. I was hearing it more frequently and with greater intensity. It seemed to carry a sense of urgency. The question took several forms: "Do you understand what I'm saying?" "Does this make sense?" "Is that nuts?" I began to listen for the questions and to wonder about them. What was really being asked? What was behind the force of these questions?

It soon became apparent that I was hearing no mere figure of speech. I grew aware of the appearance in adulthood of a child's need to make sense of the world. I was rediscovering the extent of an abused child's need to compensate for the loss of a healthy childhood. I was witnessing a strategy for dealing with an environment that lacked sane guideposts. (**Note:** Your own family experiences are bound to be somewhat different from the examples I present. They represent the many ways children figure out explanations for abuse and survive abusive situations—and how survival techniques show up later in life.) No, this was anything but a figure of speech; I was being enlisted in the survivor's attempt to comprehend a complex situation. I was being asked a vital question, "Will you help me understand?" I was being told that the world of the sexual abuse survivor is confusing. He feels that everyone else was issued a "rule book for living" and he never got one. Other people appear confident in their opinions and perceptions. They seem to move powerfully in the world, secure in word and action. The survivor feels he will never be as confident about *anything* as others appear to be about *everything*.

When a survivor asks me, "Do you know what I mean?" I take the question seriously. He is sharing his confusion and feeling of isolation. He is inviting me to help him to make sense of the world. By asking, "Is this crazy?" or "Am I crazy?" he is telling me that he goes through life *feeling crazy*. Never confident that his perceptions are accurate, never sure that other people perceive things as he does, he continually questions his normalcy and sanity. Yes, I take these questions quite seriously. When what is being presented makes sense to me, I tell him that it does and why. When it doesn't, we discuss the parts of it that are unclear to me and attempt to resolve confusion into clarity. This may involve examining the content of what is being discussed or the style of presentation. Often as not, what is being talked about is perfectly clear; all that is needed is acknowledgment.

Focus

Masks and Images

Masks have many functions. You can hide behind them, disguise or decorate yourself with them, or use them to achieve a desired effect. Many survivors, disliking what they perceive to be their "real" selves, will carefully cultivate another image—one that they feel is more acceptable, attractive, or self-protective.

The purpose of these assumed identities is to hide what the survivor thinks are his character flaws and "fool" other people into liking him. The problem with masks is that they conceal the positive as well as the negative. Masks are rigid and unchanging. They always look the same, and the wearer appears to have the same response to all situations.

A mask can also offer clues as to what lies behind it. For those who are willing to look carefully, masks reveal as well as conceal. Your choice of a persona tells a great deal about your self-image and the way you perceive the world.

Male survivors have brought a variety of images into the recovery groups. (One group member even suggested the *actual* wearing of masks during the group. It would be interesting to see what the choices would be.) Some of the more familiar masks include:

• *Blustering:* Filling the room with words, "ragtime" speech, leaving no room for anyone to pierce his fragile defenses

• *Ominous:* Silent and glowering, presenting a dark image of barely repressed violence and great physical strength

• *Invisible:* So silent and self-effacing that he seems to disappear before your eyes

• *Intimidating:* Intelligent, glib, sharp-witted, and so psychologically savvy that no one dares challenge his verbal barrages

• *Angry:* Radiating rage, criticism, and intolerance—attacking to keep from being attacked

• *Outrageous:* Shocking in word, appearance, or behavior— using the bizarre to create protective barriers

• *Placating/Pleasing:* Being so nice, caring, and helpful that all attention is directed toward others

• *Comedy:* Relying on superficiality, banter, and irrelevancies to distract attention from his underlying pain

• *Tragedy:* The Lost Cause. Presenting an image of such severe disability that no one is likely to attempt such a Herculean task as trying to help him

- *Pollyanna:* The rosy pretense that everything is just fine—this mask is usually constructed of the most insubstantial material

- *Teddy Bear:* The warm, comforting, nonthreatening, amorphous (and usually asexual) creature that is the opposite of Ominous

- *Academic:* Retreating into his head to keep from riskier contact with the emotions—often taking the form of writer, lecturer, or analyst. Tries to be observer, explainer, or co-therapist in the recovery group.

All of these masks are probably familiar to you. You may be wearing one of them right now. What they (and other images) have in common is that they get in the way of face-to-face connections. They keep us from getting to know our natural allies. But fortunately they tend to be insubstantial.

Built of flimsy materials, our disguises dissolve when exposed to powerful concentrations of caring and encouragement. As we spend more time with them, they become increasingly transparent, until not even the wearer can fool himself into believing that they still work.

We present our masks to the world hoping they will be pierced. There is tremendous relief in letting them down and revealing the true beauty behind them.

Another aspect of the insecurity felt by survivors is expressed in precision of speech. Feeling confused and inarticulate, the survivor assumes that is how he is presenting himself. To compensate for this perceived lack of clarity, he may speak with a slow, measured tone and grammatical precision that robs his message of spontaneity and feeling. Conversation takes an academic tone, which serves the double function of overexplaining and ridding the words of the frightening reality of emotion. The secondary effect is that it distances the listener from the speaker. Information is conveyed as material in a lecture rather than what it is—a profound and vital expression of the reality of a human life.

Another example of a childhood survival technique manifested in adult life is the "throwaway" style of delivery. To keep his own feelings under control, the survivor may talk about his experiences as though they were of no consequence. The most disturbing stories of brutality and neglect are told with what amounts to a verbal shrug of the shoulders. The reasons are understandable. The survivor may be convinced that his listener would be frightened off by his whole story with feelings attached. He has been trying to keep feelings at bay for so long that it has become second nature. He fears that, once opened, the flood of emotions will be uncontrollable, washing away both speaker and listener. Now that he has found someone to listen, the prospect of frightening him or her away is too great to risk.

The effect on the listener can be confusing or chilling. It is strange to hear stories of human suffering told as though they had no more significance than a laundry list. But it is necessary to understand how important it is to be heard, even in a limited fashion. With patience and understanding on the part of the listener, feelings begin to reappear and the recitation of a plot outline is transformed into a story of the genuine experiences of a real person. (**Note:** Although seemingly opposite to the previous example of precise speech, the throwaway style is identical in source. Equally common and equally disconcerting, the two may even be found together—exactitude of speech delivered with a sort of "verbal shrug.")

Why would an intelligent, articulate person be insecure about his ability to communicate? Why would he fear that his perfectly reasonable perceptions and conclusions are the ravings of a lunatic? What has so destroyed his confidence? How is his fear of being (or going) crazy another legacy of abuse? And how do these adult examples represent holdovers of childhood survival strategies?

All children must make sense of their environments. They accomplish this by watching and listening to what is going on around them. They try to understand the world by playing out what they see and hear. In a stable, healthy situation, a child has opportunities to deal with confusion. Adults in his environment behave in a reasonably consistent fashion. Inconsistencies can be resolved by asking questions. There is a sense that the world is safe and can be understood. The abused child must attempt to function in an irrational environment. Rather than explaining and reassuring, adults in his life become sources of confusion. Adult behavior is, at best, inconsistent; at worse, it is brutal and terrifying. Words of explanation and reassurance that come from the grown-ups are at odds with the child's experience. He knows "something crazy is going on!" but he doesn't have a context for figuring it out.

Focus

Examining Your Survival Strategies

Coping methods can be healthy and positive or injurious and addictive. Any repeated behavior bears some examination. Here are four questions to ask yourself to help determine whether what you are doing is what you want to be doing:

1 / How did I feel afterward?

2 / Has it helped make my life more satisfying?

3 / What have I seen other people do in similar situations?

4 / What are some other options I might try?

Trying new strategies doesn't commit you to the changes. You can always return to doing things the old way. But the more you explore options, the more you are free to take charge of your life.

The abused child has to develop explanations for what was done (and what is being done) to him. And what was done to him is *crazy*. (**Note:** I am consciously using the word "crazy" in place of more clinical terminology to present it as perceived by the child.) He has been isolated by the abuser, and has little or no recourse to normal sources of information. He can only depend on his own resources. (Jealously, perpetrators frequently isolate their victims from other social interaction in an attempt to keep the abuse secret, or for domination and control.) In light of the limited and twisted reality available to him—full of contradictory messages—it is easy to see why the child feels crazy. If he acts on what he knows to be true, his behavior will be at odds with that of other children. Again, his perception of himself as different from other kids will be reinforced (forcing him back into isolation or further abuse). Adults who are unaware of the abuse will see him as a strange and disturbed child—and he will internalize their reactions.

The abused child has no opportunity to gain perspective on his situation. Where can he learn that he is not crazy, but his situation is? There is no one to tell him: It is crazy to sexually abuse a child. The child may not even know he is being abused. He may not know that anyone lives any other way. He does know that something is wrong. Since the world is so confusing, why not believe that there is something wrong with him? Able to depend only on his own resources, convinced that these resources are severely flawed, the child works to develop explanations for what was done to him and skills for daily survival.

Extreme situations call for extreme measures. In light of the need to make sense of a crazy situation, behavior that may appear dysfunctional can be understood as an effective survival strategy. I am in continual admiration of the creativity with which children figure out ways to survive an abusive childhood. Working against powerful odds, with limited resources and incorrect information, it is amazing that they survive at all. (And, of course, many do not.) No matter that some of the adaptations appear bizarre, they are functional. They permit physical survival. The child deserves absolute respect for having figured out a way to get through his childhood. It is only later, in adulthood, when there is distance from the abuse, that the individual can contemplate change. The actual abuse is no longer taking place, he is removed from it in time and distance, and the very strategies that enabled him to survive have become barriers to a satisfying life. Strategies have turned into problems, and the survivor will most likely blame himself for creating the problems, seeing them as further evidence of his deficiencies.

But the survivor deserves neither criticism nor blame. That bravely struggling child managed to figure out a way to make it through, and for that he is eminently deserving of complete admiration. He negotiated a sea of insanity despite lack of adequate training—and with an undependable compass. His limited strategies moved him through his abusive childhood to a point where, as an adult survivor, he can begin, however fearfully and timidly, to entertain the possibility of change. This is the beginning of his process of recovery. The child as survivor must be celebrated by the adult he has become. Like that child, you are more than an abuse survivor. You are fully human, with all the attributes, imperfections, and complexities that go with that definition. You possess intelligence, creativity, humor, and ability. Proceeding with your recovery will enable you to accept your full and rich humanity.

Chapters 7 to 11 examine in greater detail some specific childhood survival strategies and their cost to survivors' adult functioning. The chapters discuss how and why these strategies were developed, functions they served, and how, when they are no longer needed to insure survival, they become impediments to achieving a satisfying adult life. I hope that, in the course of reading these chapters, you will see these strategies for what they are—creative solutions discovered by intelligent young human beings caught in terrible, senseless situations. I trust that, through this understanding, you will (as I have) come to respect the creativity and innate goodness of all survivors—including yourself.

7

FORGETTING, DENYING, DISTANCING, AND PRETENDING

The memories first appeared when I was on my honeymoon. I had a new family and I didn't have to pretend that nothing happened.
—a male survivor

It's easier to think of myself as a liar than to admit that these things really happened to me.
—a male survivor

"Wouldn't I remember it if I had been sexually abused as a child?" It is reasonable to assume that something as frightening as sexual violation would be indelibly engraved in a person's memory. But frequently this is not the case. In reaction to the trauma of childhood sexual abuse, people often forget the entire event and anything related to it. This repression can even extend to events that occurred over a period of years. (See the discussion on p. 73, Loss of Memory of Childhood.) When memories aren't accessible, the individual feels as though he is working in a vacuum. He feels that something is wrong, doesn't know exactly what it is, and will very likely assume he is the problem. He will ask questions like: "Am I just looking for an excuse for my failures?" "Am I just a terrible person and trying to blame it on someone else?" "What is wrong with me that I can't remember my childhood?"

Recovery of "lost" memories is one of the most common reasons for entering treatment. The client feels that *knowing what happened* would take care of all the confusion and bewilderment. "If only I knew for certain— then I could deal with it. It's the uncertainty that's so hard." The survivor searches for the key that will provide access to his memories. He may work with hypnosis, psychodrama, guided imagery, psychoanalysis, meditation, massage, or any other combination of mind and body work to attain the ultimate prize—remembering.

There are problems associated with setting remembering as the all-important goal. It creates a mind-set that recovery of the memories is a prerequisite to any other recovery: "I can't go on with my life until I know *exactly* what happened." Maintaining this belief distracts the individual from the task at hand—healing the hurts of childhood. He becomes obsessed with remembering. Success or failure, health or pathology, normality or abnormality—all are judged by the degree to which the abuse can be recalled.

You are understandably curious; it is human nature to want to remember your own life. But turning into a memory sleuth is more likely to be frustrating than helpful. While I understand how hard it is to live with the uncertainty of not knowing, I urge my clients to try not to focus on regaining memories. I have seen many people do profound and important recovery work despite uncertainty that anything happened to them. Continue with your recovery program. A great many survivors recall memories spontaneously while engaged in other aspects of the healing process.

To understand how memories can be recovered, it is necessary to look at some reasons they are hidden. As discussed in chapter 6, survival is the first order of business for the abused child. Possessing limited resources and faced with ongoing assaults on his physical and emotional well-being, he has neither time nor ability to weigh options. He just has to make it through. When the world is overwhelming, and the pain too intense to endure, all that may be possible is to distance himself from the situation.

This is one reason why so many of the runaways—the "street kids" of our cities—turn out to be escapees, physically distancing themselves from abusive homes. They adapt to the abuses of the streets—drugs, prostitution, violence, and brutality—because they are no strangers to abusive situations. In fact, they know little else. Harsh as life on the streets is, there is an illusion of control over their situation. They are among others who understand their feelings. They no longer have to pretend that everything is fine. They don't need to put up a facade of normality. They aren't faced with the contrast between the apparently happy, normal families of their schoolmates and their own situation. They are able to make some sense of their situation. That the price of understanding and acceptance may be further abuse, addiction, disease, and death is simply another factor to be accepted. Return to the abusive family isn't an option. If nothing else makes you understand the magnitude of the trauma of childhood sexual abuse, this should. There are "fates worse than death." For many young people, death holds less fear than the family from which they ran.

For other children, running away from the abuse isn't an option. They may be too young, scared, physically incapable, or otherwise unable to leave home. These children figure out creative ways to distance themselves from abuse while it is occurring and after it has ended. Physically unable to get away from the abuse, they remove themselves psychologically. The child may retreat to a trance state or a fantasy world. Some of the "dreamy" or "spaced-out" kids we encounter are dealing with far more than an "overactive imagination." Men in my survivor groups talk of ways they removed themselves from abuse while it was going on:

> *"I was always having out-of-body experiences. I could float up to the ceiling and look down on my father and me."*
>
> *"I imagined that it was happening to someone else."*
>
> *"I just tried to think of other things until it was over."*
>
> *"I gave myself another name and another personality."*
>
> *"I knew that they weren't really my parents. Someday my real mother and father would come and take me away with them. She would be kind and beautiful. He would be tall and strong and would lift me onto his shoulders and we would live happily ever after." (This last was said with an embarrassed smile. It seemed as though the speaker felt that, although I might find this childhood fantasy silly, it was important that I hear it—and know what it meant to him.)*
>
> *"I just focused on how much I hated him. If I could do that, I didn't have to think about what was happening."*
>
> *"I pretended that my friend Joey's parents were my real family. I spent as much time as I could over at Joey's. They were always nice to each other and laughed a lot. I tried to get them to invite me to dinner with them a lot and I always wanted to stay over. My mother didn't want me to spend so much time there. I think she was hurt that I was happier there than at home."*

Further along the continuum of ways to deal with pain is blocking it completely. With emotional trauma, this can be accomplished by *forgetting*. If I don't remember my abusive childhood, it never happened. If it never happened, I don't have to deal with it. Not remembering parts of his life that are too confusing, painful, and overwhelming enables the abused

child to deal with only as much as he can. It is logical to solve huge problems by breaking them down into manageable bits. When abuse is especially severe or ongoing, enormous pieces of childhood may be pushed
into hiding. (I am no longer surprised when clients tell me that they
remember little or nothing of childhood.)

When an adult client tells me he can't remember whole chunks of his
childhood, I assume the possibility of some sort of abuse. Memories are
blocked for a reason. That reason is usually protective. Removing a protection must be done carefully and patiently, in an environment of safety
and caring. It is unreasonable to think that getting the memories back will
take care of everything. Just as we wouldn't think of opening a physical
wound and then leaving it to become reinfected, we must have a new
strategy ready to replace forgetting. It is important to point out that the
amnesia has worked. It enabled the child to get through the abuse, and
physically survive to adulthood. The dressing on the wound was temporary, but it sufficed until something more permanent could be found. We
can appreciate the creativity of the child in figuring out how to "play for
time." He survived until recovery became possible.

The adult survivor carries the legacy of these strategies. He discovers
other ways of protecting himself from painful memories. In addition to
forgetting portions of his childhood, he may rewrite history, a strategy
that contains elements of both *denying* and *pretending*. The adult survivor
may remember his childhood as perfect. He may paint over grim details
with softer colors. When a client presents "too perfect" a picture of
childhood, it is usually a good idea to look further. When something
appears too good to be true, it often is. This doesn't mean he is lying. He
chose a view of the world that he could deal with; he created a version of
reality that allowed him to function in the face of abuse. He is getting
ready to let go of his picture of a perfect childhood and look at what
really happened.

Related to strategies of forgetting and rewriting history are ratio-
nalizing and minimizing. Like rewriting history, these techniques contain
aspects of denial and pretense. The survivor may excuse the perpetrator,
explaining why he couldn't help it, that she was driven to it, that he didn't
know what he was doing, and that she "really loved me." Justifications
include alcohol, drugs, mental illness, a bad marriage, and so forth. In
fact, all the rationalizations offered by perpetrators to justify their abuse

may also be employed by the victims to excuse it. This, too, must be recognized as a way of diminishing the enormity of abuse so that it can be handled. As such, it must be respected as a survival strategy, but not accepted as reality.

The survivor may reduce feelings of overload by denying the severity of the abuse (minimizing). "It really wasn't so bad." The most extreme stories of sexual, physical, and psychological abuse have been presented by survivors in a casual, matter-of-fact, almost throwaway tone. I'm always surprised to hear people assume that survivors dramatize their histories. (I've even heard survivors themselves worry that they're being overly dramatic—making too much of it.) It has been my experience that, if anything, survivors tend to minimize what was done to them and need slow and careful encouragement before they accept that their childhood was truly painful.

One of my clients, whose father would burn him with cigarettes, was startled when I referred to the behavior as abusive. He had never thought of it that way. To him, it was just something that Daddy did. Only when I asked how he would react if I told him that a child he knew was being burned was he able to recognize that, indeed, he had been abused.

Abused children endure grim realities. That they survive at all is testimony to their strength and creativity. Having had to cope with more than most children, they may take their coping abilities for granted. When old strategies prove insufficient to the current situation, they feel incapable of "normal" problem solving.

As much as a survivor may want to remember details of his childhood (every bit as much as others may wish to forget theirs), his mind continues to protect him from the painful memories. I believe that the only reasonable approach to recovering occluded memories is to respect the reasons they are unavailable. Memories can best be recalled when certain conditions are met:

1 / **Time and distance from the abuse.** This is why it is more common for people to be dealing with the effects of sexual child abuse when they have reached their thirties, forties, and fifties. By then enough time has passed to recognize they are no longer in danger of being further abused as children. It is unusual for men in their teens and twenties to feel the same safety. The abuse is still too

recent. Danger still feels present. Physical distance may be necessary as well to create the right environment for recovery. Several of my clients came to Boston from other parts of the country because they felt they couldn't work on their recovery at home. Only by getting away from the perpetrators (or the environment in which the abuse took place) were they able to let down their guard enough to do the necessary work. (**Note:** This argues for extending or eliminating statutes of limitation on prosecuting child abusers.)

2 / **Creation of a safe environment.** Safety has many meanings. A feeling of comfort is often mistaken for safety. Recovery work undertaken by survivors is seldom comfortable. Any environment is likely to feel scary, especially one where painful emotions are triggered. When I refer to a "safe environment," I mean an atmosphere that is nonabusive, nonjudgmental, accepting of the individual and his story, and open to the expression of a full range of feelings. Despite diversity of backgrounds, education, ethnicity, wealth, occupation, age, and life experience, men in my recovery groups struggle to create a safe atmosphere to work on healing (see chapter 17 on groups). This is no easy task, involving as it does the need to trust virtual strangers. That these strangers are also men can make it even more difficult (a) for survivors who were abused by men and (b) for those who have adopted a negative view of their own maleness. The struggle to overcome fear and suspicion and push through years of emotional isolation is intensely painful. The success with which survivors have managed to create powerful, meaningful support systems in the face of these obstacles speaks to their courage as well as the strength of their desire to recover.

3 / **Sufficient emotional discharge.** The importance of feelings and their expression is addressed at length elsewhere in this book. It is useful, however, to mention it in the context of recalling blocked memories. Part of the recovery process involves the need to express feelings. The survivor may need to cry, rage, shake, and even laugh or yawn. His need and right to do these things must be

unquestioned. In fact, it is often necessary to reassure him repeatedly that it's okay. He will be feeling fear, embarrassment, confusion, anger, resentment, and physical tension. He must be encouraged to do so. There is no timetable for getting at (or through) these feelings. It can't be accomplished in isolation; patience and encouragement from others are vital to successful recovery.

4 / **A catalytic situation or event.** Although not always necessary, many survivors point to a specific event that triggered awareness of the need to do something about their situation. This can occur whether or not the survivor has conscious memory of the abuse. The catalyst may seem mundane and trivial (such as a television commercial that evokes a childhood memory or seeing a child in a playground), or it can be a major life event (the birth of a child or the death of a family member). I have heard men say:

"When I became a father, I was overwhelmed with sadness. I knew that I had to protect my child from something terrible."

"When I saw you on that television show I couldn't stop crying. I knew that something terrible had happened to me, too."

"I was having a massage and when he had me turn over onto my stomach I began to shake uncontrollably."

These catalysts may evoke full-blown memories or simply the feeling that something happened. For many it is the first clue that they were abused.

Memories are released and recovered when the individual is ready for them. When the conditions are met, it is unnecessary to pursue specific means of recall. Memories reappear, sometimes as vague images and at other times with a blinding clarity and breadth of detail. They may return all at once or in a slow, piecemeal fashion. Just as when a piece of information is "on the tip of your tongue," going after it directly seems to make it move further away from awareness, putting your attention on something else allows it to return. The best way for the survivor to recall forgotten events is to concentrate on his program of recovery.

It is important to remember that forgetting, denying, distancing, and pretending have been valuable survival tools. The process of recovery involves finding tools that fit the job at hand. Old tools, having served their purposes, can be put away with care and respect.

John's Statement

The abuse almost killed John, a forty-eight-year-old survivor. His determination enabled him to survive.

I cannot remember, but I have been told that when I was four years old I drank ammonia. I know now that was my first attempt at suicide.

I do not remember much about my childhood except that I was mostly unhappy. I was overweight and very feminine. I can remember my grandmother asking me how I could eat ice cream knowing it would make me even fatter, and no one would love me if I got any fatter.

When I was in high school I was sent to a psychiatrist because I was suicidal.

I wanted to go to college, but felt too insecure even to apply for admission. Instead I went to trade school to learn baking. (Also, it didn't cost anything, even though my parents could have afforded to send me to college.)

I was acting out sexually, being promiscuous with older men from the time I was in junior high school. I wanted a lover, but was too needy and sexually wild. Then, at age twenty-five, I met the perfect mate.

He was a very successful older man who was in complete control at all times. He was also always angry and homophobic and he didn't give me credit for knowing enough to come in out of the rain.

This ideal relationship—I felt like dirt and he treated me like dirt—lasted twenty-one unhappy years.

I worked very hard. I had a nine-to-five job, bought and sold antiques, and in my spare time renovated houses. We had a ten-room town house and a ten-room eighteenth-century vacation house. That way we could work evenings, weekends, holidays, and vacations. Both houses were totally restored by us.

I was becoming more and more unhappy. My life was not worth living. I could think of nothing that would ever make me happy. It was getting worse and worse and the only out that I could see was suicide. I was drinking more and more and using pot, but even that wasn't working. The only thing drugs and alcohol were doing was giving me the escape of blackouts. I had days that I functioned OK, but I don't remember being there.

Then on Nantucket in May 19–, I could see no hope. I decided this was it: no more fooling around, *just end it.*

But somehow God had other ideas. I got so drunk that the police picked me up and put me in protective custody. I don't remember any of it. The next morning they didn't just let me out—they put the local psychotherapist in with me.

He suggested I go to Alcoholics Anonymous. I told him he did not understand and that the only way I stayed alive at all was through the use of alcohol and pot. He finally convinced me to go to an AA meeting. Somehow, at the first meeting I was given hope that AA could make life worth living.

Two years sober and happier than I had ever been before I still felt emotionally shut down, so I started treatment with a psychotherapist. I was also going to Adult Children of Alcoholics (ACOA) meetings on a weekly schedule.

Four months after I started psychotherapy, I was at an ACOA meeting where a man spoke of being sexually molested by his father when he was two years old. I thought it was very sad and I started to cry. I could not stop crying.

My therapist went to lunch at twelve noon, and the next day (still crying) without an appointment, I was outside his door. When he came out to go to lunch, I told him I had to see him . . . *now.*

I explained that I was still crying over the story I had heard the night before. He said that was good. It meant I must be ready to face my own past incest.

I still don't remember, but I know it happened and I know what happened. It was with my father when I was three years old.

It is now three years ago that I first became aware incest was what was in the way of my living a happy life. I have now gotten past the most difficult part. I have felt the rage and the fear. I am not finished with it, but now I know it doesn't have the power to ruin my life.

I feel I am available for love and all the good things life should be full of. I have good close friends and my life is worth living.

8

NUMBING

I never smiled until I was twenty-three years old.
—Carl, a male incest survivor

When strategies of forgetting, denying, distancing, and pretending work, they allow the child to tolerate his abusive situation by putting it out of his conscious awareness. But what does a person do when he remembers the abuse all too well, and the memories bring nothing but pain?

Part of being fully human is to be open to the range of life's experiences and emotions. To a child who hasn't been severely hurt, the world is an exciting place, full of new and wonderful things to do, see, explore, and feel. The unhurt child approaches new situations with zestful curiosity, eager to see what life has in store, confident of his ability to master his environment. He knows that the adults in his life are benevolent and ready to help him overcome the frustrations and injuries that are a part of childhood. If he is aware of dangers in the world—that people may be irrational and hurtful—he is secure that the grown-ups closest to him will protect him from the worst of these dangers. He is free to feel excitement, joy, fear, anger, grief, or confusion, because he knows they arc all temporary conditions and family, neighbors, teachers, and older friends will be there to provide guidance and comfort.

Loving parents do their best to protect their children from extreme danger, while permitting them to take some risks. Risk taking lets the child learn valuable lessons: Many problems can be solved and some can't; one's actions have consequences; adults can't fix everything; and all endings aren't happy. A child who is not permitted to take risks may feel invulnerable (perhaps putting himself in mortal danger), or fear any risk taking (ending up leading a stifled, constricted existence). Parents must push through their own natural fears for the safety and well-being of their children. Fearing the worst and knowing that even their best efforts and continual vigilance cannot insure the safety of their children, they provide what guidance they can as their beloved children begin to move out into an imperfect world.

The process of growing up involves interplay between being nurtured and becoming independent. The healthy child moves back and forth between dependency and independence. The healthy parent provides a safe base from which the child can depart, explore, return to process his experience—and then depart on another journey of exploration. When, in the course of his explorations, the child encounters pain, he learns that the adults in his life will help him understand and deal with the hurt. The child grows to adulthood with a sense of security. Confident in his ability to function in a fundamentally benign world, he greets other people as potential allies and friends. His basic self-confidence is sufficient to carry him through difficult times and allow him to enjoy the good times.

The situation is quite different for the abused child. Finding himself in a confusing and painful situation, he has no one to whom he can turn for help, understanding, and comfort. The very people who would normally provide protection often cause the pain. If they are not the perpetrators themselves, they may be aware of the abuse (consciously or unconsciously) and allow it to continue. Or the perpetrator may have effectively isolated the child from any adult who might provide protection.

There are numerous ways that isolation is established and reinforced. The perpetrator may have forbidden the child to have contact with non-family members and thoroughly intimidated those within the family, preventing them from supporting one another. He may insure the child's silence by coercion, threats, or actual physical violence. She may frighten the child with images of what will happen to him (disapproval, punishment, imprisonment, removal from the family, or even death) if "his part" in the abuse is discovered. He may likewise promise injury to himself or another figure who is important to the child if the abuse becomes public knowledge. (Remember, it is not safe to assume that the child does not love the perpetrator.) She may enlist the child in a pact, promise, or conspiracy of silence. Or he may bribe his victim into compliance. There are many ways to keep a child silent. Whatever means is used to maintain the secrecy, silence isolates the child from potential allies. He sees no way out of this situation; his isolation can last well into adulthood. Faced with the prospect of a life of chronic pain, confusion, and isolation, and (for whatever reason) unable to forget what is being done to him, the child may attempt to reduce his pain by numbing.

This is how the numbing process operates. When abuse is present, a child can become suspicious of any feeling. Emotion is so often connected with pain that, to avoid any painful emotions, he may attempt to deaden *all* his feelings. When feelings mean pain, then the absence of feelings becomes a working definition of pleasure. Based on the misinformation that all emotion must be painful emotion, the abused child sets himself the task of ridding himself of all feelings by diminishing them, destroying them, or distracting himself from them.

We have all seen numerous examples of well-meaning adults who attempt to numb (usually seen as "soothing") a child's feelings with ice cream and cookies or distract them with toys, comforting sounds, or entertaining activities. These adults have also bought the idea that feelings are to be avoided at all cost. By these means the child receives further evidence that the proper response to a feeling is to kill it. He finds an activity, object, or substance that lulls him, distracts him, and diminishes the pain, and he employs it as long as it achieves the desired effect. If a specific strategy ceases to be effective in numbing the pain, he may increase the duration of the activity, quantity of the comforting substance, intensity of the behavior, or turn to another form of numbing—one designed to be stronger or longer-lasting. If this looks like a description of addiction, *it is*. The child is setting an addictive pattern that will very likely follow him into adulthood. Unless recognized and interrupted it will persist throughout his life.

It is unusual to encounter a survivor of abuse who isn't addictively or compulsively engaged in some form of numbing behavior. Although everyone, at times, has a need to numb—to escape the pressures of life by diminishing the intensity of their feelings—the addict feels that ordinary life is so painful that, to survive, he must diminish or redirect *all* intense emotions. I am not simply referring to chemical addictions (although a high percentage of drug addicts and alcoholics were abused as children, often by addicted or alcoholic adults). I am talking about any consistent, ongoing, intensive pattern of behavior designed to numb feelings.

Clearly, some numbing activities are more socially acceptable than others. Some, in fact, may even be valued by society. Rather than being interrupted, socially acceptable addictions and compulsions may be rewarded and reinforced. These numbing behaviors are not recognized as such, much less seen as addictions. The man who directs all of his energy into his career may jokingly refer to himself as a *workaholic,* but he seldom is conscious of the import of that definition. And, of course, as his career and income increase—as others recognize and reward him as a "pillar of society, wonderful provider, and wealthy, sober, upstanding citizen"— there is no awareness of the pain underlying his drive to work ceaselessly. The workaholic's pattern is doubly reinforced: (a) the time spent at work occupies his energy and distracts him from painful emotions; and (b) appreciation by others makes him feel more worthwhile (less damaged). Of course, that very appreciation has an addictive quality, spurring him to greater achievement in his work life so that he can appear even greater in the eyes of others. The workaholic becomes trapped by the very strategy he devised to escape from feeling bad about himself. He now feels he can never slacken his drive to the top, fearing the loss of acceptance and admiration of others, as well as reemergence of painful feelings. Even when the workaholic achieves the pinnacle of success in his field he cannot rest, for fear of losing what he has achieved and because awful feelings and memories are still waiting to entrap him.

This is not to say that a person shouldn't put energy into his career. It is important to derive satisfaction from our work—one of the cornerstones of life. But when a person completely derives his identity and worth as a human being from his work, he has erected a very fragile structure. We have all seen the results of such an orientation: the executive who retires and loses all will to live, or the person who "takes to drink" after being fired. One drink doesn't make one an alcoholic, nor does being excited about and invested in one's career turn one into a workaholic. We are talking about the degree and quality of the behavior. Whenever one aspect of a person's life becomes the overwhelming focus of attention, it is a good idea to take a look at it. Most addictive behaviors taken in moderation are either acceptable to society or attract little attention. It is the nature of addiction, however, that it rarely remains at a moderate level. The solution (strategy of numbing) intensifies until it becomes a problem. That is why numbing is only a temporary solution to the problems of the survivor, ultimately creating additional problems. Addictions and compulsions are extreme extensions of any numbing behavior. Alcoholics and drug addicts face health problems, loss of family and friends, and psychological difficulties; so do the men who are addicted to their careers.

There are many other examples of numbing patterns, carrying varying degrees of social acceptability. In my groups for male survivors, I have seen recovering alcoholics and drug addicts, compulsive overeaters, gamblers, shoppers, spenders, and workers. There are men who are "addicted" to sex, masturbation, credit card use, television, danger, sleep, bodybuilding, and marathon running. There are fanatic collectors of art, automobiles, clothing, money, academic degrees, and friends. There are people who are driven to take care of others and religious fanatics of every philosophical stripe, both Eastern and Western.

Few of these activities or interests would arouse anyone's concern if kept in perspective and used in moderation. It is the quality of the behavior and the underlying reasons for it that are troublesome. When a survivor undertakes a pattern of numbing feelings as a strategy for surviving abuse, he may feel better for a while. Ultimately, the behavior gets out of control and causes more pain than it alleviates. At that point, the survivor must add one more difficult task to his program—overcoming addiction. He must learn to live without numbing and experience the range of feelings necessary to recovery and a healthy life. The way out of the pain is *through* it. Ultimately, pain can no more be numbed than it can be avoided. Instead, the survivor must find a safe and encouraging environment in which to feel his emotions, including painful ones. In this setting he gradually lets go of his numbing techniques and experiences the reality of feelings—they are rich and wonderful and nobody ever died from having them.

Carlo's Statement

Carlo, at forty-seven, is good-looking, articulate, intelligent, athletic, and popular. He owns an established business and is a devoted father. Most observers would consider him happy and successful. His statement, in the form of a letter to his friends, presents compelling evidence that numbing strategies don't work forever, and that while "masks" may conceal pain, they don't eliminate it. I include his letter because it speaks eloquently of the damaging effects of covert incest and offers a creative way to confront abuse, ask for needed support, and let trusted friends know how they can help.

Dear Friend,

I am a survivor of childhood sexual abuse. I am a survivor but I continue to suffer from its insidious effects. I was covertly and, to a lesser extent, overtly incested. The abuser was _____, my mother. In my original notes I referred to her as my "unaware" mother. That thought and even this insertion are indicative of my continuous efforts to protect her.

I've enclosed a link to a definition (actually two) of covert incest that I hope you will read. I need the definition because I have a hard time explaining the subtle yet significant implications. Part of the problem for me, and I fear for you, too, is that you will read it and say, "Yeah? So? Doesn't everyone experience this to some extent? You didn't die, your uncle didn't bugger you, tuck up your skirt and get over it!"

As you read the definition(s) think of me and what you really know about me. Try to integrate and reconcile these thoughts with the symptoms listed. I suffer—I repeat suffer—from all of them. Please read them now and come back to this letter:

www.alwaysyourchoice.com/ayc/emotional/emotional/incest_covert.php

www.sexualhealth-addiction.com/covert.htm

I carry within me a deep well of sadness traceable to my late dad. I can't tell you now whether I'm grieving the fact that we never had a relationship, or that I'm angry he abandoned me, or I'm guilty that I held him in contempt. I'm working on this—hard.

At some early age, to protect myself from painful feelings, I shut down emotionally. For forty-plus years and counting I have scuffled through life intellectualizing my relationships. I read people and react. I have only recently become aware of those forces that have guided my life. This illumination has yet to alter the fact that I am still unequipped to feel those feelings that I am led to believe make life worth living. To consider what this is like imagine going through life eating without being able to taste the food. Complicate this by adding the component that you are terrified that the taste will nauseate you. Every once in a while you will inadvertently experience a taste; and it is sweet and delicious. But you quickly catch yourself and gag before you throw up. Oh but you can remember that delicious moment and you ache to get it back.

Why have I given this to you? I don't need you to talk to me about it although I would welcome any conversation. I don't need or expect any pity. In fact I expect all of you to continue to bust my balls. I would, however, welcome your support and understanding. At this point in my active recovery there is just one thing I do need from all of you. I just need you to know. Thanks for taking the time. Thanks.

Take care,
Carlo

9
COMPARTMENTS

Everyone gets a piece of me, but no one has all of me.
—Philip, a male survivor

Throughout most of human history, daily life existed as an integrated whole. Even where there was a culturally established division of labor (men hunting and women gathering food) the divisions were known by and visible to all members of society. Life wasn't divided into work vs. play, religious vs. secular, or career vs. family. Everyone knew who they were and where they fit into the fabric of social life. Celebrations and special events formed part of the rhythm of life. Security was found in the belief that life in the present was an extension of what went before, and would continue into the future in much the same manner. When we became an agrarian peasant society, this integration continued. The family unit was the unit of work. Extended families worked the farm, ate, played, and worshiped together. Although the seasons changed, the rhythms of life remained constant. Neighbors lived in ways that were pretty similar. You not only knew who you were, you knew who everyone else was.

As we became an increasingly industrial and then technology-based civilization, the natural integration of daily life began to break down. Work became more specialized, so we no longer knew what everyone else was doing. And work began to take people out of the home, so that even family members were leading very separate lives and moving among different people. Children educated outside the home encountered schoolmates and teachers with dissimilar ideas, values, and experiences. For men, this transition was especially isolating. Men were the first group to work away from home. This was in sharp distinction to the traditional role of the man as the head of a family-based workforce, which was also the basic social, religious, educational, leisure, and celebratory unit. In modern society the schools educate, the clergy prays, and the man most frequently spends the bulk of his time at work, removed from family, neighbors, and friends. He is encouraged to keep career, family, friendships, and leisure activities separate from one another. Since everyone he knows is living the same way, it seems natural to do so. Modern man can find himself feeling isolated from those closest to him without realizing why.

When someone feels strong and healthy he strives for an integrated life. He sees himself as a whole person who brings together diverse aspects of personality, training, and experience. Although his responses to people and situations may vary, the face he presents to the world is fairly constant, whether he is currently occupying the role of worker, friend, neighbor, or family member. Of course, he will not treat an employee in the same manner as he does his child. He will certainly not interact with his child as he would a lover. But, whatever the interaction, the same basic person is in evidence. This being so, he is able to deal with those times when various parts of his life intersect (such as having the boss over for dinner or running into a coworker at a party). Part of becoming an adult involves learning how to adapt to the requirements of a range of social situations *while remaining true to one's essential personality*. It has been said "the advantage of telling the truth is that you don't have to remember what you said." The secure individual has accepted himself enough to act on the assumption that he doesn't have to change *who he is* to interact with different people. It is enough to be sensitive to the needs of the situation—and to be himself.

Most abuse survivors find it very difficult to integrate their lives in this manner. For one thing, they lack a visible model of integration. The adults who abused them showed them faces very different from those they presented to the rest of the world. Abused children are taught to pretend that nothing is amiss, and they learn to keep secrets very well. The abused child realizes early on that, to survive, he must become a master of pretense. It makes little difference when he receives conflicting information. If one experience contradicts another, he simply keeps them separate—each in its own little compartment—so they don't interfere with one another. The child, then, has learned to accept an infinite number of coexisting realities. It is small wonder he feels grounded in none of them, and reality is seen as fluid and insubstantial.

Sexual abuse leaves a victimized child with a fragmented life. He had to learn ways of keeping the parts of his life separate from one another. The sexual abuse must be kept secret, locked in a compartment that cannot be shown to peers, teachers, or even other family members. If he needs to escape temporarily from the pain of the abuse, he moves into another compartment. When an event occurs that doesn't fit into any of the existing categories, he creates a new compartment to account for it. This need to compartmentalize his life gets carried into adulthood, the survivor ending up with an adult life consisting of fragments he is unable to integrate.

Even if he is devoid of memories and numbed of feelings, the survivor of abuse lives in an isolated world (as discussed in chapters 7 and 8). He feels no one can understand him. Since he doesn't know whether he can trust his own memories and perceptions, he's not sure he can even understand himself. Carrying the perception that he is hopelessly flawed as a person, an integrated life seems beyond reach. Each social interaction, every new situation, feels completely different, and he feels frighteningly unequipped to cope with the additional demands. It doesn't feel like a matter of adapting one's experience and intelligence to somewhat different requirements. Instead, the survivor fears each new situation because it has to be learned afresh, from step one—and he doesn't know whether he is up to the challenge. Fearing new people and new situations, the survivor may find himself increasingly isolated, dealing only with the familiar, afraid to risk—reinforcing his sense of unworthiness and unacceptability.

Increasingly, even within the life that is familiar to him, the survivor may separate one part from another. Keeping all the parts of his life in tight little compartments, isolated from one another, feels both easier and safer. It is easier to act a role if you are sure of the play you're in. If you only have to interact with one person at a time, you only have to *be* one person at a time. It doesn't matter that the relationship becomes static and dull; it is safer that way. There are fewer surprises; surprises are not always pleasant. And the more compartmentalized your life is, the less information needs to be shared with any single individual. Conversely, the more information that gets out, the less control you have over how it is used . . . or abused. And, most important, if the abuse can be kept in a compartment it is less likely to spill over into all parts of your life. It can be kept under control. It's much easier when you know where the abuse is located, instead of never being sure of when and where it might pop up.

One of my clients, who is academically, professionally, and socially adept, told me, "Everyone gets a piece of me, but no one has all of me." He felt he had to maintain rigid control over who saw what, and that it was necessary to present inaccurate, intentionally distorted, and radically different faces to protect himself. It is significant that when he referred to others in his life he said, "No one has all of me," rather than "No one sees it all." It reflects the assumption that knowledge is power, and power will always be used to hurt. If people know who I am (he reasoned) they will have more control over me and I can't risk that. I know what happens when someone gets too close.

For this man the course of recovery necessitated gradually sharing more of himself, in group and individual therapy. As he did so, always terrified, always certain that openness would lead to further abuse, he began to explore the possibility of leading a healthier, more integrated life. Along with terror came the feeling that when he had revealed enough of himself to me or the other group members, he would certainly be rejected. We would then see how imperfect, stupid, evil, and ugly (all *his* words) he really is. We would be angry with him for having fooled us, and be repulsed by him. Reality was, and continues to be, quite the opposite. Freed of his need to maintain rigid control, no longer having to expend vast amounts of energy on keeping people apart and remembering who knows what about him, he could begin to relax. As he did so he became more (not less) attractive. Displaying vulnerability made him real and accessible. He found himself feeling welcome for the very first time. It is important to state that these changes did not happen quickly or easily. Each step involved moving through terror and doubt. There were times when the fear became too overwhelming and he slid back to the safety of one of the old compartments—but the compartment no longer fit and was certainly far less comfortable than it had been. So the retreats lasted for shorter and shorter periods. And, although the recovery process is not over, he is now integrating the diverse aspects of his life.

The day he told me, "You have more of the pieces than anyone else," I knew I had been given an important and valuable gift. The trust he placed in me was (and always will be) to be cherished and nurtured. As his recovery continues, his face and body relax more and more. He looks younger and less strained. He no longer needs to cringe or strike intimidating poses. His voice has become softer and he shows emotions more easily. And most important, as he allows people to get to know him, he is no longer able to accept the misinformation that helped keep isolation in place.

As long as he kept himself hidden from others, he was able to discount any expression of caring on the grounds that, whatever the other person was seeing, it certainly wasn't *him*. Whatever the reason, it wasn't real. He had fooled yet another individual into liking him. And if he could fool him—if this other person couldn't see through the act—then he surely wasn't smart enough to be of any real help. So he was faced with an apparent double bind. He felt that if he wanted people to stick around, he couldn't be real. He had to pretend, caretake, or buy friendship. If he couldn't be real with someone, why have him around? Social contact brought the feeling that his situation was hopeless. Now, as he increasingly lets go of controlling behavior, masks, and compartments, he is finding that people were attracted to him *despite* these things rather than because of them. People like him because he is a good, smart, kind, and interesting person. They like him because he is likable. They are attracted to him because he is attractive. And *that* is reality. What a challenge to trust that this might be so! What fear in testing that belief! What a relief to let down the defenses and controls! And what a triumph to turn around lifelong rigidities!

These changes are available to you. As you proceed with your recovery, you will encounter similar challenges, fears, relief, and triumph. You will experience doubt and mistrust, and you will sometimes find yourself slipping back into old compartments. But these slips are temporary. Increasingly, you will find the compartments are breaking down, replaced by something that is far more satisfying and real—an integrated life.

10

SELF-IMAGE, SELF-ESTEEM, AND PERFECTIONISM

I have two teams that I take everywhere with me: the FBI to check everything out and a film crew to record and make sure I did everything right. And they are both me.
—a male survivor

An abusive childhood shatters the survivor's self-esteem, leaving him with an unrealistic picture of himself. Regardless of how he is perceived by others, his self-image is negative. He feels ugly and unlovable. Since these feelings don't reflect objective reality, they aren't subject to change through rational argument. Despite all evidence to the contrary, the survivor "knows" he is ugly, stupid, incompetent, uncreative, weak, sick, and/or evil. When people perceive him in any other way, he takes it as evidence that he has fooled them. He can discount them because they are so easily taken in by what is, to him, an obvious deception. If they see the ugly "reality" and don't appear bothered by it, several explanations are possible—none of them positive. They are laughing at him behind his back. They are treating him kindly because they feel sorry for him. They are "losers" themselves and thus not worth his time. They are enduring his presence because they want something from him. Or they haven't perceived the full scope of his unacceptability. Any explanation that occurs to him confirms his lack of worth. That a normally perceptive and intelligent person would find him likable or desirable (in any way that isn't harmful) is inconceivable. He never entertains the possibility that others may be correct in their perceptions of him, that they like him and want him around because he is an interesting person. He has had to rely so completely on his own view of reality that the possibility of accepting any other reeks of danger. After all, look what happened when he was subjected to the perpetrator's definition of reality.

As a child, the survivor realized he had little or no control over whether the abuse would take place. Smaller, weaker, and less experienced than the adult perpetrator, he was forced to submit to his or her greater power. At best he learned to manipulate the situation to shorten the duration or lessen the intensity of the abuse. One survivor reported the following:

> *"I knew whether he was going to want sex as soon as he walked in the door. I learned how to get my mother out of the room so that we could get it over with as quickly as possible. If I did it fast enough, then he might not beat us up. I was angry with her when she didn't leave right away. It meant that he was going to hurt me more."*

This man learned at an early age that his power to control his life was severely limited—and because of his inferior position, his best chance at self-protection was to limit the scope of abuse through manipulation. Not having the ability to protect himself or significantly alter his situation led to a general feeling of inferiority and powerlessness. "If I were only smarter, stronger, quicker, or nicer [the child feels], this wouldn't be happening to me." It is clear to him that, because he cannot adequately protect himself, he is inferior. No one can preserve positive self-esteem while feeling powerless and inferior. As the survivor carries this sense of inferiority into adulthood, it is manifested in a variety of forms.

He may completely accept his own lack of positive attributes, defining himself as hopelessly flawed. Given this perspective, it seems foolish to even try to take charge of his life. Career, relationships, academic achievement, athletic prowess, and enjoyment of life all are perceived as unattainable. So why bother to even try? People will respond to him as a failure because that is how he presents himself. Any success he achieves can be written off as accidental, or discounted as incomplete—not good enough. What difference would small successes make, anyway? Only perfection would provide protection. He is safe only if he is the smartest, strongest, quickest, and best looking. This is impossible to achieve, so why bother trying? Nothing less will do. Nothing less will protect him. Nothing less than absolute perfection will satisfy him. Since no one can be perfect, his need to be so will surely destroy what is left of his self-esteem.

In these ways, feeling flawed and incomplete, believing his only protection lies in complete power, strength, intelligence, and competence, the survivor has become a perfectionist. His world is one of extremes. Relationships as well as achievements are idealized. People must be perfect or they are worthless. Since it is clear to the survivor that he is massively imperfect, he knows it is just a matter of time before other people recognize his worthlessness. Faced with division of the world into "perfect" and "worthless," the survivor finds himself in another no-win situation. The perfectionism presents itself in this form: "In order to be OK, I must be perfect and do everything right." Anything short of perfection is interpreted as further evidence that "I can't do anything right." Partial success is seen as no success at all (and humans are, after all, imperfect beings), so there is no way to overcome his shortcomings.

Focus

All-or-Nothing Thinking

To "see both sides" of a problem is the surest way to prevent its complete solution. Because there are always more than two sides.

—Idries Shah, REFLECTIONS

Abuse narrows a child's perception of the world. Having come to see people as either perpetrators or victims (chapter 2), he grows to adulthood with a similarly constricted view of life. The world is divided into black-or-white, all-or-nothing, life-or-death dualities. There is no room for flexibility or nuances in his rigid worldview—the stakes are too high. Throughout this chapter are examples of the extremes to which all-or-nothing thinking can be carried.

For the survivor recovery involves a piece of electrical work. He must remove the on-off switch that limits the way he responds to the world, and install a dimmer. Most people are neither heroes nor villains; most events fall somewhere between triumph and tragedy. When we only allow two options for any situation, two solutions for any problem (the right way and the wrong way), we are cutting ourselves off from most of life's richness.

I once commented to a survivor client that there is a vast territory between black and white. He replied, "Oh, you mean shades of gray." "Yes," I agreed, "but also red, blue, green, orange, and magenta. . . ." Expanding the possibilities we allow ourselves opens us to the rich and colorful spectrum of human experience. It lends variety to an otherwise drab palette. As survivors move through their hurts, they discover new and exciting options have opened for them. Recovery is a matter of expanding horizons.

There are four specific ways perfectionism plays out in the lives of adult survivors:

First, being a perfectionist while perceiving himself as "damaged goods" leaves the survivor feeling even more hopeless. He may respond by giving up entirely. Convinced he has no chance of success, he may not even try to achieve in school. He believes that a successful career is completely beyond his grasp, settling for just getting by, taking any job that comes along. Of course, nobody would want such a "failure" as a friend, lover, or husband—it would be foolish to even bother. Thus the prophecy fulfills itself. He becomes the failure he always knew he was.

A second scenario for the perfectionist survivor is to settle for an average level of achievement while putting himself down for his mediocrity. He is able thereby to live a perfectly acceptable life while maintaining an overwhelming sense of failure. His need for perfection doesn't allow him to take pleasure in "modest" accomplishments; they only serve to further lower his self-esteem. In this form of perfectionism, we can see most clearly the difference between the image the survivor presents to the world (external) and his self-image (internal). Outwardly, he is leading a comfortable, responsible, and reasonably well integrated life. Who would suspect he views these very things as evidence of his failure? He knows he has settled for second best.

A third manifestation of perfectionism is overachievement. Many adult survivors are tremendously talented and accomplished. They have achieved enormously successful careers, amassed sizable fortunes, become well-respected members of their communities, formed deep and long-lasting friendships and relationships, been caring family members, and done great good for humanity. They are, in the eyes of society, successful. But success brings no solace. If they are not at the absolute top of their professions, it is not enough. No level of income is sufficient to allow them to relax.

One of my clients, a single man with no dependents, said, "If I don't make over one hundred thousand dollars a year, I might as well commit suicide." He meant it. Anything less was evidence of failure. However, the fact that he earned far more than that was not seen as evidence of success. Again, it is a no-win situation.

Another client, a multimillionaire with a loving family and winning personality, found himself conspicuously amassing possessions so "people will think I'm rich."

Even if he reaches the absolute peak of his profession, the perfectionist survivor remains driven, lest he lose what he has attained and thereby reveal to the world his "true nature"—a failure.

If he has achieved a perfect career, family, friendship, or honor, the perfectionist is able to discount it by selective comparison. "I may be rich, but I'm not handsome." He compares himself to others in ways designed to find him wanting. He compares his intelligence to Einstein's while measuring his biceps against Schwarzenegger's, and his wealth to Gates's. He would never dream of doing the reverse, comparing himself to a whole person, or even not judging or comparing himself at all. He has judged himself inferior and continues to find evidence to justify the verdict.

Fourth, other male survivors become chronic "underachievers," finding themselves in menial, ill-paid positions for which they are tremendously overqualified. I have known male survivors with several advanced degrees working in clerical or manual jobs *because they felt inferior* to people with far weaker abilities and qualifications. I'm not judging the relative merits of different careers. If an occupation is freely chosen, it can provide satisfaction. But if an individual feels stuck in a job that provides nothing but frustration and confirmation of his failings, the situation needs to be reexamined.

Whether the adult survivor is a medical doctor who "feels like a fraud," a multimillionaire who worries about feeding his family, a talented musician who helps others achieve success while he remains in the background, or a skilled and insightful psychologist who moves from one menial temporary job to another, the issue is *self-esteem*. Although female survivors also struggle with career and success issues, there is a cultural bias that men are supposed to be aggressive and fearless in pursuit of professional success. Feeling passive and fearful, the male survivor is able to sabotage or discount any career achievement. An important aspect of recovery is development of a more positive self-image. This is most effectively accomplished through building trust in others. In therapy, in recovery groups, and with friends, the survivor gradually begins to accept a more accurate view of what is a reasonable and clear picture of himself. This, in turn, opens the possibility of enjoying career success as part of a satisfying, well-integrated life.

Until the survivor is ready to let go of perfectionism and accept a more reasonable self-image, his life is plagued by anxiety, tension, and the torture of self-doubt. The effects can be enormously unhealthy. Since only perfection will do, the perfectionist hates himself for his perceived shortcomings. Having set himself impossible standards, he sees he doesn't measure up to them. His unrealistic standards can lead to danger-ous behavior. Feeling, for example, that his body is ugly and unattractive, he may resort to self-destructive eating habits (including rigid dieting, anorexia, or bulimia). He may attempt to perfect his physique by compul-sive bodybuilding coupled with use of steroids. If he was once over-weight, he is ever vigilant in his war against calories. No evidence of mirror, height–weight charts, or reactions of others will convince him that he is not grossly obese or in imminent danger of becoming so. One client, who would be described by almost anyone as tall and elegantly slim (perhaps verging on gaunt), showed me photographs of himself taken many years ago as evidence of how fat he *is*! He feels he must con-tinually purge himself of food (a condition known as bulimia) so he doesn't show the world his true nature.

The catch-22 of this situation is that it also feels dangerous to appear too attractive. If other people find the survivor attractive, he believes, they will abuse him. The compulsive overeater may feel his obesity is a buffer, providing insulation from a dangerous world. Food, for the overeater, serves many purposes. It provides nourishment and depend-able comfort. It numbs negative feelings. The resultant obesity keeps people from taking a sexual interest in him, and provides visible evidence confirming his negative image of his inner self. He feels he is (always was and always will be) ugly. He uses this "evidence" as another stick with which to beat himself. Attempts to bring his weight under control evoke massive terror. That the only way he can still the fear is with food destroys any hope of success. Again, his sense of failure is confirmed. It is important to understand that the survivor feels a need to project an image at odds with his self-image. He faces two conflicting pressures: (a) the need to be (and appear) perfect to conceal his perceived flaws (imperfections) from the world; and (b) the need to conceal anything that would make him attractive, so he will not invite abuse.

If the survivor is to be attractive in any way, he must find something to protect him from the resultant threat of abuse. Thus, the bodybuilder may attempt to protect himself by presenting a powerful and intimidating image to the world. The martial arts expert tries to be the best so no one can overpower him. Perfectionist survivors are likely to be obsessive and extreme in their athletic pursuits. Runners are drawn to ultra-marathons or triathlons. The underlying, often unconscious goal may be safety; it may be acceptability. Neither feels attainable. And it isn't attainable, because (to the perfectionist) safety means *total security* and acceptability means *complete and absolute acceptance.* These do not exist in the world, yet the perfectionist continues to struggle, gives up completely, or berates himself for his mediocrity. His insistence on absolutes prevents him from achieving a reasonable, healthy level of self-esteem. Healthy self-image and a satisfying life are attainable, but not without giving up unrealistic standards of perfection.

Living at the extreme of shame and hopelessness, the survivor sees no way to overcome his monumental deficiencies. Ultimately, if his level of self-esteem falls low enough, he may be led to contemplate or attempt suicide. At this point of despair, killing himself seems to him to be a reasonable option. He feels he could give up trying, let go of the pain, and the world would no longer have to put up with him. He could put an end to striving, frustration, failures, and self-hatred. And, he feels, no one would really care anyway. People could go on about their lives and stop wasting their time on the likes of him. Thus, the logical extension of his unrealistic perfectionism is, "If I can't be perfect, then why should I *be* at all?" Survivors frequently report feeling like killing themselves. Many have attempted suicide; some have succeeded.

Focus

Suicidal Feelings

If you have ever felt this way, then you know that it is almost impossible to move out of the suicidal feelings by yourself. You need perspective on the painful emotions. That perspective can only come from outside you. Survivors need to be able to express the hopelessness that leads them to consider doing away with themselves. They need to share mistaken notions like: "Everyone would be better off if I were dead." "It would be the ultimate solution, I wouldn't feel the pain anymore." "I could finally relax and just stop struggling." This is another reason why contact with other survivors, therapy, and participation in recovery groups and workshops are so important. Sharing the struggle with other survivors provides a safety valve for suicidal thoughts. It shows you that you are cared about—that whether you live or die makes a difference. Survivors need to talk about their hopeless times, and what they have found useful in moving out of despair. They may create their own "suicide hotlines," making themselves available to receive phone calls or visits from one another when things get too overwhelming.

If you feel like killing yourself, call someone—a friend, a neighbor, a counselor, a crisis hotline—and move yourself away from your suicidal isolation. Make a contract with your therapist (or a friend) that you will not act on suicidal feelings until you have spoken face-to-face. Give yourself a chance to turn your life around. Your feelings of low self-worth are the outgrowth of the way you were abused. *If you kill yourself, then you are letting the abuse win!* Don't allow that to happen. No matter how bad you feel about yourself, you are worth more than the abuse! The painful emotion and the low self-esteem can be overcome. Recovery is real. You can heal. And the results are worth the effort.

Your process of recovery will involve gradually breaking down misguided perfectionism. It will entail learning to distinguish reasonable goals and expectations from unreasonable ones. All people must come to recognize that to be human is to have human flaws; this is as true for you as for everyone else. During your healing you will discover that people *do* like you, not because of the perfect face you struggled to present to the world, but *despite* that facade. By testing your perceptions against those of others—in individual and group therapy, with friends and allies—you will find out who you really are. You will understand how childhood experiences led you to accept misinformation as truth. You will be better able to spot negative, self-defeating thoughts as soon as they appear, and learn to contradict them. The face that stares back at you from the mirror will come to look less like a hideous monster and more like an ordinary person, with a range of interesting strengths, weaknesses, talents, and problems. You will begin to explore the rich and varied landscape between worthlessness and perfection.

Steve's Statement

Pushing through his fears of not being good enough and his desire to minimize, deny, and numb, Steve, a thirty-eight-year-old survivor, shares the importance of his feelings.

My name is Steve, and I almost did not write this. Not that I could not; as you can see, I can write. Nor that I should not; my experience of being sexually abused by my father for well nigh ten years, followed by my road to recovery, the insights gained as a result of those experiences, as well as extensive research on the subject, make me well qualified. No, it simply boiled down to the fact that I know, deep down, I cannot write it well enough to say what needs to be said, to reach those who need to be reached. It simply had to be perfect, and I know I am further from being perfect than any man.

That demand for perfection in myself, while forgiving any and all frailties and foibles in those around me, is just one of the character defects I know I must have. Low, nay, a lack of self-esteem, self-worth, and self-confidence, as well as inabilities to trust, to form intimate relationships, to engage in sexuality, or even admit to my sexuality, are all common residues of my incest trauma that I share with many others.

Also, like many others who have experienced incest, I have adapted so well to these deficiencies they often go unnoticed. It is only when I am in a group of other survivors that, seeing the ravages of incest in their lives, I can clearly see it in my own. To see a need to control in others and then to find it such a pervasive trait in myself is truly eye-opening.

None of this should be so alarming to survivors or those who wish to help them as to prevent them from beginning or continuing down the road of recovery. Usually the trauma is so extensive that all areas of the person's life are in some way affected. This need not rule out recovery; rather it underscores the difficulties and obstacles along the way. To hope never to feel the pain and anger and sadness is not a realizable goal of recovery. Not to have the sadness, anger, and pain prevent one from truly being happy, loving, and caring is.

11
SEX, TRUST, AND CARING

When Reason knows the heart and soul are troubled
But thinks that happiness would look better
And Reason makes the body react accordingly, then
Reason is unreasonable.
—a male survivor, from his poem
"Something Old, Nothing New"

It has been widely noted that rape is a crime of violence, not a sexual crime. However, since the anger, hatred, fear, and violence are acted out sexually, many people continue to view rape as an act of sexual passion. I raise the subject to emphasize how easily a connection can be made between two different phenomena when they occur in close proximity or have common aspects. Some time ago on a television comedy special, Carol Burnett asked Robin Williams, "Are you laughing at me?" He replied, "No, I'm laughing *near* you."

The distinction between laughter and ridicule is not readily apparent to someone who has experienced the humiliation of being laughed at or teased. To someone who has been attacked by a dog, *all* dogs, no matter how cute and friendly, may be objects of terror. A child who was subjected to beatings for talking during mealtimes may, as an adult, become a morose, uncommunicative dinner companion. He may not realize why dinner table conversation makes him uncomfortable, but it does. The connections were childish connections, perfectly logical in the context of his limited experience, carried unconsciously into adult life. Similarly, sexual child abuse delivers a message to the child that equates caring with sex. A trusted adult violates a position of responsibility by sexually victimizing the child. An adult who is supposed to care about the child becomes his attacker. The child learns to mistrust any caring overtures, fearful they will lead to further sexual victimization.

These associations aren't necessarily made consciously—we aren't always aware of lessons we are learning—but the connections are made.

Childhood perceptions, accurate or incorrect, are incorporated into the way we view and respond to the world.

Any form of child abuse generates confusion, which profoundly influences adult relationships. I have spoken of how children make logical assumptions based on what they are told and what they experience. People in the world of computers are familiar with the phrase "Garbage in, garbage out." When the child receives correct information, he is able to draw accurate conclusions. If, however, he receives misinformation, he will develop a worldview that—although consistent—is based on inaccuracies and distortions.

The sexually victimized child makes many connections based on the abuse. When a protective, caring relationship becomes sexualized, the child concludes that any expression of caring will lead to sex. Conversely, he feels that, to be cared for, he must be willing to submit to sex. All touching (or a particular type of touch—gentle or violent—depending on the situation) may be interpreted as sexual. If physical violence was part of the abuse, then touch, caring, and/or sex may feel like a violent act. If touch means sex, and sex means abuse, the child may feel anxious whenever anyone touches him. Having incorporated this misinformation into his understanding of life, he goes out into the world fearing and avoiding any expression of caring. When treated affectionately, he reacts with mistrust, becoming withdrawn, suspicious, or antagonistic. Alternatively, having learned to connect caring with sex, he might attempt to sexualize the interaction—becoming confused when his behavior is considered inappropriate. After all, that is what was demanded in the past.

Acting on internally logical conclusions based on boyhood sexual abuse, the child (and later, the adult he becomes) receives confusing messages from the world—and, in turn, behaves in ways that are strange and confusing to people who were not victims. If he manages to learn appropriate behavior and isn't seen as a misfit, he may still be confused. He goes through the motions without really knowing why his behavior is appropriate. He learned to give people what they want without questioning their desires too closely.

In her workshops, Claudia Black refers to how children raised in alcoholic families develop the ability to shift their reality at a moment's notice. The survivor, sometimes from an alcoholic family himself, must also develop this skill. He learns it to survive. He becomes adept at figuring out what people want so he can supply it. If the other person doesn't want anything—or doesn't want anything *sexual* from him—he is confused. Convinced that all displays of caring and affection must become sexual, the individual who doesn't want to be sexual is viewed with distrust. "He/she must want *something* from me. If it's not sex, what is it? If it is sex, why pretend it isn't?"

On the other hand, the absence of a sexual response may feel like rejection. When a person thinks his only value is as a sexual object, and his partner isn't interested in sex, he feels he has no value at all. Although he may not want to have sex, the survivor may redouble his efforts to sexualize the social interaction. He learned "what people really want." If the other person yields to his pressure, the survivor is confirmed in his belief that, after all, all closeness is sexual. Resistance to sexual overtures is interpreted as abnormality, denial, or rejection. When someone chooses not to sexualize an interaction, the survivor is likely to interpret it as recognition of his undesirability. "Of course she/he doesn't want to have sex with me. Who in their right mind would be attracted to someone as messed up as I am?" Once again he is faced with a no-win situation.

Sex is seen as inevitable, whether desired or not. But even when sex is not involved, the survivor considers himself undesirable. He is *only* a sexual object, attempting to prove his worth and desirability through repeated sexual encounters that are neither satisfying nor uplifting. Or, if he doesn't engage in sex, he sees himself as worthless, unattractive, and undesirable—again confirming a negative self-image.

If negative and erroneous messages about caring, affection, and sex are not powerfully contradicted, the abused child carries them into adolescence and adulthood. Studies of sexually promiscuous teenagers, prostitutes (male and female, teenage and adult), and sexually compulsive adults turn up large numbers of individuals who report childhood abuse. Many survivors describe themselves as not liking to be touched while, at the same time, engaging in compulsive sexual activity. This appears contradictory only to someone unaware that sexual abuse leads to sexualizing any expression of caring. It is consistent because it represents genuine needs—to be cared for and to be close. Compulsive sexual activity depersonalizes sex, making it possible to engage in physical closeness—and even the appearance of caring—without requiring the survivor to be intimate. Intimacy involves trust, which is too threatening for the survivor to risk.

Trust is the paramount issue for a survivor. Since the information he receives from external sources so strongly contrasts with his own experience, trust is a stranger to him. Why, indeed, should he trust? Who could he trust? He feels that all trusting ever got him was abuse. Having learned to depend on his own resources for survival, he sees nothing but danger in trusting others. This lack of trust and dependence on misinformation about caring are carried into all adult relationships. I say "misinformation" because he hasn't experienced true caring. Genuine caring respects an individual's needs and boundaries. Abusers put their own desires ahead of the well-being of their victims. Regardless of the justification, or how gentle the behavior, it is harmful.

It will take time and effort to learn that people do care. It takes longer to distinguish true caring from the perversion of caring he learned from the perpetrator, and trust that his perceptions are accurate. It involves slow building of trust, learning to form intimate (not necessarily sexual) relationships with caring people who will respect intimacy and not violate his trust. Building trust and establishing intimacy are difficult tasks, but they must be done. If they aren't, the survivor will continue to have unsuccessful relationships informed by his abusive childhood.

In my work with survivors I have encountered five common patterns:

1 / **Isolation.** Fearing and distrusting intimacy, the abuse survivor distances himself from any relationships, living a lonely and isolated life. He may not know why he is unable to connect with people, seeing it as further evidence of his own unworthiness. Other people seem happier, smarter, and better adjusted. Relationships may be perceived as ideal states, perfect and perfectly inaccessible to someone like him. He sees his inability to "figure out" how to sustain relationships as further proof of his stupidity.

2 / **Short-lived and volatile relationships.** Some survivors push through their isolation and enter a series of short-lived, highly volatile relationships. Suspicious and afraid, they wait for their partners to abuse them. Some goad their partners beyond

endurance, never realizing they are behaving provocatively. Expressions of caring are rejected, as trust is necessary to accept such intimacy. Since they have learned to mistrust words, open communication is impossible. Partners who attempt to discuss problems in the relationship are met with silence, hostility, or withdrawal. Finally, the survivor finds sufficient justification to leave the relationship, often abruptly and without explanation. He feels hurt and misunderstood, but quickly moves on to another relationship that follows a pattern virtually identical to the one he just ended. If he remains in the relationship, the survivor may unconsciously push his partner away. Through silence, criticism, unreasonable demands, emotional outbursts, promiscuity, or other means, he may wear down his partner's will to keep trying. Since there is little open communication, these issues aren't worked on. When the partner, hurt and confused, leaves the relationship, the survivor feels—once again—abandoned. He has received further evidence that nobody cares; people can't be trusted; he is unable to find someone who will really love him; all women/men are undependable; all anyone wants from him is sex; relationships are impossible; and/or he is totally unlovable. No insight or understanding comes from the breakup because neither trust nor communication was involved.

3 / **Abusive relationships.** In other cases the adult survivor enters into abusive relationships. Whether he is the victim or abuser in these relationships, they follow a pattern similar to the original abuse. His chosen partner may resemble the perpetrator physically or in behavior, mannerisms, occupation, age, voice, or personality. He might find someone who reminds him of himself as a child and treat her/him as he was treated. This relationship may continue for some time if the chosen partner was hurt in ways that lend themselves to acting out her/his chosen role. It creates a neat fit, with the partners agreeing about how each should act. Or the partner may rebel against the victim (or perpetrator) role, demand change, or end the relationship. Whether the survivor or his partner ends this type of relationship—or if it continues for a considerable duration—it provides confirmation of the survivor's belief

that relationships must be abusive. Little understanding can result from an interaction that doesn't allow open discussion between individuals who trust each other's basic caring and good intentions.

4 / **"Settling for crumbs."** Another type of relationship involves settling for very little. Not trusting that anything better is possible, feeling useless and inadequate, believing he is lucky to have any relationship at all, the adult survivor may find a partner in a tedious, unsatisfying, unchallenging, and humdrum life. The survivor interprets this existence in a variety of ways. He may see it as all he can hope for, since he is such a boring person. He might find a humdrum life infinitely preferable to one of violence and abuse. He may feel that this represents normalcy. Or he might see his life for what it is, but feel inadequate and powerless to change it. If his partner feels similarly, the relationship may continue in its grinding dullness for a considerable length of time. He may hate his life but feel bound to his partner, their children, or his ideal of commitment. If one or both partners are dissatisfied with the arrangement, it still is necessary to communicate the dissatisfaction in order to effect change. This is no easy task, as this type of arrangement isn't based on open discussion. If the survivor leaves the relationship, it is with feelings of guilt and inadequacy about his ability to sustain a nonabusive relationship. If his partner leaves, he is confirmed in his isolation and the feeling that, to endure, relationships must be abusive. He is left without even the meager partnership that he had.

Focus

What If I Enjoyed It?

It is not unusual for sexually abusive experiences to arouse some degree of pleasure in the victim. For many survivors, these pleasurable sensations are more upsetting than painful ones. This response to an otherwise negative experience confuses the meaning of enjoyment and the understanding of pleasure. It is likely to set off a chain of emotional reactions leading to mistaken conclusions about the nature of abuse. If you have been confused about pleasure or arousal during sexual abuse, you may have gone down one of the following paths of reasoning.

One faulty path arrives at the belief that if any part of it was pleasurable, it wasn't really abuse. That you can even consider this possibility is evidence of how sexual child abuse warps reality. It allows perpetrators to confuse their victims into thinking that the child's participation in the abuse was of his own volition.

The truth is quite different. There is no such thing as a "willing victim"—to be a victim is to have your will destroyed. The act of victimization damages the human spirit. An element of physical pleasure does not diminish the destructive nature of sexual child abuse.

"You enjoyed it" is a self-seeking statement by the perpetrator, who attempts to mask the nature of abuse and enlist the victim as an accomplice. You enjoyed a physical sensation that represented the kind of closeness that you needed—not the abusive act itself.

Human beings deserve pleasurable experiences that do not rob them of autonomy and self-respect. It's how you should have been treated and is a legitimate goal of your recovery.

A second mistaken connection leads you to the belief that pleasure can only be found in abusive situations. Having experienced some enjoyment from the original abuse, you may have allowed the abuse to continue (and even sought out further abusive encounters to re-experience some degree of physical pleasure, however small). Thus, the perpetrator not only inflicted abuse directly, she or he set up a pattern of victimization that continued into adulthood.

Where this pattern exists, recovery requires breaking the connection between abuse and enjoyment. As you explore nonabusive means of experiencing physical pleasure, you open the possibility of leaving victimization behind.

A third conclusion arises from confusion about what it means to be an abuser. It leads to a logical but *false* progression of thinking about your role in the abuse. The progression moves this way:

1 / If I enjoyed it at all, then: (a) I'm a perpetrator; (b) I'm a bad person; (c) It's all my fault. This leads to:

2 / If I get any pleasure at all from sex, then I'm bad. Sexual pleasure has been connected to abusive behavior. The ultimate extension of this derailed train of thinking is:

3 / If I derive any enjoyment from life, there's something wrong with me. Any positive experience is a source of suspicion, self-doubt, mistrust, shame, or fear—because it raises the possibility of abuse.

A child who is given love and protection feels secure in his enjoyment of life. Boundaries and distinctions between caring and hurtful behavior are clear. Even an abused child has a fundamental understanding that things should be otherwise. An adult survivor told me, "Do you know when I got up the courage to tell my mother about the abuse? It was the first time that I started to enjoy it."

It is vitally important that, as an adult recovering from sexual child abuse, you do not punish yourself for whatever pleasure you were able to derive during the abusive experiences of childhood.

You did nothing wrong. You deserved better treatment. It was wrong that you were subjected to a damaging environment that blurred the distinction between loving and child abuse. You can gain perspective on the abuse by thinking back to your childhood and asking yourself:

• What was I really needing?

• What was I really enjoying?

• What was I settling for?

• What do children deserve from adults?

Understanding these distinctions helps you move toward acceptance of the healthy pleasures life offers.

5 / **Two-survivor relationships.** There are many situations where both partners in a relationship have experienced childhood sexual abuse. Just as significant numbers of adult children of alcoholics end up together, it is common for survivors to establish relationships with other survivors. Although there is little information available about two-survivor relationships, it is likely they face challenges and strains similar to adult children of alcoholics. (There are a number of excellent books on that subject.) If your relationships have tended to follow the other patterns I described, you may be hooking up with other survivors. For two-survivor relationships to be successful, it is necessary that both partners work on their own healing. It is not enough for one of you to recover. You can't do the work for your partner, and you certainly can't expect your partner to do your healing for you. But you can use each other as resources, supporting each other in a program of mutual growth and healing. Having had similar experiences, each of you is likely to understand what the other is experiencing. This won't be easy, but it will be rewarding—and you won't have to do it in isolation.

The picture presented by some of the preceding paragraphs reflects the feelings of many adult survivors. Contemplating "normal" sexual relationships, friendships, intimacy, and trust only underscores their difference from the rest of humanity. They fail to recognize gestures of caring, or can't trust that they are genuine. Sex feels like too confusing a topic on its own, without the frightening additions of caring and trust. Options feel extremely limited—to remain in isolation, accept abuse as a given in relationships, or go through the motions of what they perceive as "normal" sexual relationships without ever feeling caring, understanding communication, or trusting what is going on.

I don't want to end this chapter without providing balance to the tone of hopelessness. Healthy relationships are difficult for anyone to achieve, requiring continual dedication and hard work. Even though this is particularly true for people who were abused, many adult survivors learn to maintain healthy, satisfying relationships. You can do the same. This achievement requires time, patience, and understanding of the issues by both partners. It cannot be done in isolation. After all, it was isolation that first set you up for misinformation and hurt. You must be able to test your thoughts, ideas, feelings, and reactions in a safe, welcoming, nonjudgmental environment. You need people to listen as you work through confusion and fear. (Information for people who are in relationships with survivors is provided in chapter 22.)

You are starting to recognize your positive qualities, figuring out the world based on new information, and learning that this information can be trusted. You will meet people who believe you, instead of treating your memories as sexual fantasies. You will need to test, sounding out your perceptions in an understanding arena, asking question after question. You will doubt that friends have the patience or interest to listen to all you have to say, and respond to all you need to ask. Indeed, some will not, but others will be steadfast in their caring. Opening to trust is usually slow and tentative—at times you will retreat into old patterns—especially when you feel that you have gone too far or someone has come too close. When old feelings take over, you may want to withdraw or lash out. This can occur just when things seem to be going well. Forgive yourself when it happens. Understand that those developing feelings of trust and caring, so unfamiliar and threatening, trigger the reaction. You are learning to build healthy, trusting, caring relationships.

It is vital that the pace and intensity of trust-building is completely in your hands. You are in charge of your recovery. Too much change at too fast a pace is overwhelming and will lead you to shut down and retreat. Survivors have an excellent sense of how much is too much, and when they need to speed up, slow down, or take a rest. Trust your own timing. Allow friends to facilitate your recovery by listening to you, providing nonjudgmental feedback and respecting your physical boundaries. It's okay for friends to make mistakes and have conflicts. What is a friendship without them? Remember that mistakes aren't usually disastrous; disagreement is a normal part of a relationship. It may be necessary to reassure yourself that difficulties can lead to understanding and strength.

Building trust in relationships will take other forms. Just as you must regulate the pace and intensity of sharing your ideas, perceptions, and feelings, you need to be in charge of your physical world. Since the abuse involved loss of control over your own body, you must be completely in charge of when, how, and by whom you are touched. Because touch was sexualized during childhood, even casual touching can feel threatening to the adult survivor. Having the freedom to decide whether or not to engage even in such "innocent" interactions as a handshake or an arm around the shoulder helps provide you with an atmosphere of safety. Under no circumstances should a friend engage in physical exchanges that rob you of control over your body (such as tickling, bear hugs, pinning you down, or hugging you from behind). State your needs clearly, assuming that your friend wants to be as helpful as possible. Let him or her know that, no matter how playful the motivation or how innocent the intent, these behaviors can be a source of intense restimulation of negative memories. The healthy guideline isn't "no touching," it is "no touching without permission." Any touch should be by mutual consent, with either person having the complete right to terminate it at any time. If touching—or limitations on touch—brings up feelings, it is helpful to take time to feel them and talk about them without negative self-criticism. The greater the degree of communication, the more helpful and loving it is. Learning to communicate in relationships contradicts isolation and leads to insight and understanding.

When a relationship has a sexual component, it is even more important to think clearly and communicate openly about what feels (and what is) abusive. Each partner must determine what is acceptable to him (or her). When there is doubt it is always appropriate to err on the side of caution. If you are not comfortable with something your partner wants, it is best to refrain from doing it. If it feels abusive to you or your partner, talk about it. It is neither loving nor sophisticated to pretend to feelings you don't have. Abuse is never a loving act. You can always do more in the future, but behavior can't be undone. A loving partner communicates how he or she feels and encourages the other person to do the same. Questions like "May I touch you this way?" "How does this feel?" "How do you like to be touched?" are always appropriate and aid in communicating caring and consideration for the needs of one's partner. Letting your partner know what you enjoy and what you find unpleasant allows him/her to be a more sensitive lover. Thus, opening communication enhances the sexual experience as it increases the level of safety and trust in the relationship.

It is far from easy to overcome fear and reach out to other human beings. It takes time to unlearn years of misinformation and isolation. There are inevitably slow periods, mistakes, and setbacks. But it doesn't have to be figured out all at once. And it doesn't need to be done alone; lots of help is available. It is worth all the effort to learn that people can express feelings in ways that don't cause harm. The struggle to separate the mistaken connection between intimacy and abuse leads to healthy, affectionate interactions. Establishing and maintaining satisfying relationships is a primary goal of recovery.

Ellen Bass and Laura Davis, authors of *The Courage to Heal,* talk of needing to open wounds to clean them out and heal them. This cannot be done with your old tools. New tools are required—suited to the task of healing. Some of these tools for recovery, and their uses, are discussed in the chapters that follow.

Part Four

ABOUT RECOVERY

12

IS RECOVERY POSSIBLE?

My eyes are open, but I want to blink.
—a male survivor at a recovery workshop

I'm not going to keep you waiting for an answer to the question posed in the title of this chapter. This isn't a mystery novel, and the question is too important to play games with. My response to that question is a resounding yes! Absolutely. Unequivocally. Without a doubt. Recovery is possible. And not only is it theoretically possible, it is possible for *you*.

In earlier chapters, when I wrote about the nature of sexual child abuse and its effects, I wasn't attempting to prove their existence. Children are sexually abused. That is a fact; it happens all the time. My purpose in describing sexual child abuse and its aftermath was to give you a basis for understanding your experience and offer a framework for your healing. Similarly, I do not doubt the reality of recovery. That, too, is a given.

This book is meant to provide you with tools, resources, and encouragement in your recovery process. When Ellen Bass and Laura Davis called their book *The Courage to* **Heal** [emphasis mine], they presented their confidence in the availability of healing. In the same way, this book, *Victims No Longer: The Classic Guide for Men* **Recovering** *from Sexual Child Abuse* [emphasis mine] proclaims the reality of recovery.

How can we be so certain that healing and recovery are possible? From our experience of working with thousands of survivors and talking with thousands of counselors and therapists who work with survivors, we have seen the reality of recovery. We have seen many survivors grow and change—creating better, healthier, more satisfying lives. I speak confidently about healing because I've witnessed it. I know it is true. Growth and change are available to you. It isn't quick or easy, but it is real. The remaining chapters of this book do not attempt to prove the existence of recovery; instead, they offer specific guidelines to assist you in recovery.

Many people consult me professionally because they know I work with adults (particularly men) who were victims of childhood sexual abuse. They hear about me from various sources: referrals from professional colleagues, television and radio appearances, workshops, newspaper interviews, and word of mouth. Whatever the source of the contact, when men come to see me for abuse-related issues, they display a certain kind of urgency. It isn't difficult to understand why they feel this way.

Survivors have lived with pain and confusion since childhood. They try many ways of getting past the experience. They numb themselves (see chapter 8) with alcohol, drugs, sex, food, or any number of other addictions and compulsions. They attempt to change their view of life through religion, various psychotherapies, meditation, mysticism, and philosophies (both Eastern and Western), workshops, retreats, and personal growth practices. Many throw themselves into work or play with intensity incomprehensible to anyone except another survivor (see chapter 10.) They try diets of deprivation or overindulgence. They seek serenity through yoga, release through marathon running, and protection through martial arts. They attempt to escape geographically, some moving several times a year or whenever feelings get too overwhelming. Some change their appearances, jobs, friends, and lifestyles. Many pursue academic degree after degree (often in psychology or other human services) to gain understanding of their situation. They avoid (or pursue) men, women, children, authority figures, older people, friends, and lovers. Some of these practices prove helpful, providing significant relief, learning, and comfort, but there always seems to be something missing. And through it all they try and try to *think* their way out of the feelings they have never been able to shake off completely.

No doubt some of this list is familiar to you. Whatever strategies you undertook to help you endure, survive, identify, fit in, or feel better, they (and you) deserve complete admiration and respect. That they are no longer what you need doesn't negate one simple fact—they helped you survive to this point. Appreciate yourself for having figured out a way to get yourself here—ready to dare to take the next step in your recovery.

When you undertake recovery, it must be a conscious decision, arrived at through a great deal of soul-searching. Having attempted every imaginable way of working around, over, and under the feelings, you reluctantly concluded that the only way out of the pain is straight ahead . . . through it. Abuse and the pain created by abuse need to be confronted directly. Those awful feelings must be felt. This is no easy matter. Even though it is unlikely that anyone ever died of feelings, it can *feel* like dying. (There are those who have chosen death rather than face what they believe will be a lifetime of pain.) It takes tremendous courage and determination to undertake this confrontation, especially when you feel there is no guarantee that its outcome will be any more successful than all the other things you tried. Beginning a recovery program may not lessen the pain immediately. In fact, it often feels worse before it gets (and feels) better. But it does get better. And it continues to improve as you move from surviving to *living* and *thriving*.

An alcoholic, to recover, must first admit to being powerless over the disease of alcoholism. He must let go of the illusion of control to take genuine charge of his healing. Control is equally central for the survivor. Like the recovering alcoholic, the recovering survivor must relinquish rigid control of his feelings—and familiar avenues of escape—that feel like his only protection against being overwhelmed by terror, rage, or grief. He must risk depending on other people's experience, judgment . . . and caring. It may be necessary to think, react, and behave in ways that feel impossibly dangerous. When a survivor first comes into my office, his level of anxiety, tension, and fear is often so high that it feels like a physical force in the room. He overcame the impulse to cancel his appointment or just not show up, and probably is struggling not to bolt out the door. My first question, "How do you feel being here?" may come as a relief or as confirmation of his worst fears: "He is going to force me to *feel*." I listen carefully to his answer, and I believe it. It gives me some gauge of his anxiety level.

In the face of fear and distrust, the survivor has decided to move forward. Indeed, he may feel that he tried everything else, and this is his last resort. He doesn't want to be here; he needs to. Since he has to be here, and knows it's going to be a terribly difficult experience, he wants to get it over with as quickly as possible—preferably yesterday. While understandable, the desire to speed through recovery is unrealistic. Recovery from sexual child abuse is a long-term, ongoing process. It takes time. I wish it were otherwise, but I know of no other way. (I keep several "magic" wands in my office, and offer to try waving them in hope of an instant solution. But the wands seem to be defective, only succeeding in eliciting an occasional smile. Maybe that's enough to make them worth waving.) Although I understand my clients' feelings of urgency, I try not to buy into them. I try to help the survivor arrive at a realistic picture of what he can expect of his recovery process. Realistic expectations make the prospect more bearable. They allow structure, order, and reassurance. They take recovery out of the realm of the imagination and put to rest some of the worst fears. ("Other people have been through this. There are things that have worked for them. Maybe . . .") This perspective permits him to set specific, realistic goals—something that wasn't possible before.

In addition to impatience, survivors undertake recovery with feelings of anger and resentment. ("It just isn't fair that I have to go through more pain. After all, I was the victim. The perpetrator doesn't have to pay money, spend time, and feel pain to get over this. And it was her/his fault!") These feelings reflect unfortunate fact. If the survivor waited for the perpetrator to apologize, repent, and make amends, he would very likely be waiting forever. It truly isn't fair, but it is necessary that his recovery be his alone. (This does not mean he must go through the process in isolation; it means his recovery cannot depend on anyone else's actions or inaction.) I wish it could be otherwise—that there was some way I could reach in and extract the pain. If there were, I would do it without hesitation. But that is beyond the scope of a therapist. I (and others who care about survivors) can only provide my best thinking, experience . . . and caring. I reassure my client that, although he has to go through this experience, he has allies in the struggle. He doesn't have to experience it again the way he did as a child: He now has protection. His resources are real and powerful. There are paths through the woods. When he returns to look at the hurts of childhood, he does it as an adult man, able to reassure a frightened child that he will survive. He is, of course, living proof of that survival.

The most important reassurance I can offer the courageous individual who embarks on an odyssey of recovery is that, although there is pain, it is not unceasing. There are times of rest, relief, and even joy. Recovery can be undertaken with humor and humanity. There is time to forge ahead and time to stop, look back, and gain perspective on your progress. When the task feels too daunting, or the progress too unimportant to matter, it may be time for rest or a celebration. After all, a major part of recovery is learning to be kind to yourself. As you accept the fact that it is all right to feel good, enjoyment of life ceases to be some far-off goal—to be realized only after "completion" of recovery. In small steps you unlearn all-or-nothing thinking. Enjoyment of life no longer represents time taken away from recovery. On the contrary, taking pleasure means participating in life. It is evidence that recovery is working.

Once recovery begins and you accept its reality, you start to see that change is possible. Even tentative acceptance of the possibility of change ("Well, I'm not sure I believe you, but you haven't lied to me yet") represents a major step toward taking charge of your life. This is not the old rigid need for absolute control. Rather, it is recognition that human beings have the ability to make decisions that affect their lives . . . and the power to put their decisions into action. This is a tremendously important insight. Power to change your life seemed inaccessible—something only available to other, healthier beings. Although you may not feel it completely, you are now ready to move out of isolation and make decisions about living your life.

Having accepted that change is possible, it is difficult to control the desire to change everything at once. Although you may be making changes at breakneck speed, you feel that things aren't progressing nearly fast enough. How can you be comfortable with "small" changes when you want "everything" in your life to be different? You are tempted to consume change with the fervor of a starving man at a banquet. If this enthusiasm gets out of hand, it leads to disappointment. It is necessary not to fall prey to all-or-nothing thinking. Unrealistic expectations set you up for failure. To achieve a healthy life you must determine which goals are realistic. It is important to turn to other people for help in goal setting and checking your progress. This helps you cut through isolation while providing perspective on what is reasonable. Setting reasonable goals makes them possible to achieve. Thus, success builds upon success, and each successfully attained goal is further evidence of the reality of recovery. It keeps the process from becoming overwhelming.

Focus

Four Myths That Interfere with Recovery

One of the most intelligent, self-aware, and insightful men I know frequently describes himself as "stupid" because he can't think his way through his abuse history.

Men are taught that logic and rational thought will solve any problem. This is a persistent and frustrating piece of misinformation that impedes recovery for men.

If sexual child abuse yielded to clear thinking alone, most male survivors would have gotten over their boyhood traumas long ago. The reason it doesn't work is not a matter of intelligence; more than logic is required. Other pieces must be added to the logic.

All too often men attempt to reason their way into denial and minimization of abuse. They "think" it really wasn't so bad, or the pain they are feeling isn't so terrible. They are hesitant to take the next "logical" step toward understanding their situation, fearing what might be stirred up. A vitally important step for male survivors is letting go of the following myths:

myth 1. Vulnerability = Weakness
myth 2. Rigidity = Strength
myth 3. Comfort = Safety
myth 4. Under Control = In Charge

Many men talk about being "afraid to be vulnerable," as though vulnerability were some hideous flaw. Fearing what might occur if he were to allow himself to be vulnerable—what uncontrollable destructiveness would be unleashed, what dire aspect of his character could be revealed, what further abuse he would open himself to—the male survivor seeks to maintain tight control over his emotions and behavior.

He may attempt to adopt the image of the rigid, unfeeling, taciturn, self-sufficient, macho male that our culture so frequently mistakes for strength. But this posturing is not true strength, and deep in his heart, the survivor knows it. If he is really that strong, why does he feel like a scared little kid?

True strength lies in risking vulnerability—for vulnerability is not weakness, it is openness. To be vulnerable is to open yourself to feeling pain and looking at uncomfortable, unpleasant realities. It is letting go of the need to control all situations. It means showing yourself to other people and inviting their responses, allowing your feelings to be felt—finding the safety to experience uncomfortable emotions—sadness, fear, anger, shame, embarrassment—even joy.

Feelings are not the enemy, they are important healing resources. Allowing yourself to be vulnerable won't happen instantly. It took a while to shut down your feelings; you've been holding a rigid pose for a long time. It takes time and courage to open in this way, but it is the path of recovery. Undoing the myths and stepping out of emotional isolation provide you with genuine information to "think through."

When all the misinformation has been contradicted, you will see rigidity for what it is—a feeble attempt to portray strength you don't feel you possess. You can risk vulnerability, realizing that it represents genuine strength. Comfort and safety take on their correct meanings—so you find genuine safety instead of comfortable illusions. Having learned that being "in charge" means responding flexibly to the demands of a given situation, you cease to substitute rigid control that you mistakenly thought provided strength and safety. In short, you have achieved genuine strength and safety; you truly have taken charge of your life.

The combination of taking charge of your life in specific ways and breaking through isolation by reaching out for support represents powerful and profound growth. It makes possible a host of other changes. You will achieve perspective on how your coping methods kept you stuck. You look at how to replace them with healthier, more satisfying behavior.

As you shift your outlook on life, you question other premises. Having accepted that the world is not a totally dangerous place, you explore, with other people, ways to distinguish genuine dangers from irrational fears. You talk about safe boundaries—how to set and maintain them. And you learn to "check out" your feelings. Instead of "mind reading" (assuming that you know what other people must be thinking and never finding out if your assumption is correct), or "separating" (believing that you must be the only one in the world who has these feelings and perceptions), you find you can talk about what is going on in your mind. You are less surprised to discover that others share your thoughts, values, and perspectives. Recovery brings increased inclusion and participation. In gradual, sometimes small steps, you achieve tremendous growth and change. Although not always dramatic, your recovery is real and impressive.

Paul's Statement

At sixty-two years old, Paul is living evidence that recovery is real and that it's never too late. His statement describes the feelings that followed a major step in his recovery.

It is the day after a workshop for male survivors in Santa Cruz, and I want to write this while the reactions and feelings are still fresh—if I wait too long, I am afraid they will fade away, so here goes.

As I write this, I am sitting in my garden—a beautiful and peaceful environment of flowers, oak trees, and surrounded by tall Monterey pine trees. I am listening to Beethoven and enjoying the company of two neighborhood cats who have come to visit. I am at peace for the moment. Not so this morning as the weeping which started on the drive back continued. Actually, the tears began to flow during the workshop—I remember the shame over my "lack of control"(!), but my attitude toward those tears is changing. They are *my* tears, which are the expression of *my* sadness, and I am trying to be grateful for being able to weep for and *with* my child within. I cried uncontrollably for a long time in the car and then, miraculously, began to scream and rage at the people who "took care of me" when I was an infant and a child. I say "miraculously," as I have been unable to express my anger and rage—I've had no difficulty with expressing pain, fear, and sadness, but have been terrified of my own and others' anger. After I had exhausted myself with the yelling and raging in the car, I had a short period of relief—a feeling of having empowered myself! However, the tears resumed until I got home to the peace and serenity of my little house in the pines. And then a long phone call with a woman survivor friend here, who patiently allowed me all my tears and feelings that the workshop had released in me— she didn't try to "fix" me—just listened and shared some of the similar experiences from her own history. The workshop *was* a gift—to hear the pain, sadness, joy, and hope of the other men touched my heart—for a short time I got out of my "intellectualism" and grandiosity and opened my heart (the tears are starting again). Also the sight of that many men, *straight* and gay, being patient, open, and cooperative with each other, really moved me. To share with all these other gentle, wounded, and, I think, brokenhearted men, certainly contributed to my healing— not to mention the warm and supportive way in which the leaders conducted the workshop. Enormous feelings of love were surfacing for me during the course of the workshop—feelings that I have kept buried and hidden for many, many years. I had almost given up ever feeling or expressing love—I had no concept of what that word meant—after all the years of receiving(?) their "love."

I couldn't understand why I wasn't experiencing euphoria at the close of the workshop. I don't know where I got the idea I was *supposed* to feel euphoria! I was simply in touch with *my feelings,* and I am getting closer to being able to let go and just *feel* without censuring or blocking. So for now my hope and faith are invested in that process. I pray that I have the courage to survive the days (and nights) which may be painful or uncomfortable due to surfacing feelings—the workshop leader did warn us of the temptation to resume our addictions (mine being alcohol, pornography, and sex), and I remember shaking my head to indicate to you that it could not happen to me (more grandiosity). I have changed my mind after experiencing the emotional roller coaster of the past three days (the day before the workshop, the workshop, and the day after, today). I am going to pray for the courage to go through the healing process and to find the appropriate people and resources, as I know I cannot do it alone. I certainly *want* to do it alone, as I have survived alone most of my life—but the isolation has become too uncomfortable to endure.

I know it's not "too late" to recover, and now I have feelings of hope. My goal is to love and cherish "little Paul" in order to allow the loving, caring, and creative adult Paul to emerge—released, finally, from all those shame-based "caretakers" of the past. I want to return all of the shame to *them*—they are entitled to it—it was never *mine*.

I certainly hope these are not just words on paper—I pray that I mean them, and can maintain my resolve to persevere in the healing process. P.S. The touching image of the grown men cuddling teddy bears is still with me.

A loving survivor,
Paul

13

BREAKING SECRECY

There are no secrets in families, only denial.
—Terry Kellogg, M.A., family systems specialist and author

Secrecy is the cement that holds abuse firmly in place. It allows sexual victimization of children to continue despite the presence of concerned family, friends, neighbors, and child protective legislation. It is certain that the extremely high incidence of sexual child abuse would be greatly reduced by open discussion. As long as the subject remains hidden—a source of shame and embarrassment—children will continue to be victimized in great numbers. Like mushrooms, abuse grows and spreads when kept in the dark. We know this is true, yet not nearly enough has been done to bring the subject out into broad daylight.

Before writing this book, I asked several people to read my outline and offer comments. On the topic of secrecy, one survivor wrote: "What is it that makes this subject so difficult to talk about—not only within the family in which the abuse took place, but with friends made and kept in adulthood? For the victim, having been abused is like having cancer— something he doesn't want to admit; and for others, something they don't want to acknowledge—for fear of 'catching' it? I suppose the answer is obvious, but it wouldn't hurt to spell it out in some detail." I'm not sure I agree that the answer is obvious, but I know there is a great deal to be gained by discussing it . . . out loud, often, and "in some detail."

To create an environment where he or she can abuse a child without getting caught, the perpetrator must make sure that no one who might interfere with the abuse knows about it. The first step is to make certain that the child won't tell anyone. There are any number of ways that silence is installed and maintained. The perpetrator may make direct threats to the child, promising dire consequences if he were to tell anyone. The abuser may threaten to kill or hurt the child or his loved ones. There may even be the promise that harm (imprisonment, violence, or death) would befall the perpetrator if the acts were discovered. At first glance this would appear to be reason for the child to speak up. But it must be remembered that the perpetrator is often someone very important to the child, and the fear of losing him/her is enough to insure silence. At times, threat of harm is reinforced with actual violence expressed against the child or other family members. Many children bravely endure abuse to protect siblings or other loved ones from harm. In this situation the child soon learns to suffer in silence rather than risk the threatened consequences of seeking help.

If it is in their power to do so, perpetrators insure secrecy by physically isolating their victims. Children are jealously kept from contact with playmates and, later, not allowed to date or participate in social activities. In extreme cases, abusive adults have literally held children prisoner. If this treatment is explained to the child at all, it is usually presented as punishment for his wrongdoing or evidence of his being a bad boy. As with physical violence, physical and emotional isolation add another harmful dimension to the sexual abuse of children.

The perpetrator may also tell the child that nobody would believe him—he would be called a liar and punished if he told anyone. Unfortunately, this is often true. Adults are reluctant to believe that anyone they know would harm a child. Because of their own denial (or sometimes through bewilderment, helplessness, or fear), they refuse to believe that the story is anything more than the result of a child's lurid, overactive imagination. The child may even be chastised for making up "such an awful fib." This confirms the child's view of himself as an evil person who needs to keep his "true nature" hidden. Even if the report is believed, the trusted adult may be too frightened, confused, or uninterested to take appropriate action to protect the child. It doesn't take long for the child to get the message that there is nothing to do but accept the situation. He learns that it is easier to go along with abuse than make futile attempts to stop it. Since there is no help to be had, he sees as his best hope behaving in ways that will minimize the abuse—get it over with faster and with less violence. Ignoring or disbelieving a child's story reinforces and perpetuates abuse, effectively isolating the child with the perpetrator. In so doing, it constitutes further child abuse. Whatever problems may result from giving credence to and investigating a child's report of abuse, they are insignificant compared with the harm that comes from allowing abuse to continue. It takes tremendous courage for a child to disobey an adult's commands and risk the anger of a large, intimidating figure. When a child's pleas are ignored, he is unlikely to take further risks.

Perpetrators do not always resort to threats or violence. Secrecy may be maintained with bribes—actual or promised. The child who accepts such gifts or special treatment (bribes are not always material) in exchange for his silence about abuse grows up feeling like a coconspirator or prostitute. (This may even become a self-fulfilling prophecy. Few prostitutes do not report a history of sexual abuse.) And the gifts may not be interpreted as bribes. As one survivor said, "When you've got nothing at all, anything feels like something."

Another way to insure that the child will maintain secrecy is to misrepresent the nature of the abusive situation. Desperate for love and comfort, the child will accept an adult's words of assurance: "This is our special secret" or "This is how a father loves his son." By the time the child realizes that he has been lied to, he is too ashamed, intimidated, or hopeless to tell anyone. One of my clients, after years of working on feelings of anger and loss, was finally able to let go of his attachment to the perpetrator when he discovered that he was not unique. A sense of betrayal overwhelmed him when he found out that there were other victims. "He always told me I was special. Now I see that this was just another way I was lied to. He never cared about me. He only wanted his own pleasure." Coming to this realization allowed this man to give up his remaining illusions about the abuse and move on with his life.

Mistaken notions of family loyalty (sometimes taught by the abuser) further reinforce the silence. When a family shares abuse, it is kept as a family secret. A facade of respectability effectively masks chaos within a family. "Everyone thought we were the perfect family. My father was a deacon of the church. He was a Boy Scout leader. We looked like *Father Knows Best*. Who would ever believe that Jim Anderson would be having sex with Bud?" Thus, not always consciously, the entire family cooperates in sacrificing one or more members to the abuse. Incest becomes truly a "family affair," affecting all family members. When the incestuous behavior is interrupted, family unity (based on accommodating an abusive system) is destroyed.

For healing to take place within the family context, all family members need extensive help. This takes time, resources, and commitment. It is more common for the family to be torn apart, sometimes blaming the victim and forcing him out of the family. "Whistle-blowers" are seldom rewarded in our society. The incestuous family that has settled for "comfortable" does not take easily or kindly to the family member who insists on embarking on the uncomfortable road to health. The more family members ally with one another and insist on ending the pretense (no matter the cost), the greater chance that the family will recover intact. It is far more common, however, for family members to continue to accept the abuse until each is in a position to escape it alone. The abused child learns to keep his own counsel. He may never discuss the abuse with anyone—even his own siblings, who very likely were also victimized. The adult survivor who chooses to violate the family conspiracy of silence and pretense is likely to be defined as "the problem":

> *"You always were a difficult child. You were never happy. Nothing seemed to satisfy you."*
> *"You never knew when to keep your mouth shut."*
> *"Can't you ever leave well enough alone?"*
> *"Things were fine until you started in with this business."*

If this happens to you, don't be confused by these tactics. Things *haven't* been fine until now. The family hasn't been "well enough"; it's been sick. You know very well how to keep your mouth shut—you've been doing it for many years. Accusing you of having been a "difficult" child is unconscious recognition of the effect of the abuse. *You are not the problem.* The problem is sexual child abuse and its effects. It must be acknowledged if it is to be dealt with. You are right to break the secrecy. But it is difficult. What you are doing is contrary to all you were taught.

The abused child grows into an adult who knows how to keep a secret. He plays his cards very close to the chest, and may feel uncomfortable about disclosing any information, no matter how harmless. How much more dangerous it feels to share his shameful secrets. The adult survivor learned his lessons well. Convinced that he is a severely flawed person, he maintains secrecy to keep others from discovering just how bad he is. The pattern of protecting the perpetrator is so deeply ingrained that it can persist even after the perpetrator dies or otherwise is no longer a threat. The survivor is certain that "normal" people would be unable to hear his story. They would find it too shocking, disgusting, or frightening. They would scorn, reject, or, even worse, pity him. At best, the survivor sees no good coming from telling his story.

Even when talking to other survivors, he can find reasons to maintain his silence. These can range from "My story is less important than anyone else's so I'll keep quiet" to "My story is so much worse than anyone else's that I'd better not tell it." He feels that no one is really interested or that they would derive morbid pleasure from hearing details of the abuse. Finally, although logic tells him he is now physically safe from being abused, it still feels too frightening to risk. The initial breaking of secrecy may be the most terrifying—and most important—step in recovery from the effects of sexual child abuse.

Focus
Finding Your Voice

The taboo against talking about incest is stronger than the taboo against doing it.

—Maria Sauzier, M.D.

It is no accident that

- the national support organization of incest survivors calls itself VOICES in Action

- many survivors find loud sounds upsetting and loud-voiced people intimidating

- survivors often find it impossible to yell or shout.

Perpetrators of sexual child abuse must silence their victims in order to keep them powerless and allow the abusive behavior to continue. Many survivors carry memories of raised voices inaugurating a cycle that led to their being sexually exploited. In adulthood if they speak loudly, they feel as though they are being abusive. When someone else raises his or her voice, the situation feels dangerously out of control.

There is a phenomenon that is so common that I try to be alert to it when talking with a new client. Although I know of no research about its frequency, when I mention it to others who work with abuse recovery, they recognize it instantly.

It is so familiar that I've named it. I call it "The Voice."

Survivors often speak in slow, measured, soothing, lulling tones. They have cultivated a soft and pleasant voice quality which, when combined with precise word usage (it is quite common even for uneducated survivors to select their words with accuracy and precision), produces a calming, hypnotic effect.

When I feel as if the person talking to me is soothing me, that I'm receiving a "verbal massage," I wonder if the speaker has a history of abuse.

If I have to strain to catch the words, lean forward in my chair, or regularly ask the speaker to repeat himself, there is a possibility that I am talking with a survivor. Any interaction where loudness and/or emotions are expressed can feel unsafe; "The Voice" represents his attempt to calm a potentially volatile and dangerous situation. "The Voice" is used to prevent anger from getting out of control.

Male survivors fear the consequences of unbridled anger— their own or someone else's. Being men, they fear that their anger, if released, will be a harmful, destructive force. "My anger is so strong that if I let it out I'll kill somebody." They fear that any expression of anger, however small, will be so over- whelming that it can never be brought under control.

When men in my recovery groups first begin to express anger—whether directed at the abuser, their families, the leader, or other group members—they are certain there will be dire con- sequences. Even a harsh word can feel like a devastating attack. It takes a long time to realize that strong words and a powerful (even angry) delivery are not necessarily abusive.

Since a person's voice reveals a great deal about him, it is no wonder it plays a major role in the life of survivors. One man in a recovery group talked of feeling as if "everyone can hear the conversations that go on in my head. I feel like I'm talking all the time." (In fact, he seldom spoke in group, but watched and listened carefully to the other group members.) Another survivor reported that he loses his voice when he is frightened. Several group members said that they use their voices to "control" other people.

An important aspect of recovery is finding your authentic, full voice, literally and symbolically. You may need to spend time regaining your ability to yell. (If the prospect of shouting terrifies you, it is almost certainly called for.) You can start by speaking with your full voice when you are alone at home. Try a shout or two in the shower.

Having practiced on your own, try it out wherever you have a good opportunity. Ask a friend if you can practice yelling at him or her; try raising your voice in your individual therapy or recovery group, and notice the feelings it brings up. You can shout into a pillow or someone's shoulder to muffle the sound. (Some of my clients suggested that it feels more comfortable to yell in their cars on the highway, or have their shouts muffled by ocean surf or forest foliage.) You may begin with sounds, words, or phrases.

As you become more comfortable with your newly rediscovered voice, allow yourself to attach feelings to your speech. Don't be surprised if you find yourself crying, shaking, or laughing as you do it. Don't let the feelings stop you—keep on shouting, raging, crying, and/or laughing—at full volume.

Once you learn to do this, you can experience the exhilaration of telling your story—out loud—with the full power of your voice. As you move on to loudly expressing your anger at the perpetrator, you will be amazed by how spirited you feel.

After growing more comfortable with expressing your voice, you will find that your everyday speech is stronger and more confident. Finally, you will find a forum for your voice. It may be expressed in helping others to recover their voices, or simply by making your voice heard more powerfully in every aspect of your life. However you choose to do it, I encourage and celebrate your moving ahead with your recovery—at full voice.

When someone who is being (or has been) abused asks, "What should I do?" the best answer is "Tell somebody." Survivors and therapists who work with them insist that this is the essential first step toward recovery: "Find somebody," "Tell your story," "Break the silence."

This may sound like simple advice, but it is not easy to accomplish. To break the silence, you must defy years of training in isolation. You may already have tried and been disbelieved, rebuffed, or punished. This is not a course of action you will enter lightly. What if you are still not believed? What if they think you are weird or sick? And what good would it do to talk about it now? Fighting the pulls to keep silent, you face the question of who to tell. Again, the simplest answer may not be as easy as it sounds. Not everyone is willing or able to listen to reports of sexual abuse. Some might respond in an unhelpful or even hurtful manner. A person with the best intentions may have neither the resources nor ability to respond helpfully to the revelation.

So who *do* you tell? Sometimes the answer provides itself. Someone raises the subject of abuse or identifies him- or herself as a survivor—and your story comes pouring out. The subject of abuse is increasingly being addressed in books, articles, films, and television programs. Regardless of the quality of these programs, they help to create an atmosphere where it is all right to discuss the topic. Your story has been waiting for years. Sometimes all you need is a catalyst. Whoever is around becomes the first person to hear your story. It isn't unusual for the first person learning of the abuse to be a total stranger. You may open up to someone sitting next to you on a bus or to the friend of a friend. "Something about the person" feels safe, or the situation is right—who knows why? In fact, the very impersonality and anonymity of a passing acquaintance can create a safe enough setting for disclosure.

Who do you tell? The answer must be: "Somebody," "Whoever you can." What is most important in breaking the secrecy is not who is the first one to be told, but that you tell *someone*. The logjam of silence, fear, and intimidation must be broken. Where you start is less important than that you start. You don't have to wait for the perfect person or the best possible circumstances. Tell someone. If she or he is unable to listen, tell someone else. Get into the habit of disclosure. Share information all over the place. If the abuse is still happening, keep on talking about it until you find someone who can help. If the actual sexual abuse has ended, the effects remain.

Talk about them. You will find someone who can listen. You'll probably be surprised at how much support there really is in the world.

Don't worry about getting the story right. All the details aren't necessary. You may not even know them yourself. It is important to start the process by reaching out to someone. It is good enough to tell someone, "Something happened to me." If that is all you know for certain—or is all you're able to say—then it's enough for now. If you don't know that much, it is enough to say, "It feels like something could have happened to me." Just once. Once the first log or two starts to move, it is amazing how quickly the others follow until finally the jam has broken up completely and the logs flow easily.

Once the silence is broken—and the world has not ended—it is important to maintain the momentum. Tell your story again and again. Repeating your story:

- makes it more real to you

- emphasizes that it is important

- allows for shifts of focus and access to new perspectives on your experience

- permits a forum for more feelings to come up

- provides a reality base that continually contradicts the lie that talking about the abuse will result in dire consequences.

Don't assume you have found the only person in the world capable of listening to you. Rather, begin with the assumption that you have a right to speak and that people are eager to hear you. If anybody is unable to listen, don't assume that no one wants to hear you. Look for someone else. The fact that not every conversation or social situation is appropriate for discussing abuse doesn't mean that it is never okay to talk about it. Keep talking, and you will find a helpful support network. You will create the safety. Once secrecy is broken, you never again need to return to isolation.

Each time the story of abuse is told—whenever a survivor is listened to with caring and awareness—another piece of healing takes place. As the story is repeated, more details are recalled. Whole chunks of childhood that had been forgotten can be recovered. It is not always a pleasant experience, but is immensely valuable. This is especially true as the story is told with more and more feelings attached to it. When survivors first start to tell their stories, descriptions are often delivered in a flat, lifeless, or factual tone (as though the topic being lectured on was of purely academic interest, without personal connection to the speaker). It reflects the degree of fear attached to talking about abuse. The survivor is so terrified of unleashing powerful and painful emotions that he keeps his voice (and feelings) under rigid control. His detached presentation is an attempt to establish distance from his emotions. The subject may even be presented in a light, offhanded, and almost joking manner—as if it were no more important than baseball scores. This delivery serves the double purpose of keeping feelings at bay while reassuring the listener that she or he doesn't have to worry about this story—or even take it too seriously. "Don't worry [the survivor seems to be saying], I won't lose control. It really wasn't that bad." The listener may be left more confused than reassured. The content of the story is shocking; the presentation is calm, lighthearted, or devoid of feeling. Which is to be believed? Don't let concern over confusing your listener stop you; it doesn't matter how the story comes out. Any confusion can be straightened out later. For now, it is important that your story be told to someone any way at all.

As you become more comfortable with talking about the abuse, you will attach more feeling to your story. Beginning with a few tears, a nervous giggle, or a slight shudder, you gradually connect your emotions to what was done to you. This is a true exercise of trust. For some survivors it comes relatively quickly. For others, it takes years to create sufficient safety. Some men succeed in sobbing, shaking, or raging their way through their stories. For others, having a "funny feeling" when talking about abuse represents a tremendous accomplishment after years of feeling nothing at all. Encourage and celebrate whatever emotions are accessible to you. Feelings are the lubricant that allows recovery to move forward. All survivors (including you) need to tell their stories over and over again—in as much detail as they can recall—with as many of the feelings attached as are accessible. It is no use pushing for the feelings. They will arise spontaneously when sufficient safety has been created.

When you first break silence about the abuse, you will experience powerful and conflicting emotions. You may feel frightened that you (or someone you love) will be hurt. You are likely to think of yourself as having betrayed someone close to you. Disclosure can feel like weakness of character. You may feel as though you are falling apart or going crazy. You may have panic attacks or fall prey to periods of worry. You may struggle with bouts of depression. Changing the pattern of secrecy that you have depended on for so long can leave you confused and disoriented. Disclosure is no picnic. But these effects are temporary. Gradually, as you tell more and more of your story, as more emotions become available, and as your isolation is replaced by healthy interaction, healing progresses. You see that change is possible. As your self-esteem increases, you accept the possibility of something that had only seemed available to others: Hope. The process is often slow and takes a long time; there are setbacks. But overall growth is consistent and the rewards are real. It all begins with breaking the secrecy.

In summary, it is important to break secrecy for many reasons:

- If abuse is still going on, talking about it will help to stop it. It can solidify a family and lead to healing.

- Talking cuts through isolation and creates support. By building support you learn that not all trust is abused. You learn to trust.

- Through breaking the silence you bring up feelings and, by doing so, help to heal your wounds.

- Telling your story is an important part of taking charge of your life. It leads to greater self-confidence—a key important aspect of recovery.

- Talking about it leads to greater public awareness of sexual child abuse and its effects, creating an atmosphere that is more responsive to the needs of people in recovery.

- It helps others by paving the way for them to tell their stories— reassuring them that they are not alone.

Once your silence has ended, recovery has begun in earnest. The pattern of abuse has been broken. Nothing will ever again be quite the same.

Ed's Statement

Ed's story is one of courage and perseverance in the face of family denial, pretense, and resistance. At twenty-three years of age, his determination and success in standing up to abuse provide a model of healing.

I was molested by my oldest brother when I was nine and he was fifteen. I can remember it like it was yesterday, because my mother caught us the very first time it happened.

My brother had crawled into bed with me and started fondling me. I didn't know what to do. I was scared and excited at the same time. How many nine-year-olds know about sex? I lay there and let him do it. As far as I was concerned, he knew what he was doing and it couldn't be wrong. He was my older brother. I trusted, respected, and loved him. I couldn't believe he would do something to hurt me. Was I wrong.

My mother came upstairs and caught him. She ordered him out of bed and downstairs. She didn't say anything to me, but the look in her eyes was enough to let me know that something terribly wrong had happened.

Later on that day, she pulled me aside and told me if he ever did anything like that again, I should tell her. I promised her I would. I wish I had kept that promise. If I had, I wouldn't be writing this. But he came back and I didn't say anything.

When he did it again, I pushed him away and told him what our mother said. He told me that it wasn't wrong, but that I shouldn't tell her. It had to be our secret. I didn't know what to do. Could my mother be wrong? My brother said she was. I looked up to my brother, so I told him I wouldn't say anything. I didn't want to hurt my mother. I knew I would, if she found out. She would be mad at me. He told me that. I believed him.

I learned about sex when I was nine years old. I was giving blow jobs at ten. While other kids were out playing with guns, I was learning how to "please" a man. I was taught how to be a "woman."

My brother liked to act out fantasies in which he was the "man" and I was the "woman." That was fine by me. When I acted out these fantasies, I was somebody else. It wasn't me taking the abuse. I wasn't feeling the pain. I built up a wall as high as possible. It protected me from the hurt. When that wall went up, I felt nothing. I still use it. When it goes up, nobody can get in.

Unfortunately, it didn't protect me as much as I wanted it to, because I soon started to have bad feelings. Guilt, shame, anger, hurt. I hated myself for what was happening. I started blaming myself for letting it happen. I hated myself for liking it. There were times when I actually enjoyed it. That usually lasted about five minutes.

But liking it made me hate myself even more. If I initiated it by going to him, I would cry after it was over. I told myself it would never happen again. But it did. I'd go on lying to myself every time.

One night he brought some friends over and proceeded to tell them that I gave great blow jobs. I had to go down on his friends. I was ten at the time. I also started having sex with some cousins, both male and female. Sometimes I would initiate it, sometimes they would. I had sexual fantasies about other members of my family. I thought that was how it was; I didn't know any differently. The only sex I knew was with family members.

My first thoughts of suicide occurred when I was twelve. I knew what was happening was wrong. The feelings inside were often too much for me. I wanted to die. I convinced myself that I would be better off dead. It would be easy, right? Wrong. I don't know if it was a survival instinct, but every time I wanted to kill myself I always chickened out. It wasn't until I was almost sixteen that I actually cut myself. Again, I got scared about dying and I stopped. Once I got into my car, locked all the doors, started the engine, and began to fall asleep. I was happy that it was going to be over. Fortunately, some friends found me and talked me out of it. But the thoughts about killing myself stayed with me for a long time. I was bound and determined to end it sooner or later.

I thought of ways to make myself unattractive, especially to my brother. I was always depressed, but that didn't stop him, so I turned to food. It "helped me" during my depression. Not only did it help to make me a *little* happier, it also helped me gain 120 pounds by the time I reached freshman year in high school.

The abuse had gone on nonstop during my twelve years of school. High school was the worst. I already felt like a different person. Nobody else was doing things with their brother. I was the only one this was happening to. Who would understand? I weighed close to 300 pounds in high school so, naturally, I was the brunt of a lot of cruel jokes.

Of course, I hated myself even more for this. A lot of times I would come home in tears, or close to it. Sometimes I would tell my mother what was happening and she would tell me to just ignore it. I don't think she ever fully understood how badly I was affected by the kids at school.

I started seeing a counselor at school. He was a nice guy but, because he was a man, I couldn't trust him. I was being hurt by a man so, to me, men couldn't be trusted. I never told him what was happening to me.

When I did turn to him and told him I wanted to die, he told my mother. When my mother asked me why, I couldn't tell her. I told her it was because of the kids at school. She told me to ignore it. Later, after she came from the shopping mall, she handed me a white stuffed baby seal and said, "You think you have problems, just think what this poor thing has to go through."

That was the end of it. But my thoughts of suicide didn't stop. The incest didn't, either. Through four years of high school I was being used by my brother. It would happen during the day or at night. It didn't matter if the rest of the family was home or not.

If it happened while my family was home, I would pray that we would be caught. Then it would finally end. But my brother knew what he was doing and made sure there was no chance we would be caught.

If no one was home, I knew it would happen. I sometimes wanted it to happen. There were times when I enjoyed it. "Enjoyed?" No, not really. As I got older, it was the only sex I knew and, as my own sexual desires surfaced, I turned to my brother. There really was no joy in it. I would go until I had an orgasm, then it would be over. Right after I had an orgasm, the feelings would all come up. Guilt was the major emotion. Even now, if I am having sex with a partner, my partner has to reach orgasm first or I just shut off.

It would start in different ways. If I was in bed, my brother would come in and start rubbing my leg, moving up my body until I woke up. The first time someone else did this to me while I was sleeping (this was after I had moved out), I must have jumped about twelve feet, screamed, and scared the hell out of the person who did it.

If I were awake when he came home, he would go into my room and lie on my bed, or I would go into my room and pretend to be looking for something. He would come up behind me, reach around, and start fondling me.

Other times he would knock on the wall separating our bedrooms. This was my signal to go into his bedroom. If I were taking a shower, he would come into the bathroom, tap on the shower curtain, tell me to get dried off and "get ready." To "get ready" meant to go to my bedroom, lie down naked, and wait for him to come in.

If we went on a vacation, my brothers and I would share a room. I would end up in the same bed with my oldest brother. My second oldest brother would be in the next bed. At that time I didn't think he knew what was going on. Now I remember he did. It happened between us only once. He is a year older than me. We were in his bedroom and I gave him a blow job. I can't remember who initiated it, but it happened.

I wanted it to stop, but I felt powerless to stop it. A couple of times I told my oldest brother "no more," but it would start again. One time, when he was trying to have anal intercourse, I started crying. It was just too much. He asked me what was wrong. I couldn't believe he was asking me what was wrong. I told him we couldn't do this anymore. It was wrong; we were brothers. I pulled away from him. He looked at me and said, "We are not brothers. We are lovers."

That devastated me. He saw me as his lover. I said, "No way." I had to walk away or kill him. I was going to stop it. I had to. It was killing me emotionally. And I wanted to kill myself.

It stopped for about three months. Then he came into my

bedroom one night and started again. I let him. I don't know why I couldn't stop it. Why couldn't I just tell him that he was the biggest asshole I'd ever met and walk away? Maybe I'll never know, but at that time I couldn't do anything.

When my brother informed the family he was getting married, it was the happiest day of my life. If he was getting married it meant he would be moving out. I didn't have to stay awake nights wondering if he was going to come into my bedroom, or finding someplace to go, or worrying about how I was going to fight him off if my parents went out. I could go on with a "normal" life.

The night of my brother's bachelor party we had sex. We had to drive someone home. I went for my mother. She didn't want my brother driving alone, since he had been drinking.

On the way back he pulled a rubber penis out from under the seat. I groaned in . . . pain, can only describe it. I didn't want to. I had enough. He put it up to my lips and told me to suck it. I didn't want to, but we were alone on a deserted street and I was afraid of what he might do if I refused. I was afraid of him. I did what he wanted me to. I sucked on that for a while, then he told me to suck him.

When I went down on him, I wanted to bite it off. It sickened me to know that he was getting married in two days, yet still wanted me to satisfy him. I couldn't wait for him to get out of the house. I wanted to be left alone.

After he was married, I only visited a couple of times, always making sure my sister-in-law was there. Once I went over and she wasn't there. I started it; I wanted it. We had sex in his bed. After that time it never happened again during his marriage. A year after he was married, his wife left him and he moved back home.

I moved into the bedroom downstairs, and when I found out he was moving back, I freaked. My parents slept upstairs. When he came home, he could come right into my room. I wanted a lock on my door, but my mother refused. I couldn't explain why I wanted one. I was sure she wouldn't believe me and/or blame it on me. I was in my senior year of high school. I was seventeen years old. I didn't know what to do.

I wanted to move out, but I only had a part-time job and there was no way I could afford to get an apartment. What could I do to stop it? Kill him? I thought about it. But I didn't have the courage. I trained myself to stay awake until he came home and went up to his own bedroom. Sometimes he wouldn't come home until one or two in the morning. I would stay awake until I was sure he was asleep. When my alarm went off at quarter to seven, I would be exhausted.

My schoolwork wasn't that great and it got worse. My mother yelled and screamed at me to do better work. I was more worried about my brother than my schoolwork. A couple of times he came into my bedroom. I would tell him I wasn't feeling good, or I would let him do what he wanted, then tell him to leave.

Around the time I was seventeen I went through a major change. I did a lot of thinking about myself. I had a girlfriend for a while, but it didn't work. Yes, I loved her very much, but I had mood swings. I wouldn't tell her anything for days, then I'd want to share everything with her. It got to the point where she couldn't take it anymore, and I don't blame her. I knew it would end, anyway. What sex we had, I always felt there was something missing. I thought it was either a phase I was going through or it was because of my brother. Maybe I just had to find the right girl? But I knew that wasn't it. I was different from other guys at school. I found men attractive. I wanted to sleep with them. I acted more like a girl than a guy. I knew I was gay. I also knew this was something else I couldn't tell my parents.

To my family homosexuality was a sick, abnormal disease. Gay people were jokes. I was trapped. I had no one to tell. I sank more deeply into myself. I couldn't stand looking at myself in a mirror. When I walked by a store window, I couldn't look at my reflection. I loathed my appearance. I hated myself and I was convinced everyone else hated me. I was a Failure.

It was at this lowest point in my life when something good happened. I was accepted to a women's college. Although it was small, it was a good school. The best part was that it had recently gone coed. I would be comfortable; I would "fit in," and I did.

Although it was occurring only once or twice a month, the incest, however, didn't stop. Despite this, college was great. I was in the human services field. I wanted to be able to help people. Even though I couldn't help myself, I wanted to be able to help others in some way.

During this time I met someone who would help me more than anyone. I met Mary through another friend. After we met the second time, we clicked. Although she was seventeen years older, I could talk to her. She listened and she cared. We were out together one night when she asked me to move in with her. I knew she was living with another woman, but that didn't seem to matter. She needed me just as much as I needed her. I, however, couldn't move out of my parents' house unless I could afford it. Mary told me I could move any time I was ready.

By the time I reached my second year of college, I had basically stopped the incest. If my brother came into my bedroom, I would tell him to get out. If he pleaded, I would refuse. Without my parents or anyone else knowing, I got a gun. I vowed that if he ever tried to force me, I would shoot him. If I were watching TV and he came home and started, I would walk out. Sometimes I would walk the streets for a couple of hours. Other times when he failed, he would go right to bed and I would go back and watch TV. As far as I was concerned, it would never happen again. If it did, one of us would die and I was through thinking it would be me.

It was also my second year of college that I met a really nice guy, someone who would change my life. I dated this guy for four months before we went to bed together. I put him through a lot with my moods, but he stuck by me. I finally agreed to sleep with him only because I was afraid of losing him. It was the night before Easter and we went to a motel.

The night was wonderful. I finally felt fulfilled. This was what I had been longing for. I finally had a real man. He was the exact opposite of my brother. Tall, slim, great personality, very handsome, and I loved him. All of this did not prepare me for the next day.

The next morning we said our good-byes and agreed to meet

that evening. I went home and called Mary. She asked me how everything went. I told her good, but I wasn't feeling good. Everything I had ever felt after my brother was done, I was feeling now. I felt so guilty about making love. I felt ashamed—like I had done something wrong to someone I loved. During the whole day I felt that way. I wanted to be alone. I went out for a drive. When I got back, I stayed in my room. I didn't want to see or talk to anyone.

I had promised to meet this person at the club we frequented. Mary and some other friends were meeting us there. I knew I had to go. All the hate I was feeling toward my brother, I was directing toward this guy. I knew it wasn't his fault, but I felt I couldn't see him. All day I went back and forth about going. I finally decided to go. Maybe seeing him would make me realize it wasn't him.

When I got to the club, he and my other friends were all at the downstairs bar. I went down, took one look at him, turned around, and went back upstairs. I couldn't face him. It was too much. I sat down at a table.

Mary and another friend of mine, Alice, came upstairs. They wanted to know what was wrong. "Nothing," I told them. It was obviously something. My "lover" was upset. He didn't know what he had done. He hadn't done anything. It was me.

I looked at the two of them. They were angry and concerned, but I didn't know what to say. Could I trust them? Would they believe me? Would they still love me? A million questions ran through my mind. I didn't know what to do. All I knew was that I couldn't go on like this anymore. I wanted to be able to have a normal relationship. If this happened every time I had sex with a man, I knew I had to get help. But who to trust?

I told Mary and Alice because they were women and because I couldn't take it anymore. I gathered any strength I had in me, took a deep breath, and told them.

"I was molested by my brother."

I cried, torrents. I cried like I had never cried before. Alice held me in her arms and let me cry. Mary said she was going to tell my "lover" that it wasn't his fault and that I just needed some time. It felt so good knowing they believed me and didn't hate me. Alice asked me if I wanted to get professional help. I said yes. I needed it. I knew the only way I was going to live a halfway normal life was if I got help. Alice said she knew a therapist who might be able to help me. I agreed to meet him.

I had to tell my mother. She had to know. But would she believe me? Just because my friends did, didn't mean she would. I would have to take my chances.

The following week was the worst. I couldn't concentrate on anything. My schoolwork suffered. I was only a couple of months from getting my Associate Degree, but my studies were going downhill. I cried constantly. When people asked what was wrong, I swore it was nothing. By the end of the week I couldn't stop crying. I couldn't stand it anymore. I had to tell my mother. I was scared, but I knew it had to be done. I decided to do it that night.

All the way home I changed my mind several times. I was afraid that my brother would be right and my own worst fears confirmed. I was, however, on the brink of a nervous breakdown and, no matter what the outcome, I had to tell my mother.

When I got home, I brought her into my room. As gently as possible, but without beating around the bush, I told her. Through her tears, and my own, I explained how I was affected. I also told her that my brother may have been molested.

When I told her this, she said she knew who probably did it: her brother, my uncle. Ironically, this uncle was the first person I talked to about being gay. I also had gotten together with this uncle to discuss the molestation. Again I was hurt, betrayed, by a man I trusted. Never again would I let that happen. From then on, I decided, I wouldn't trust a man unless I knew him for a long while.

Anyway, my mother was hurt, naturally very upset, and mad at me. Not for telling her, or for letting it happen, but for not telling her in the first place.

"Why didn't you tell me sooner?" was the only question she asked. I explained why I couldn't. I had been convinced she would hate me and blame me. She took me in her arms and we held each other and cried. She told me that she loved me. I really needed to hear that from her. It was probably the best thing she could have said. I told her I was gay. I figured, why not? I might as well lay everything on the line. We discussed everything I had told her.

I moved out that night. I hated leaving her alone, but I couldn't stay there any longer. I drove over to Mary's and rang the doorbell. She opened the door and smiled, but immediately stopped smiling when she saw my face. She asked what was wrong and I said that I had told my mother about my brother. We talked about it for a while, then she went to bed. It was about one A.M. and she had to work the next day. I lay down on the couch but couldn't sleep. There were too many thoughts running through my mind. What would my dad do when he found out? Would he defend my brother? Would he turn against me when he found out I was gay? I didn't know. I was scared.

When my mother confronted my brother, he denied it. She wrote me a note saying that she had to believe me and she had to believe him. I was very angry at her. Didn't she know that he was going to deny it? She made me feel like he had been right when he told me that she wouldn't believe me. I was the one suffering and he was the one getting away with it. I couldn't speak to my mother. I had always considered her my friend. Now she, too, was betraying me. I never wanted to see or speak with her again.

While I was living with Mary, I started seeing a therapist. He was very gentle, very caring. The only problem was that he was a man. He promised me that he would in no way ever try to molest or hurt me. How could I believe him? I had been hurt, very badly, by two men I had trusted. I couldn't trust this therapist. Not unless he earned it.

I tested him. I would sit in his office for forty-five minutes without saying a word, staring out the window. I was convinced that sooner or later he would ask me to leave and not come back. I was trying to prove to myself that no man could be trusted and that I wasn't worth it to anyone. I'm glad I was wrong.

My therapist proved himself to me and as I got to know him, to trust him, to love him, I opened up more and more until forty-five minutes wasn't long enough. We worked together on some things. He made me work alone on others. I always knew he was there for support. He put up with a lot from me, and I kept thinking that one day he was going to turn around and say good-bye, but I knew deep down that wasn't true. I hope it's not anyway.

In the meantime, I had been living with Mary for nine months when some trouble started at the apartment building and we decided to move. At first we were going to try and find a place together, but I decided to save some money and try later. I didn't know what I was going to do. I couldn't move back home, not with my brother there. I asked my mother to phone an aunt to see if I could stay with her. My aunt said, "Okay."

My dad was a little upset because I wasn't moving back home. My mother made me promise I would never tell him about my brother because "it would kill him." My dad has a bad heart. Reluctantly, out of guilt, I promised. Previously, my dad accepted the fact I was gay with no problems, but now I had to "protect" my father. By doing so, I was protecting my brother.

I lived with my aunt for a while, then moved in with a cousin. Unfortunately, I couldn't stay there very long and had to leave. The only place left was home. I asked my mother if I could move home. She said yes. I made some rules. I wanted a lock on my door. I wanted to be able to come and go as I pleased. I had been on my own for almost a year, and I had gotten used to doing things my way. I was twenty-one and felt I should be able to run my own life. My mother still insisted my father not know about my brother. I still protected my brother by not telling my father.

I was home for a couple of months when I met a really nice guy. He was possibly someone I could trust. Before we started seeing each other, I explained about my brother and how I dealt with things. He promised me he would stick with me. I moved in with him. Things were rough at times, but we managed. He even came to therapy with me once to try and get a better understanding.

The only problem was that I still didn't trust people. I didn't trust him most of all. I couldn't; I was in love with him. One night he decided to go out alone. I had to work. I didn't want him to go. We got into an argument about it, and I told him I didn't trust him. No more was said that night.

For three days we didn't speak and I was falling apart. On the fourth night I had to work and he was going out. I got home early and tried to wait up for him, but fell asleep around midnight. When he came home the smell of liquor was so strong I felt sick.

The next day, I called him at work and asked if we could talk that night. He agreed. I asked if we were going to be okay. He said he didn't know, but that we could talk.

He picked me up after work. We drove to the dead-end street and he told me he wanted me to leave that night. I tried to make him change his mind, but I knew he was right. I called my mom again and cried, trying to explain what happened. She told me to come home.

I left his apartment that night. I walked part of the way home vowing never to trust anyone again. People who weren't my true friends could go jump in front of a speeding truck. Trusting people wasn't worth the pain. I called my mom again from a pay phone. She picked me up. I got home and fell asleep on the couch.

The next day, I was sitting on the picnic table when my dad drove up in his truck. He got out and said hello, and I said hello. He asked me if I was going to live at home again. I said yes. He said we needed to talk.

We went inside and my dad told my mother and I to sit down. At that moment my brother walked in and my dad told him to sit down. I knew right away what was going to happen: a confrontation.

I had already confronted my brother again with my mother there. That time he admitted molesting me and also admitted having been molested by our uncle. He refused, however, to get help. Apparently he didn't have a problem. His beer, coke, and pot made him happy. But he had "no problem."

When we were all seated, my father asked me why I didn't speak to my brother. I have never started to shake so badly in all my life. I could barely hold my cigarette.

I looked at my mother, who looked at me as if to say, "Please don't tell him." I looked back at her thinking, "To hell with you. He has to know and I won't hide it anymore."

Surprisingly, my brother started it by telling my father it was something that happened a long time ago. With tears streaming down my face I explained what happened. Dad was dumbfounded. He was also very hurt. He didn't say anything for a while. Then he quietly asked me why I hadn't said anything before.

I had never felt close to my father, not only because he was a man (another one I didn't trust), but also because I never felt like he loved me. Maybe it was just me, but my father and I always fought. If I couldn't tell my mother, who I loved more than anyone, how could I tell him?

I explained to my father that when one of my cousins talked about being molested, she was thrown out of the family. My dad said the reason he didn't talk to my cousin was because of the way she treated her father. I couldn't believe he didn't know. I told him that she treated her father like that (not talking to him, not even caring if he were alive) because he molested her.

This surprised my dad. He really hadn't known. There was so much happening in our family, but none of the adults seemed to notice or, if they did, they ignored it. Keeping the "Family Secret" quiet is an old tradition in my family, one that's being broken down now as more and more of my cousins come out about who molested them.

I told my dad about our family and who had done what. I told him about the aunts and uncles who molested my cousins. I told him about the brothers who molested sisters or vice versa. I told him a lot. Not everything, but what I felt he could handle. I was becoming drained emotionally.

After I finished, he turned to my brother and told him to get some help. My brother insisted he didn't need help. I tried to tell my dad that a person can't be forced to get help; he has to want to get help. Unfortunately, my brother doesn't want help. He still insists he has no problem. I know he does, but I can't force him to get help, either. I've learned to worry and care about myself.

Every day is a fight to survive. In therapy, I was told that incest survivors view their lives as failures. Some are underachievers and some are overachievers. I am an underachiever. I don't do half of what I can. Things that I do usually fail because of something I've done to screw them up.

I am trying to get my life together. I have a couple of cousins who I can talk to. One lives in California. She works with incest survivors. I hope to do the same someday. I call her for advice and/or support. My therapist is a great help still. I don't see him that often because of work. When I do see him, however, forty-five minutes is still not enough time.

I'm taking one day at a time. I feel I'm becoming stronger every day. I want to put what happened behind me. I'm so . . . gung-ho about incest and sexual molestation and getting it stopped, especially in my family, that I'm trying hard (sometimes too hard) to get people to talk about it. In this area I feel I'm overachieving. I want it stopped. It messed up my life and I want to stop it at my generation. Maybe someday my family will all get along and love each other. Maybe there won't be any denial in my family, someday.

My parents don't talk about it. I do feel that if and when I need support, my dad will be there for me. My mother is deep in denial. We were talking one day about the incest, and she admitted to being molested by an uncle of hers. I asked her why she never said anything. She said she couldn't. I believed her. When my mother was seven, incest and molestation were not talked about at all. If it had been talked about, it probably could have been stopped a long time ago.

My mother freaks out every time I mention it. If I say I'm going to talk to someone, she gets mad and asks why. She still feels it shouldn't be talked about. I don't think she'll ever understand that the only way to stop it is to talk about it. She's so afraid something will come out about the family secret that she doesn't want me to say anything. Her motto is forgive and forget. God will take care of it. I'm not going to wait until people die to say anything or to get the incest stopped. I want them alive so they can get help and maybe help others in their family. Helping is much better than hurting.

14

RELATIONSHIPS AND SOCIAL SUPPORT

Child abuse can exist in adult relationships.
—a thirty-three-year-old man in recovery

Allies aren't a crime.
—a male survivor

The previous chapter discussed why breaking secrecy is necessary to begin healing. Since the abuses are committed in private and the child feels he has to maintain silence, he is effectively trapped by (and with) the perpetrator. The abuser may even convince the child that she or he (the perpetrator) is the only one who cares about him.

An abused child feels isolated in a world that he is helpless to change. Adults are either unaware of the abuse or unable (at times unwilling) to do anything to put an end to it. Someone who is isolated in this manner cannot learn to trust. Suspicious of others' motivations and doubtful they could do anything even if they cared enough to try, he becomes an adult who relies only on his own abilities and resources. Offers of help and support are viewed with suspicion. "What will they demand in return?" Friendships only go so far. If someone gets too close, the survivor shuts down emotionally, grows cold and distant, or ends the relationship. People say things like, "You can only get so close to ————. I've been his friend for years and I don't feel as though I really know him."

To maintain the relationship, friends will respect the survivor's emotional boundaries, avoiding topics that make him uncomfortable. These limits on intimacy are not discussed; the survivor is probably unaware of their existence. But they work as effectively as the moat around a fortress. The survivor maintains absolute control over when and for how long the drawbridge is lowered. At any hint of danger, it is quickly raised again, leaving the friend standing bewildered on the outside. If the friend becomes worn out by having attempts at intimacy repeatedly rebuffed, the survivor interprets the diminished friendship as proof that people can't be depended on. Here, he thinks, is further evidence that caring about someone only leads to abandonment and pain. Not having a model of trusting, nonabusive relationships, he has no way of seeing how his behavior contributed to the estrangement. "After all," he reasons, "my behavior was no different than before."

The survivor is left where he has always been—emotionally isolated, confused, and fearful. He is once again dependent on his own resources, viewing the world through a lens clouded by his history of abuse. He always needed intimacy, but sexual child abuse prevented him from getting the nurturing he required. These unmet childhood needs cause problems in the survivor's adult relationships.

Focus

Isolation

Themes of isolation permeate the life stories of child victims and adult survivors. They appear in memoirs and poetry, stories told during individual counseling, group therapy, recovery workshops, and the survivor Statements in this book.

Recovery requires only one thing of a survivor: whatever is hardest for him. That most difficult challenge is not the same for everyone, but has certain common features:

1 / It rarely turns out to be what the survivor imagines when it is first considered.

2 / The prospect of taking it on generates feelings of confusion, anxiety, and/or fear.

3 / It feels unsafe to work on this issue. At worst, it can trigger flashbacks.

4 / He always feels resistant to the idea.

5 / It was established early in his childhood.

6 / It feels so central to the survivor's self-definition that changing it seems impossible.

7 / Successful completion of this heroic task results in huge positive changes in his life.

For many (although not all) male survivors, overcoming isolation is a significant component of recovery (see Focus: Combating Isolation, p. 322).

The sources of isolation are complex, as are its effects. Isolation (both physical and emotional) appears in many forms in a survivor's life, including:

- *A precondition of abuse.* Some form of neglect or abandonment almost always precedes the sexual victimization of a child. Lack of love, protection, and healthy attention makes a child feel lonely and unlovable, leaving him vulnerable to the attentions of a sexual predator. Conversely, abusers will target an isolated child as easy prey. Paradoxically, the child victim may attempt to alleviate his painful isolation by seeking the continued attention of the abuser. Indeed, if he experiences sex as the only time he isn't alone, the prospect of ending the abuse can seem like banishment to a life of loneliness.

- *A means of maintaining secrecy (thus allowing the abuse to continue).* Isolation is often encouraged and reinforced by the abuser's attempts to keep the abuse secret. There are many reasons why a child victim would cooperate in this endeavor (for example, to protect his family; to protect the abuser; as a response to threats, coercion, or bribery; to avoid being shamed or blamed; because he feels that his situation is hopeless; because his past attempts to tell someone have failed). Regardless of the reason, a child's isolation is never his fault. (It is sadly interesting that isolation can be both a contributory factor and an effect of sexual child abuse.)

- *A survival strategy.* As I observed in chapter 5, "When a child feels that his only safety is in isolation, it seriously impairs his ability to respond to others. Protecting himself from abusers by keeping to himself, he misses out on the possibility of positive, healthy social interaction." He has created an illusion of safety, but illusions can be costly. Like many survival strategies, its initial purpose is protective—a creative temporary solution that (again, through no fault of the child) later becomes a problem.

• *A barrier to recovery.* Patterns established in early childhood, often as strategies for survival, are the most resistant to change—especially when they are reinforced by later experiences. How does a socially isolated adult survivor learn that not all intimacy is sexual (let alone abusive)? Why would he risk putting himself in danger? It is never easy to reverse long-term behaviors, however important it may be to do so.

• *A means of reducing tension.* When it feels as if safety is only found in solitude, social settings (however safe they may be) evoke confusion, anxiety, or fear. Even when inter-actions are pleasurable or exciting, the survivor may experi-ence unendurable tension. The unknown—new people and situations—can be frightening. Restoring the familiar (in this case, a return to his solitary existence) is one way to reduce the tension. Thus isolation is another numbing strat-egy, possessing both the benefits of analgesia and the risks associated with long-term numbing.

• *A retreat from the intensity of recovery work.* Recovery is difficult. Often intense, frustrating, and emotional, it can be mentally and physically exhausting. Even though an experienced counselor will encourage survivors to be in charge of the pace and intensity of their work, it isn't always possible to follow this advice. There are times when the recovery work itself feels overwhelming. Accurately or not, isolation might feel like a vacation. That's okay, as long as withdrawal isn't interpreted as failure. The survivor can always return to his recovery work; capable therapists will leave the door open for his return.

Basic to human survival are the needs to love and to be loved. When a child's basic needs to be loved *and be allowed to love* are stifled, they do not disappear. When a parent doesn't love his or her child (or when that love is perverted into sexual abuse), the child continues to search for love. He seeks a loving parent in all relationships. The need for parental love has become "frozen." A *frozen need* is any unmet childhood need that is carried into adulthood. It is incapable of being filled, no matter how hard the adult survivor (or his partner) may try. Difficult as it is to accept, you can never get the love that you missed when you were three years old. No one will ever be able to parent you as a five-year-old, because you are no longer five. This does not mean you cannot be loved, just that you can't be loved *as a child.* There is an important reason to relinquish the frozen childish need for parental love. Not only is this need impossible to satisfy, it interferes with something more important. As long as you insist that your partner become your loving parent, you prevent him or her from being able to offer you genuine adult love. Even if she or he tries to meet those frozen needs, the effort is doomed to failure. Your partner isn't the one you needed love from when you were a child. It is only possible for her or him to love you now, as you are, in the present.

At the same time that he fears intimacy, the adult survivor yearns for close human contact. Humans are social beings. Although we occasionally crave solitude, to be solitary is to be something less than human. Children raised in isolation don't learn the social and emotional skills necessary to live healthy lives. The isolation of abuse deprives the child of normal experiences necessary to the establishment and maintenance of warm, caring, and mutually satisfying human contact. Although he has not developed the ability to form these relationships, he is aware of their existence. He sees other people who seem to enjoy normal friendships. He knows of relationships that appear to be satisfying. He reads and watches and listens, and wonders whether he will ever experience the closeness he so deeply desires—and fears.

Intimacy demands trust. The conflict between wanting and fearing closeness is a central theme in the life of the adult survivor. Since his most powerful interactions have been chaotic and abusive, he wonders if caring, nonabusive relationships aren't just a Hollywood myth. If he accepts that human intimacy is theoretically possible (or even actually attainable by others), he assumes it is unavailable to him. Seeing other people who seem to be happy becomes further proof of how flawed and unattractive *he* is. That he cannot "figure out" how to form relationships confirms his feeling that he is stupid. If he decides to try to get close to someone, he doesn't know how to go about it. How could he? Where would he have developed the skills? If he begins to move close to somebody, perfectionism takes over—at the first sign of a problem he is ready to give up. Any conflict is proof of failure. Accustomed to idealizing friendships, he hasn't had the opportunity to learn that no relationship is perfect; they all require work and have problems. But his experience with closeness has been limited to the perversion of intimacy. He is an expert on the subject. And he is always looking for signs that he should run and hide. He tries to protect himself in situations where he is in no danger. He misreads signals because, in the past, they always meant danger. Or he unconsciously seeks out abusive relationships because they are more familiar and less confusing to him.

Adult survivors have told me that they can never hope to sustain successful relationships because their needs are too great:

"When someone pays attention to me, I just want to hang on and never let go."
"I feel like I'd fall apart if he left."
"I wanted her with me every minute. I was jealous of her friends, I resented her job, and I wanted us to do everything together. When she wanted to be alone, I felt like she didn't love me and wanted to leave."
"I get so scared and I feel like a little kid. I just want to hold on tight."

This intense, clinging neediness is easy to understand. The first expression of warmth and affection after a lifetime of deprivation feels precious and unique. It feels like your only chance at a happy life. The stakes are impossibly high. "If I blow this opportunity I'll never get another chance." Part of that perception is correct—human connections *are* precious. They should be treasured and nurtured so they can flourish. Each relationship is representative of what can happen when people connect with each other. What is learned from one can be applied to others, but no relationship has it all. A full life contains a rich variety of human interactions. No one person is capable of fulfilling your every need. That he or she is unwilling or unable to do so is not failure, nor is it evidence that the person doesn't love you enough. A profoundly loving partner may not be able to bake a cake or understand world politics. She or he might have no interest in folk music or be passionately involved in something that you find boring. This is not proof of incompatibility. Nor is it abandonment if your partner chooses to pursue some of his or her interests with other people. Relationships flourish in an atmosphere of encouragement. Each partner supports the other's interests without needing to share every one. Time spent apart, alone or with other people fosters diversity of experience. Rather than pulling the two apart, it can allow each to develop strengths they can then utilize in helping the relationship to grow. Instead of being two frightened children clinging to each other for comfort, they become strong, independent adults who have chosen to share parts of their lives.

When someone clings to another person—overcome with jealousy, frightened, and needy—it usually has very little to do with present reality. Insisting that your lover be "the parent you never had" leaves both of you feeling frustrated and unhappy. Caring between two adults, although it can never replace what was lost in childhood, is a wonderfully affirming experience. To achieve it, it is necessary to stop blaming your partner for not being what she or he can never be—and begin to appreciate what is possible. It isn't fair that you were never loved the way you deserved to be. Nevertheless, you must let go of the insistence that somebody must love the little child you feel yourself to be. Giving up this frozen need isn't easy, but doing so opens the door to accepting support in ways that hadn't been possible.

There is another aspect of blame that you have to let go. To move ahead with recovery, you need to stop blaming yourself for not having been a lovable child. Many adult survivors find that an important component of their recovery involves acceptance of themselves as children. *No child ever deserves to be abused!* Although you can accept this truth about other people, you probably have difficulty believing it about yourself. As you look back to your childhood, it is a fair bet that you don't like what you see. You may have accepted the lies that you were ugly, stupid, evil, unlovable, manipulative, seductive, or otherwise "deserving of the abuse." It isn't comfortable to remember a small, frightened, and confused little child. It is understandable that you want to distance yourself from association with your abusive childhood—and the child who reminds you of it. But getting to know that child in a new way—befriending him—can prove to be a key component of creating a supportive environment for the adult you have become.

Understanding that your "child within" always deserved to be loved moves you toward being able to accept yourself as a lovable adult, deserving and capable of achieving healthy adult relationships.

As an abused child you had no guarantee that your struggle to survive would be successful. You got through the abuse the best way you could, relying on your intelligence, creativity, and courage. That you survived at all is an accomplishment deserving respect. That you became a functioning adult is testimony to the resiliency of the human spirit—reason for admiration and celebration. (I discussed my admiration of the strength, courage, and creativity of survivors in chapter 9, but I believe it needs to be repeated again and again. Are you starting to be able to hear it?) It can be a powerful experience to go back to your childhood and befriend yourself as a child. Reassure and appreciate the child within you. Tell him that he is fine and brave and good. Assure him that he is right to expect to be treated with respect and caring—that it wasn't fair that he was treated abusively. And you can let him know that he will survive his situation. After all, you are living proof of his survival. *You* can be the loving, nurturing adult he (you) always needed. In short, you can break down his isolation and form a loving, respectful relationship with him. By cherishing yourself as a child, you give up demanding that others do so. Relieved of the burden of parenting you, their energy is freed to provide you (and yours to accept) the support that adults can offer one another. Your adult isolation is broken down, opening a path to healthy adult relationships.

Having taken care of the needs of the past, it becomes possible to address present concerns. As you support yourself, you reach out for realistic support from others. You still may not be able to get support from your family. They may remain abusive and chaotic, locked in denial and pretense. Or they may not be physically or emotionally accessible. Some survivors have made great progress in joining with their families in sharing the difficult journey to reconciliation and recovery. Others continue to battle to extract recognition and caring where none exists. They have taken on a thankless and hopeless task that leaves them trapped in isolation. Still other survivors decide that, since their biological families are incapable of providing the needed support, they will create their own "families." These support systems take many forms. They may consist of only those biological relatives who are able to respond in an open, caring way. They may be just the survivor's spouse and children. Or the family may be formed of unrelated people who commit themselves to thinking and caring about one another. New "families" may be made up of survivors who decide to support one another.

Focus

Finding the Child Within

One of my clients carries in his briefcase a framed photograph taken when he was a child. He treats the picture with respect, keeping it wrapped in a soft cloth and handling it gently. Sometimes we look at the photograph together, while he tells me about himself as a boy.

Another client will sometimes prop up an early boyhood photograph on the sofa during his session, as a reminder of a time before the abuse.

Thom Harrigan, codirector of The Next Step Counseling, asked each member of a men's recovery group to bring in a childhood picture. He reported to me that most group members showed up with several pictures of themselves and sometimes snapshots of their families. They all knew that it was important to them to make these connections.

Part of your recovery work needs to focus on your childhood. That is, after all, when the abuse took place. The boy you were is an important source of information about the man you have become. You carry him with you in the form of memories, feelings, reactions, attitudes, personality, and physical characteristics. There are a number of reasons to get to know him.

At times you still feel like a scared, lonely, abused child. Part of your self-concept was frozen at the time that you were abused. Emotionally, you don't recognize that you have gotten through the ordeal. The world still feels like a risky place. When you are confronted with a difficult or frightening situation, try to ask yourself, "How old do I feel?" Chances are that you feel young, small, and weak. Returning your attention to childhood helps you to get a better picture of who you were—and who you are.

Initially, you may have some difficulty finding something positive to say about your younger self. Many survivors have carried their negative self-images from childhood. They blame themselves rather than the abuse for their unhappiness, shyness, fear, confusion, and isolation. Nothing could be further from the truth.

The fact that you survived into adulthood is proof that, as a child, you were resourceful, creative, and strong. (Yes, I'm talking about you!) You owe a debt to that little boy. It is because of his courage and determination that you are moving on your recovery today. And it is a debt that you are able to pay. He deserves your respect and friendship. You are an adult he can count on absolutely. You are living evidence that he will make it through his difficult, lonely childhood. Recognize that he was working by himself with limited resources, and he overcame tremendous odds. What a terrific little guy! If he could do all that without help and support, imagine what he could have accomplished with the right kind of care, love, and encouragement. Getting in touch with the reality of yourself as a child will help you turn around your equally inaccurate picture of your adult self.

There are many ways to reconnect with the child within you. Here are some suggestions:

1 / *Make use of photographs.* If you can, take a look at pictures taken before you were abused as well as afterward. Notice how they are different.

2 / *Write a letter to yourself as a child.* Tell him how wonderful he is and that he never deserved to be hurt. Reassure him that he will survive, and that the abuse will not go on forever.

3 / With the help of friends, or in a workshop or group, *create a drama or fantasy about your childhood:*

• You can have someone else take the role of you as a child while you reassure him that he is fine and everything will be OK.

- You can play out returning to the scene of the abuse as your adult self, protecting the child by standing up to the perpetrator. Take along allies or reinforcements if you like, but be your own hero.

- You can set up a scene of yourself as a child the way it always should have been. Imagine a safe childhood, peopled with kind, loving, protective adults.

4 / *Learn new ways to play.* Don't worry about appearing foolish or feeling silly. That's what it's all about. There's nothing like playfulness to bring out the child within you.

I recently saw a lapel button that said "It's never too late to have a happy childhood." While you can't change the past, you can forge a new perspective on it that will allow you to have a happier adulthood. Befriending and reassuring the child within strongly reinforces adult recovery by creating new insight into past experiences.

I'll describe one interesting (and unexpected) example of how this type of support system can come into being. Some of my first time-limited recovery groups for male survivors spontaneously turned themselves into longer-term groups. All the group members elected to continue for an additional cycle, allowing no room for adding new participants. What occurs in these continuing groups is extremely powerful, speaking to the advantages of ongoing work in an environment of established safety. These groups move from retelling their histories to exploring specific life issues. Members present more details of their current life struggles, enlisting group support in dealing with them. In this way, the continuing groups resemble general issues groups—but with a very specific difference. For recovery group members, safety is grounded in a level of trust that comes from everyone having experienced boyhood trauma. (It is similar to the intensity of support felt by groups of Vietnam combat veterans.) Although it is important that this trust eventually be extended beyond the group, that can be dealt with later—with the active assistance of the other group members.

Members of these ongoing groups make sense of their experiences, using their insights to bring about real changes in their lives. They are more likely to go out for dinner or coffee together after the meetings. They invite one another to parties and meals at their homes. They send one another notes and e-mail and exchange phone calls. Group members provide active support during intimidating life situations, such as accompanying one another to medical and dental appointments, attending court appearances and funerals, helping with preparation for job interviews, attending family events—and confronting perpetrators. During the breaks between the end of one cycle and the beginning of the next, group members meet informally as an interim support group. It is clear to me (and to them) that something very special is happening. These adult survivors are taking genuine charge of their recovery. They are accomplishing this feat by creating a healthy, functional *family*. This is the way family always should have been. On some level they've always known it, and now they are figuring out what to do about it. They are actively rejecting the experiences that told them there is no closeness without abuse.

It is no exaggeration to say that, in accepting support from one another, they are rediscovering their capacity for love. They are reaffirming what they originally knew—the possibility of nonsexual, nonabusive loving of other human beings. This is a profoundly thrilling discovery, opening infinite possibilities for male survivors. What has been done can be repeated. They recognize that if trust and love are possible here—with this group of men—they can be found elsewhere as well. Survivors, now starting to *thrive,* can say (with the certainty of experience), "Change is possible. I have the ability to turn my life around." The power of this transition from surviving to living—from hurt to health—deeply affects all who experience it. I feel touched and privileged when I witness what these men have accomplished. And this is only one (admittedly special) example of how survivors support one another by creating new families. There can be any number of foundations for these associations. They may be religious, neighborhood, school, or special interest groups. Most frequently, the new families are less rigidly defined, deriving support from a range of safe, caring friends, wherever they can be found. Creating a support network requires trust. Like trust, social support develops slowly, one interaction building upon the next as relationships are formed. This development of adult support systems is crucial to recovery. It means that you are no longer alone.

The route to recovery begins with putting an end to your isolation. The only way out of isolation is, of course, the company of others. The logical question is, "How do I go about it?" You may feel as lost and unskilled as a child. Asking you to form intimate relationships seems as unrealistic as expecting an infant to talk or a five-year-old to write a sonnet. This is not an idle comparison. Asking a child to behave like an adult is unrealistic in the extreme; to require him to do so is cruel. The basic information and social experiences—the building blocks of relationships—simply aren't in place. It is shortsighted to expect the survivor to know intuitively how to negotiate the confusing tangle of emotions, expectations, and skills involved in maintaining an emotionally satisfying social life.

Your situation isn't hopeless. It is not stupidity or incompetence that keeps you isolated. You never had the opportunity to develop normal social skills. Social relationships are possible; skills can be learned. But it can't all be accomplished at once. Moving toward other people must be done in gentle, logical steps. Whenever a new bit of progress is achieved it must be examined, felt, considered, and savored. The only way to tackle an overwhelming task is to break it down into manageable bits. When one step feels solid, it is possible to move on to the next. Now and then it makes sense to stop and look at what you have accomplished. If you only focus on what you still need to do, the task will always feel impossible. Looking back at where you were last year or three months ago allows you to see the progress you've made.

Building a relationship takes time and experience. Everyone makes mistakes, and very few are fatal. When people are willing to acknowledge that something went wrong—and don't waste a lot of time blaming others or themselves—they can get on with the business at hand. That is the business of correcting mistakes, figuring out a better solution, and thereby forging a stronger relationship. Human interactions that have survived tests can be more solid for them. By meeting challenges together, people forge a history of successful communication that they can fall back on when things get rough.

Harry's Statement

Harry, a forty-year-old survivor, tells of removing himself from abusive situations through out-of-body experiences and running away—and how he stopped running to start healing.

I am five years old. My parents have just completed their umpteenth screaming match. I've gotten used to it. I can fall into a trance while they fight, a state bordering on sleeping and waking.

A noise grows out of my own heartbeat. It squeaks and thumps in regular rhythm, getting closer and closer. It's at the window now.

I get out of bed and move toward the door. My terror grows. If I can just reach Mom and Dad in time—I make it to the hall and run. Run, Harry, run!

I can feel the floor begin to slip under my feet. A creature I cannot see is getting closer. I can see the kitchen light and the shape of my mother's head. My mouth forms a soundless scream. There is no escape.

To this day, terror stuffs down the word "help" when I need it. Sometimes my soul still spins into a half-dreaming, half-waking state as my mind conjures up monster-movie dreams.

I am a forty-year-old gay male, a musician by trade. The forty-year-old part is not a pleasant prospect. I'm still running.

Looking back I can see a lot of reasons why my life has gone the way it has. My father left when I was four. The unspoken reason: marital separation.

I couldn't grasp any of the situation except the fact that he was gone. I began my own brand of separation: mental separation.

Dad is gone. I am lying in bed for a winter's nap. I gaze at the sun filtering through the "webs" at the base of my fingers and drift away. Soul leaves body.

My mother and I joined my father in Houston a year later. Together again! But drinking and fighting begin. Violence erupts into our outwardly *Ozzie and Harriet*-type family life.

Mother senses trouble the first time Dad drinks heavily. He

picks at her with a cold sarcasm. The sounds begin to crescendo and Mom and I head for a motel to weather the storm.

A day later we return to an absolute shambles. Furniture is broken, musical instruments smashed, and clothes thrown about. In later instances we stay home and learn to take it.

I also learn that anger can destroy, and I reject it as a valid expression of emotion, become a true Southern gentleman. Little do I realize that the depression I adopt to survive can maim, cripple.

A similar process operates at school. I have a difficult time adjusting socially, and am labeled "underachiever" by teachers. My father circles grades under an "A" in red. On the other hand I am beaten up by other kids for being "bookish."

My mother has a long history of drinking. She began as a teenager when her stepfather made life miserable for her; perhaps she was a victim of abuse. She drinks day and night by my eleventh year. I return home from school to find a locked front door, the television blaring, and Mom passed out in front of it. I learn to leave my bedroom window undone so that I can get in. Basically the neighborhood streets and the field behind our house become home.

Earlier, I mentioned my separation technique. I perfect it so I can disappear at school, too. By my fourteenth year, my guidance counselor has me classified something like "out the window." She asks often if anything is wrong at home. I answer no. I have learned my lesson well.

In this same time period I return home one day to the usual scene. Mom is snoring away in front of the television and I feel a wave of rage. I don't need to think twice about what I am going to do. I grab a butcher knife out of the kitchen drawer, creep to the sofa, and raise the knife to her throat. I falter, redirect the knife to myself. Again I falter. The separation starts. I don't know how long I have been staring at the knife while soul left body.

I join Scouts at age eleven, hoping for some escape from home. I work hard to earn the money and rank so I can attend my first summer camp. My reward: a scoutmaster, male hero-image, sexually molests me. The major part of the experience is in an outhouse and we are totally silent. I learn sex is a dirty, secret experience.

I feel guilty, afraid, responsible. I leave the troop and join another, attempting to escape my shame, but run headlong into a group of older boys who are drawn to me like radar. I can read their thoughts: new meat.

I am initiated into the troop the following summer by five members of this older group. My next-door neighbor is within earshot and I listen to his screams as he receives a "normal" initiation consisting of being blindfolded, rolled in mud, sprayed with shaving cream, and receiving a series of punches and whacks.

J———, who I am fellating while my neighbor screams, whispers, "Isn't this better than what he's getting? Now relax, kid."

Relax.

N——— continues to scream. I relax as soul separates from body.

In high school there is not much to report. I try to reform myself in this new place, but I am too far gone. I live up to my underachiever status most of the time, except in music and drama.

In my late teens, however, I discover religion and become part of an Episcopal church that bears the earmarks of a cult. There is a system of extended families and I become a part of one in order to find safety for myself. My separation ability becomes spiritual experience, my ability to separate is sanctified. My inwardly directed anger and self-hatred are redefined as self-mortification and perfection.

It is possible that the separation experiences are willful attempts at psychotic split, the ultimate refuge of the tortured. However, the depression continues, deepens. Suicide looks pretty good as an alternative.

Finally at age thirty-three I leave community life, determined to discover what my long-repressed gayness is about. As far as I can tell from the behavior of those around me in the late seventies and early eighties, one is supposed to sleep around. I discover a certain prowess in that activity. My musical and acting abilities developed in music school and perfected in the church community serve me well as I now perform in bed, often to packed houses in gay baths, rest areas, parties, but always with strangers.

Every time someone gets too close, I move and/or change jobs. I've had eight jobs in three countries during the last ten years, and have lived in forty-seven homes in my lifetime. Panic alternates with depression, despair with hopelessness. I am alone in crowds. But I keep running.

After watching a television show describing the long-term effects of child abuse on its victims, I talk to a counselor whose name is advertised in a local gay newspaper. We review my symptoms, compare them with those of adult incest survivors and I enter group and individual therapy. I begin to change certain unhealthy life circumstances.

It has taken me a long time to plug into the group and to trust even my therapist. But at last someone understands my horror story and does not minimize it, nor allow me to. I am slowly allowing a few people into my life in significant ways, sharing feelings while they happen. I'm working at committing myself to living in the Boston area and putting a stop to the running. I have a new job (church music!) where I feel professionally significant and socially accepted.

I am in the middle of establishing a monogamous, mutually life-giving relationship with another survivor. We know each other's assets and liabilities clearly, try to live openly and honestly. We blow the whistle on the trade-off game each of us learned to play in order to survive.

I have recently taken the HIV test. The result: positive. But I feel pretty good physically and mentally.

I am determined to feel whatever is left of my life rather than separate and dream it away. I look for hope in tiny doses. Hang on, Harry, hang on.

15

SEXUAL FEELINGS

It's hard to be passionate when you're trying to maintain control.
—a male survivor

One of the most perplexing questions faced by a survivor of sexual abuse is, "What should I do about sexual feelings?" In spite of all he has done to ignore, deny, control, redirect, hide, discount, or explain away his sexual feelings, they have a way of appearing, unbidden, with alarming persistency. I mentioned some elements of his consternation in earlier chapters:

1 / He has come to associate sex with abuse. When sexual feelings arise, he fears he is about to be abused—or, if he acts on the feelings, he will be abusing someone else.

2 / Since displays of affection were inappropriately sexualized, any show of affection has the potential to be sexually charged. This can cause avoidance of any kind of affectionate interaction, lest it lead to arousal and then to inappropriate behavior. Finding himself aroused in situations that have no obvious sexual component makes him feel like a pervert—sex-obsessed and out of control.

3 / The abuse was committed by someone who was unwilling or unable to recognize and respect normal boundaries. The perpetrator, in meeting his or her own sexual desires, taught the child that people act on impulse, regardless of the pain that the action may inflict on others. The survivor learned that any arousal will inevitably result in sexual activity. Never having had the power to keep the perpetrator from abusing him, the survivor feels powerless to prevent his feelings from leading him into sex—whether or not he wants them to.

4 / The idea that it is necessary to act on all impulses blurs the distinction between feelings and behavior. Thinking about murdering someone is not the same as committing the crime. Wanting to hit someone raises no welts. Similarly, sexual fantasies are not the same as sexual acts. When he has not yet learned this distinction, a survivor punishes himself for crimes he hasn't committed. He has "lusted in his heart" and feels like a rapist or sexual deviant. His sexual feelings become, for him, further proof of his wickedness.

5 / Fear of his sexual feelings can lead the survivor to excessive preoccupation with sex and arousal. Having a commendable wish to behave toward others in a nonabusive manner, he finds himself without adequate guidelines as to what constitutes abuse. He has been lied to in the past. If he talks about it, what will people think of him? Will they suspect that he is having these feelings and expose him to ridicule and punishment? Thrown back on his own resources, the survivor becomes increasingly scrupulous about monitoring and controlling his feelings. Every impulse is scrutinized and judged. Each thought is examined for potential sexual content. The prophecy has fulfilled itself. In his attempt to avoid becoming a perpetrator, the survivor has become obsessed with sex. He can't seem to get his mind off the subject—which he sees as further proof that he is flawed beyond recovery.

6 / To avoid sexual arousal the survivor may attempt to deaden all feelings. He avoids situations that have the potential to be arousing. He may deny that he has sexual feelings or, when they do appear, label them as something else. In his distrust of sexuality, he goes to great lengths to protect himself and others from his sexual feelings.

Many survivors keep sex rigidly compartmentalized—separate from other areas of their lives. They confine sex to solitary masturbation, thus protecting others from being sexually "victimized." Masturbation has the powerful secondary benefit of being completely under one's own control. Since the only other people involved are fantasy objects, they present no physical threat. Ironically, even this harmless form of sexual release can become overwhelming. As it turns into patterned, compulsive activity, it becomes one more part of life that feels out of control. The masturbatory fantasies may replay aspects of the original abuse, reinforcing the feeling that sex—even when performed alone—is abusive. There is a vast body of pornography dedicated to fantasies of sexual and physical abuse. The term "self-abuse" becomes, in this case, a description not of the act but of the feelings attached to it. It underscores loneliness and provides survivors with further proof that they are unacceptable human beings with no hope of normal relationships. (I do not mean to criticize masturbation, which is not necessarily an unhealthy activity. In fact, masturbation may be the only safe way that the survivor has been able to allow himself to enjoy sexual feelings. My concern is when the activity becomes a compulsion, isolating the survivor and reinforcing his negative self-image.)

Another form of compartmentalizing confines sexual activity to situations that are purely sexual in nature. These range from frequenting prostitutes and massage parlors to anonymous—sometimes furtive—encounters in parks, public toilets, or highway rest areas. What these activities have in common is that they are divorced from any other area of the survivor's life. There is no need to develop a relationship. There is no requirement of tenderness, humanity, or self-revelation. It is simple gratification of a sexual urge. Or is it? There would be no problem if it could be accepted as simply meeting a physical need. But there is more to it than that.

Compartmentalizing sex reflects the belief that it is wrong, dirty, evil, and abusive. That is why it must be hidden. "Nice, normal" people must be protected from this activity. The old morality that states "good girls don't" carries the corollary that "bad girls *do*." The next logical step is easy to take. If only the dregs of humanity engage in this kind of sexual activity, and if the survivor's sex life is limited to it, then surely (he reasons) he is beneath contempt. (These beliefs may not be held consciously. The survivor may feel himself to be a completely liberated individual, and yet be unaware of how severely he is judging himself.)

Taking this belief system a bit further shows how seriously it can affect the survivor's life. Having defined himself as flawed or perverted, he tries to protect other, "better" people from contamination. Assuming that his sexual feelings are dangerous to himself and others, he backs away as soon as he begins to feel them. Any attempt to add a sexual component to a relationship is met with suspicion and fear. His illusion of control is threatened. Order must be restored. This is accomplished by running away. The survivor finds a reason to end the relationship abruptly, leaving his partner bewildered—particularly if she or he doesn't share or understand his situation. If he does become sexual with his partner, he may negate all other aspects of the relationship, redefining it in keeping with his previous sexual experiences. His abuse history, then, has sabotaged a potentially satisfying relationship, relegating it to a meaningless sexual encounter.

To lead a satisfying life you have to figure out what to do with your sexual feelings. You must break down the barriers that keep sexuality separate from the other parts of your life. This is a process of acceptance and integration. It is never easy, but there are ways to accomplish it.

As with breaking the silence about abuse, you begin to deal with your sexual feelings by talking about them. As long as sexual feelings and activities remain hidden, they become shameful secrets. It is hard to share them; feeling like a horrible confession of your sins or an embarrassing revelation of weakness. It may be easiest to begin by sharing your feelings with a counselor or therapist. In this setting you are assured of confidentiality and (it is hoped) not being judged. An experienced, sensitive counselor will provide safety and encouragement as you explore your sexual feelings. (Chapter 16 includes a discussion of how to find the right therapist for you.) As you grow more accepting of your sexuality, you begin to communicate thoughts and express feelings. During this process you discover that others have concerns, fears, and interests similar to yours. It is especially helpful to share your thoughts and feelings with other survivors. (Chapter 17 explains why interacting with other survivors is a powerful aspect of recovery.) As you become more comfortable with your sexual feelings, they won't need to be kept hidden. Neither will they be constant intrusions that prevent you from relaxing and enjoying life. It will become easier to accept them as another part of the richness of human experience. Acceptance of sexual thoughts and feelings paves the way toward integration of healthy sexuality into your life.

I don't mean to present this simplistically. It isn't simple. Sexuality is a highly charged topic for everyone. None of us is as "cool" about sex as we would like others to believe. Sex is still fraught with embarrassment for many of us, and it is common to attempt to cover it up with pretense or jokes. It may take years before you are comfortable with your sexual feelings. But the benefits of taking the first steps are numerous. You start to reap these benefits long before the process is complete.

To talk about feelings is to acknowledge their existence. You may be asking yourself, "OK, now that I've acknowledged them, what do I do about my sexual feelings?" The answer, at first, appears painfully simple. When stated, however, it may seem to be the reverse—simply painful. The best thing to do about feelings, sexual or otherwise, is *feel* them. This idea can seem threatening and feel frightening. As a survivor, you have experienced what happened when feelings weren't kept under rigid control. They always were acted on—and the actions were abusive. You are rightly suspicious of any suggestion that you allow yourself to feel sexual. Wouldn't that make you an abuser, too? The answer is a resounding *no!* You have been given misinformation. You have been lied to. Feelings are not the same as behavior. (And sex is not the same as abuse!) You are not at the mercy of your feelings. You don't have to act on them unless you choose to do so—*no matter how it feels.* Learning to acknowledge them, accept them, and even enjoy them allows you to stop being a victim of your own feelings. Again, feelings are to be felt. Nothing more. There is no harm in that. Neither are feelings alone the best basis for action. The most useful guide to behavior is your own best thinking, taking into account all available data, including (but not limited to) your feelings. When you accept that, you cease to be afraid of your feelings. Only then does the novel concept of enjoying your sexual feelings make sense.

Talk about your feelings to someone who will listen (and share) without judgment or criticism. As you allow yourself to have sexual feelings, to share them and even celebrate them—as you accept that you have choice as to which of your feelings you put into action—you will see how it is possible to be a feeling, caring, *and* sexual person. As you recognize that you have the choice not to act on all of your feelings, you accept that it is possible to act on some of them. You are in charge of when you will be sexual and when you will not. Sexual feelings—even sexual arousal—do not have to lead to sexual activity *unless it makes sense for you and your partner.* This revelation is tremendously liberating. It enables you to explore all ranges of feelings and activities at your own pace and in your own way.

Having given up rigid control over your feelings and actions, you are

free to take charge of your life. You experience what it is like to touch and
be touched in ways that don't automatically lead to sex. You learn that a
hug can be enjoyed as a warm expression of human caring. Instead of
responding to every touch by tensing up or drawing away, you allow yourself to be held, caressed, and reassured physically. You express (and
receive) affection on many levels, and make the distinction between abusive contact and caring touch. Most important, you can state clearly when
(and how) you want to be touched, and when you don't. Recognizing that
everyone has a right to absolute control over his or her body, you exercise
that right without worrying about hurting someone's feelings. Having
given up the fear of your feelings, you let go of another piece of the
tyranny of an abusive childhood. Knowing that it is OK to feel, and that
you can decide what to do with your feelings, a world of possibilities
opens to you. You explore a range of feelings, activities, and affectional
choices (including sex) that are free of abuse.

16

INDIVIDUAL COUNSELING

I want to put up a sign that says, CLOSED FOR REPAIRS.
—a male survivor

WHY THERAPY?

The idea of going into counseling or therapy can be very intimidating. You may have been raised with certain ideas about therapy. If, for example, you were brought up to believe that "people should be able to solve their own problems," asking for help feels like an admission of defeat. Further, you may have been taught "only nut cases need shrinks." This leads to the idea that if you see a therapist, you are admitting to yourself (and the world) that you are crazy. Finally, you may think of therapy as an extreme measure, to be turned to only as a last resort.

Movie and television portrayals of therapy and counseling don't ease your mind. Therapists tend to be presented as severe, unresponsive, forbidding types who sit silently behind their patients—out of sight—taking notes and occasionally asking probing questions. The patient lies on the therapist's couch for years, delving deeply into the obscurities of his infancy and childhood, spending small fortunes and endless hours to discover that the severity of his toilet training caused him to loathe his mother. Although some therapeutic situations resemble this scenario, they are rare. The Hollywood image is parody—most counselors and therapists create a far more human and welcoming environment. But old images persist. Even if you know that the movie version isn't real, it can be intimidating enough to make you want to stay away.

This chapter discusses some specific issues and problems that confront the adult survivor in individual counseling. It offers guidelines for finding the right therapist. But before doing that, it may be useful to address some widely held myths about counseling and therapy.

There are many different types of psychological counseling and therapy. These are sometimes legal distinctions, which vary from country to country, state to state, and among different professional groups. For our purposes I will not distinguish between *counseling* and *therapy*—or between *counselor* and *therapist*—but will use the terms interchangeably. They refer to a one-way helping relationship with someone who possesses particular skills, training, and experience in dealing with the effects of various life experiences on emotions and behavior.

Let us look at some reasons people avoid seeking counseling:

1 / **"I should be able to do it myself."** The idea that we should be capable of thinking our way out of any psychological difficulty is a strange one. People who would readily consult experts to repair broken furnaces, fix their television sets, service their cars, or give them advice on major purchases are strangely reluctant to seek the help of someone with special training and practice in dealing with psychological issues. And that's really all a therapist is—a man or woman who, by virtue of having had specialized education and experience, has developed particular skills and insights into certain areas of human life. Not the least of the benefits of a counselor is that she or he sits outside the problem, providing a perspective that someone within your situation (you, your friends, and family) can't. You go to a barber to have your hair cut, a mechanic services your car, and a plumber fixes your sink. Why, then, would you leave your emotional well-being in the hands of amateurs? Are you any less important than a toaster oven?

2 / **"If I go for psychological help, I'm admitting failure."** This assertion is difficult to support by any kind of logic. If you had a broken leg you wouldn't expect it to heal itself; having it set by a doctor is not evidence of your personal shortcomings. On the contrary, it is the appropriate response to the situation. It makes sense to get the help you require.

3 / **"It's not that bad." "It's not serious enough to require treatment."** How bad does it have to be? How much pain is too much?

How many years of isolation and unhappiness do you have to endure before going for help? Many people view therapy as a last resort. Couples, for example, often wait until separation or divorce is imminent before they seek professional counseling. Waiting that long makes the job much harder. The couple (as well as the counselor) must wade through additional accumulated frustrations and resentments before getting to the underlying issues. Recognizing problems early on—while they are still manageable—makes them a lot easier to deal with. Ultimately, by seeking assistance before things get "too bad," you are saving time, money, and energy. Perhaps the situation would be easier to accept if therapy were viewed as "maintenance" instead of treatment. Something that is important to you deserves to be well taken care of. People who would never dream of waiting until their car broke down before changing the oil—who would be shocked at the idea of not cleaning their house until the Board of Health forces them to—who scrupulously schedule an annual physical examination—see nothing illogical in waiting until they are in crisis before seeing to the care and maintenance of one of their most valuable possessions—their emotional well-being.

4 / **"It's too expensive. I can't afford it."** It is true that psychotherapy can be extremely costly and protracted, but it does not have to be that way. While some mental health professionals charge upwards of $125 for a forty-five-minute session, these are the exceptions rather than the rule. And high cost does not mean that the care will be of higher quality. There is a wide range of services available to you, from private psychotherapy to organizationally, religiously, and publicly funded agencies, hospital programs, and clinics. Mental health counselors, social workers, psychologists, psychiatrists, pastoral counselors, and nurses offer services. In addition, there is a range of nontraditionally trained (but often very able) professionals and nonprofessionals. These services range in price from very expensive to free, and many are covered in total or in part by health insurance. In an effort to make services more widely available, some practitioners will adjust their fees to the financial situation of their clients. Don't be afraid to

inquire, and don't feel that you will be looked down on or receive inferior treatment if you pay less for it. Don't deny yourself the attention you need. You are worth it, and there are high-quality professional services available at affordable prices.

5 / **"I don't want people to know I'm in therapy. Everyone will think I'm wacko."** No one has to know. Psychotherapists have a professional responsibility to protect the confidentiality of their clients. This means that therapists require permission from their clients before revealing their clients' identities or any information about them. It is necessary to face realities of life no matter how irrational they may be. One of these irrational realities is that some prejudices still exist against people receiving psychological counseling. It makes no sense to punish someone for dealing with his problems while rewarding someone who ignores or hides his difficulties. But prejudicial attitudes aren't based on reason. This is why active drunks continue to find social acceptance while recovering alcoholics participate in programs that are "Anonymous." It is why professional sports figures who try to overcome their drug habits by entering treatment programs face the possibility of losing their careers. The message is: "Do whatever you want as long as no one is forced to notice it." This attitude—which assumes that there is something shameful about rebuilding a damaged life—is clearly mistaken. But unfair as it is, we must recognize reality. Some jobs would be jeopardized if it were known that the jobholder is in therapy. People still gossip and engage in character assassination. It would be wonderful if all the survivors of all types of maltreatment could stand proudly—openly proclaiming their identities and determination to put the abuse behind them. But this is not yet possible. When people finally recognize that abuse, not recovery, is shameful, they will encourage survivors to get the help they need. Then the subject will come out of the shadows. That time is coming, but it is not yet here, and responsible professionals recognize the need to protect the confidentiality of their clients.

There are some parts of the country, types of careers, and other environments that are less open to psychological counseling. Not every city is like Los Angeles, New York, or Boston, where it is almost embarrassing to admit that you are *not* in therapy. One of my correspondents wrote, "... there is a 'Midwest' mind-set that begins somewhere west of Allentown, PA, and ends just east of Reno, NV, which says that talking directly about personal problems and asking for help from 'outsiders' is suspect." Although the writer may have more direct experience than I with that attitude, I don't think it is unknown on the East and West Coasts. Nor is it found everywhere in the Midwest, as the excellent work done by counselors in Minnesota, Illinois, Wisconsin, Texas, and many other "heartland" locations will attest. Some of the best pioneering work on recovery from abuse is coming out of the Midwest. Narrow-mindedness is neither a Midwestern nor a rural phenomenon.

Until psychotherapy is more widely accepted in all geographical areas, social classes, occupational and ethnic groups, it is important to insure that your confidentiality will be protected. You should have absolute control over who hears your story, when they hear it, and under what circumstances. Ask your therapist to give you that guarantee. She or he is ethically committed to doing so.

6 / **"I don't want some shrink telling me what to do." "I'm afraid it will completely change my personality."** These concerns usually represent a fear of giving up control—a fear that is quite familiar to survivors. In reality, you can always be in charge of the pace, direction, and intensity of your recovery. An experienced, able counselor will help. You and your therapist work together toward your taking full charge of your life. You will still be yourself after therapy, and will derive greater satisfaction from being who you are.

Beginning a program of counseling or therapy is, at best, somewhat intimidating. At worst, it can be terrifying. This is particularly so if it is your first encounter with a therapist, or if you have had negative previous experiences in therapy. You approach the situation with fears and questions. "Who is this person?" "Will I be able to trust him?" "Does she know what she's doing?" "Is he experienced in the areas where I need help?" "Will I be able to let down my guard enough to open up to her?" "Can therapy do any good at this point?" "Will he like me?" "Will she think I'm weird?" "What should I say?" "How much should I reveal?" "How will I know if it's doing any good?" These questions are legitimate. It is normal to have doubts, and reasonable to ask for information and reassurance. Share your concerns with the therapist. The way he or she responds will give you information that will help you decide whether this is someone with whom you want to work. If your initial fears are dismissed as unimportant, it is unlikely that the therapist will address your deeper concerns adequately—or that you will be able to open up the way you need to. A later part of this chapter offers suggestions on what to look for in a therapist. But unless you can express your fears to your therapist—and feel that they are being listened to and taken seriously—it will be difficult to form a useful therapeutic alliance.

IMPORTANT CONCERNS ABOUT THERAPY

In addition to the anxieties faced by anyone embarking on a counseling program, there are particular feelings that the therapeutic setting brings up for an abuse survivor. It is important that the therapist and the survivor be aware of these feelings and discuss them. Not doing so can seriously hinder recovery. I will raise some of these concerns, with suggestions as to why they are important and what can be done about them.

The Setting

Most counseling sessions take place in private, with only two people present. The door is closed and sometimes locked to eliminate the possibility of interruption. There is agreement that what goes on in the session is kept confidential. The client may even be expected to sit on a couch. For the survivor this can be frighteningly reminiscent of the original abusive environment. Most abuse takes place in secret. There are seldom other people present. The perpetrator usually makes sure that secrecy is maintained. It is easy to understand how a survivor feels uncomfortable in such a setting, without being consciously aware of why. How is it possible for you to be relaxed and trusting in a setting that restimulates the abuse memories? How can you face putting yourself into this situation week after week?

A counselor who has experience with abuse issues is more likely to raise these questions. She may discuss with you possible ways of dealing with the problem. If the counselor fails to do so, initiate the discussion yourself. (Sometimes it's necessary to educate your therapist so that he can do the best job for you.) If the therapist shows respect for your concerns and is willing to explore ways of addressing them, you have taken the first steps toward forming a helpful therapeutic alliance. Unwillingness to do so may be evidence of rigidity that will interfere with your progress. Recovery from the effects of sexual child abuse is a recent area of therapeutic concern. Therapists must be open to putting aside preconceived notions, and seek solutions that work best for the survivor.

What, then, can be done about the challenge of the therapeutic setting? It can be met with flexibility and openness. Sometimes awareness of the issue is enough. Recognition of a problem is the beginning of a solution. If you know that you can talk about a problem whenever it arises—no matter how often it comes up—you're well on your way to getting over it. You can agree that if your counselor senses that you are shutting down emotionally (or appearing nervous) she will ask you what is going on. Remember that you may be unaware that it is happening. Asking your therapist to raise the issue is doubly helpful. It confronts the problem while inviting someone else to think about you.

Some simple physical adjustments to the therapeutic setting can make a tremendous difference to the safety level. You may wish to keep the door unlocked. You might find that it feels safer to sit on a chair rather than a sofa. It can be helpful to increase the physical distance between you and the therapist until you feel comfortable. You may feel safer at particular times of the day and schedule your sessions during those hours.

You may want to discuss with your counselor what would allow you to feel most in charge of your sessions. Perhaps you'll feel safer walking around the room as you talk, instead of remaining in your seat. You can request reassurance (as often as you need it) that he will remain in his seat and never touch you during a session. It is important that you and your therapist do whatever lets you get to the necessary work. Creating safety is a vital part of that process. Don't worry about your counselor taking offense at these precautions. They are no reflection on his trustworthiness; they represent an attempt to build trust.

If, after talking about the issues and making the physical changes, the one-on-one counseling setting still feels too threatening, you may want to discuss with your counselor the possibility of including another person in your sessions. You may wish to ask a trusted friend to attend one or more sessions. It might not even be necessary to actually follow through on this suggestion. It is sometimes enough just to know that you have your therapist's permission to do it. It reassures you that the therapy session doesn't need to be kept secret—nothing abusive will go on. It is an option that you can exercise whenever you feel the need. If having another person actually in the room doesn't seem right for you, you can always bring someone along with you and have them remain in the waiting room or somewhere else "within shouting distance."

As you can see, there are many possibilities for altering the setting to better fit your needs. No doubt you and your therapist can come up with adjustments that work for you. (I would be happy to hear about other creative solutions discovered by readers of this book.)

Money

The feeling that your counselor is "only doing it for the money, and doesn't really care" about you is hard to overcome. It touches on several issues for the survivor. It raises echoes of having had to pay for caring and affection. It doesn't matter that the current payment is monetary rather than sexual. It still feels like paying to be cared about. No one could love you for yourself alone. Doubting that your therapist genuinely cares about you leaves you questioning whether you can believe anything she says. The issue becomes one of suspicion. "Can I trust caring that I have to pay for?" This creates a dilemma for both therapist and client that isn't solved by abolishing payment. Seeing therapy as "paying someone to love you" is a distortion. You aren't paying your therapist for love. You are paying for her to think about you. She has invested considerable time, effort, and expense in receiving training and developing the skills of a professional. It is appropriate that this professional commitment be compensated. The fact that she has chosen to work in this emotionally demanding field can be seen as evidence of caring. Competent therapists display their caring by obtaining the very best training available, keeping abreast of current developments in their professional area, exchanging ideas and information with colleagues, maintaining their own physical and psychological well-being, and bringing their experience and best thinking to the issues raised by their clients.

The double bind for the client looks like this: If the therapist charges for her services, then she doesn't really care about me. If, on the other hand, she lowers or waives the fee, she won't provide the same quality of care given to someone paying the full fee. It is the old theory of "You get what you pay for." The survivor feels that he is in a no-win situation.

The solution to this problem is simple—communication. Cost of care is not the best gauge of its quality. Individual psychotherapy is offered on a "fee for service" basis. That is, you have a contract with your therapist that for an agreed-upon fee she will provide you with psychological counseling. This fee should be negotiated at the onset of treatment. Both client and therapist should agree to it. Therapy should not begin until both parties accept the financial arrangement. If you can't come to a mutually satisfactory agreement, it may be necessary to find another therapist. If either party proposes changing the financial arrangement, ample time should be given to discussion of the reasons for the change and exploration of alternatives. Once this financial situation has been agreed upon, it is best to accept it and adhere to it responsibly, so you can devote your attention to the real business at hand—your recovery.

Power

By definition, the therapist-client relationship is unequal. By entering therapy, you are putting yourself in the unusual situation of having to open up to a relative stranger. You are expected to share intimate details of your life, thoughts, and feelings with someone who does not share his personal life with you. In other words, you are to trust your story to someone you barely know—someone in authority. This is not easy for anyone to do. For an abuse survivor, it is tremendously difficult. You have had the experience of someone in authority abusing that trust in a damaging way. Someone known to you—someone who was supposed to love and protect you—hurt you. If someone that close to you could violate a position of trust, what can you possibly expect of a virtual stranger?

Power, control, and abuse have been linked by your experience. It is understandable that you would be wary of letting down your guard against those in power.

The way to handle the question of power is to *take your time*. Move very slowly, step by step, stating your fears and suspicions whenever they arise. Talk about it! If you feel that your therapist is being manipulative, tell him. If you think that she is pushing you in ways that don't make sense for you, let her know it. If you feel weak or childlike in his presence, it is important to talk about it. Your therapist isn't a mind reader. You can't expect her to guess what you are feeling. The more you talk about your feelings, the more you learn that it is okay to do so. A good therapist remains open to his client's interpretations of the therapeutic relationship. If your counselor isn't prepared to accept the possibility that she made a mistake, that he may be unconsciously manipulating or controlling the situation, that her ideas may not be appropriate for a particular client, then you probably don't have the right therapist for you. But before you decide that it isn't working, you must communicate your feelings.

Counseling is a relationship. Two people are involved. Don't assume at the first sign of disagreement that the relationship has fallen apart. Learning that two people, acting in good faith, can overcome disagreements and build trust is an important revelation. It is a lesson that is learned slowly.

A responsible driver enters a superhighway cautiously, first checking for obvious dangers, then moving into the slow lane. As he becomes familiar with the road, he judges the flow of traffic before picking up speed. He signals before moving into a faster lane. Only the most reckless of drivers would charge full-throttle across three lanes of traffic without checking for danger. Similarly, the best way to build trust is to proceed carefully and patiently. Don't move any faster than makes sense for you. If you are not comfortable with the direction or speed of the therapy, slow down and read the signs or ask for directions. In that way, you learn the route. It becomes yours. You understand the components of trust and create trusting relationships.

Instead of looking at your counselor as someone who is telling you how to run your life (a sort of psychological backseat driver), you can view him as an expert consultant: someone who may have traveled this route before, knows how to read the road map, and is available when you feel lost. No doubt you both will make mistakes, take some wrong turns. But it's good to have someone around to help you figure out how to get back onto the highway.

To be mutually satisfying a relationship needs reciprocity. Both parties must feel that they are getting something from the interaction. But the exchange doesn't have to be exact. If each of us gives the other ten dollars, not much has happened. We might as well have kept our own money. But if you give me a gift and I perform a service for you, we each have acquired something new. And we have each offered something to the other—that is reciprocity. By the same token, it is not appropriate for a counselor to use the therapy session to work on her own personal issues. The reciprocity is of a different order. It is a professional relationship, not an interaction of friends or lovers. Treated responsibly, with mutual respect for the nature of therapy (and its boundaries and limitations), your relationship with your counselor can be profoundly important and immensely helpful.

Direct Experience

You may wonder whether somebody who hasn't been abused can really understand what you're going through. For a therapist to be helpful, does she have to be a survivor? On the other hand, can someone who was sexually violated ever develop enough distance from the abuse to offer a realistic perspective on your problems? There isn't one absolutely correct answer to these questions. Advantages and disadvantages need to be weighed—and viewed in light of your particular situation.

I have heard people insist that it is necessary to be a survivor of abuse to work effectively with other survivors. I think that is a somewhat misleading perspective. But, like most heartfelt opinions, it contains an element of truth. The accurate part, of course, is that the best way to know about anything is to experience it. Only another survivor of abuse can truly claim to know what it is like to be in that situation. Even if the specifics of the abuse were different (they do vary tremendously) the effects are remarkably similar. The benefits of communication and interaction with other survivors cannot be stressed enough. But does this mean that your therapist has to be an abuse survivor? I don't believe it does. While it is true that no one who hasn't had a burst appendix can know what it feels like, few people would insist that their surgeon display his appendectomy scar before performing the operation. A therapist doesn't need to have experienced a problem in order to treat it. She does need to learn about the issues involved, including (and nothing is more important than this) the subjective effects of sexual abuse on the victim. (Sexual child abuse is more than a physical assault. Therapy must explore the way you feel about yourself and what was done to you.) Some information about abuse can be obtained from courses, workshops, and reading. The most important part, however, can only be learned from survivors. You are the expert. You must be listened to. You must be encouraged to talk—to tell your story over and over again. And your therapist must listen very carefully—with an open mind and complete respect. Through this process, your counselor learns how best to be helpful to you.

Feelings of hopelessness lurk behind assertions that only other survivors can provide adequate counseling. They sound very much like, "No one can really understand me." Implied in these statements is, "I'm so flawed that only someone who is equally messed up can begin to understand what I'm going through." They reinforce the survivor's sense of isolation. Building an alliance with a therapist who is not a survivor can be a powerful contradiction of those feelings of hopelessness and isolation.

There are also advantages and pitfalls in having a counselor who is an abuse survivor. Empathy and understanding that grow out of direct experience are precious assets. You may feel that you are being understood for the first time in your life. Nothing is more valuable than that feeling; it is important that you experience it, either with your counselor or with other survivors. However, one potential problem of working with a therapist who is also an abuse survivor is the blurring of boundaries. Although there are similarities of experiences and effects, it cannot be assumed that all survivors are alike. Life experiences vary greatly. Despite the similarities, there is great variety in the effects of and responses to sexual child abuse. There is a risk that a counselor who is also a survivor will identify too closely with your story, assuming it is the same as her own—that she knows what you are feeling without checking out her assumptions. This form of "mind reading" is seldom helpful to the client. It is important that a therapist who is also a survivor has worked extensively on his own abuse history, so that he can bring perspective and objectivity to the therapy along with empathy. If your therapist hasn't worked through enough of his own abuse issues, it will be impossible for him to provide the help you need. She will bring her own issues into the therapy (whether or not they are yours), thus leading you in inappropriate directions. Or he will overidentify with your issues, creating a situation where there are two clients in the same room and no therapist. You will then find yourself in the unhappy situation of needing to counsel your therapist. While this can be an interesting experience, it is not why you are there.

Whether or not your therapist is a survivor, she must be careful not to impose onto the therapy a pace or focus that is not right for you. The counselor must remain aware that you are not "just a victim." You are a human being, possessing a wide range of skills, attributes, feelings, and experiences. It is a serious mistake to look at anything less than the whole person. There will be times when you will want to work on topics unrelated to the abuse. This is not only appropriate, it is essential. Sexual abuse is something that was *done to you;* it is *not who you are.* Don't be pushed to spend every minute of therapy working on abuse. Your counselor must see you as a whole person, and encourage you to view yourself the same way.

There are advantages and difficulties with any therapeutic situation; none is perfect. It is less important to find a therapist who is (or isn't) a survivor than that you get the best available care. Be aware of the qualities that are important to you in a therapist, and keep searching until you find a satisfying counseling situation.

Gender

"Should I see a male or female therapist?" There are no hard-and-fast rules here. When therapists first began to recognize issues of sexual abuse, it was assumed that all perpetrators were male and all victims female. Because of this mistaken assumption, many counselors concluded that a survivor can only feel safe with a female therapist. When male survivors began to seek help, the counseling profession was slow to accept the reality of their situation. Recognition of the existence of female perpetrators was even longer in coming.

Many factors influence the choice of a male or female therapist. For some, the question of gender is irrelevant. You may not care whether your counselor is male or female, but just want to find the best person for the job. On the other hand, you may "just feel more comfortable" with a woman or a man. There is nothing wrong with trusting your feelings on the matter. While it is possible to treat your feelings of discomfort as "clinical issues" to be worked out in therapy, you don't have to. Entering therapy is sufficiently anxiety provoking. If choosing either a male or female therapist makes you feel more comfortable, by all means do so. You can always work on your feelings about men or women in other ways—or choose to work with a different therapist some other time.

Not everyone has the luxury of wide choice. You may live in an area where there are very few therapists, or only one who has any experience working with abuse survivors. You may have to go with the "only show in town." Or the best choice may be someone of the "wrong" gender. You may even find that there is no counselor with relevant experience in your area. Don't despair. Not so long ago no one knew anything about these issues. Our knowledge is increasing rapidly. Find yourself a smart, caring, dedicated professional and encourage him to learn what he needs to know in order to be effective as your therapist.

All other things being equal, you will feel safer choosing a therapist who does not remind you of the perpetrator. This would suggest that it might be better to begin with a therapist of a different gender than that of the person who abused you. But this is something to consider, not a rule. Gender is not the only attribute or quality that might remind you of the perpetrator. Other aspects of appearance, such as voice quality, speech mannerisms, gesture, style of clothing, and age, can evoke powerful memories. If you feel comfortable with the individual—if he is intelligent, insightful, well trained, responsive, and encouraging—gender doesn't matter. You have found yourself a valuable resource.

Type of Therapy

"What kind of individual therapy is best for me?" This is a complicated question. There are many models of counseling and psychotherapy, reflecting different ways of interpreting human behavior. Although some basic knowledge of counseling theory and methods can be helpful, it won't be possible for you to do a thorough exploration of all schools of psychological thought.

Like recovery itself, psychotherapy is a house with many doors. How you enter the house is less important than actually getting inside. Some doors may be more convenient than others, some more difficult to open, and others too small to get through or too heavy to move. I think that, although some types of therapy may be better suited to your purposes than others, the choice of therapist is more important. If he is competent, insightful, flexible, and encouraging, you have found someone who will be effective in whatever modality he has chosen. A rigid, controlling, unimaginative person will be a bad therapist no matter what training he has received.

Find someone you feel good about and ask him about his theoretical orientation. You don't have to be an expert yourself. When you interview prospective counselors, ask them what kind of therapy they practice. Ask them what they see as the main issues involved in working with survivors of sexual abuse. Ask them how they go about setting up a program of counseling. How would they work with you? Put the questions in your own words. If you don't understand the answers, ask for clarification. Therapy should lead to understanding, not further confusion. It isn't necessary to hide behind clinical jargon. If they try to do so, they either don't know what they are talking about or don't know how to communicate directly. Neither makes for good therapy. Ask as many questions as you have to. Keep on asking until you receive answers that are satisfactory. Don't be afraid that you are wasting their time. Few decisions are more important than this. Give your choice of a therapist at least the same care you would when selecting a new house or car.

Misuse of Therapy

That there are many different helpful therapeutic styles does not mean that all therapies are helpful. Not everything that is called therapy is therapeutic—some so-called therapeutic practices are, at best, counterproductive for the survivor. At worst, they can be abusive. Some of the most glaring examples of the misuse of therapy follow. Watch out for them and avoid them, no matter how anyone attempts to justify them:

1 / **Sex.** There is never a legitimate reason for a therapist to have sex with a client. It is harmful to the client and destructive to the

therapy. For a therapist to engage in sexual interaction with an abuse survivor is an inexcusable violation of a position of trust. Unscrupulous individuals attempt to justify sex between therapist and client. They have called it by various euphemisms, such as "bodywork." They have attempted to legitimize it by saying it is a way to "get at feelings," "open up" the client, or even to "teach" the client "how to achieve intimacy." None of that is true; these are lies or self-deception. A therapist who initiates sex with a client is predatory. It replays the original abuse, taking advantage of the survivor's vulnerability to serve the personal ends of the therapist. It is natural to want to please your therapist. It can be flattering to feel that your therapist finds you attractive. It is all right to have sexual feelings for your therapist. It's a normal part of the therapeutic process, often referred to as *transference. Acting* on these feelings destroys the safety of the therapeutic alliance. If a counselor suggests or condones engaging in any form of sexual activity with you, leave immediately. You are being abused; this time you have the opportunity to do something about it.

2 / **Re-creating the abuse.** As an abuse survivor, you must never be revictimized. Whether the victimization is actual or symbolic, it is harmful. You have already spent far too much time in that position. Any role-playing, psychodrama, guided fantasy, or other technique that simulates the original abusive situation *with you in the role of victim* will be frightening and destructive to your recovery. This does not mean that role-playing or psychodrama can't be useful techniques. They are therapeutic tools. Like any tools, they do a good job if used correctly and appropriately by someone who knows how to employ them. But their proper use requires training and awareness of the requirements of the task at hand. For example, it can be helpful to role-play a situation where you stand up to the abuser and take charge of the situation. A psychodrama that portrays how things should have been for you as a child can elicit powerful emotions and insights. You may wish to rehearse confronting the perpetrator. You can engage in fantasy and imagery of what it would be like to be fully powerful and self-confident. These, and any number of other techniques, can be useful because

they move you into a position of taking charge. Rather than reenacting weakness, they focus on your strengths. Instead of forcing you back into the role of victim, they show you a way out of it. You are correct to resist any attempt to rob you of power by re-creating the victimization.

3 / **Inappropriate touch.** When you were abused, you were robbed of physical control. Part of your recovery demands that you be in complete charge of your body. You have the absolute right to decide who can touch you, and to set limits on when and how you are touched. You can always say no. This right extends to hugs, pats on the shoulder, and even handshakes. Although hugs and other physical contact can be reassuring, comforting, and healing, they can also be frightening to an abuse survivor. No one should be able to touch you without your permission, no matter how well intentioned they are. Beware of any therapy that *requires* you to be touched. The key to appropriate touching is permission. Do not be coerced or manipulated into doing anything that isn't right for you. If you don't want to be touched, then it isn't okay to touch you. If you're not sure you want to be touched, it is probably best to wait. You can always do it later; you can't undo it. You don't have to acquiesce to please someone else. You don't even have to explain your reasons. Your body is yours. That is enough. If your therapist can't accept that, he shouldn't be working with survivors.

4 / **Authoritarianism.** You've had enough of people telling you what to do. People who insisted that they knew what was best for you did you a great deal of harm. Recovery means being in ultimate charge of your life. A program that is imposed from outside, by someone who claims to have all the answers, may be very tempting. "How nice it would be to give up control and let someone else make all the decisions." But it doesn't work. Beware of any counselor who tries to take over your life. Even if he has the best intentions, it just isn't helpful. You need autonomy over your life. A good therapist will help you to explore options. After examining possibilities with you, she will encourage you to take charge of making your own decisions.

5 / **Unresponsiveness.** Some therapists provide virtually no feedback to their clients. The client is left to imagine what the therapist is thinking, projecting his own ideas onto the counselor. Direct questions are turned back to the questioner unanswered. While this style of therapy may be useful for some people, it isn't very helpful for survivors. You lived much of your life in that kind of isolation—thrown back on your own resources, guessing at reality. You are looking for contact: communication and understanding. When an abuse survivor asks a question it should be respected as a legitimate inquiry that deserves a response. To do less leaves the survivor feeling isolated and crazy. A therapist can't have all the answers, but he should be able to help you discover some of them. You need to question and test reality with someone who is open to exploring the world *with* you, without doing it *for* you or leaving you to do it alone. When you interview therapists, make sure they respond like real people.

6 / **Criticism and judgment.** You are an expert at self-criticism and negative self-judgments. You don't need to pay someone else to do it for you. People who are committed to only one point of view can be critical of any perspective that differs from their own. Whether the perspective is religious, political, academic, or therapeutic, it indicates single-mindedness and rigidity. It is impossible to relax and open up to someone prone to constant judgments and criticism. Look for a therapist who, regardless of his personal beliefs, is open to a range of possibilities. It will be invaluable in helping you overcome your own rigidities and any tendencies you have toward "black-or-white" thinking.

FINDING A THERAPIST

Once you decide to see a therapist, how do you go about finding one? How do you know whether the person you've found is competent, professional, and knowledgeable? And how do you determine whether this person is the right counselor for you? These are important questions. You will be entering into an intimate, trusting relationship with your therapist, and you want it to be a good one. This isn't something to be decided by closing your eyes and picking a name out of the Yellow Pages.

It's important to go into your search for a therapist with your eyes wide open, using your best judgment, and availing yourself of all possible resources. The following suggestions may be helpful.

1 / **If you have been in therapy previously, think about what that experience was like for you.** What was difficult about your relationship with the therapist? What did you find useful? What were the problems? Was your counselor patient, caring, reassuring, open, flexible, and accepting? Is she someone to whom you would want to return? If so—and if she is still available—you might decide to reenter therapy with this counselor. The advantage of this option is that the two of you have already established a history and a working relationship. If you don't wish to return, it is useful to figure out why. If you know what you want in a therapeutic relationship, you are far more likely to find one that meets your needs. If you like and trust your old therapist, but he is unavailable for resuming therapy, ask him for suggestions and advice on finding someone else. If your former counselor is inexperienced in treating the effects of sexual abuse, he may refer you to someone who has that expertise. This is not rejection, but professional responsibility. You wouldn't bring your broken refrigerator to someone who only works on telephones, no matter how good he is at fixing your phone. Make sure you let your old counselor know what you are looking for—and why—and be sure to ask why he recommended these particular therapists.

2 / **Talk to trusted friends, family members, and business associates.** Ask them about their experiences in counseling and therapy. This can be particularly helpful if you are new to the process. You may discover that more of your associates than you thought have been in therapy. If you have friends who are therapists, ask them for recommendations—and ask them why they suggested these particular people. Once you have gathered suggestions, your search isn't over. Not all therapeutic settings are right for everyone. Neither are all therapists. A counselor who is just the right match for your best friend may be quite wrong for you. Ultimately, you have to trust your own judgment.

3 / **Contact local agencies and organizations that deal with sexual abuse issues.** Ask for recommendations of counselors who have experience with survivors. Even agencies located at some distance from where you live may be able to suggest resources in your area.

Among these important resources are women's centers and rape crisis centers. Yes, these can even provide resources for a man! Since women have been at the forefront of dealing with sexual abuse issues, a women's center will probably be able to steer you toward a compatible counselor. Don't worry about being refused assistance because you're male. The issue is abuse, not gender, and most women's centers know that.

In addition to women's centers, some district attorneys' offices have victim assistance programs or sexual abuse units. The workers in these units can furnish information and referrals. There are also local government agencies—departments of social services, child protective units, and the like—that have referral sources. Some religious and educational organizations have resources for helping survivors of abuse. Finally, you may be able to obtain referrals from local chapters of professional organizations, such as the National Association of Social Workers, American Psychological Association, American Psychiatric Association, and American Counseling Association.

4 / **Contact national, regional, and local organizations established to support and educate people about sexual abuse.** National organizations may have local chapters or contact persons in your area. They keep referral lists of local counselors who have experience or interest in working with survivors. At the end of this book there is a resource list of many of these organizations. Remember that inclusion on a referral list does not automatically guarantee the quality of service.

5 / **Think about what you need and want in a therapist.** What expertise is important to you? What personality traits? Examine your wildest hopes as well as your realistic expectations. Then make a list of requirements. Decide which items on your list are

most important to you—which are essential and which would simply be nice to find. If you are aware of your expectations and preconceptions, you are less likely to be disappointed.

6 / **Draw up a list of questions to ask the therapist during your initial interview.** Don't be afraid to show up with an extensive list. Write them down so you don't forget any. The questions on your list can include practical details (What are your fees? Do you accept health insurance? Do you have evening or weekend hours? What is your policy on cancellation of sessions?), information about the therapist (What is your theoretical orientation? How long have you been a counselor? What is your training? What is your experience with abuse survivors? Do you receive supervision in this area?), details about your proposed therapy (How long do you anticipate that I will be in therapy with you? What form will that therapy take? Will you give me specific feedback about my progress?), and other crucial issues (Can you assure me of complete confidentiality? Do you think sex between therapist and client is ever beneficial? [If you get any answer other than no, this is not the right therapist for you.] How do you feel about crying, raging, etc.?).

A responsible therapist will be happy to answer any questions you have. If she does not wish to answer a question, the counselor should, without defensiveness, explain to you why she believes that the question is inappropriate. If a therapist is unwilling to provide you with the information you need, find one who will.

7 / **Shop around.** Selecting a therapist is an important decision. Don't settle on the first person you find. Talk on the telephone with several counselors, and set up interviews with those who sound best to you. If you need to schedule a second interview with one or more therapists in order to decide, do so. If none of those you've interviewed is satisfactory, keep looking. This may be more expensive initially, but it is a wise investment in your recovery. Don't let embarrassment keep you from shopping around. A responsible therapist will want to help you find the best person for the job. Take the time to do it right.

8 / **Trust your impressions.** If something feels wrong with the "fit" between you and a counselor, that can be sufficient reason for hesitating to select that person. You may need more information. You may be picking up on something that requires further exploration. You don't have to be able to explain your reasons—they don't need to be rational. If you feel unsafe with this person, maybe her voice quality reminds you of your mother's or he wears the same aftershave as your father. Whatever the reason—no matter how nice the person is—if you feel unsafe, it will be harder for you to open up. Raise the issue. A good counselor will not feel threatened by your honesty, and will be willing to discuss your hesitations and reservations. Although not an insurmountable problem—it can even be an opportunity—it is not necessary to take on every challenge. You have the option of staying with this therapist and working out whatever is eliciting those negative feelings, or you can find another therapist—one who feels more compatible. However you resolve the question, it is best to address it openly.

9 / **Come to a decision.** Although shopping around is important, it is also important to get on with the business of recovery. Beware of getting so involved in the process of finding the "ideal therapist" that you never get to the work you need to do. Don't let perfectionism get in your way. Just as you have to accept that it is okay for you to make mistakes, you need to understand that your therapist is human. No doubt you will both make mistakes. What is important is not perfection, but a mutual commitment to figuring out what went wrong, and how to solve the problem. If you find someone who is smart and caring, patient and accepting, skilled and flexible, stop searching. You have found the "perfect" therapist.

17
GROUPS AND WORKSHOPS

*I used to think that I had to talk all the time in order to be heard, but
I can be quiet and hear my story from the other people in the group.*
—a male survivor

"It was hard enough to tell *you* about my father. I could never talk in front
of a whole group!" The thought of sharing personal information with a
bunch of strangers is intimidating to most people. It is especially so for
survivors. You are not alone if you feel terrified at the prospect of joining
a survivors' recovery group. You've lived for years under a burden of
shame, guilt, and denial that kept you silent about the abuse. You've been
afraid of the consequences of admitting that you suffered sexual violation. You feared that disclosure of your history would lead to humiliation,
disapproval, punishment, and further isolation. You avoided the subject
because talking about it brings up pain and sadness. If it's this hard to
deal with your own story, how on earth could you stand listening to a
roomful of other men sharing similar histories? It would be too immediate—too painful—too real. And where will it end? It took great strength
and courage to admit the abuse to one person. Even promises of confidentiality aren't very reassuring, so it's understandable that you recoil at
the thought of taking this process further—making it "public knowledge." You wonder how anyone who cares about you could even suggest
the possibility of a survivors' group. You wonder whether you're ready
for such an emotionally charged experience—whether you'll ever be
ready.

Group participation is not a substitute for one-to-one counseling; it
is another aspect of the recovery process. When used in conjunction with
individual therapy, a group is a powerful means of moving you toward
your goal of taking charge of your life.

In this chapter, I discuss different types of groups and address questions of how to decide what kind of group is right for you, how to find a group, and how to know whether you're ready.

WHY JOIN A GROUP?

As discussed in chapter 13, the first step in recovery is to tell someone. Telling your story to a supportive, encouraging person establishes the basis of a trusting relationship. Beginning such an interaction, however tentatively, is an act of healing—in the best sense of the word it creates a therapeutic relationship. When you undertake this trusting relationship with a competent, caring professional counselor, it becomes the foundation for forming other relationships. When you learn that you can trust someone, and not have your vulnerability abused, it opens the possibility of establishing important ties with other people. As your relationship with your therapist deepens and strengthens, he should encourage you to widen your circle of trust and intimacy. As you feel stronger and more positive about yourself, you are more willing and better able to reach out. Each time you tell someone about the abuse—every time that information is respected—it is easier to feel welcome in the world. Participation in an adult survivors' recovery group is an important way to experience that welcome.

It is impossible to overstress the benefits of sharing your feelings and experiences with other survivors. There is no more powerful contradiction to isolation than telling your story to people who:

• Can listen to what you're saying (and are even *eager* to hear it)

• Believe you

• *Know* you're telling the truth about the abuse and its effects, *because they have had similar experiences.*

Their histories won't be exactly the same as yours. It isn't really important whether the perpetrator was male or female, blood relative or not, one or many persons. The age of the survivors at the time of the victimization, and the frequency and intensity of the abuse make little difference. I have found no clinical justification for ranking the severity of different types of sexual child abuse. The similarities of the effects and feelings are important, not the specific details of the abuse. I stress this point because I have found that survivors are able to latch on to any excuse for feeling that they don't belong in the group. They feel isolated because they are the oldest/youngest, most/least successful, richest/poorest, best/least educated; having been older/younger at the time of the abuse; having no specific abuse memories/remembering it in great detail; having been abused by a close/distant/nonrelative; having had no/little/much violence attached to the abuse; having experienced "only" a single incident/prolonged abuse; having been abused by a single/several perpetrators; having enjoyed/hated the abuse. These are all minor distinctions. It is important that you not let the differences make you lose sight of the enormous similarities. Assume that you belong; don't yield to the pull to isolate from potential allies.

As you tell your story and listen to others sharing theirs, you realize that you are not alone. Feelings you've carried with you for so many years—the numbing, isolation, and sense of failure—are not evidence that you are a sick or evil person. They are the results of your having undergone a terribly traumatic experience—which would deeply affect any normal person. If the survivor of a shipwreck can do nothing more than cling to a floating piece of debris, who would blame him for not swimming to shore? It is normal to do whatever you can to survive. Meeting other worthwhile, lovable people who, like you, have spent a great deal of time clinging to flimsy supports can give you significant perspective on your own situation. It can also provide glimpses of hope. "If they deserve better—if they are able to make changes and take better charge of their lives, maybe there is hope for me." It may be for these reasons that the men in recovery groups so actively support one another. It becomes important to each group member that the other men in the group successfully attain their goals. Each time someone takes charge of his life, it underscores the reality of recovery for everyone. Therefore, it is no wonder that I have witnessed men in my groups actually standing up and cheering one another's successes.

The group also provides a safe haven. It is a place where you don't have to explain why you feel the way you do, or why you've done the things you have. The group setting allows you to feel connected without exposing yourself to the risk of being abused. You explore your feelings in the company of others who are doing the same thing. You see your similarities to and differences from the other group members in a non-judgmental context. Group participation is an important means of finding out who you really are and what you can become.

Even though a group is a safe place to be, it is not always comfortable. You've spent a good deal of time and energy trying to avoid reminders of the past. You have steered clear of anything that elicits memories of abuse because of the painful feelings evoked by such recall. "Why then," you may wonder, "would I ever want to look for more pain? I'd have to be nuts to join a survivors' group. Not only would I be feeling my own pain, I'd be forced to listen to other people's stories. I don't know if I can take it." No, the group is not comfortable. No sane person would choose to spend his time dredging up painful memories in a roomful of other people who are doing the same thing—unless there is a powerfully compelling reason to do so. There are lots of other, more pleasant ways to occupy your life. If pain were all you had to look forward to, you would indeed be crazy to undertake a group. But there is lots more to the group than painful emotions. The purpose of bringing up these feelings is not to learn to live with them, it is to *get through them*. It doesn't do any good to avoid or ignore your feelings. You know that. You've tried it, and you continued to feel bad.

The group doesn't cause the distressing feelings; it creates safety that allows them to be felt. Once the pain is felt in a nonabusive atmosphere, it can be examined, understood, put into perspective, and diminished. There will be times during the course of the group when you will feel anxiety, fear, confusion, and anger. There will also be periods of calm, elation, excitement, and even joy. Although any of these conditions may be helpful, none is the ultimate purpose of the group. The group uses the feelings, both positive and negative, to lead to greater awareness. This awareness, in turn, leads to changes of thinking, responding, and behaving. The ultimate goal is a more satisfying life. To the extent that you achieve that goal, you are rewarded for the discomfort of group membership. Being a member of a recovery group for survivors can be of inestimable value. Connections made by group members frequently prove to be among the most meaningful of their lives. They may be intense, volatile, and disturbing. They will sometimes be confusing. At times you will want more and at other times you'll wish you had never taken this on.

Group members have said, "I have to force myself to show up every week." "I sometimes think I'll just run out the door and never come back. But I keep coming back week after week because I know that I need to be here." Group participation will always be important, but rarely comfortable. That is why it is necessary to make—and continually remind yourself of—the distinction between "comfort" and "safety." The safety of the group—*genuine, uncomfortable safety*—provides what you need to do the work of recovery. "Discomfort" is temporary. Like "survival," it is a stage in an ongoing process. Eventually, recovery leads you to relationships that are both safe and comfortable.

KINDS OF GROUPS

There are many types of groups, ranging from loose, informal, "drop-in" gatherings open to anyone, to highly structured therapy groups that require a long-term commitment. Groups can be led by a professional therapist, a survivor without formal training, or they may be "leaderless." The stated purpose of a group may be therapy, support, education, or some combination of the three. They may be time-limited or ongoing. Group membership may be fixed at a certain number of people or open-ended. The population can remain relatively stable over time or change from week to week. A group may focus only on sexual abuse or address more general life issues. The form of the group can vary as much as the content. In other words, there are infinite possibilities for a group experience. The type you choose will depend on your needs, preferences, and the availability of services in your area. Some localities have developed virtually no services for survivors. Others are relatively rich in resources. If there are no groups currently available near you, all is not lost. You can satisfy some of your needs within the context of a general issues group, or start a survivors' group yourself. Before you attempt that you may want to attend workshops and conferences for survivors.

A word of caution: I urge you to think seriously before starting a group of your own. Many survivors are chronic caretakers. They put everyone else's needs ahead of their own. The result is that the only need that ever gets met is their need to take care of other people. If you are this kind of person, starting your own group is a setup. You will find yourself giving what you hope to receive, satisfying everyone but yourself. Make sure that you are not sacrificing yourself to a pattern of caretaking.

My recommendation is: first establish a solid relationship with an individual counselor. With her help, explore the resources in your area. If a group exists, make sure that the group leader spends enough time with you to answer your questions *fully* before you join the group. In addition, be certain that your individual therapist has spoken with the group leader. The more open their communication, the better it is for your recovery.

There are advantages and problems with any type of therapy, individual or group. In the following pages, I discuss some types of groups— what to look for, and what to watch out for. (See the Focus later in the chapter for the rules established in my recovery groups.)

Peer or Self-Help Support Groups

These groups are set up by and for adult survivors. Leadership is usually informal. There may be a designated leader or leadership may rotate among group members from meeting to meeting or at specific intervals. A group may even consider itself "leaderless." They meet weekly, biweekly, monthly, or sporadically. The purposes of such groups include personal support of their members, educating themselves and the larger community, and advocacy for social and political recognition of the needs of survivors. Format of the meetings also varies according to what the group wishes to accomplish. Meetings may involve discussion of specific topics (relationships, sexuality, violence, fear of success, disclosure, confrontation), or guest speakers might be invited to address the group. Group members may have the opportunity to share their own stories. The meetings can follow a specific agenda or be quite loose and openended. Some support groups are part of a specific recovery program, such as Survivors of Incest Anonymous. In many places there are peer support groups for survivors formed on the model recommended by VOICES in Action (see "Other Resources," p. 378). Some support groups limit their activities to group meetings; others sponsor social gatherings, educational and fund-raising events, and encourage group members to form friendships that extend beyond the meetings.

Fees for group membership are usually quite nominal, and many are free of charge. Since rules for membership vary widely from group to group, it is important to get the information you need before joining one. At the very least, make certain that your confidentiality and personal boundaries (physical and emotional) will be respected by the other group members.

Peer support groups can be tremendously helpful to survivors. In addition to cutting through the isolation felt by most survivors, these groups contradict a common self-image—that survivors are flawed, helpless people who can't function on their own. Thus, the self-help group provides a means for taking active charge of your own recovery. A peer support group can be a valuable supplement to your individual (and even your group) therapy. Great advantage is derived by standing up to your ingrained feelings of powerlessness and inadequacy and joining with other survivors in forming peer support groups.

Although there are many advantages to self-help groups, there are some problems to be aware of and try to avoid. I believe it is important that a group has a designated leader, convener, or facilitator. This is someone whose responsibility is to think about the group as a whole. This person should be aware of the "flow" of the meeting: whether people are getting enough group attention (so the meeting isn't dominated by more assertive individuals while less outgoing members get lost); whether anyone appears to be in crisis; that the rules of the group are adhered to; and that the meeting begins and ends at the agreed-upon time. Someone should also be thinking about the continuity of the group from meeting to meeting. These functions can be invested in a single person for a period of time, or shared by group members on a rotating basis. However it is done, having someone think about the overall welfare of the group can be critical to its success.

Another potential pitfall for peer groups is the immediacy of the abuse for all participants. When heavy emotions come up—and they do—it is important to have someone who is not going to get hooked by them. If everyone in the group becomes overwhelmed and sinks into despair, you end up with a roomful of victims instead of a gathering of survivors. Someone with a different life experience may be able to recognize more quickly signs of becoming overwhelmed and provide the group with a perspective that keeps it from getting stuck in feelings. In the absence of such perspective, the group must be aware of the possibility of "shutdown," and figure out strategies for dealing with it. If this is not done, the group probably will not last. Dealing with this issue enables the members to build a truly solid and effective support group.

Another challenge for self-help groups is screening new members. Not everyone is able or ready to function as a responsible group member. For some survivors, effects of the abuse include acting in antisocial ways. They may be violent, verbally abusive, hypercritical, or otherwise prone to inappropriate behavior. An individual's neediness may be so extreme that he or she monopolizes the meetings, not allowing anyone else to receive group attention. It is commendable to want to exclude no one from group membership; survivors know what it is like to be isolated in pain— kept from getting the help they need. They don't want to put anyone else in that position. However, including a deeply troubled individual can destroy a group. The enormity of his neediness drains the resources of the other group members until they are unable to derive any benefit from the group. An individual who is that needy will not get enough from the group to be of any real help to him. He isn't ready to function as a group member. He will eventually move on, feeling that this is another example of people failing to meet his needs. In the process, he may destroy or severely damage the group. He needs extensive individual therapy before he has enough available attention to be responsive to the needs of others.

Since few peer support groups have adequate resources for pre-screening potential members, they must be alert to the possibility that the group will be faced with such a situation. Although this problem is certainly not unknown in more structured therapy groups, an experienced counselor will have evolved prescreening procedures that lessen the possibility of including inappropriate individuals. He will also have experience in handling individuals who behave inappropriately in group settings.

Finally, we must look at the issue of control. We know that control is an important theme for survivors. A leaderless, unstructured situation can be terribly frightening. Some deal with the fear by shutting down, numbing out, or leaving. Others attempt to diminish their anxiety by taking control of the meeting. Taking control in this manner reduces their anxiety level, but it also prevents them from deriving much benefit from the group. It keeps the other group members at a distance. By taking over the group, a survivor isn't forced to confront the very issues and feelings that brought him to join. This behavior can lead to power struggles and resentment within the group. Power struggles can be devastating to the survival of peer support groups that have no mechanism for dealing with them.

Good planning can solve some of these problems. Other issues are simply risks inherent in self-help groups. Awareness of these potential problems can help you respond more effectively should they arise. No situation is risk-free, and the problems I raised are not sufficient reason to keep you from participating in this type of group. Instead, keeping these cautions in mind, I encourage you to explore peer support groups as a resource for your recovery.

General Issues Groups

This type of therapy group is usually long-term and ongoing. Membership may be all male, all female, or a mix of the sexes. Upon joining, group members are usually asked to make a commitment to remaining in the group for a significant period of time. As you might expect, a general issues group can address any subject that interests its members, including the dynamics of interaction within the group. Depending on the group leader's philosophy, he will either make sure that members stay focused on relevant issues and each person receives his or her share of attention, or he will not interfere, allowing participants to establish their own rules and problem-solving strategies.

Most cities and towns of any size have a therapist who leads groups. Many hospitals and clinics have general issues groups, as do some schools, religious organizations, and community centers. Some are quite inexpensive. In the absence of specific abuse survivor groups, you can take advantage of existing resources and tailor them to meet your needs.

Another advantage of a general issues group is that you are not forced to limit yourself to abuse-related issues. This can keep you from feeling as though all you are is a victim. It allows you a wider perspective on your life and gives you a broader context in which to explore the abuse. The negative side is that the topic of abuse may never be raised. You may find yourself reluctant to talk about sexual abuse with people who aren't survivors themselves. People who want to avoid a subject can always find reasons to do so. You can spend months waiting for "the right time" to bring it up. And, unlike in a survivors' group, it is unlikely that the topic will be discussed here unless you raise it. The other group members will have issues that are "far more pressing" than yours. If you do raise the topic, you might encounter reluctance from the other group members (or even the therapist) to talk about abuse. There may not be the encouragement, safety, and understanding that you need to work on your recovery. You may feel as isolated in this group as you do in the outside world. This can be a useful situation, enabling you to work on those feelings of isolation—but only if the problem is recognized and confronted directly.

At the very least, before joining a general issues group, discuss abuse recovery with the group leader. Make sure that she knows that this is a major part of your reason for joining the group. Be certain that her responses make sense. Ask the leader to help you talk about your abuse history in the group. Let her know how she can be most helpful to you. Don't proceed until you are fairly certain that you will be welcome in the group without having to conceal any part of your life, least of all your recovery.

Ideally, you should join a general issues group *after* you have been in a group specifically for survivors. Once you have worked on the abuse in a specific group context, a general issues group may be a logical next step. You can take what you accomplished in the laboratory of the survivors' group and test it in the general issues group, as you move toward greater participation in the outside world.

In summary, although not ideal for dealing with recovery from sexual child abuse, a general issues group may be the best group resource available to you right now. If perfection is not available (it rarely is) it doesn't mean you have to settle for nothing. Even though it may not be just the right thing for you, a general issues group can be quite helpful.

Special Issues Groups (Other Than Sexual Abuse)

If there are no groups specifically for sexual abuse survivors in your area, you may want to join an existing group for other recovery issues. Even if there was no drinking, addiction, or battering in your family, you have a great deal in common with people who were raised in alcoholic, drug-abusing, or violent households. Many of the ongoing effects are quite similar, and it can be encouraging to see that you are not alone in your feelings of isolation and low self-esteem due to a traumatic childhood.

The largest, best known, and best organized of these organizations sponsor "Twelve-Step" groups throughout the nation. They include Alcoholics Anonymous (AA) for recovering alcoholics, Al-Anon and Alateen for those who are (or were) in relationships of any kind with an alcoholic, and "Adult Child" groups (ACOA or ACA) for people who were raised in alcoholic families. Following this model, many communities have developed related groups, including Narcotics Anonymous (NA), Narc-Anon, and Overeaters Anonymous (OA); Sex and Love Addicts Anonymous (SLAA) for people with sexual compulsions; Debtors Anonymous (DA), and Spenders Anonymous (SA). Twelve-Step programs for survivors include Survivors of Incest Anonymous (SIA) and Incest Survivors Anonymous (ISA). All these groups share the recognition that their members were exposed to destructive family patterns they were help-less to overcome. By acknowledging the hurts of the past, joining with peo-ple who have had similar experiences, and undertaking a program that has a proven track record, they move toward taking charge of their lives.

It isn't necessary to embrace these programs entirely. You needn't become a "convert" or overwhelm your life with meetings. Proceed at your own pace. No doubt you will have some reservations. There will be some aspects of the program that you will find less useful than others, but don't make the mistake of discounting a program entirely because it isn't perfect. Stick with it for a while and use the parts that are useful. Tailor the experience to meet your needs. Use it to supplement your ther-apy. It is helpful to know that you have a range of available resources. Many abuse survivors find that the meetings and literature of Twelve-Step programs start them on their own roads of recovery. You can find AA and Al-Anon groups listed in your phone directory; most also have Web sites (see "Other Resources," p. 384).

There are many other types of groups that are helpful to survivors. Resources vary widely. Explore both national organizations and local groups to locate ones that are best for you. (**Note:** Be wary of any pro-gram, group, or meeting that discourages you from expressing your feel-ings. Even if they are more comfortable, they will be less helpful.)

Special Issues Groups (Sexual Abuse)

A wide variety of groups address the needs of survivors of sexual abuse. Many are for women only, others are mixed, and some are just for men. They may be specifically for rape victims, adults abused as children, or limited in other ways. There is also a wide range of philosophy, focus, procedure, rules, and *quality*. Group leaders have all sorts of motivations for starting groups; group members have many reasons for joining. At worst, a group leader may be abusive. The leader may not have dealt with her own sexual abuse history, and may be trying to use the group for these purposes. Don't assume that just because someone is leading a group he is competent to do so. Investigate carefully. Ask all the questions you need to, and if you aren't satisfied with the answers, don't join the group. Check out the responses you received with another professional whose judgment you trust. Be particularly wary of hidden agendas. There are, for example, organizations whose philosophies include keeping the family together at any price. All too often, in an incestuous family, that cost is the physical and emotional well-being of one or more of its members. It is too high a price to pay. Not all families should remain together; forgiveness and reconciliation may not be appropriate goals for you—at this time in your recovery or ever. Don't be coerced into accepting any program that doesn't make sense to you.

"Short-Term" or "Ongoing" Groups

The question of whether to join a time-limited (eight-, ten-, twelve-, sixteen-week) or long-term group is a matter of the availability of services and your personal needs and preferences. There are advantages and difficulties with any option. For many survivors, a commitment of even a few weeks feels too frightening. If this is true for you, consider starting with a single workshop (see the end of this chapter for information about workshops), or a group that has a "drop-in" format, with no need to commit to more than one meeting at a time. A disadvantage of such an arrangement is that the population of these groups can be unstable, shifting from meeting to meeting. It is harder to establish safety and intimacy. You never know whether people will be there or not, and it's difficult to get on with the necessary work if you have to start over again each time someone new shows up. Sometimes, however, the drop-in group provides you with the right degree of freedom, allowing you to make a long-term commitment "one day at a time."

A long-term or ongoing group is one where the participants agree to commit to group membership for a significant period of time, often years. (At The Next Step Counseling, Thom Harrigan facilitates several male survivor recovery groups that have been meeting, with some changes of membership, for over a decade.)

Advantages of such a group include the depth of trust and intimacy that is established over time. Rather than exploring only abuse-related issues, a long-term group has time to deal with group dynamics. Interaction among the group members becomes the basis for understanding and improving relationships in the outside world. When handled properly, membership in an ongoing group provides perspective on the past, a solid base for present activity, and a jumping-off point for future changes. When a new person joins an ongoing group, he benefits from the collective experience of those who have been there longer. The older group members receive from the newcomers fresh perspectives, as well as a sense of how far they have moved since joining the group.

Focus
Rules and Agreements for Group Members

The rules for my recovery groups are few in number, but very important. I'll list them briefly, along with my reasons for them.

Before joining the group, all participants are expected to:

1 / **Have established an appropriate (nonabusive) relationship with an individual therapist, preferably of at least six months' duration, and have been actively working on the abuse issues.** They sign releases allowing me to exchange information with their therapists, so we are working together toward recovery. The reason for this requirement is that what comes up in the group is so

powerful and intense that one and a half hours once a week, divided among six to eight men, isn't enough. Friends and family can't (and shouldn't be expected to) deal with it all. Individual therapy is the proper setting.

2 / **Be dealing effectively with substance abuse problems.** This means that, if they are alcoholics or addicts, they have been sober/drug-free for six months to a year and are actively working a recovery program. The reason for this rule is that it is important that the intensity of the group experience not jeopardize their sobriety.

3 / **Not have had a major psychiatric hospitalization for a year before joining the group.** This gives them the opportunity to reestablish an everyday routine before they take on the intensity of a group experience. There is always time to join a group after one's life has stabilized.

4 / **Not be in the midst of a *major* life crisis.** I consider the group experience to be a major crisis in their lives. Any more would constitute overload.

5 / **Not be currently living in an abusive environment or abusing another person.** (I make the distinction between *feeling* like an abuser and actually *being* one.) Recovery is not possible while being abused—or abusive.

As group members, participants agree to the following rules:

1 / **Complete confidentiality.** Group members may share their own experiences with anyone they choose, but agree to do so in a way that completely protects the identity of all other participants. This is not the same as secrecy. It is about respecting the privacy of group members. Participants are free to talk about anything I say or do, but they agree to protect one another's confidentiality.

2 / **No touching one another without permission.** Both parties must agree to even a handshake. Sexual child abuse violates personal boundaries in the most destructive way. A survivor's right to control over his own body must be respected absolutely.

3 / **No sex between group members.**

4 / **No physical violence.**

5 / **Any contact with other group members outside the group, even a phone call, must be mentioned in the group.** Within the limits of these rules, I encourage group members to socialize and support one another in exploring nonabusive friendships. But it must be done with complete respect for one another's boundaries and pace. Everyone has the right to decline to extend his participation beyond the group meeting time.

6 / **Attend each session on time, sober and drug-free.** Give ample notice of necessary absences and call in case of emergency.

Honoring these rules helps to establish a safe environment for recovery.

Clearly, not everyone is ready or willing to make a long-term commitment to a group. For those who are, it can be a mainstay of recovery. For some, the group represents the first stable "family" they have known.

Most survivors' groups have a time-limited contract. This means that the group members agree to attend a fixed number of sessions over a specific time period. The length of these contracts varies, but they average ten to sixteen meetings. Barring an emergency, participants agree to attend every session, and the population of the group remains stable from the first or second session to the last. Short-term groups usually have more structure than ongoing groups, sometimes focusing on specific topics or goals. Because they are time-limited, there is little opportunity for exploration of group dynamics. The ongoing group can evolve gradually according to the interests and paces of its members; in a short-term group they are likely to feel a sense of urgency to "get down to business." It will end on a specified date, whether or not it has accomplished what it set out to do. This can be strong motivation for getting on with it. Time-limited groups tend to be intense and powerful, and often are a bridge between drop-in meetings and long-term groups. It is amazing to see what can be accomplished in twelve weeks of hour-and-a-half sessions divided among eight men. Short-term groups make up in intensity what they lack in duration. For some men, a twelve-week commitment feels like a lifetime. Others think they "won't even be able to scratch the surface in twelve weeks." The information is there for you to examine; see what is available in your area and make your own decision.

All-Male or Mixed Groups

This, too, will depend in part on the available resources. I know survivors who had the experience of being the only man in their recovery group. For some, this felt like a safe environment; others found it isolating and uncomfortable. Where there are few resources for male survivors (and that has been more the rule than the exception), groups are likely to be for women only. If a group is open to men, it is probable that you will be part of a very small minority. Even if you don't find this situation to be perfect, it may be better than nothing. Ideally, there should be more than one man in a mixed group, and the group leader must take care that the male participants do not become the repository of everyone's rage against male perpetrators. No matter how much you feel like a perpetrator, it is important that you not be treated like one by your group.

On the other hand, an all-male environment (especially if you were abused by a man) may be more than you are willing or able to take on right now. Ultimately, you must weigh the potential benefit against the terror and decide what kind of group is right for you. An all-male group, although frightening to contemplate, can make for a special kind of unity and understanding. In addition to comparing experiences, its members can explore their feelings about sexuality and about women without worry about being oppressive or exploitive. The rules of the group and the mutual support that develops become the basis for forming nonabusive relationships with men—a major step in your recovery.

Sexual Orientation

The clearest way that I can discuss the question of separate or integrated recovery groups for heterosexual and gay male survivors is by sharing my own experience and relating how my ideas evolved. I hadn't originally intended to separate the groups by sexual orientation. My intention was to screen prospective members for active "homophobia" and "hetero phobia," and include both gay and heterosexual men in my first group. When it turned out that I had about equal numbers of self-identified gay and "straight" men who wanted a group—and enough people to form two groups (and over the objections of a few prospective group members who felt unwilling or unable to make that choice)—I decided to start separate heterosexual and gay groups. My reasons for doing it this way were that sexuality and sexual orientation are highly charged issues for most men, needing to be explored in a safe, supportive environment. I felt that the heterosexual men needed the safety to explore their own fears about being gay—or being *labeled* as gay—perhaps including voicing antigay feelings without worrying about offending other group members. But it isn't helpful for gay men to have to listen to expressions of homophobia. I also thought that the gay men needed to talk about their sexuality—including sexual practices—without having to censor the information for fear of being judged or criticized. I was curious to see whether there would be any major differences between the groups.

At the time I thought that, even though there were far more similarities than differences between the two groups—and there was no reason to insist that heterosexual and gay men be in separate groups—it would be helpful to make the separation. The two groups were quite similar in the nature of the issues that they dealt with, and the way their members supported one another on all issues, including questions of sexual confusion.

Since those first groups, I have had the opportunity to offer groups that were not segregated by sexual orientation. My ideas have changed based on my experience and that of my colleagues. I am now convinced that the benefits of heterosexual and gay men working together toward mutual recovery far outweigh any difficulties. Male survivors have demonstrated again and again that we are dealing with issues of sexual child abuse, not sexual orientation. I continue to be moved by the solidarity with which group members and workshop participants come to that understanding, supporting one another in their diversity—and their recovery.

If you want an all-heterosexual or all-gay group and there isn't one available to you, I suggest that you consider joining an integrated group. You may be pleasantly surprised by the experience. Although it isn't ideal to be the only gay man in an all-heterosexual group or the only straight man in an all-gay group, even these situations can be worked out so you have a worthwhile group experience. Discuss your concerns with the group leader before joining a group. Be honest; don't sabotage yourself. Offer as much information as you can, and ask for all the information that you need. This provides the best foundation for beginning any group.

Age Range

Because it is necessary to attain some distance from the abuse before undertaking recovery work, it is unusual to find men working on abuse-related issues before they are in their thirties, forties, or fifties. For men in their teens and early twenties, the abuse is too close—they feel that their survival is still in doubt—and a group of adult men can be very threatening. For this reason, it is better for teenagers to be in a group of their age mates, whether all male or of both sexes. When teenagers, in the company of their peers, take charge of their own recovery, the results are impressive. The same consideration is useful, though not quite as important, for men in their twenties. Although I have seen men in their early twenties make great strides in groups where they were significantly younger than the other members, it is more difficult than in peer groups. The power differential feels too great.

Age doesn't appear to be a significant factor for men in their thirties, forties, and fifties. Perhaps this is because they either feel like scared children all the time or have taken on adult roles since they were quite young.

As with the other factors, you may have little choice of whether to be in a group of age mates; don't let concerns about age keep you from getting what you need.

Other Factors

If you have the uncommon luxury of a wide range of choice, consider whether to join a group that is led by a survivor or a nonsurvivor (or whether you even want to have that information about the leader). You may consider groups with a single leader or two coleaders—male, female, or one leader of each sex. These are options to consider; none is a major stumbling block. If you are in the happy situation of having a range of available services, by all means exercise your freedom of choice. But, when you have explored the options, *choose*. Don't grow old waiting for the perfect group to appear; join an adequate group and make it right for you. Doing so will give you a tremendous sense of your own power.

FINDING A GROUP

Just as you did to find an individual counselor, as you would before making any major investment, shop around. Ask friends and colleagues. Ask your individual therapist and other mental health professionals. Consult with organizations for survivors, rape crisis centers, women's centers, hotlines, social service agencies, and other community resources. Contact the national and local offices of various advocacy organizations. Finally, in the absence of existing groups, consider becoming a contact person for other survivors who want a group. Then go out and hire yourselves an experienced group leader. If there is sufficient demand, there are ways of meeting it.

ARE YOU READY FOR A GROUP?

This is a tricky question. The answer depends on what you mean by "ready." If you're wondering whether you are able to deal with the demands of group membership, or if you just need to focus on yourself for a while, talk about it with your individual therapist. Explore the question together and come to a decision not based on some "absolute" criteria, but on what is best for you. I recommend that you join a group only after working on the abuse in individual therapy for a significant period of time, at least six months to a year. But this is simply a suggestion, not a rule. Let your own best thinking, in consultation with the best information you can obtain, and the advice of your individual counselor, determine your course of action. (If the group leader does not think you're ready to join this group, try not to take it as personal rejection. Ask him why he thinks so, and attempt to listen to his reasons without defensiveness. You don't have to agree with the leader's decision, but you may benefit from knowing what considerations went into making it. You can then decide to wait a while before joining a group, or to look for another one.)

On the other hand, you may be ready but not *prepared* to join a group. If being ready for a group means that you can sail through it without feeling a thing, you'll never be there. Groups generate powerful emotions in their members. Sitting numbly through a dozen meetings won't do you much good. If you alternate between loving and hating the other group members, if you sometimes feel totally bewildered and out of control during the sessions, if you leave some of the meetings in turmoil, then chances are that the group is doing its job. As we said before, the goal is recovery, not comfort. You can't completely prepare yourself for giving up control. Like standing at the edge of a diving board, at some point you have to trust that you're ready—all your training has led to this moment; now is the time, go for it! Anticipation is usually a lot worse than reality. Trying something new is never completely risk-free, but once you have done it, it will never again be quite as frightening.

My opinion must be obvious by now. I strongly believe that a group experience constitutes an extremely important component of recovery for male survivors. The recovery group provides a laboratory for investigating and testing life changes before you put them into operation in the outside world. Once you have been a group member, it is extremely difficult to return to the same degree of isolation and confusion that you experienced before. Your direction is now forward, and the group provides much-needed fuel. Remember that you are taking this on for yourself, and everyone benefits from your progress.

WORKSHOPS

Recovery workshops are a very special type of group experience. These powerful events differ from groups that meet regularly over a specified number of weeks, or open-ended groups that meet weekly for years.

Workshops are onetime events, beginning and ending at specified times. They vary widely in scope and focus. Recovery workshops may be limited to men or women, or open to both. They may be general, allowing participants to work on any areas of immediate concern, or focus on specific topics or experiences (for example, relationships, ritual abuse, anger, sexuality). Some workshops are brief, lasting only an hour or two, perhaps offered as part of a larger conference or other activity. Most are more extensive, lasting a full day, a residential weekend, or longer.

Recovery workshops offer a number of benefits:

- They provide an opportunity to do a focused, intensive piece of work—removed from (and uninterrupted by) one's daily life. Workshops that are held some distance from a survivor's home area may feel safer and more anonymous than a local group.

- Because there is a specified starting and ending point, many survivors find it easier to commit to a workshop than to join an ongoing group.

- A *male* survivor workshop brings men together in a safe environment of mutual healing and support. This, for many, is an unprecedented experience that contradicts old messages about masculinity.

- The contained nature of the workshop setting (especially residential retreats) offers a survivor safety to do intense emotional work without needing to "pull himself together" right away.

- Workshops allow the survivor to see that his feelings and experiences are shared by others, of diverse backgrounds, locations, ages, races, religions, classes, sexual orientations, educational level, professions, and other categories.

- They multiply the number of people who know the survivor's story, thus extending his support network.

- They provide information about further recovery work. Participants learn what others have found helpful and decide whether to try some of these resources for themselves.

- Participating in a workshop gives many survivors a "jump start" when the momentum of their individual or group therapy seems to have stalled. Stalled or not, some men participate in workshops frequently to achieve this boost to their progress.

- Receiving the respect and admiration of the other participants (yes, this will happen to you) challenges old negative messages, replacing them with a clearer picture of reality.

- The presence of other survivors at various stages of their recovery demonstrates vividly that recovery is an ongoing process, not an event.

- Participants often leave the workshop with renewed energy, hope, and ideas about changes they wish to institute in their lives.

- Most importantly, many survivors report that, during a workshop, they get a glimpse of how their lives will be when they are past the agony of their current situation. Once a survivor experiences this "glimpse of recovery," the world is never again quite the same. Even if the dark curtain comes crashing shut, he retains an image of what is possible—what is in store for him as he continues his important work.

You must decide whether (and when) you will try your first workshop. Most who do so are surprised to discover that they look forward to repeating the experience. But it can be frightening to contemplate subjecting yourself to such an undertaking. It can feel like deciding to walk a high wire without a safety net. The actual experience is quite different. After pushing through their fears, applying to a workshop, and undergoing the initial terror of sitting in a room filled with strangers (especially male strangers!) most survivors end up wondering why it took them so long to give themselves this amazing gift.

I have been conducting recovery workshops for many years, and never fail to be moved by the power of the experience—power that is generated by the courage, intelligence, strength, creativity, insight—and love—of the survivors who participate. I always learn something new and am always pleasantly surprised. I return to everyday life renewed and invigorated—reminded of why I do this work. Judging from the feedback I receive from participants, I'm not the only one who feels this way.

Like other groups and healing experiences, not all workshops are alike. Workshop leaders vary in quality, experience, and skill. If you are considering trying a workshop, ask questions similar to those you would before starting individual therapy or joining a group. Talk it over with your therapist and with other survivors—especially those who have attended workshops. Get the information you need before making your decision. But understand that no one can anticipate what the workshop will be like for you. It's necessary to be open to surprises (surprises aren't always negative). Each year before my summer male survivors workshop, some individuals ask me to tell them *exactly* what they will experience every minute of the weekend. I reply that I can't even tell them exactly what the weekend will be like for me, let alone predict *their* experience. My colleagues and I (and other experienced workshop leaders) try our best to provide a safe, respectful, encouraging environment. When we do that, and then get out of their way, survivors create brilliant, profound experiences.

Perhaps the clearest way to demonstrate the possibilities of a workshop is with some direct quotes from participants. I assure you that these responses are far more the rule than the exception. I hope they will lead you to consider attending a workshop.

Here are six examples, excerpts from letters written by male survivors after attending men's recovery workshops:

"... how moved & changed I was by the weekend experience. I ... feel much freer & safe with myself ... such a caring & safe space & tone. I felt accepted and cared for and gently invited to move forward in life."

"I left the workshop as an adult ... feeling at peace with a new freedom never felt before."

"... how much this weekend meant to me. On my way back home Sunday afternoon, I realized that for the first time in as long as I can remember, I had no 'knot' in my stomach. I didn't feel alone in the world, and I felt relaxed and 'at peace.' "

"... a safe space ... I was able to face some assumptions (about men and about myself) as well as allow myself to feel/not suppress/connect. I was also afforded the opportunity to discover an awesome group of strong, courageous, life-affirming guys. I gained so much power this weekend looking into other men's eyes, hearing their stories, telling mine, feeling their pain/sorrow/hope/desire/ anger/tears and having them feel mine. I'm going to keep this weekend in my heart as a touchstone—my shield, armor, sledgehammer, hug, high-bar, soft landing."

"For one weekend . . . when the rest of the world kept doing its thing, my world was turned upside down. . . . In less than forty-eight hours, I found new meaning to words like courage, strength, survival, acceptance, and love . . . especially the kind we can offer ourselves. Nothing is really all that different, but somehow everything has changed."

"I shall ever be grateful for having this 'safe' experience to share from the depths of my soul. As I continue on this journey, my spirit has been renewed, refreshed, and strengthened! I truly never realized what an impact forty men would make on my life. *This was powerful!* . . . It felt good to cleanse my soul."

18

CONFRONTATION

I needed to love my mother and father. . . . I could not afford to address them directly about the felonies committed against all of us. I could not hold them accountable.
—Pat Conroy, PRINCE OF TIDES

Confronting the perpetrator is a difficult and complex issue. You must give a great deal of thought to why you would want to do it—and whether confrontation is in your best interest. If you choose to confront, it is important to consider when (and under what circumstances) you want it to take place. There is no general rule about confrontation. It is a highly individual, personal decision. For some people it is a logical next step in recovery; for others it could be a dangerous, self-destructive act. To be helpful, your confrontation must come from a position of strength. It is unlikely that you will be feeling powerful when you first undertake your recovery work. But as your healing continues, you will come to recognize that you have great power, certainly far more than the perpetrator—a dysfunctional individual who abuses children. By the time you are prepared to confront the perpetrator, you will have much strength on your side. You will possess a sense of certainty—a readiness to insist that the abuser be held accountable for his or her acts. There are ways of bringing yourself to this point of self-confidence. If you take the time to prepare, your confrontation—whatever specific form it takes—will be a powerful and healing event.

Survivors have all types of relationships with those who abused them. Some have had no contact whatever for a significant period of time—through their own choice or due to external circumstances. Others remain financially, physically, or emotionally dependent on the perpetrator. Feelings toward the abuser run the gamut: love, hate, anger, fear, confusion, shame, guilt, embarrassment, tenderness, and protectiveness are often intertwined in a confusing emotional jumble. Because of this complexity the decision to confront cannot be taken lightly. While I can't tell you whether confrontation is the right course of action for you (that is for you to decide), this chapter provides information to help you make your decision.

THE MEANING OF CONFRONTATION

When I speak of confrontation, I'm not necessarily referring to a direct encounter with the abuser. The real meaning of confrontation is *standing up to the abuse*. You are giving voice to the determination that you are no longer willing to submit to victimization *in any form*. It is a statement of self-respect and self-determination. Confrontation, in this sense, is a major aspect of recovery. It represents your recognition that:

- What was done to you was abusive.

- Sexual child abuse is wrong.

- You never deserved to be abused.

- You were not responsible for the abuse.

- People are accountable for their actions.

Confrontation, then, proceeds from a position of growing strength that recognizes that every human being deserves respect. Each person has the right to control his or her body. This includes *you*!! Whatever form it takes, and regardless of the outcome, healthy confrontation is an act of self-respect. When it is approached assertively (instead of passively or aggressively), you are left feeling better about yourself—more able to move ahead with your life.

Sometimes, when survivors first experience abuse memories—or decide to do something about them—their impulse is to rush to confront the abuser. There are many reasons for wanting to do this, but it is rarely a good idea. Like recovery, confrontation is a process that takes time. It calls for careful, thoughtful preparation. Rushing headlong into confrontation without adequate planning is foolhardy, reducing it to the level of acting out a male revenge fantasy (a John Wayne gunfight or a Rambo-like search-and-destroy mission). Although this might feel satisfying at the moment, it reinforces the stereotype that problems can be solved by aggression and violence—the very attitude that allows for the existence of sexual child abuse. Confronting a perpetrator on his or her own terms makes it harder and scarier than it needs to be. You will be far better off setting up the situation in the way that is best for you—making certain that you are ready, feeling strong and self-confident.

PREPARING TO CONFRONT

With proper preparation and planning, confrontation can be a healthy, important step in your recovery. It makes good sense to keep confrontation in perspective. There is a great deal of work to be done first.

Laying the Groundwork

Your most important preparation involves examining your own experience with abuse. This examination consists of everything that has been discussed in previous chapters: telling your story to someone, repeating it in as much detail as you remember, adding details as they appear, attaching whatever feelings are accessible to you, finding people who will listen and believe you, sharing feelings and histories with other survivors, establishing an appropriate therapeutic relationship, entering a group for survivors if one is available, and building a solid support network. These preparations take time, but they are necessary if you are to be clear about confrontation.

Before you undertake confrontation, you want to be as honest with yourself as possible about how you feel about the abuse, the perpetrator, and yourself. Confrontation is not a magic wand that will make everything all right. Although you have survived scarier and more difficult challenges, it is likely to be an exhausting, highly charged emotional experience—bringing up lots of material to be dealt with afterward. The perpetrator will not become your therapist. She or he won't suddenly become the loving, protective parent figure you always longed for. If you begin with the expectation that confrontation will magically solve all your problems, you will be disappointed. You owe it to yourself to be prepared. It is essential to understand your motivations and expectations. You accomplish this by being as clear as possible about sexual abuse in general and your abuse history in particular. The more secure you are about who you are—the more you believe that you are a good person who was in no way responsible for the abuse—the less likely you will fall victim to defensiveness, fear, and self-doubt. Work on understanding your situation until you think the time for confrontation is approaching. Don't depend on anyone else's time schedule; you are the primary expert in deciding what is right for you. Making these decisions for yourself will help you take charge of your life. The fact that it is your decision doesn't mean that you have to prepare for it in isolation. There is a good deal of information, support, and encouragement available to you, and it is always a good idea to remind yourself that you are not alone.

Many other survivors have confronted abusers—with a wide range of results. Although their situations aren't the same as yours, you can benefit from hearing about their experiences with confrontation. Other survivors have chosen not to confront. You may want to learn their reasons for that decision. It might be helpful to read the pamphlet called "How to Confront Your Perpetrator: Dead or Alive," by Lynne Lamb Bryant and Pat Dickman, available from VOICES in Action (see "Other Resources," p. 378).

In addition to learning about the confrontation experiences of other survivors, you can talk over your ideas and feelings with friends, sympathetic family members, and your therapist. These discussions don't have to be limited to realistic planning. (Remember, you haven't yet definitely decided whether or not to do it.) Allow yourself to express your wildest, most irrational fantasies of how it will be, both positive and negative. You aren't committing yourself to anything; indulging in fantasies can uncover your unconscious expectations. Whether or not you ultimately decide to go ahead with the actual confrontation, this preliminary process can be very enlightening. Sometimes it even proves to be enough.

Remember: Confrontation is not the goal of recovery. However, it can be a tool for recovery. Like any tool, its value is in how it is used. You deserve to take enough time to make the best decision for yourself. You can change your mind about confrontation at any time during this process. You can decide to put it off because you aren't ready, or do it sooner than you had planned. You can determine that it just isn't something that makes sense for you to do at all. You can change your mind from minute to minute. The choice is always yours. Don't worry about disappointing anyone else; you're doing this *for yourself.*

Practice

There are a number of ways to rehearse confrontation, just as there are many ways to confront the perpetrator.

1 / **Letter writing.** You may want to commit to paper your thoughts about the abuse and feelings toward the perpetrator. This can take the form of a letter to him/her, to a friend, a family member, the authorities, or even a newspaper. You can write several different letters, polishing them as you explore your feelings. You may or may not ever mail any of them. For now, the point of writing them is to learn more about yourself. You structure your thoughts and ideas and create a concrete document you can refer to. Letter writing provides a useful perspective. If you choose to proceed with face-to-face confrontation, your letter can help you stay on track. When you have written the letter, take the opportunity to read it to some friends. Ask for their reactions—how does it sound to them? The more feedback you get, the better. Accept what is useful to you and ignore the rest. Even if you never use the letters directly, you may want to keep them. It can be helpful to reread them from time to time to see how your ideas and feelings have developed.

2 / **Guided fantasy.** Your therapist may be able to assist you in creating a fantasy picture of the confrontation. Ideally, this will be a symbolic creation of a situation *where you are in complete control.* It doesn't have to mirror reality; it can be pure fantasy. You can imagine yourself twelve feet tall with the strength of Hercules. You can be bigger, older, smarter, and stronger than the perpetrator. You can bring reinforcements with you, real or fictitious. (Often children employ make-believe protectors like Mighty Mouse, Superman, Wonder Woman, or Big Bird. They might select a pet dog, a family member, sports figure, or movie star. You can

choose one or more of them, or select your own hero. This hero can even be *your adult self,* going back in time to befriend and protect yourself as a child.)

Whatever form your guided fantasy takes, it should not reenact the original victimization. If your fantasy includes the perpetrator trying to abuse you, envision yourself clearly and powerfully thwarting the attempt. The picture should be of moving away from the helplessness of the abused child into your full adult power. Take time afterward to discuss your feelings about the guided fantasy. What was helpful? What would you change? You can, if you wish, go back and do it again and again until it feels exactly right. You may be surprised by the changes this kind of exercise produces. For some, it is all the confrontation they need. Others use it as a confidence-building step leading toward direct confrontation.

3 / **Role-play.** You can rehearse any number of confrontation scenarios, using friends, other group members, even dolls or clay figures to represent the perpetrator(s) and other relevant people from your childhood. Through role-play (or "psychodrama") you can try out various means of confrontation, and experience your responses. You are able to look at "ideal" situations as well as confrontations that don't turn out as well as you'd like.

Getting Support

One of the most important aspects of preparation for actual confrontation is making certain that you provide for support at all stages of the process. You need to know that there are people you can call on for company, understanding, feedback, reality testing, and even physical protection before, during, and after the confrontation. You deserve support, encouragement, and protection *whether or not* you are in physical danger from the perpetrator. Anticipate the possibility that you will be feeling very small and vulnerable. Good allies reflect a more powerful reality to you, contradicting intimidating feelings.

Plan for logistical as well as emotional support. You might want someone to drive you to and from the confrontation. Even if you choose to confront the perpetrator alone, it may make sense to have someone within sight or earshot. This is essential if you might be at some physical risk from the perpetrator, and it may be desirable in any case. If the confrontation is to take place at some distance from your support network, you can arrange to have people waiting at telephones for your call, and meeting you upon your return. You can find out whether there are members of VOICES in Action or other support/advocacy organizations in the area where the confrontation will take place. You may also ask for help in arranging transportation, meals, and lodging.

Even though you are capable of doing this all yourself, consider letting other people help you. It will probably be a new and challenging experience for you. Just because you *can* do something doesn't mean that you *need* to—or even that you *should*. (Survivors carry around so many "shoulds." Accepting support and assistance helps you to remove some of them.) Power and strength are found in community. Set yourself the challenge of availing yourself of that support. Finally, make sure to set up a session with your therapist, counselor, or closest support person as soon as possible after the confrontation. You will probably want to schedule extra follow-up sessions to deal with the results of the confrontation.

IMPLEMENTING A FACE-TO-FACE CONFRONTATION

Once you have decided to go ahead with in-person confrontation of the perpetrator, set it up in the way that is most useful to you. (I have tried to avoid using the phrase *"your* perpetrator" in favor of *"the* perpetrator." Using the possessive pronoun creates a sense of alliance between abuser and victim. This can inhibit the work you are doing to break the connection to the abuse. Words are important; they can be binding or liberating. Try to practice using words that enhance your sense of yourself as a strong, smart, capable adult.) Although you cannot have complete control over the situation, there are things you can do to increase the likelihood of getting what you need out of it. Confrontation won't be easy for you, but don't make it any harder than necessary.

Arranging the Meeting

Think about the advantages and disadvantages of letting the perpetrator know that this meeting is about to take place. If you choose to provide advance notice, consider how much information to supply about the subject of the meeting. Remember, this confrontation is for your benefit alone. You don't have to protect the person who abused you; he/she didn't protect you. Giving some advance notice is, of course, necessary if you have no other way to ensure that the perpetrator will be there, or if you have to travel to the meeting. It can also increase the perpetrator's anxiety level, making him/her more vulnerable to confrontation. On the other hand, it can allow time to prepare cover-ups, denials, and even counterattacks. (These are likely to occur anyway; be prepared for them.) Think carefully about what you need in this situation before making your decision. If you choose to, you can make arrangements without going into detail about the content of the meeting. Arrangements can be made by letter, e-mail, or telephone; consider the advantages of each. Make setting up the meeting part of a process that increases your strength and self-confidence.

The Place

No setting for a confrontation is likely to feel comfortable, but it can (and must) be physically safe. Choose a meeting place that will provide you with a maximum degree of security. It is hard enough to think clearly when you are nervous without having to worry about protecting yourself from violence or further sexual assault. I strongly urge you to avoid setting up the confrontation at the location of the original abuse—or anywhere that reminds you of that place. Just being with the perpetrator will bring up old fears; being together in the place where he or she abused you is likely to be overwhelming. You will feel a greater pull to regress to a more juvenile, helpless condition, robbing you of the strength that you need to keep on course. Therefore, choose a place where you are relatively comfortable, and feel adult—whether it is your home, that of a trusted third party, or neutral territory. It is a good idea to select a place that is familiar to you. You can choose to meet in a public place, such as a park or restaurant, where you can be aware of other people. In such settings the intensity of your reactions to the confrontation will more likely be kept to a manageable level.

In a public setting you aren't forced to be alone with the perpetrator, and you can leave anytime you like. You can have trusted allies within sight but out of hearing range, ready to be summoned if needed. On the other hand, a public place may feel too exposed. If the meeting takes place in private, you may choose to have someone, a friend or family member, present as a witness to the confrontation. This person can also play an important part in processing the experience afterward, validating your perceptions and providing another perspective on what occurred. If you prefer to meet the perpetrator alone, try to have supportive people waiting nearby, where you can summon them easily. It is essential to be realistic when you assess the potential of physical danger presented by the abuser when confronted. Take precautions to insure your safety and provide an extra degree of comfort. There's no such thing as being too safe.

Your Presentation

Remind yourself that you are doing this for yourself. How do you want it to be? This isn't a debate or a jury trial. There is no need to argue. You don't have to present "both sides" or protect the perpetrator from painful feelings. You have prepared for this moment carefully, thinking about what you want to say and what you hope to achieve. You decided whether you are seeking to express your anger, make accusations, or set the groundwork for reconciliation. You played out "ideal" as well as "worst case" scenarios. You considered possible reactions, and the possibility of responses that will surprise you. Now is the time to present what you have to say.

State what you *know* to be true (and, perhaps, what you think happened and which parts are unclear). You can tell the perpetrator how the abuse affected you. You don't have to go through this experience calmly or numbly. If feelings arise, give yourself permission to feel them. You have a right to feel sad, afraid, or angry. Crying will not weaken or invalidate what you are saying. On the contrary, it may help clear your mind so that you can present your thoughts more coherently. If you want or need to hear from the perpetrator, you can ask for it at this point.

If you find yourself becoming increasingly anxious or panicky, slow down the pace—take some slow, deep breaths; take a few minutes to cry, shake, or giggle; picture something calm and beautiful; think about someone who cares about you; imagine a friend, hero, or the members of your survivors' group standing by your side. Take all the time you need; you've been waiting a long time for this moment. Don't proceed until you're ready—then continue until you are finished. Don't allow yourself to be interrupted or distracted. There is time for response, afterward. When you have finished, take the time you need to pull yourself together. Don't rush to soften what you said; resist the temptation to protect the perpetrator from the impact of your words. Be clear about when (and if) you are willing to listen to a response. You are in charge of what you do in this situation. Take good care of yourself—you deserve it.

Possible Reactions

There are a number of ways perpetrators respond to confrontation. As much as you think you know a person, you cannot be one hundred percent certain that he or she will react in predictable ways. For this reason, prepare for the possibility that the confrontation will not proceed precisely according to plan. As much as you thought about what will happen—and did a lot of planning, fantasizing, and role-playing—be ready for some surprises. If proceedings don't follow your script to the letter, it doesn't mean that everything has fallen apart. When you have made all the reasonable preparations, try to relax and remain open to what happens. This will feel like loss of control and may be frightening, but you will learn far more by doing it this way. You discover that flexibility—the ability to adjust to the requirements of a situation—makes you feel more powerful than rigid attempts to maintain control. Try to remember that the perpetrator will be at a psychological disadvantage, and you are proceeding from a position of strength. In most cases, when you are adequately prepared for confrontation, you really need not be afraid. Here are some responses by perpetrators when they are confronted:

1 / **Denial.** The most commonly reported response to confrontation is that the perpetrator denies the abuse took place. Denial can be total ("That never happened"), or coupled with an attempt to explain away the memory ("You are probably remembering a bad dream"; "You always had a vivid imagination"), disprove it ("We didn't live in that house when you were five"; "There was no sofa in the attic"), or deflect it ("There was a neighbor who used to hang around the park. I always thought there was something

funny about him"). Other forms of denial include outrage, bluster, and "guilt-tripping" ("How dare you accuse me of such a monstrous thing?" "How could you even think that I would do something like that?" "You are sick! You've always had it in for me!" "After all I've done for you!"). Denial may be accompanied by an offer to assist the survivor to "get help" in dealing with his delusions. One male survivor reported that, when confronted, his uncle responded, "That never happened . . . and, besides, you can't prove it." Be prepared to encounter denial. Don't let the situation turn into an argument or debate. Don't allow a perpetrator to talk you out of your memories. She has lied to you before. Stick to your guns and don't get trapped in an exercise in frustration. You don't have to convince the perpetrator that something happened. He knows it did. Saying that something didn't happen doesn't erase the truth. For many survivors, the purpose of confrontation is to tell the perpetrator clearly, "I know what happened, and I'm telling you that I know it." This can be particularly important if you think the perpetrator is (or will be) harming someone else. You don't need acknowledgment of the abuse or permission from the perpetrator to proceed with your recovery. Your memories aren't invalidated by denial; you confronted the perpetrator. You stood up to the abuse.

2 / **Ambiguous responses.** These can be the most difficult to deal with, leaving you feeling as though nothing happened. After putting all this time, energy, planning, and emotion into the confrontation, it appears that you are left no better off than you started. Ambiguous responses are a form of denial, without actually stating that nothing happened. They include variations of "I don't remember." One man reported this response by the perpetrator: "I don't remember, but I can't imagine that I would do something like that." Also in this category are attempts to evade the question, change the subject, or distract you from the confrontation. Perpetrators are very adept at these techniques. Don't be fooled by them. When you replay the situation afterward, removed from the immediacy of the feelings, you will see that evasion, confusion, distraction, and claims of lack of memory are

simply more subtle forms of acknowledgment. If they truly believed that nothing happened, they would say so, simply and unequivocally. Looking beneath the surface, you see that what had seemed ambiguous gives you a clear message.

3 / **Acknowledgment.** Abuse can be acknowledged in many ways, ranging from reassuring to terrifying, supportive to abusive. I'll mention some of the more common responses, so you can think about ways to deal with them.

One of the more difficult situations arises when the abuse is acknowledged without acceptance of responsibility or expression of remorse. This situation occurs all too frequently; perpetrators are masterful at avoiding responsibility for their actions. Rarely do they seek help unless they are forced to. The most blatant and vicious forms of assault leave some perpetrators unmoved. This form of response is some variation of "Yeah, it happened, so what?" It may even carry with it a challenge (or thinly veiled threat), as in ". . . and what are you going to do about it?" Your decision about what to do next should include understanding that a sociopathic personality does not feel remorse. Although you might obtain legal redress of damages, you will probably never receive a heartfelt apology from such an individual. If you wait for that to happen, you will be disappointed. Consider the source of the response and move ahead with your recovery.

A perpetrator may acknowledge that the abuse took place, but try to minimize it:

- "It happened so long ago."

- "It only happened once/a few times."

- "Nobody was really hurt by it."

- "It wasn't *that* bad, was it?"

- "All right, it happened, now can't we just forget about it?"

- "Let's just put it behind us."

- "I didn't mean any harm, I thought you liked it."

These minimizing responses are attempts to evade responsibility for abusive behavior. You know what the effects have been. Don't allow your memories and feelings to be so easily dismissed. You deserved better treatment then; you deserve better treatment now. The question of forgiveness may not be one that you are prepared to deal with at this time. Don't let yourself be pushed into anything before you're ready.

Focus

Am I Making the Family Crazy?

I know that some part of telling is wanting to heal the family.
—a male incest survivor

If there's a fire and I call the engines—so who am I double-crossing? The fire?
—Judy Holliday in the film BORN YESTERDAY

Some time ago, during an appearance on a television show, I received a phone call from a young survivor. She said she was afraid to talk about the abuse because it would "make everybody in the family crazy." She was probably correct in thinking that dealing openly with the abuse would send her family into an uproar. But it is a mistake to believe that she would be responsible for anything other than focusing attention on a serious problem. The family is already "crazy."

It is crazy to sexually abuse children. Calling attention to abuse is an act of sanity. Members of a dysfunctional family cooperate in maintaining the dysfunction. It is necessary to destroy a system of denial so ingrained that it will sacrifice a child to keep things running smoothly.

Putting things right is more important than looking good to the outside world. The person who blows the whistle on abuse is rarely appreciated for it. Nevertheless he is performing a valuable and courageous act by initiating healing the entire family. The abusive situation, not the healing process, is "crazy."

Don't let concerns about upsetting family stability stand in your way; stability is no substitute for health. Neither is a false image of respectability. Don't allow other people's fear or pathology to interfere with your recovery. Don't be "guilt-tripped" or intimidated into silence; you know their ploys by now. Keep talking; you have a right to be heard. Continue to insist that what is right takes precedence over what is comfortable. It is the only way to free you from abusive family patterns. If you can't get the support you need within your family, find it elsewhere. But keep insisting on your right to be heard—your right to recover.

Acknowledgment can also be turned around into an accusation, the perpetrator attempting to blame you for the abuse. Here, the perpetrator acknowledges his or her actions, but tries to shift the responsibility because "You liked it," "You wanted it," "You looked for it." It is hard to avoid being trapped by this perversion of the facts, particularly if you found any part of the abuse pleasurable. But this response is simply another form of denial—blaming the victim. No matter how "attractive," "seductive," or "sexy" you were, this adult had a responsibility to protect and nurture you. Any other interpretation is a self-serving distortion of the facts. You never deserved to be abused—no matter what.

Another category of response involves acknowledging the abuse and then, in one way or another, attempting to repeat it. The most overt forms include seduction, fondling, and even rape. (One survivor—see Philip's Statement, p. 83—decided to meet with his father many years after the original prolonged, violent, and vicious abuse. He agreed to a restaurant in broad daylight as the location of their meeting. Later, as the survivor sat in a car with his father, the perpetrator once again violently abused his son. The public nature of the setting did not lessen the traumatic effect of this encounter.) If there is a possibility of further victimization, it is essential to protect yourself. There is nothing rational about child abuse; rationalizations don't make it permissible. Abusers do not protect their victims; it is up to you to make sure that you are in no danger of assault.

There may be dangers of nonsexual assault. Know whether the perpetrator has a history of (or potential for) violence. If confrontation carries the risk of physical attack, consider abandoning your decision to confront in person. If you decide to go ahead with it, make certain that you are adequately protected. At the very least, tell someone about the confrontation and *let the perpetrator know* that you have done so. Sometimes the presence of witnesses is enough to prevent violent behavior; in other situations, further precautions are necessary. The perpetrator may also resort to *threats* of violence, particularly when fearing disclosure. Threats may be empty attempts to keep you silent, or can represent genuine danger. To avoid intimidation, take time beforehand to think about whether the danger is real and how you could respond to threats to yourself or others.

Violence operates both ways. If you think you might be in danger of losing control and physically attacking the perpetrator during confrontation, stop and think. Will the satisfaction of hitting, injuring, or killing the abuser undo the pain and suffering he or she caused you? Do you want to risk losing all you have accomplished so far? Isn't prison too high a price to pay for momentary satisfaction? Will you feel guilty afterward? Do you really want to perpetuate a pattern of responding to other human beings in an assaultive manner? You know what maltreatment did to you; do you want to be the kind of person who inflicts pain? I urge you to consider these questions very carefully, and focus your energy on your own recovery instead of the fleeting satisfaction of revenge.

Other, subtler ways to perpetuate abuse include attempts by the perpetrator to engage you in an alliance. The rationale might be keeping silent to protect others:

- "If this came out it would really hurt your mother."

- "Your father has a heart condition; finding out about this would kill him."

It could be an appeal to loyalty or sentiment:

- "Can't we keep this our secret?"

- "You know that there's always been a special bond between us."

- "Even though I've made mistakes, I'm still your uncle."

- "I love you and I know you love me."

Or it might be a plea for "understanding" or protection. Recognize these ploys for what they are—desperate attempts by perpetrators to protect themselves from the consequences of their abusive behavior. By allying yourself with the perpetrator, you run the risk of accepting some of the responsibility for the abuse. Doing that is a mistake that will interfere with your recovery. You did nothing to deserve what was done to you. Don't confuse acceptance of abuse with forgiveness. True forgiveness does not arise from denial. It can only occur when there has been complete acknowledgment, including the nature of the wrongs and where the responsibility lies. For the perpetrator there can be no rehabilitation without admission of responsibility and feelings of remorse. Your recovery isn't complete until you fully accept your responsibility to yourself. What is in your best interest is also best for those who truly care about you.

Finally, when confronted, the perpetrator may acknowledge and *apologize* for the abuse. This may, on the surface, seem to be the ideal response. But, although you have longed for this moment, it raises its own questions. What does the apology mean? Can it be trusted? You have been lied to before. Are you able to believe it this time, no matter how much you want to? Unfortunately, there are no easy answers. Consider the response in the context of everything you know about this person—and everything you know about yourself. What does an apology mean to you if it is real? What if it is false? Take all the time you need to consider your feelings.

Genuine or not, you are under no obligation to respond to an apology. No apology requires you to forget the abuse. It is only a step toward forgiveness if you choose to make it so. Don't do it a minute before you are ready. Pretense is never a useful tool in recovery. If, after careful thought and exploration of your feelings, you decide to accept the apology, you retain the right to determine the nature of any future interaction with the perpetrator. You may decide never to see the person again. That is your right. What do you want? What are realistic expectations? The decision is yours. If you choose to have a relationship, it will have to be a brand-new one, built slowly and with awareness. Apologies don't create instant trust. Think carefully about what you need to establish a relationship that will be healthy for you.

Even an unsatisfactory response can provide useful validation of your thinking about the situation. Sexual child abuse is the act of a disturbed person. Don't expect that confrontation will produce a sane, predictable reaction. A crazy response can confirm that what was done to you was in fact abusive. This affirmation can help you move on with your recovery.

Follow-Up

Don't try to return to life as usual directly after the confrontation. You need time to react, relax, and process what happened. If you can, take some time off from work. Spend the time in ways you find pleasant and life-affirming. Visit with friends, whether or not you talk about what happened. Schedule extra sessions with your therapist and/or arrange to meet with other survivors. But also take time to play. Take a walk in the country; go for a bike ride; see a film—treat yourself well. Put yourself into situations that remind you that there is a world outside the abuse, and you have a place in that world. It will be some time before you understand the full import of the confrontation; being kind to yourself reminds you of why you are going through all this.

IMPLEMENTING OTHER TYPES OF CONFRONTATION

Not all confrontations can or should involve face-to-face interaction. The perpetrator may have died or otherwise be unavailable for direct confrontation. Even if she is physically accessible, there are reasons why it might not make sense—now or ever—to face the person who abused you. Consider all the options, and remember that the choice is always yours. What follows is a brief discussion of some alternative means of confrontation.

1 / **Symbolic confrontation.** Earlier in this chapter, I wrote of symbolic ways to confront the perpetrator, including letter writing, guided fantasy, and role-playing. For some survivors it is sufficient to stand up to the abuse in symbolic form. Doing so provides

enough release and perspective that they no longer feel it is necessary to confront the perpetrator directly. They are able to move on with their lives. Examine your thoughts and feelings after you have confronted the abuse symbolically. Decide whether your need to confront has been satisfied or further action is required.

2 / **Mailing a letter.** If you want to confront the abuse without facing the perpetrator directly, you can send a letter. Letter writing has many advantages. You can take your time, preparing as many drafts as you wish, polishing and editing your message, pausing to feel, rest, and consult with allies before deciding on a final version. Take as long as you like, and change your mind whenever you want. In addition, you don't have to worry that interruption or intimidation might keep you from completing your statement. Since this form of confrontation takes place at a distance from the abuser, you don't need to deal with his immediate reaction; you can resist any pulls to protect her feelings. Keep copies of your letter, so you can refer to it if there is an attempt to distort your words. And, regardless of the response, you control whether to follow up the letter in any way. Confrontation by mail can be a good way to "just get things off your chest," or put the perpetrator on notice that you will no longer stand for his abusing you or anyone else. (See Ivan's Statement, p. 276.)

3 / **Legal action.** Some survivors have confronted perpetrators by pressing criminal charges or pursuing civil suits for redress of damages. Recent examples include many lawsuits by survivors of sexual victimization by priests (see chapter 19). Litigation is tricky, not to be undertaken lightly. For some survivors, a lawsuit is a public statement of their intention to force abusers to make amends for their actions; for others, it becomes another form of abuse. Think about it carefully; get all the information you need. Recognize that legal proceedings can be costly, protracted *public* proceedings. There is no guarantee of success. Cases are tried on the basis of what is "legal," not what is "fair." Opposing lawyers will attempt to break down your story, sometimes by attempting to portray you as a liar, promiscuous, or crazy. Judges and juries may not be sympathetic. Should it come to trial, you will have to face

the person who abused you, in public, under stressful conditions. Despite these limitations, some survivors have proceeded with legal action. Before you decide to do so, consult with your therapist about how the experience may affect you. You will need more than therapeutic advice. Meet with one or more attorneys who have experience with sexual abuse cases. Learn what the laws are. (They vary widely.) Know the statute of limitations for sexual abuse cases. Ask whether there are legal precedents, and what their outcomes were. Ask your attorney to give you a realistic idea of what you will be going through and to estimate your chance of success. Weigh the possible gains against the stresses and sacrifices. Think of who else will be affected by this course of action. Think about what you stand to gain and what you might lose. Then make the decision that is right for you.

4 / **If the perpetrator is dead.** If the abuser is no longer alive you may still have a need for confrontation, and it is still possible in some form. Although you cannot effect a direct, face-to-face interaction, there are other ways to accomplish it. Many survivors have visited the cemetery where a perpetrator is buried and talked to him at the grave. This can be as powerful and emotional an event as confronting a living person, so be prepared for an outpouring of emotions. You can prepare what you are going to say, or trust that the right words and feelings will present themselves. You can speak directly to the perpetrator, to God, or just speak for yourself. If you feel that talking to a dead person would be too embarrassing to do in front of someone, do it alone. Otherwise, you may choose to have someone accompany you to the cemetery. You might want a hug, shoulder, or sympathetic listener afterward. Or you may need to be alone for a while. Set up the situation to get what you need.

There is much to be gained by this type of confrontation. If (and when) it is right for you, go ahead and do it. One of my clients said that, after visiting his uncle's grave in the Midwest, everything in his hometown took on a new perspective. He was apprehensive because he had to visit his parents' home immediately afterward for a family gathering. These events had, in the past, been scenes of great discomfort for him. He was concerned that he would be too upset or emotionally drained to participate in family interaction. But there seemed to be no way around it—he went. To his surprise he discovered that, by having gone to his uncle's grave, crying and telling him how it had hurt, expressing his grief, fear, anger—and love—he was able to let go of what had kept him from being a part of his family. He understood that he had been resenting his parents for not protecting him from the abuse. He felt freed of the need to live with the abuse. He had returned the responsibility for the abuse to his uncle. A weight had been lifted from his shoulders, and he moved ahead with his life. Upon his return to Boston, he immediately effected major changes in his life.

If you don't know where the grave is, or don't wish to do a graveside confrontation, you can employ other representations of the perpetrator. Possibilities include speaking to an old photograph. Looking at her image can stir up emotions that carry you through this procedure. You can also imagine talking to a deceased perpetrator by using some of the role-playing techniques mentioned earlier. Or write an obituary or eulogy of your own for the perpetrator, incorporating whatever needs to be said. There are many ways to evoke the image of an abuser. Ask your therapist, other survivors, or friends to support you in discovering what works best for you. As with any other confrontation, take sufficient time afterward to process the experience and appreciate yourself for having done it.

5 / **Confronting "nonperpetrators."** Confrontation does not have to be limited to the individual(s) who directly abused you. Confrontation is a way of standing up to the abuse, not just to the abuser. In doing so you are standing up for yourself. You may need to confront other family members who failed to protect you. Did they know what was going on? If they knew, why didn't they put an end to the abuse? If they didn't know, why didn't they? The person or persons who acquiesced in (or encouraged) the abuse also reinforced your isolation. You have a right to feel betrayed; you don't have to protect anyone from your feelings—or theirs. Say what you need to say. Don't continue to sacrifice yourself to

the pain of silence and pretense. When you stand up to abuse, everyone benefits. People who care about you want to help you heal the wounds.

As you can see, the question of confrontation is not easy. Whatever you choose to do about it, know that you have a right to be respected for your decision. Take the time you require, get the information and support you need, and proceed in the way that makes the most sense for you.

Focus
Why Didn't They Do Something?

A question that plagues survivors is, "Why didn't somebody do something to stop the abuse?" When the adult survivor examines his childhood, he questions the role of the nonabusive parent and/or other adults in his life. Did they know what was going on? If they knew, why didn't they do something about it? If they didn't know, why didn't they?

These questions speak to the power of denial. People frequently ignore what they don't want to deal with. Nonprotective parents often know that something is wrong, whether or not they recognize the true nature of the situation.

There are many reasons why people fail to take action against child abuse. A dysfunctional family can create an "everyone for himself" atmosphere. Family members are too concerned with their own survival to pay attention to anyone else's. They feel they have to escape alone, without encumbrances. They compete for scarce emotional resources and don't want to tip the balance against themselves. Other family members may even feel jealous of the abused child for receiving special attention. They may fear for their own safety, be confused about what to do, or simply not care.

While ignorance, fear, confusion, and apathy are explanations for inaction, they are not excuses. Adults have a responsibility to protect children from harm.

An adult survivor may feel a greater sense of betrayal by nonprotective parent figures than by the actual perpetrator. His feelings of anger at this form of abandonment are appropriate. To allow abusive behavior through inaction is to condone it. It constitutes neglect, another form of child abuse.

Nonprotective parents can best help a survivor's recovery by accepting their role in the abuse. Attempting to make excuses, deflect the anger, or minimize the problem only serves to inflict more guilt and shame. It is a continuation of the abuse. Accepting the anger as justified may be more painful—and may deepen the rift between the survivor and the nonprotective adult—but it is better than a false closeness based on denial and pretense. Ultimately, it contributes to healing. There is no way to undo the past, but genuine help can be offered in the present. For an example of a survivor and his father achieving successful understanding and reconciliation, read *Half the House* (see Books, Articles, and Pamphlets, p. 398).

Ivan's Statement

There are many ways to confront abusers without face-to-face interaction. In this letter to his mother (which he edited for confidentiality), "Ivan" confronts the abuse clearly and powerfully. He invites her to participate in the healing process, but will move on with his recovery whether or not she is willing or able to do so. Notice the confusion created by being abused by someone he loves, and how this boy dealt with it by thinking of his mother as two different people.

June 30, 198———
Dear Mom,

I'm sure you've noticed that I haven't been in touch with you lately. To be honest, the reason is that I've been avoiding you. I've just needed that space, and have enjoyed it. I want to keep not having contact with you for a while, maybe a long while, but I don't want to feel like I'm avoiding you. So I want to tell you why.

At last, I have the strength and safety in my life to begin to face the facts about what it was like to grow up with you. Some of the facts are good. Yes, we did go on vacation a lot, and Jim and I did get a lot of encouragement from you, and I *know* it wasn't all bad. But dammit, that wasn't all. It is very hard to face the fact that it wasn't *all* good, that some of our past is downright ugly and terrifying to go back to. But I have to go back, because these ugly things have long-reaching, powerful effects on my feelings and behavior and ability to trust today. I am in the business of making myself grow, of developing an ability to trust, to crawl out of the mindless terror of my life, that all began with you. So here I am, writing to you.

What is he talking about? I hear you ask. I am talking about child abuse, and nothing minor at that. I realize that you may find some of this hard to remember. Often you were drunk when this kind of thing happened. Usually you were in a state of intense rage at my father, or me, or somebody else. And all of it is so very scary that I found it easier to "forget" about it for decades. So you may have done the same. Whatever you've chosen to do with your memories, I can't stand mine anymore. This really happened. To me. So, if you draw a blank, reach back and try to see it.

Let's get down to specifics. Most of this, the worst, happened before we moved south, from my birth to age four and a half. From there it continued, but in less intensity. By then I had developed some survival mechanisms, and Jim's birth meant that you and I weren't alone as much.

In these early years I thought you were two people: "Mommy," and "Scary Lady." "Mommy" was nice and fed me and hugged me and put me to bed, and loved me. "Scary Lady" was violent and erratic. She would attack me sexually and physically, and I was so scared of her that I would literally freeze in terror.

I will give you a description of one specific incident, one that is particularly clear to me. It is also the one that has been the very hardest for me to accept, that someone who was supposed to love me, my mother, could ever do such an ugly thing to me. This is what happened:

1966, Anytown, USA. I saw you yelling at Daddy, really mad
at him for something. You pushed him out the door, hitting him.
He tried briefly to stay, but left. Still confused and angry, you came
to me, and picked me up. I believe this was in one of the upstairs
rooms, one that faced toward the lake. I remember the morning
sun coming in the window, warm. You had a knife or razor blade
in your right hand. You were mad, yelling and moving your head
around a lot. Your hair was all tousled, and your eyes were wide
open but jerking around in a funny way. This was "Scary Lady."
With a quick jerky movement, you cut my left hand between my
first finger and my thumb with the knife. It was a good-sized cut,
nothing minor, and it bled a lot. It hurt. You were surprised, and
scared, and you dropped or put me down on the hardwood floor.
You had blood all over your white or rose-colored blouse, and
blood on your hands. You reached back down to me, I don't know
why, but all I saw was your bloodstained hands coming at me
again. I screamed and curled up. You ran out of the room, closing
the door behind you.

I was very, very alone. I saw a small puddle of my blood on
the wooden floor, next to where I lay. I saw blood coming out of
my hand, warm and horrifying, like it would never stop. I didn't
know how to apply pressure, I was only four; on the contrary, it
hurt and I didn't want to touch it. I flailed around yelling and
crazily moving my arms around. This lasted forever. Slowly, I felt
my strength ebb, and my shock gave way to faintness. I passed
out, still bleeding, lying in my own blood. You were long gone.

So I don't know how long I was passed out before you came
back to clean up your mess. What strikes me all the more is my
luck. As incoherent and angry as you were, you cut me wherever
you could. If you had cut me an inch lower, on one of the veins on
my wrist, you would have come back to find me DEAD. I'm sure
that's what your first thought was when you came back into that
hellish room. You really nearly killed me.

Do you remember this? I used to think that it was just a
coincidence that I fainted often, especially at the sight of blood,
and that I was afraid of knives. But, no. This is why. And the

crappy thing is that this isn't all I remember about what you did to me. I remember much more, and there are half-uncovered memories that I'm still too afraid to face.

Furthermore, this early stripping of my self-esteem and power led to a childhood in which four other people sexually abused me, including a very violent episode which resulted in my hospitalization for a urethra/bladder infection, my head-banging frustration in school, and my years of therapy with Dr. C——. These four are responsible for what they've done, but I never would have been as vulnerable to them had you not attacked me before they did. You really set me up for them, and I hate you for it. And I hate you for what you did yourself.

I wonder how you're feeling as you read this, but I really don't care now. I keep not wanting to tell, to force a weak "I love you," to do anything to protect you from your responsibility. I do hope you have the sense to seek help, to talk to a friend about this. But help or no help, sooner or later, you must face up to the reality of your violence against me.

What do I want from you? I mainly want you to know that I know, and that I am not remaining silent about this anymore. I want you to understand that I don't want to see you because I am angry at you. I want you to know that this was not just "in the past." There are long-term struggles that I face every day which make my life far more painful, difficult, lonely, and impoverished than it would have been without your abuse. I want you to know that therapy, which has saved my life, is expensive. It is my single largest expense next to rent. But I'm worth it, even if I'm the one who has to pay.

I would like some acknowledgment from you, even an apology. Ideally, I would like you to pay for my recovery expenses. Unfortunately, I don't expect any of this, I don't expect anything more from you than minimization and denial. Keep these to yourself, if you can stand them. I challenge you to exceed my expectations, to take some responsibility for your past actions. If you can do this, write me. Otherwise, I don't want to hear from you. And don't expect me to reach out to you anymore, not now. I like this space, and intend to keep it.

So, this is why I'm not in touch with you. I know that deep down inside, you know what I'm talking about.

                                            Very much alive,
                                            Ivan

                        Copies sent to
Minister   Brother   Father
Uncle   My therapist   Selected friends

19

CLERGY ABUSE

This new chapter on sexual abuse by clergy was the hardest one to write. Some of the difficulty arose from the especially sensitive nature of the material. An individual's spiritual beliefs and practices are personal, emotional, and sensitive. They are less likely to be questioned than other areas of one's life. Any questioning of them by another—particularly someone who does not share one's particular faith—may be interpreted as an attack, and resisted defensively.

It is not the role of a counselor or therapist to argue the merits or validity of a client's religious beliefs and practices. It is important, however, to understand that any aspect of one's life can support or interfere with healing. When a survivor's beliefs or the requirements of his religion impede his recovery, he must identify the conflict and explore ways to resolve it. At the very least, the survivor has to understand that the conflict exists; the therapist must respect his client's belief system as well as any conflict it engenders. The choice of what to do about it is the survivor's to make; his therapist can support him through this difficult process. This chapter offers some suggestions about potential areas of conflict and their resolution.

Adding to the difficulty of writing this chapter is its timing. We are in the midst of a spate of revelations of massive sexual abuse of children and teenagers by Roman Catholic clergy throughout the United States. To varying degrees, other countries and religions are addressing clergy sexual abuse within their own communities. The past year brought news of clergy sexual abuse in Canada, Australia, New Zealand, Great Britain, Ireland, and Europe. Sadly, there is no doubt that sexual child abuse by clergy is a huge problem worldwide, and is limited neither to English-speaking nations nor to the Catholic Church.

In the United States, recognition of the prevalence of clergy sexual abuse is dawning. A *Washington Post* article (February 1, 2003) about a rabbi convicted of sexual child abuse contains the following:

> While Catholicism has been hardest hit, almost every major religion in the United States has grappled with cases of child sexual abuse by clergy.... In recent years, for example, the Episcopal Church has revised its disciplinary code and extended its internal statute of limitations to encourage victims of abuse to come forward, while the Presbyterian Church (USA) has eliminated its time limit on such complaints. The United Methodist Church recommends that two unrelated adults be present with any child or group of children.... Lawyers who have specialized in suing Catholic dioceses are turning their sights on other religious groups, including Mormons and Jehovah's Witnesses.... State legislatures are requiring clergy of all faiths to report allegations of child sexual abuse.

Increased public awareness of the scope and severity of clergy sexual abuse offers hope to survivors and all who care about protecting children. This chapter contains many examples of positive change; it also demonstrates that, as a society, we have far to go to solve the problem.

It is impossible to address the needs of survivors recovering from the effects of clergy sexual abuse without attempting to understand the social/political/economic context that gives rise to the situation. I claim no expertise in sociopolitical analysis. My intention is to offer neither a definitive analysis nor an attack on religious institutions. As in the rest of this book, my primary focus is on the recovery needs of male survivors. Any discussion of religion and church hierarchies is presented in the context of exploring the very particular ways that clergy sexual abuse affects victims and survivors. The material is offered in an attempt to help create an atmosphere of healing.

I live and work in Boston, Massachusetts, the city and Archdiocese where an enormous clergy abuse scandal was uncovered, largely due to the persistent efforts of the investigative staff of *The Boston Globe* newspaper. Few days pass without new disclosures of abuse by sexually predatory priests and other Church workers, and the systematic covering up of their predations at all levels of the Church hierarchy. Widespread shock and dismay greet reports of the extent to which Church officials knew of this behavior. Not only was the Church aware of the abuse, but there is ample evidence that these crimes were actively hidden for many years. Some victims were even paid for their silence while offending priests were being transferred to parish after parish, each time finding a fresh crop of victims.

Fr. Andrew M. Greeley is a sociologist and Roman Catholic priest in the Chicago Archdiocese. In his review of the book *Betrayal: The Crisis in the Catholic Church* by the Investigative Staff of *The Boston Globe* (*The Boston Globe,* July 7, 2002), Fr. Greeley wrote, ". . . the investigative staff of *The Boston Globe* has done the Catholic Church an enormous favor. It has forced reform on a reluctant Catholic hierarchy. It has revealed to the Catholic laity the ignorance, arrogance, stupidity, and insensitivity of the hierarchy. It has bared a pattern of sinfulness that has been a cancer eating at the church and has forced the bishops to excise it. If it had not been for the *Globe*'s investigation, the bishops would never have enacted the 'Charter for the Protection of Children and Young People' at their Dallas conference in June. Much less would they have appointed a lay supervisory board to assure compliance in the respective dioceses."

Greeley continues, "[Considering] celibacy and homosexuality to be the sources of the problem [plays] the game of Catholic ideologues on the left and right. In fact, the problem is caused by bishops sending back to parishes known abusers."

This is no small or simple problem. It seems to grow more convoluted with each fresh disclosure of abuses and coverups. Understandably, the extent of the revelations can generate a sense of hopelessness. However, the situation is far from hopeless. Thousands of people of good faith—from all walks of life and systems of belief—are advocating for accountability and healing. Tremendous power and significant change result when "ordinary" people join to fight abuses of power. Concerned individuals, survivors and their allies, continue to come together to condemn clergy abuse, support victims and survivors, and help to heal their wounds. Some work within the structure of a resistant Church, others from outside the system. Several organizations of and for survivors of clergy abuse existed long before the current scandals broke into public awareness. In the United States, these groups include The

Linkup, Survivors Network of those Abused by Priests (SNAP), Inter-faith Sexual Trauma Institute (ISTI), and Survivor Connections. (For more information, see "Other Resources," p. 380, and my Web site: www.victimsnolonger.org.) Others, such as Voice of the Faithful, arose in direct response to the current crisis.

Members of other religions are organizing as well, such as The Awareness Center, which focuses attention on issues of abuse and recovery within Jewish communities (Web site: www.theawarenesscenter.org). Survivors of Spiritual Abuse (SOSA) is "dedicated to all those that have been abused by anyone in the name of a religion or spiritual belief." (Their Web site is www.sosa.org.)

Some advocates for victims and survivors of clergy abuse see signs of hope in recently stated changes of Church policy regarding removal of priests who abuse children, response to child victims and adult survivors, preventive measures, and boards of inquiry. Others are more skeptical that adequate changes will be implemented, withholding judgment until they see actual improvement. Regardless of your perspective on these issues, the atmosphere surrounding clergy abuse is difficult and often painful for survivors and their allies.

Fr. Gary Hayes, a Catholic priest, is past president of The Linkup, an organization for survivors of clergy abuse. He assumed the interim presidency following the death of the organization's founder, Fr. Tom Economus. Fr. Hayes generously permitted me to quote from his tribute to Tom Economus that appeared in the Spring–Summer 2002 issue of *Missing Link,* The Linkup's newsletter:

> Tom spoke the truth to a "Church" immersed in secrecy, lies, cover-ups, distortions, and half-truths. A "Church" more concerned about preserving its image than protecting its children. A "Church" that paid hush money to keep victims quiet, intimidated and bullied victims, and vilified victims in the press as money hungry lunatics looking for a fast buck because the "Church" has deep pockets.
>
> The late Bishop James McHugh of the Diocese of Camden, NJ, called victims "Terrorists" and their desire to confront their abuse with the truth a "new kind of terrorism" in the Church. A "Church" that ignored warning after warning for over 17 years about priests who abused children and the ramifications for the "Church." A

"Church" that transferred offending priests from parish-to-parish and diocese-to-diocese and sometimes country-to-country giving those priests glowing recommendations that hid their perpetrations. A "Church" that paid millions of dollars for treatment centers and treatment for abusing priests and often times grudgingly paid for limited counseling for victims.

One has to wonder why there are no treatment centers established by the "Church" for the victims. There are fourteen treatment centers for priests who abuse, zero treatment centers for victims of the priests who have abused them. One can easily see where the priorities of the "Church" lie.

Andrew Greeley, Tom Economus, and Gary Hayes are three among a great many people of faith—clergy and laity—who commit their energy and dedicate their lives to goodness, morality, and righting wrongs perpetrated against the innocent. It is a tragedy that the hierarchy's focus on protecting the Church's image (and thus the predators) has resulted in distrust of the credibility and good work of dedicated people of faith.

I have found that the clearest perspectives are often provided by survivors themselves. In the statement he sent me, Rick, a survivor from the Midwest, wrote:

These are some of the things being sexually abused by a member of the clergy has done to me: fear of my own memory, fear of friendships, fear of sexuality, fear of love, fear of touching, fear of being touched, fear of being alone, fear of being with others, hatred of religion, hatred of religious people, and hatred of myself. I'm not sure which of these is worst or even if one can be worse than another. They all cut me off from society and normal growth. I stopped growing and simply became defensive and insular.

Beyond these consequences, though, there is one which I can identify as the worst: the destruction of my faith in God.

Rick identifies powerful fears generated by powerful losses. Sadly, his experience is far from unique, and certainly is not limited to abuse by Catholic clergy. As with any profession, all sorts of individuals enter the priesthood, ministry, rabbinate, and other religious pursuits. They do so for a wide range of reasons—not all of them good or healthy. Again, as in any profession, some clergy are good, kind, moral, even "saintly" and "holy." A few are monsters, committing acts of evil while cloaked in a disguise of sanctity.

The vast majority of clergy fall between these extremes. Like the rest of us, they are human, possessing the range of strengths and failings that humanity encompasses. They try to do as much good as they can, sometimes succeeding and sometimes failing. All of this is logical; only gods can be expected to be godlike. The best we humans can do is our *human* best. That's often pretty good. (See chapter 10 for a discussion of the difficulties of perfectionism.)

When we have reasonable expectations of our institutions, religious as well as secular, and of our religious practitioners, it is possible to treat them as we would anyone in a position of trust and responsibility. We can set and enforce standards of conduct, institute procedures for monitoring behavior, and prevent (or punish) misconduct. We can require that no individual is above the law, and every institution bears the consequences of wrongs committed in its name or under its auspices.

We create serious problems, however, when we set any individual or institution above these considerations, conferring upon them unreasonable power, unrealistic trust, or the expectation of unattainable levels of sanctity. We are aware of the saying "Power corrupts, absolute power corrupts absolutely." Yet we can all cite examples of blind trust of untrustworthy people and institutions—of wholesale abdication of critical judgment leading to collusion (conscious or unconscious) with unspeakable evil. It is only necessary to think of the Holocaust to realize the atrocities that ordinary, good citizens are capable of ignoring, denying, or even "normalizing."

Although abuses of position and power are found within all institutions, traditions, and religions, certain conditions allow (and encourage) them to flourish. Whether we are looking at the family, schools, businesses, governments, or religious institutions, abuse is more apt to be accepted where rigid rules are dogmatically regulated by a powerful, entrenched hierarchy.

Individuals whose belief systems encourage them to take responsibility for their own behavior are less prone to abdicate their critical thinking by blindly accepting a "priestly ruling class." They are more likely to trust their own judgment about the actions of their religious leaders, challenging what they perceive as wrong or harmful. Although such environments don't guarantee that children will come to no harm, there is greater possibility of recognition that everyone shares a responsibility to protect the vulnerable.

Traditional patriarchal hierarchy of many cultures (and their religions) devalues those without power—notably women and children, the poor and uneducated, and those not belonging to a cultural, racial, religious, linguistic, professional or hereditary elite. A system that places one individual or group above another sets up the "lesser" one for harm. Those in control establish teachings, laws, rituals, and agencies of enforcement to keep hold of their power. Everyone understands these standards of belief and behavior; opposition is met with punishment or banishment (excommunication). The more rigid, absolute, fundamentalist, "traditional" the institution, the less likely it will countenance dissent. Speaking for the weak and vulnerable is perceived as a challenge to duly constituted authority; punishment is swift and sure. Just as incest is not about the worth of the institution of family, the current scandal is not only about clergy abuse or the Catholic Church. The deep harm arises from arrogant misuse of power.

When hierarchical power is couched in religious terms, dissent is perceived as opposition to the Word of God. It takes tremendous courage to stand up to that much power, no matter how heinous are the crimes committed in its name. **A child who is abused by an adult identified as the representative of God feels like he is being abused or abandoned *by* God.** The child's fear and self-hatred can be enormous: how bad he must be to deserve this treatment! If he can't even trust God, how is any trust possible? He may be told that if he discloses the abuse, he will be betraying God. Many who manage to overcome their fears and tell an adult are not believed, punished for lying, told to keep silent, or abused again. Where in the universe can a boy find safety when its most powerful forces seem to be aligned against him?

Adding to this already bleak picture is the fact that many children abused by clergy began as those most obedient to the teachings and practices of their religion—and therefore the most trusting of its clergy. Some survivors of sexual child abuse turn to religion for solace and healing. Where does a child abused by clergy turn? Along with his trust, clergy abuse can destroy a child's faith, sometimes irreparably.

Focus

Ten Thousand Children: A Tipping Point?

*Richard Hoffman graciously gave permission to reprint the fol-
lowing essay, which originally appeared in* Voice Male, *the magazine of the Men's Resource Center of Western Massachusetts.
He addresses many important points about clergy abuse and
other harsh realities of the lives of so many children. He brings
our attention to the numbers of child victims, and urges us not
to narrow the focus of our attention to the Scandal of the Week.
He ends on a note of hope. It is the duty of all of us to turn that
hope into a reality.*

*For more information about Richard Hoffman, visit his Web
site www.abbington.com/hoffman/index.html. Information about
the Men's Resource Center is at www.mensresourcecenter.org.*

In every struggle there is a moment that is afterward recognized
as the point when the tide began to turn, when success became
sure. Those who have struggled, over the past two decades
especially, to bring the reality of children's widespread sexual
exploitation to light can only hope that the present attention to
the assault on children by Catholic priests may serve as such a
tipping point.

Until now, the spotlight (quite literally, The Boston Globe
Spotlight Team) has been on the Archdiocese of Boston and its
protection of serial child rapists. Perhaps this is as it should be;
after all, the only thing worse than a wolf in sheep's clothing is a
wolf in shepherd's robes. However, in the discussions that have
followed, the focus has been on the Church, on the nature of the
priesthood, on the psychology of the perpetrators of this recur-
rent atrocity, and on who knew what and when. But the most
important thing for the public to understand is the real scope of
this tragedy, and the number of children who were harmed.

For years we have been hearing that incidents of child sexual abuse are few, that wild-eyed fanatics have created social hysteria, that most children pass into adulthood without encountering such psychopaths. But let's do some simple arithmetic.

As of this writing, the archdiocese has turned over the names of 90 priests to District Attorneys. Does this mean that 90 children were sexually assaulted? Not at all. Therapists who treat sex offenders, law enforcement people, and forensic psychologists all know that most men who violate children are serial offenders. The coach who raped me when I was ten turned out to have had more than four hundred victims over a forty-year period. Like most predators, Christopher Reardon, youth minister at St. Agnes parish in Middleton, Massachusetts, kept records of his many victims. When arrested, he had a list describing the private parts of 250 boys. Christopher Reardon had not reached the age of 30 when he was arrested. Many of the priests among the 90, on the other hand, are quite old.

Let's err on the safe side, though, and say, oh, ten victims per year for ten years or five victims per year for twenty years; in other words, 100 victims each. That's 9,000 children. Oh, and then there's John Geoghan's 118. And James Porter's 70. Let's not forget Reardon's 250. That's nearly 10,000 victims of those predators whom we know of.

So far we have only been talking about abuse within the Catholic Church. It would be a grievous mistake, however, to view the sexual exploitation of children as an issue existing only within the Catholic Church. We must not be diverted into discussions of celibacy, of the culture of the Church, of the ordination of women. A quick survey of news articles during the past year makes it clear that we should also be talking about sexual assault by teachers, by camp counselors, by youth workers, by scout leaders, and by coaches.

The point is that sexual violence, actual and threatened, is a constant feature of children's lives. Are we ready to grasp this reality, or shall we remain a community whose children are forced to bear on their bodies, in their souls, the knowledge that adults, with our state-of-the-art denial systems, refuse? When confronted with an incident of child sexual abuse, most people profess, each time, a shock that only serves to underscore their ignorance. So far we have been acting like good white Jim Crow Southerners minding our own business undisturbed by the occasional "strange fruit" hanging from the nearby trees.

Maybe this is the tipping point in the struggle to end the sexual exploitation and abuse of children. Maybe this is the moment when hesitation and hand-wringing give way to outrage and action, when, having grasped the magnitude and scope of this hidden crime, adults stand together, across whatever political divides, and say, "No more!" on behalf of our children. I surely hope so.

Recovery for survivors of clergy sexual abuse is largely the same as for other survivors, and is addressed elsewhere in this book. In this chapter, however, I want to place special emphasis on two areas that carry particular relevance for those who were abused in a religious context—*forgiveness* and *legal redress*.

Forgiveness

Although I discuss forgiveness in chapters 18 and 20, it is important to reemphasize it here. A number of religions stress the *spiritual* importance of forgiveness. Some present it as a moral imperative, urging believers to forgive those who have harmed them. Survivors who hold this view of forgiveness may feel conflicted. On the one hand, they feel hurt, betrayed, frightened—and angry at those who harmed them. On the other hand, their religion instructs them to move past these feelings and forgive the abusers—usually without offering guidance as to how to negotiate this process. If they are not ready, able, or willing to forgive, they feel shame. The survivor may interpret this "failure" as further evidence of his weakness, powerlessness, worthlessness. Whether the judgment is external or self-imposed, it is unfair—another example of blaming the victim. To be effective, forgiveness must be genuine. It cannot arise from obligation or coercion. One comes to true forgiveness (or does not) as part of a healing process; there is no absolute obligation to forgive. Some survivors consider forgiveness to have been a crucial aspect of their recovery; others have found it of little or no relevance. In any case, any decision must be arrived at honestly, at a pace that makes sense to the survivor, and not according to some arbitrary schedule.

An apology from a perpetrator may move a survivor to forgiveness—or it may not be sufficient. Many feel that an apology alone, without sincere commitment to changing one's behavior and making amends, is an empty gesture. Regardless of its sincerity, an apology does not require a given response, nor does the response have to be immediate.

On January 31, 2003, *The Boston Globe* ran an article about a priest's meeting with—and apologizing to—the adult children of a woman with whom he had conducted a long-term sexual affair. A number of news reports relate the specifics of the profound and irreparable harm inflicted upon the woman and her family by this priest's actions. After the meeting, one son was quoted as saying, "He told us he was sorry for the pain and anguish he had caused our family, and he asked us to forgive him. I'm not sure we're ready to do that. We need more answers before we talk about forgiveness."

This man's response makes sense. Just as a valid apology must be heartfelt, forgiveness is a choice that must be a product of soul-searching. It is too important a matter to be arrived at lightly. Anything less negates its importance, and is a form of pretense. Take the time you need to arrive at a reasonable decision. If you are in conflict about what to do, it may mean that you aren't ready to do anything. Trust your own timing. By honoring your recovery process you are far more likely to arrive at a conclusion that satisfies you. You may be more inclined toward forgiveness later on in your recovery, or may never choose this option.

Another perspective maintains that forgiveness isn't a choice. The Reverend Anne Fowler is an Episcopal priest with extensive experience working with survivors of clergy abuse. She is also a trusted colleague whose expert and insightful suggestions have improved the quality of this book. After reading an earlier draft of this chapter, Anne wrote, "I don't think forgiveness is a choice. I think it is grace. Sometimes it happens, sometimes it doesn't. And it happens mysteriously, not on anyone's schedule. You can't force it, and I don't think it's helpful or pastoral to suggest that it's something volitional. I thought the most obscene moments of the day of [Cardinal Bernard] Law's resignation were when the press kept asking survivors if they forgave the Cardinal."

Whether you see forgiveness as a choice, as "grace," or even as a desirable goal, please try to examine the question honestly. Your forgiveness is *yours*. Don't allow it to be mandated by external pressure.

The nature of the offense and the severity of the injuries suffered are not determinants of whether a survivor must (or should) offer forgiveness. In the earlier example, the priest in question stands accused not only of violating his vows of celibacy, but while doing so resuming his sexual relationship with a mentally ill woman after she had been lobotomized, possibly fathering two of her children, and abandoning her while she died of a drug overdose, only phoning for help after fleeing the scene. Clearly, this is an extreme situation, but its severity is not what determines whether forgiveness is the valid response. In fact, I hesitated before deciding to include specific details of this case, not wanting the reader to compare their severity to his own abuse history. Regardless of the specifics of what was done to you, you have the right to come to your own decision.

In considering the question of forgiveness, you can ask for help from your support network—therapist, spiritual advisor, other survivors, groups, friends, and/or loved ones. You don't have to do it alone, but please understand that your conclusion doesn't have to please anyone else. Your decision, once made, may not free you from conflicting feelings. If you are in that situation, your allies may be able to help you to understand and perhaps resolve (or at least diminish) these conflicts.

Reverend Fowler offers the perspective that "the benefits of forgiveness accrue chiefly to the *forgiver,* not the *forgivee*. It's burdensome to remain endlessly angry and resentful at someone, but it does much more harm to the one who can't forgive than to the perpetrator. And so very often, particularly in these clergy cases, the perpetrators seem to be unrepentant." While this is no doubt true, it doesn't constitute a requirement that you forgive the abuser. If entrenched anger and resentment are interfering with your recovery, it is essential that you examine these feelings. You may come to the conclusion that forgiveness will allow you to move forward in your life. Or you may discover that understanding and moving beyond your anger and resentment have nothing to do with forgiving those who harmed you. Again, there is no universal rule or easy answer concerning the role of forgiveness in recovery. You are left with the need to follow the path that is healthiest for you.

Legal Redress

The legal system presents another area of concern for survivors of clergy abuse. Although legal action is addressed briefly in chapter 18 ("Confrontation"), further discussion is necessary in light of certain responses to the flood of lawsuits against individual clergy and religious institutions.

It is essential that a survivor understands the risks and dangers before deciding to undertake legal action. It is a minefield and must be negotiated with extreme caution. This is true not just for survivors of clergy abuse but for any survivor who is contemplating a lawsuit. If you are considering this course of action, you must do all you can to protect yourself. Do your homework. Get all the information you can. Discuss possible risks and rewards with those closest to you. Talk with other survivors, both individuals who have undertaken this process and those who have chosen not to. Consult with your therapist, attorneys, and survivor support groups. Here are some important considerations:

1 / The legal process is quite different from a therapeutic environment. In a counseling/therapy setting, you have a great deal of control over personal information. At the very least, you can expect assurances of confidentiality. Barring a few specific exceptions (which your therapist should explain to you during your first meeting), you are assured that your personal information is confidential. The therapist cannot disclose the information without your written permission.

The same is not true in a lawsuit. The opposing attorneys have the right to "depose" you. That is, they are permitted to question you (in the presence of your lawyer) in preparation for presenting their case in court. Depositions are taken under oath, and you must be truthful in your answers. This can feel like a tremendous violation of your privacy, perhaps eliciting overwhelming feelings or flashbacks. If a deposition taken in a lawyer's office makes you feel like a helpless child being attacked by a cruel adult, the experience can be even more intense in a more public setting—the courtroom. Although you have done nothing wrong, and have nothing to be ashamed of, being questioned by the opposing attorneys can leave you feeling guilty and ashamed. Their job is not to present a fair and balanced picture; it is to win their case.

Before a deposition or trial, your lawyer will instruct you as to how to respond to questions, but once the procedure begins, you are largely on your own. Some survivors, having successfully negotiated these challenges, report that having done so left them feeling more powerful and in greater charge of their lives. Others have felt revictimized and retraumatized. Unfortunately, there is no way to guarantee what your experience will be. That is why it is essential to prepare yourself as completely as possible before following the legal route. Although there may be much to gain by pursuing legal action, there are many risks as well. A lawsuit is not therapy. Ideally, you will be well advanced in your recovery before undertaking a lawsuit. Sadly, this is not always possible. Statutes of limitations, not survivors' needs, can dictate the timing of legal actions. There will be more information about this in a later paragraph.

2 / The lack of privacy in legal settings is not limited to you. A number of people in your life will be deposed and/or called as witnesses. They may be questioned about parts of your life that don't seem relevant to the matter at hand, or that you would rather not have made public. Facts and events may be twisted to portray you in a negative light. It is possible that you may even begin to question your own view of reality.

3 / At this writing, many professionals who work with survivors are protesting a legal tactic that would severely compromise the safety and effectiveness of the therapeutic setting. Lawyers for the Boston Archdiocese are demanding to depose therapists of clergy abuse survivors who bring suit against the Archdiocese. The lawyers argue that, by bringing suit, survivors are "going public," and the Church has a legal right to mount a vigorous defense. This right, they maintain, includes gaining access to the survivors' therapy records.

Opponents of this tactic argue that while the Archdiocese may have a *legal* right to therapeutic information, there are *moral* and *ethical* considerations as well. The Church presents itself as a moral and ethical authority, committed to promoting healing for victims and survivors. It has encouraged survivors to seek therapy and counseling, and established an "Office of Healing and Assistance Ministry" to provide counseling resources for victims and survivors. Clergy abuse survivors feel betrayed and revictimized when the very content of their therapy is treated as fair game by attorneys for the Archdiocese. Survivors and their advocates have characterized this legal tactic as a "thinly veiled threat" that if the victims don't settle their lawsuits, their therapies will be subject to invasion. In a classic example of blaming the victim, the survivor is told that by continuing the litigation, he is responsible for his own suffering. Fortunately, fewer and fewer survivors are deceived by this threadbare tactic. (I don't know whether this conflict will be resolved by the time this book goes to press. Further information—and the text of a letter sent to Bishop Lennon and a list of its signers—can be found at www.Boston.com [*The Boston Globe* Web site]. I have also posted it on my own Web site, and will add other matters that relate to it.)

4 / I firmly believe that it is essential for survivors to be in charge of the pace and intensity of their recovery work. I have noted elsewhere that there is nothing to be gained (and much to lose) by attempting to work in a manner that isn't right for you. If you take on too much too quickly, you risk being overwhelmed, overstressed, and feeling hopeless. Each step must be taken only when you are ready; attempting to move from where you wish you were, instead of where you are, is likely to be an exercise in frustration and futility.

Unfortunately, the legal system doesn't work that way. Once you begin the process, you may lose control over both its timing and intensity. Schedules will be set for you, and you may not be permitted sufficient time to feel, examine your feelings, bring the issues that are raised into your counseling sessions, or just take a break for needed rest. In fact, this very loss of control has pressured some survivors to drop their lawsuits or settle for less than they feel is fair. Make certain that your attorney understands these issues and is respectful of your recovery, helping you retain the maximum possible control over the process.

5 / Another legal reality that pressures survivors to take premature action is the "statute of limitations." Many jurisdictions impose a specific time limit on how long after a crime was committed legal action can be initiated. Survivors and their allies have advocated (sometimes successfully) to extend or eliminate these statutes when they involve cases of sexual abuse of children.

   If you are faced with the impending expiration of a statute of limitations, you may experience pressure to move before you are ready. While acting prematurely is always risky, you may be forced into a choice of "now or never" where the legal system is concerned. Again, you are in a difficult position: each option carries the potential for disappointment and further pain. There is no universally correct solution. I can, however, reassure you that **no one's** recovery depends entirely on whether or not they take an abuser to court. There are many different roads to recovery. If one proves to be a dead end, there are other possibilities available to you. Setbacks can be overcome. Take heart, and remember that it was your strength, resilience, and creativity that brought you to this point. You are fully able to discover the direction that works for you, and you have many allies to help you figure it out.

6 / These are all matters to be discussed extensively with your therapist, lawyer, and other members of your support network, so that you can arrive at a reasonable decision about whether to litigate. Your attorney should be up-to-date about the legal issues and precedents in clergy abuse cases. He or she should also be willing to explain fully what you can reasonably expect to happen. Your therapist can help you explore the emotional and psychological risks and benefits, both before you begin legal proceedings and throughout the process. Whatever you decide, please remember that success is measured by how well you pay attention to your needs. As in every aspect of recovery, victory does not depend on any particular course of action, but rather on how well you con-

tinue to take care of yourself. As with other forms of confrontation, the validity of taking legal action isn't judged by the outcome.
What is vital is that it be right for you. This is true when making
the initial decision about whether to commence legal action, and
at every other point in the process. There is no shame or failure
attached to any decision. Despite whatever pressure you may be
facing, it is always good to take the time to feel. At every stage it is
important to be aware of how you are feeling, how you feel about
yourself—and what you genuinely need.

Damage from abuse by clergy is profound, bearing a special weight
of spiritual loss. A significant number of clergy abuse victims have not
survived, driven by despair to suicide or fatal harm. Many who do survive
never fully regain their former trust—in the religion of their childhood,
or any belief system. If religion or spirituality is an important part of your
life, you will need to find ways to repair the damage. This will take time,
but you need time to heal. The more important an area of recovery is to
you, the more essential that you devote sufficient attention to its repair.
When done correctly, fully respectful of your individual needs, the repair
will be permanent. Pay attention to what you know is meaningful to you;
you deserve no less.

Some clergy abuse survivors recover their spirituality within another
religious context or system of belief and practice. Others, such as members
of the groups advocating for sanity and healing of their religious institution, refuse to leave their church, insisting that they will not be forced out
by those who cause harm to children. Whichever path you choose, you
deserve encouragement and respect for your decision. Just as no one has
the right to tell you what you must do *therapeutically* to heal from sexual child
abuse, decisions about your *spiritual* recovery are yours alone.

Recovery from the effects of clergy abuse is difficult, but possible.
Many have accomplished it, none without painful emotions and deep
soul-searching. If you undertake this quest, please try to have patience
with yourself. It will take longer than you wish, and be harder than you
imagine. As with other aspects of recovery, don't attempt your spiritual
healing in isolation—it can't be done. There are many others on paths
parallel to yours; sometimes your paths will even intersect. Having allies
on this journey won't make it easy, but it is wise not to make it any more

difficult than necessary. Experience the power to be found in numbers—power that doesn't belong only to the abusive. Create your own recovery "congregation."

Finally, as I have urged readers elsewhere in this book, try to avoid measuring the severity of what was done to you against the experience of other survivors. Clergy abuse survivors are no more or less "damaged" than others who were victimized. Again, Reverend Anne Fowler presents her perspective clearly, saying, "I agree with you that measuring degrees of victimhood is not a winning ticket. However, I do think this. Church or synagogue is a place we would hope people (we) could go to find sanctuary when we have been abused or recollect memories of abuse. But if the abuse has been perpetrated by the 'guardians' of the sanctuary, that refuge is threatened or destroyed. Also, people's ability to worship or even to form images of God is often destroyed as well. This is another dimension of abuse."

This chapter was not included because other forms of sexual child abuse are "not as bad" as clergy abuse. Rather, it is intended to address specific issues of clergy abuse survivors, in the hope of pointing toward paths of healing. Resist any thoughts that would separate you from your allies. *All* survivors need and deserve attention—including you.

As your trust in yourself grows, you will discover that you know better than anyone else what specifics of recovery work best for you. This is as true in the realm of spiritual healing as in any other. Accept no substitutes for what you know is right—no matter how attractively they are packaged. You merit no less. Chapter 23 contains information about prayer, meditation, and spirituality in recovery. Approach it as critically as you do any other aspect of healing. For now, be gentle with yourself. Try to remember that you never deserved to be harmed in this way. You can recover in all dimensions of your life.

Josh's Statement

I received a number of deeply moving, often shocking statements by survivors of clergy abuse. I wish I could have included more of them. I selected the statement by Josh, thirty-nine, because it portrays many themes common to abuse by clergy: emotional isolation of the child, "grooming" of the vulnerable victim by a predatory adult, linking of God/religion with abuse, perverting of religious teachings, manipulating the faith and needs of the child, installation of secrecy, shame and guilt, possible ignoring of the abuse (collusion) by nonprotective adults, abandonment by the abuser leaving the child even further isolated, and increased vulnerability to further violation.

Fortunately, Josh begins his next forty years with determination, resources, a support system, and hope.

I was born in ———— in 1963. I grew up in a small north side neighborhood. I had what to the outside appeared to be a "normal" family life. However we were not a close-knit family, and I often felt emotionally detached from them. Physical display of affection was rare.

My father was often away on business trips, and I often sought attention elsewhere. I remember craving emotional closeness. But it just wasn't part of the picture.

As a boy, I attended ———— church in my neighborhood. I recall riding my bike to and from the playground there often in the warmer months. I was about 8–9 years old. Sometimes I would play there with friends, but more often alone. I remember a priest approached me one afternoon (this would have been in June of 1971) and befriended me. He asked if I'd like to play catch with him. His name was Father "Roy," or so he said. I took an instant liking to him. He was really nice and very friendly, like one of the guys. He also became emotionally available for me. I thought he was really special. On one occasion he invited me into the rectory for lemonade and ice cream. What little kid could resist that offer on a hot July day? I greedily accepted. I remember him teasing my hair and saying "sit with me on the couch and we'll enjoy our treats." I didn't think it amiss at all when he put an arm around me and said something like "You know, you're a really nice kid. What would you say if I personally trained you to be an altar boy? Would you like that?" I readily said yes. I was very excited. It seemed like a special honor to a little boy.

So we started meeting clandestinely on certain afternoons, mostly Saturdays. I remember him saying to me not to tell my family about it, in order that it might be a special surprise for them later. I went along with it. I trusted him implicitly. After all, I grew up learning that a priest was the next best thing to GOD. Sort of the link between me and the guy upstairs. He would pace me through all the motions, ritual, and terminologies necessary for the position of altar boy.

One day he said that in order to be ready for mass one must cleanse themselves spiritually and physically. I only had a vague notion of what he meant. He told me I must pray to God to absolve my sins and then to take a shower. He told me the two of us would have to do this together so God would see that he was instructing me properly, and that it would be a bad thing to anger God. He said the water was special holy water and it would purify our bodies. I never suspected anything bad when he told me this. I guess I was so excited by everything that it didn't seem strange. He told me we should undress and enter the shower. I felt a little awkward, but he reassured me that "God made our bodies beautiful and that we should display them for him so that he could see the fruits of his labors." He had me help him "soap up" and vice versa. He even managed to manipulate me into washing his penis, telling me that it was the "rod of procreation" and needed to be especially cleansed and handled as it was "God's most special gift to man." I didn't of course realize it then, but he had succeeded in seducing me into mutual masturbation. He had told me it was all part of God's plan, and as a naïve, trusting child I of course believed him. Besides it didn't hurt or anything. It actually sort of felt good. He even got me to fellate him by telling me "in order for me to have the special seed necessary for procreation (when I got to be a man, of course), he had to implant it inside me . . . that God gave it to him to give to me." So when he ejaculated this weird stuff into my mouth and made me ingest it, he said that "I had done well and had pleased God very much!" I remember thinking it was like sour milk or something but still I never thought or knew it was wrong.

These sessions would be repeated several times over the next year and a half, all the while in secret. Until one day he must have gotten carried away in his pleasure while playing with me in the shower and slid a fat finger into my anus and I remember it hurt like hell. Suddenly everything changed. This felt like a violation. I remember struggling to free myself from his grasp around me. Suddenly it wasn't fun and good anymore. It was creepy and dirty. I felt terrified and betrayed. I broke free and I believe I shouted "WHY DID YOU DO THAT???" I was shaking and crying and upset that this man who I thought was my friend had hurt me.

He got angry and chased after me, tackling me on the bed. He said, "You are making God very angry right now, do you want to burn in hell forever? You should never disobey me. I was only showing you that one needs to learn to handle pain to be strong. God wants us to be strong." I was devastated and really scared. I think I asked him, "But w-w-why did you not tell me?!" He really got crazy. When I think back on this incident, he seemed like he had snapped and wasn't making any sense. But as a 10-year-old I only knew that he had turned on me. And I was confused and didn't understand.

Anyway, he then said to never question him again. He said, "Now you're going to be punished for your sins." And then he grabbed me; pinning me to the bed, he spit on his hand and grabbed a bottle of lotion from the bed stand and stuck his fingers in me and then forced his thing inside me. It was like nothing you could imagine. I think I blanked out from the pain of his having penetrated me. He told me that if I ever said anything to anyone that God would take me away.

At this point I'll dispense with the story; suffice to say he continued to abuse me for about another month off and on until one day he was just gone. I dissociated and buried away the memories of this for a long time.

I came to find out through later investigation that he in fact was only a novice priest at the time, and that when he seemingly just disappeared, that he had finished his training and had been assigned a parish in another state.

I also want to note that when he was abusing me, there never seemed to be any other priest around at the time. He must have been really slick and knew just when it would be safe for him to get away with it.

I went on to be abused by two other adults before I was fifteen, but that is another story. I spent a long time in and out of counseling and have been steadily in sessions for the past eighteen months, since recovering the memories of my abuse some nine years ago. I finally told my sisters about my past abuse, and just recently told my parents for the first time. Next year I will turn forty and hopefully can begin my life anew.

20

ABOUT FORGIVING

There are no verdicts to childhood, only consequences,
and the bright freight of memory.
—Pat Conroy, PRINCE OF TIDES

Even the best-intentioned people may not know what to do when they
see or hear about traumatic events. As caring individuals they want to be
supportive and encouraging but have no idea of what constitutes a helpful response. It is hard to see someone in physical or emotional pain. It is
natural to try to do everything you can to make the hurt go away. People
want to help because they truly care but also because the situation restimulates painful memories of times when they were hurt. Caught up in their
own painful emotions, they are unable to think clearly, and may resort to
clichés and other patterned responses. These unthinking reactions, while
motivated by love and caring, often serve to increase pain by telling the
sufferer that he must stop feeling bad. Unfortunately, in order to accomplish that, it would be necessary to stop feeling altogether. When bad
things happen, it is appropriate to feel bad—and to express those emotions. This is an essential part of healing. However, because these emotions are a response to trauma, they get confused with the hurt itself. The
mistaken idea is that if the person would only stop *expressing* the pain, he
would stop *feeling* it—and it would go away. Well, it just doesn't happen
that way. Crying is not grief; it is a way to get over the grief. Trembling is
not an expression of cowardice; it is a means of moving out of the paraly-
sis engendered by fear. But our culture tells us otherwise. We are uncomfortable with our emotions, and that discomfort is reflected in our
behavior.

Whether the individual is an adult undergoing the loss of a loved one
or a child who has skinned his knee in the playground, the most frequent
reactions he encounters are attempts to distract or "comfort" him—by

getting him to turn off the expression of his feelings. A hurt child needs loving attention while crying, shaking, and talking his way through the feelings that come from having been injured. When he receives that kind of attention, recovery is quite rapid. Having discharged the feelings and processed the event, he can return to playing—clearheaded and happy. But most adults are disturbed by a child's tears and attempt to stop his crying. They may do it with bribes and pacifiers. ("Here, don't you want an ice cream cone?" "If you stop crying, I'll buy you a toy.") This technique not only informs the child that it isn't okay to feel, it teaches him that adults are so upset by tears that he can manipulate them by crying. Adults may try other distraction techniques ("Let me kiss it and make it better" or "There, there, stop crying . . . look at that big doggie over there"). Or they attempt to shame, ridicule or criticize the child into calm ("Big boys don't cry," "You're acting like a little crybaby," "You weren't really hurt *that* badly," "You made a big crack in the sidewalk"). Finally, the adult may attempt to turn off the child's uncomfortable expression of feelings with threats of punishment ("If you don't stop crying I'll give you something to cry about") or actual violence. All of these responses aggravate the hurt. At best, a child who has been bribed, distracted, ridiculed, or punished remains cranky and irritable. He feels misunderstood, rejected, and isolated. Having had his difficulties belittled, he feels that help is unavailable. In the future, believing that he has no right to his feelings, he avoids seeking help—retreating instead into "self-sufficient" isolation. Or he becomes increasingly needy, seeking comfort and understanding in inappropriate ways. In either case, feelings of inadequacy and shame have been reinforced, further shaking the child's confidence that it is possible to take charge of his life.

We have all experienced these responses to childhood trauma. When we encounter them as adults, they have a familiar ring. We are likely to stop thinking about what we need, and react in ways that we learned when young. Although not the most helpful approach to pain, this regressive behavior is a self-protective response. When we have upsetting experiences in adult life, we are less likely to be able to say, "I need you to just be there and allow me to cry" or "Just hold me." We were taught to be "good soldiers" and not show our feelings. We know how to keep our own counsel, protecting others from our feelings. Survivors are particularly well trained in keeping people calm. Male survivors, carrying the additional cultural disapproval of men who cry, are extremely unlikely to express their feelings in the presence of others.

It is natural to want to create distance from painful emotions, whether one's own or someone else's. When the painful experience occurred in the past—as is the case with childhood sexual abuse—adults will attempt to relegate it to the past. In the grip of their own painful feelings about sexual abuse and emotional expression, they are unable to think clearly; they cannot respond appropriately to the survivor's needs. Instead, they resort to giving advice that only serves to isolate him further.

The most frequent form of advice is some variation of "You need to learn to forgive" or "It happened so long ago, why can't you just put it behind you?" They truly believe they have the best interests of the survivor at heart, but they are doing the emotional equivalent of telling someone who was bitten by a rabid dog, "If you just ignore it, it will go away." Not only does this response reflect a total lack of understanding of the ongoing effects of sexual abuse, it delivers a clear message to the survivor. Aware of the listener's discomfort, he receives confirmation that what was done to him was so horrible and disgusting that he had better keep his mouth shut about it or he will drive everyone away. As a child he learned to pretend and protect the feelings of others; as an adult he is certain that he must continue the pretense. No one, he feels, could stand knowing who he really is. The inability of his listeners to tolerate his story and his feelings is seen as evidence that *he* is intolerable.

Nor is the inherent criticism in statements like "You should learn to forgive" lost on the survivor. If he were a "better" person (stronger, more forgiving, kinder, more mature, more spiritually evolved), he reasons, he would be able to put all this behind him and embrace the perpetrator. His inability to do so becomes yet another corroboration of his personal failings. This is harmful, and easy to buy into—since it reinforces the survivor's existing feelings of shame, self-blame, and responsibility for the abuse. This misguided advice buttresses the wall of secrecy and silence—the very wall that needs to be torn down.

There are effective ways of helping someone who is having a rough time. One is simply to listen to him. Although our programming tells us "Don't just sit there, do something!" the reverse is likely to be far more helpful. Instead of rushing headlong into inappropriate advice or action, "*Don't just do something, sit there!*" Sitting and listening to a survivor *is* doing something. It is doing something important. Showing that you care—that what he has to say deserves to be listened to, and he has a right to have feelings about the abuse—is an important contradiction of internalized negative messages. How many times have any of us had the wonderful experience of someone listening to us without offering judgment, criticism, advice, or blame? How often have we seen someone looking at us with love and approval while we talked about what it has been like for us? When has someone just held us as we shook, taken our hands as we cried, without trying to stem the flow of feelings? Those of us who have experienced this expression of caring know how therapeutic it is. For an adult survivor it is vital to receive aware, loving attention. No, listening to someone is not "doing nothing." Active, aware attention is a special skill. To develop that skill and offer it to another human being is a valuable gift. It makes a world of difference to the survivor.

As an adult male survivor, you have to let people know how to be more effective allies in your recovery. You need to teach them to listen, giving them feedback about what isn't helpful—*as well as appreciation and encouragement for what is*. It isn't enough to criticize what they haven't done. If you only do that, they will eventually give up out of frustration. Don't expect them to guess ("If you really cared about me you'd know how I feel"). They are friends, not mind readers. Talk to them, show them, consult with them. If you don't know what's best for you, admit your confusion and try out a number of possibilities. One of them might work. The caring is what is most important; work out the details together.

FORGIVING

In the preceding paragraphs I wrote about how the concept of forgiveness can be used in unhelpful, avoidant, and punitive ways. Now we can look at what remains. Is forgiveness ever appropriate? If so, under what circumstances? Do you, in fact, need to "learn to forgive" the perpetrator? Again, I won't make you wait for an answer. I will tell you, clearly and emphatically, that *it is not necessary to forgive the person who abused you*! Do what makes sense for you. Forgiveness may never be the right course of action for you. The choice to forgive or not to forgive is entirely yours.

Forgiveness—like any other aspect of recovery—is an individual matter. There isn't one answer that fits all survivors. The issue is complex.

It requires time and careful thinking before even deciding whether the concept of forgiveness is relevant to your situation. Some survivors feel that forgiving the person who abused them allowed them to let go of ties to the past and move forward with their recovery. For others, forgiveness seems like acceptance of the abusive behavior. Many survivors are not ready even to consider the possibility. You are the only one who can determine what is right and what is possible for you. It is important that you not proceed according to someone else's values and agenda. The concept of "forgiveness" is open to a wide range of interpretation. Examine the idea within the context of your own moral, ethical, religious, and cultural values to make the decision that is right for you. And, even if you accept the idea of forgiveness, you must be the one to decide whether or not the time is right. Don't be pushed. If it is to be right, it must be genuine. I can't tell you what to do, but here are some suggestions to help you feel better about your decisions:

1 / **Take your time.** Don't rush to forgive. Whether or not forgiveness will ever be relevant, it is not appropriate in the early stages of recovery. There is too much work to do first. Part of that work involves identifying your feelings about the abuse *and the abuser,* and allowing yourself to feel the hurt, fear, and humiliation. As you recognize the unfairness of your childhood—in the course of regaining your power—you will probably need to express outrage at what was done to you and at the individuals who were responsible. These initial steps cannot be taken in an atmosphere of forgiveness. If forgiveness is to come, there is time for it . . . later. For now, you have other priorities.

2 / **Protect yourself.** Beware of getting trapped by pity. Be careful not to yield to the inclination to protect or take care of the perpetrator. Even if you care for him deeply, he is not in need of your protection—you are! Premature forgiveness revictimizes the survivor by minimizing the abuse or sharing responsibility for it. Remember that everybody benefits when abuse is stopped (including the perpetrator; acting abusively is never a healthy mode of human behavior). Your recovery is in everyone's best interest. Don't sacrifice it to misguided feelings of pity, protectiveness, or responsibility.

3 / **Explore your authentic feelings.** Consider forgiveness. What feelings arise when you do? You may be surprised to discover that you already have some feelings on the subject. Pay attention to those feelings; they came from somewhere. No one has more information about your situation than you. Planning to forgive is less effective than figuring out how you really feel about it. Examine your heart—you'll know if and when you're ready to forgive.

4 / **You can change your mind.** Recovery is a dynamic process. Things change. What is appropriate at one point in your recovery may be counter-indicated or irrelevant at another. Right now you may feel that you will never forgive the perpetrator and later on find that your feelings are quite different. Or you may attempt forgiveness only to discover that you are unable to do so. It is all right to change your mind; you are figuring out what is right for you. You are trying on alternatives to select the one that fits you best.

5 / **Forgiveness takes different forms.** If you choose to forgive the perpetrator, there are a number of ways to do so. You can say so directly. This will allow you to get an immediate response. As with confrontation, be aware that the response you receive may be quite different from what you anticipated. There will be no Hollywood-style reconciliation scene with music and flowers. Declaring forgiveness may be a beginning step in building a viable relationship. Or your forgiveness may be rejected or misinterpreted.

If you don't want direct contact, you can declare forgiveness on the telephone or by letter. The latter, of course, allows you to state what you wish without the possibility of interruption. You can also forgive someone without telling him directly, manifesting it through a change in your behavior. Finally, it is possible to forgive in your heart, without doing anything about it directly. It is your decision, to be shared only if you want to—with only those you choose to.

6 / **It isn't "all or nothing."** Forgiveness doesn't have to be total. A little can go a long way. You can experiment with a little bit of forgiveness, just to see whether it's right for you. You can move

closer gradually or dance back and forth according to your needs. Remember, once again, your primary responsibility is to your own well-being.

7 / **Think about what you mean by forgiveness.** When forgiving a person, it is important not to *condone* the abuse. What was done to you was wrong. Child abuse is always bad. If you forgive the perpetrator, it must be with the understanding that you have decided to bear no malice toward someone who committed a grievous offense against you. It is an act of pardon, not exoneration.

REVENGE

Revenge has been a forbidden topic. Although children fantasize about "getting even" with their parents, expression of their fantasies is greeted with shock and dismay. As an adult survivor you may be frightened by images of revenge. You may feel that your fantasies are wrong—that you should be above such base desires. But there is nothing wrong with feeling like avenging the hurts you have suffered. You are correctly feeling outrage at an outrageous act. And you need the freedom to express your desire to punish those who abused you. A survivor recovery group or workshop is a particularly appropriate place for you to do so. One of the most exciting aspects of the group experience occurs when a participant first shares his thoughts about taking revenge against the perpetrator. These can range from lurid fantasies of torture and physical violence to elaborately thought-out plans for confrontation, public exposure, and/or legal action. Whatever their form, revenge themes are evidence that the survivor has stopped blaming himself for the abuse and is demanding that the perpetrator be held accountable for his or her actions. It is a powerful stance—the anger is that of righteous indignation. When a male survivor voices revenge fantasies to the group, he is surprised by the energy with which the other members support, encourage, and even build upon his ideas. Genuine bonding occurs as group members cheer one another on to more powerful behavior. You will find yourself encouraging the revenge fantasies of the other group members.

Putting these revenge fantasies into effect is another matter. Although the saying tells us "revenge is sweet," it has a way of turning bitter. Some forms of retribution carry severe penalties. You have been hurt enough; be careful not to do anything that will result in further pain. Revenge is not necessarily a bad idea, if it can take a form that will further your recovery, not set it back. Delicious as the prospect of killing, injuring, or even abusing the perpetrator may be, acting on those feelings is almost certain to be harmful to your well-being. You have been punished enough; don't risk further pain for the momentary satisfaction of getting even. There are other sayings about revenge: One is that it is "a dish best served cold." If you choose to pursue revenge, it may ultimately be more satisfying to seek redress through such indirect means as public exposure or litigation. It will certainly be safer. Perhaps the most realistic saying is "living well is the best revenge." Creating a satisfying life is certainly the sweetest aspect of overcoming abuse. Enjoying your own recovery, helping others to effect theirs, and then working together to put an end to sexual abuse, while less immediate and dramatic, will provide profound and lasting rewards.

SELF-FORGIVENESS

Without question, this is the most important need of all. As long as you continue to accept blame for what was done to you—as long as you buy any of the lies you were told—the abuse continues. Although having been abused does not call for forgiveness of others, it *is* necessary to "forgive yourself."

Self-forgiveness is a tricky and confusing concept, because you did nothing wrong. Therefore, the word "forgiveness" is inappropriate. I use it only in the sense of "letting yourself off the hook"—a hook you never deserved to hang from. If you haven't been blaming yourself, self-forgiveness isn't necessary. But if (like most male survivors) you assume responsibility that isn't yours, you have more work to do. You need to excuse yourself for all the wasted time, withdrawal, depression, and failures of your life. You need to "pardon" yourself for having behaved in ways that brought pain to others. You must forgive yourself for self-inflicted pain.

It is often helpful to do this in the company of other survivors. They make sure that you don't turn the process into another form of self-punishment. Self-forgiveness must not be a further assigning of blame.

Instead, it is an acknowledgment of your basic goodness and a celebration of your survival. It represents a decision to include yourself in the kindness and respect that you extend to the rest of the world. As you stop blaming yourself, you are standing up to the abuse. Self-forgiveness is an important way to recover your self-respect. When you delight in who you are—as you respect your own perception, judgment, values, and timing— you are well along in your recovery.

21

MOVING ON

And this morning I thought of the Resistance surfacing after the War (the tyrant's body hanging in the public square), restoring the rightful names of the capital's streets, renaming the places where the old names now mean little.
—Richard Hoffman,
from his poem "Yesterday. Last Night. This Morning."

TEMPORARY SETBACKS, ONGOING RECOVERY

There is no specific moment when recovery ends—no instantly recognizable goal. As you undertake healing the wounds of sexual child abuse, you begin a journey of exploration and education. In the course of this odyssey you gain insight into yourself, your experience, and the world. You realize that you are not alone. Sharing your story with others, you find people who can listen to you, understand what you are saying, and believe that you are telling the truth. You discover that many other people have undergone similar experiences. Encouraging one another to share your stories, you forge a support network of fellow survivors and other caring individuals (VOICES in Action calls them "prosurvivors"). Individual counseling and group therapy are laboratories where you experiment with trusting other people—practicing in a safe environment until you are ready to take further risks in the wider world.

Breaking free of isolation and developing support systems, you move ahead with healthy social interactions. You make new acquaintances, develop friendships, and even form nonabusive loving relationships. In the course of recovery you discover strengths, capabilities, and resources you hadn't realized you possess. You learn more about the benign aspects of the world—where you can turn for help, information, and protection. And you find that the world isn't a completely dangerous place. You learn to distinguish between real and imaginary dangers—how to protect yourself from genuine risks without needing to insulate yourself from life.

You give up the defensive stance that forced you to see the world in all-or-nothing terms; you accept that the world is neither completely safe nor totally dangerous. And you find that an imperfect world can be quite wonderful.

Over time, you build self-esteem, realizing that you have a right to a full, rich life. As you treat yourself with respect, you come to expect respectful treatment. And you notice that the world is treating you better. Feeling deserving of the good things in life, you find yourself taking steps in your education, career, community, and personal life that didn't seem possible before. (In fact, they weren't available when you were trapped by the effects of the abuse.) When you look back at where you were, you are astonished by the extent of the change. Life hasn't become perfect, but it is livable—and sometimes even satisfying.

Be gentle with yourself and keep in mind the following issues:

1 / **Discouragement.** Change doesn't come easily. Recovery takes time. It's an ongoing process that requires courage and determination. You will feel pain and confusion. There will be times when nothing seems to be happening; at other times you'll be discouraged and want to give up. Sometimes you'll wonder if the rewards are worth the pain, and doubt that you're up to the struggle. Even when good things happen, old feelings of fear and mistrust will arise to undermine your gains. If you are feeling vulnerable, any setback can cause you to believe that you haven't really made any progress. A relatively small disappointment appears to undo all your accomplishments. Expect that there will be times when you feel exhausted, overwhelmed, and hopeless. The wounds of sexual child abuse are deep; recovery takes time. For every fast, exhilarating period of forward movement, there are times of slow, difficult growth, and plateaus of apparent inactivity. All are necessary parts of your recovery. If you understand their importance, you can anticipate them—not with relish, but with acceptance that they are temporary.

2 / **Perspective.** The road to recovery is rarely direct, and is never a superhighway. (It usually feels more like an obstacle course.)

Although you are experiencing general forward movement, a temporary setback can cause you to lose perspective. Feeling that all your work has been negated, you are tempted to give up. For this reason you must stop periodically and take stock of the situation. Times of inactivity are perfect for this endeavor. Stop, rest, and take a look around you. Think about where you were at this time last year, two years ago, three. Think about the changes you have made and the people who care about you. Despite your current bad feelings, does the present disappointment really negate all the progress you've made? Take time to chronicle your recovery; a diary or journal provides you with visible evidence of how your thinking and feelings have changed. When you feel discouraged, take time to test reality. Talk to friends and other survivors. Share your feelings with them, and ask them for feedback. They may remind you of things you've forgotten. Go to a meeting or social activity; get back in touch with your support network. It helps to talk with someone who has just recently begun to deal with his abusive childhood. Seeing him going through the initial agonies of discovery, offering your experience and insight, will help him, while providing you with a useful perspective on your own progress.

3 / **Relaxation.** Feeling discouraged and overwhelmed provides you with another message. This business of recovery isn't easy. You've been working too hard. As much as you want to get through this all at once, it doesn't happen that way. You need time for rest, relaxation, and play. Vacations aren't charity; they were established for a reason—a rested worker is more productive. They are given to employees because they are good for business. Taking time to recuperate from the rigors of everyday life allows you to return to the struggle with renewed energy. When I suggest to a survivor that he take time to play, he will often reply that he doesn't know how to relax. When I encourage him further—asserting that learning to enjoy life is part of recovery—he is likely to say, "Okay, I'll *work* on it." I respond, "*Play* on it." You don't have to wait until the work of recovery is complete before you enjoy life. Allow

yourself pleasure along the way. It will remind you of why you are doing all this. Relaxation is not a distraction from the task at hand; it is an important part of that task. A well-rounded, satisfying life includes play as well as work, leisure as well as activity. If you don't know how to enjoy yourself, it's time you learned. Enlist the help of people who know how to play—what more pleasant favor could you ask of someone? Do things you've thought about but never tried because they were too silly/frivolous/juvenile/foolish/wasteful. Recovery is serious, but it doesn't always have to be heavy. You always guessed that there is more to life than pain and struggle. You were right. Accept that you deserve to take part in the pleasures of life, not just the pain. Accept my assurance that rewarding yourself is an essential aspect of your recovery.

4 / **Acceptance of progress.** There will be times when you question whether the rewards of recovery are worth all the effort. You wonder whether you possess the stamina to sustain a project that promises to go on forever, even though you know that there really isn't any other choice. You tried withdrawing, numbing, and a host of other strategies, and the pain remained. You're doing this because you have to. It's the only course of action that makes sense. Once you've begun to recover, difficult as it is, there's really no turning back. You know, deep down, that you're on the right track. But the knowledge doesn't keep you from sometimes feeling uncertainty, discouragement, and doubt.

When you experience self-doubt, it helps to get a good healthy dose of appreciation. It can come from friends, other survivors, or yourself. You need acknowledgment that what you are doing is very difficult. You need reassurance that it is understandable that you are feeling discouraged and overwhelmed. And you deserve admiration for having decided to end the way abuse has ruled your life. Accept that the progress you have achieved is genuine. Bask in the appreciation, admiration, and encouragement of those who know what you've accomplished. If you're ready for it, ask for a hug or two. Look in the mirror and see how you have changed. Admire what you have done and what you are going to do.

WHAT WE'RE UP AGAINST: OPPOSITION AND "BACKLASH"

Earlier chapters addressed the need to join other survivors (and allies) for mutual support, understanding, and affirmation. Beyond this personal aspect of recovery, there is another important reason for survivors to work together. Ideas and attitudes of the overall culture toward sexual child abuse must be reshaped. This can only be done actively and cooperatively. Laws must be changed, books and articles written, and outcry heard in all quarters. It must be shown that we will no longer tolerate a society that ignores or romanticizes abuse and thereby sacrifices its children.

The only way that these fundamental changes can be accomplished is through strength of numbers. Moral outrage isn't enough if only a few people express it. Powerful forces hold abusive attitudes firmly in place; dislodging them will take considerable strength and concerted action. Even if you don't think of yourself as "political" or as an "activist," it is easy to see why you must help bring about these changes. As long as abuse continues to be ignored or condoned—as long as children are sexually violated—you will be faced with an ongoing reminder of what was done to you.

It has been said that no one can truly be free as long as anyone is enslaved. Sadly, entrenched attitudes don't change easily. Change must be fought for and won—often at great cost. African-Americans, women, Jews, and trade unionists had to struggle for recognition of their rights (and must continue fighting to consolidate their gains and keep moving forward). Gay men and lesbians, people with physical disabilities, mental patients, some ethnic, religious, and racial minorities, and other groups are actively engaged in trying to effect widespread recognition that there is a problem, and that it is up to *all* of us to solve it. It is to everyone's advantage to bring about these changes for our children, our loved ones—and ourselves.

Who, then, stands in the way of these changes? Wouldn't everyone agree that sexual child abuse is a serious problem that needs to be remedied? Unfortunately, there are many forces opposing change (some are conscious and active; others support sexual child abuse through denial, minimizing, and apathy).

Backlash

Not everyone receives the information in *Victims No Longer* or the growing survivor movement with equal enthusiasm. Wherever people try to overcome past hurts, face problems, and improve the human condition, they meet opposition and hostility. There is a strong, often vicious backlash against the survivor movement. Dr. Jon Conte, past president of the American Professional Society on the Abuse of Children (APSAC), in his presidential farewell message warned of the virulence and sophistication of this backlash, urging all helping professionals to stand up to those who deny the problem exists or resist creation of services for victims and survivors ("On the Backlash," *The Advisor,* APSAC, Chicago, April 1989).

In past years, especially since the initial publication of this book, I have encountered the backlash from:

- deniers of the existence (or frequency) of sexual exploitation of children

- those who view abuse recovery as "this year's fad," assuming that "all the fuss" will die down

- those who think males are always perpetrators and never victims

- those who refuse to acknowledge that women as well as men sexually abuse children

- apologists for sexual child abuse and intergenerational sex

- people who minimize or romanticize the harmful effects of sexual child abuse

- profiteers from the sexual exploitation of children—unscrupulous individuals who have created a multimillion-dollar worldwide child sex and pornography industry and powerful "pro-abuse lobby"

- institutions that cover up abuse and protect abusers

- misguided media figures who believe that all issues have two equally valid sides.

To combat the backlash successfully, we must understand its many manifestations:

1 / **Those who fear to deal with the issue at all.** It is too ugly, too frightening, too distasteful a "can of worms," and they don't want to touch it. If pressed, they resort to excuses like "It isn't really that widespread a problem." The response to that bit of nonsense is that sexual child abuse is epidemic, affecting millions of people. Even if only one child were being abused, it would be wrong, hurtful, and cause for outrage. But sexual abuse of children is widespread; for centuries we have accepted a system that fosters harmful attitudes. Now is the time to stop it. Ignoring or denying a problem has never made it go away. The world turned its attention away from Nazism, allowing millions of Jews, Catholics, gays, the mentally ill, Poles, Gypsies, the physically handicapped, political opponents, and others to be slaughtered. More recently, Roman Catholic officials "treated" sexually abusive priests by reassigning them—providing them with fresh victims. *Denying reality condones abuse.* It is everyone's responsibility to eradicate sexual abuse.

2 / **Powerful economic forces working to keep us from putting an end to child abuse.** Multimillion-dollar industries depend upon sexual exploitation of children. One need only look at mass media advertising to see children being portrayed as seductive objects of adult sexual desire. Displaying sexual exploitation of children in this manner condones it. We are allowing ourselves to be titillated by the outrageous and repulsive. In addition to the "acceptable" forms of exploitation, fortunes are made in child pornography (which has been dubbed "kiddy porn" by the media—a cute diminutive that softens the reality in the same way as calling a weapon of mass destruction a "nuke" or an abuser a "perp"). Runaway and "throwaway" children, boys and girls, in increasing numbers, become prostitutes. Rather than seeking to protect these children, society's institutions ignore them, leaving them vulnerable to exploitation by the unscrupulous for personal economic gain. What has been called the "pro-incest lobby"

stands in the way of implementation of child protective legislation. We cannot continue to allow profit at the expense of our children and our collective well-being.

3 / **Individuals and groups that seek to justify gratification of their sexual desires.** There are those who argue that sex with children is acceptable, consensual, or even beneficial. When their activities are criticized, they create smoke screens, crying about freedom of association and individual rights. They fool many well-meaning people into seeing this as a "civil rights" issue, rather than what it is—sexual abuse of power, exploiting children who are unable to advocate for themselves. They join with the economic exploiters of child abuse in railing against the "erotophobia" of a society that denies that "children are sexual beings." They stridently attempt to obscure the distinction between sex and sexual abuse. This perversion of the concept of civil liberties limits protection to the perpetrators, ignoring the rights and needs of children for nonabusive nurturing. Thus pedophilia becomes acceptable and children become sexual playthings. We must not continue to sacrifice children to gratify adult sexual desires.

4 / **People who attempt to justify sexual child abuse by cloaking it with the concepts of privacy and sanctity of the family.** This is a tricky and touchy area. It is within their family that most children are first exposed to cultural, religious, moral, and social values. Because of the inarguable primary importance of family, we developed a social system that supports it with laws, protective agencies, tradition, economic support, cultural mythology, and community feelings.

The family is a quasi-sacred concept, and we are reluctant to interfere with it on any level. Any attempt to do so is greeted with outrage at the infringement of human rights by an unfeeling government, media, or other outside agency. Unfortunately, this well-meaning defense of the right of a family to determine its own beliefs and activities is based on the concept of a healthy family— dedicated to the well-being of all its members. In that instance, while one might disagree with some of the family's values and ideas, they can be respected as evidence of the diversity of a large,

pluralistic society. Interference would constitute a major violation
of the right to freedom of belief. Assistance would take the form
of a system of excellent, affordable child care. But when abuse
enters the picture, the need for protection of children supersedes
the right of parental control. It is a time for direct, decisive action
in the child's best interest. This does not mean that the rights of
the family can be ignored. On the contrary, we must take great
care to determine that the situation is indeed abusive and that we
are not simply facing a disagreement about child-rearing philosophies. We must understand all we can about sexual child abuse and
its effects. We must develop clear, reasonable definitions of abuse
and procedures for dealing with it. But children must be protected
throughout this process.

Champions of "family unity" at all costs are misguided. All
too often, that cost is the welfare of one or more children sacrificed to an image that doesn't reflect reality. A dysfunctional (alcoholic, violent, neglectful, sexually or emotionally abusive) family is
harmful to children. All children have the right to the protection
of a healthy, loving family. Where such a family does not exist, it is
up to society to protect the child from harm. We begin by stop-
ping existing abuse as completely as possible. Wherever feasible,
we should work to help families recover from dysfunctional patterns so they can become whole. When this isn't possible, we must
establish healing environments for the victims—as soon as abuse
is discovered. (Our current foster care and child protective systems are woefully inadequate. Removal of a child from a destructive family without placing him in an environment that is
substantially healthier does not improve his situation. Worse,
removing him instead of the abuser reinforces the child's feeling
that he did something bad and is being punished for it.)

On a larger scale, we must all cooperate in changing some of
our ideas about family, from an authoritarian, patriarchal model to
one based on cooperative encouragement of all its members
toward competence, confidence, and self-esteem. The unity of
such a family doesn't need to be legislated; its harmony is a natural
outgrowth of mutual respect.

How, then, can we accomplish the monumental task of changing our society to one where sexual child abuse is nonexistent? If the idea seems overwhelming, chances are you're feeling that you have to do it all your-self—yesterday. Although the task is large, our resources are extensive. You don't have to do it all, and you aren't alone. If each of us undertakes what we do best, we'll make it. For some, this will be a matter of public activism: lobbying for child protective legislation, picketing, or running for public office. For others, the best course of action will be changing public attitudes through education: speaking and/or writing in class-rooms, the media, and to community, educational, religious, and profes-sional organizations. For all of us, it is a matter of reexamining our ideas, priorities, and behaviors, changing those that need to be changed, and helping those around us to do the same. This could mean resolving to spend more time with children, attending more meetings, talking about abuse and recovery whenever you can, perhaps sharing some of your own experiences, or simply determining to treat all children and adults (includ-ing yourself) with respect.

Yes, changing the world is a tall order, but I believe it can (and must) be done. Just think of how empowering it will be when we accomplish it. If you have any doubt of the importance of this undertaking, take a few minutes to stop, close your eyes, and imagine a world free of child abuse. Picture the results of treating all adults and children with respect and con-sideration. Think how all aspects of society will be affected—family, community, education, religion, business, the military, art and literature, politics, entertainment. Can a world that truly nurtures its children have room for nuclear war, murder, violence, rape, homelessness, poverty, famine, or bigotry? Can we really cherish our children, hoping that they will face the future safely and confidently, while building larger and more frightening weapons of destruction? (Dr. Leslie Fenn, a Boston-area psy-chiatrist who works with survivors, encourages people to recognize the direct link between the way we treat our children and the ever-present threat of nuclear devastation.) Will it be possible for people to starve while food rots in silos? Will we keep poisoning our environment, know-ing that succeeding generations could perish for lack of healthy air and clean water? Will it even be conceivable to keep someone from enjoying a decent life because of race, gender, religion, nationality, sexual orientation, social class, language, physical appearance, age, state of health, or level of intelligence? Obviously, the answer is "No, of course not." If your image of an abuse-free world looks better than the one we have now, the choice is clear. Dedication to learning to love ourselves—to treating ourselves with exquisite respect and care—requires us to join forces to put things right. Making a commitment to world survival, we move to another level of recovery.

Focus

Combating Isolation

One of my clients is a male survivor of a childhood of extreme physical brutality, parental cruelty, and sexual abuse. Through his strength, courage, creativity, and fierce determination, he survived the horrors of his childhood. His dedication to recovery led to long-term sobriety. As an adult, he is intelligent, charming, competent, and physically powerful. Afraid of no one, he is undaunted by physical danger.

He acknowledges that if I were to tell him that wrestling a grizzly bear bare-handed is essential to his recovery, he would leave my office immediately, in search of the nearest grizzly. However, when I suggest that his recovery requires stepping out of his isolation by letting people into his life, his face takes on a "deer caught in the headlights" expression, and he attempts to change the subject. This man is neither a coward nor a weakling. Indeed, everyone who knows him appreciates his courage and physical strength. But trust and emotional vulnerability still feel impossibly threatening. There are good reasons why this is so. It will be a while before he is able to complete this task, but he will accomplish it. Not because I tell him to; because he knows it is necessary.

He will be successful; his courage and determination will see him through. Afterward, he will be truly liberated from the pain of his childhood.

It is certainly possible (although difficult) to confront and ultimately overcome isolation. Following certain guidelines increases the likelihood of your success:

1 / Remember that the pattern of isolation was established early and has been in place a long time. Things won't change overnight. It takes time to recognize and unlearn a long-standing practice; replacing it with healthier behavior takes even longer. Give yourself a break. Try to have reasonable expectations.

2 / Proceed slowly and carefully. Be aware of your emotions throughout the process, feel them, and talk about them with your therapist and other allies. You will notice a change in your feelings as you progress from isolation to inclusion.

3 / There is more to overcoming isolation than breaking silence and ending secrecy, but these are important steps toward this goal. Telling your story, again and again, to people who want to hear it, helps to heal the shame that kept you isolated.

4 / Some manifestations of isolation are subtle. You may discover that certain behaviors that appear to be social are facades that keep you hidden from others (see Focus: Masks and Images, p. 98). The more you step out of isolation, the more you will notice these subtleties. Try not to be discouraged. This is evidence of progress, not a setback.

5 / Not all solitude is isolation. Time spent alone can offer welcome, restorative freedom from life's pressures. Meditation, prayer, reading, writing, dreaming, and hobbies are among many healthy activities that can be practiced in solitude. But the benefits of solitude are not the same as leading a solitary existence. Most humans need time to themselves, but we are essentially social

beings. You can learn to enjoy periods of solitude as part of an integrated social life. It is a matter of balance.

6 / Just as not all solitude is isolation, not all isolation occurs in solitude. It is painful and confusing to be in the company of others and still feel alone. If this happens to you, try to remember that these are just feelings and do not reflect reality. It is the residue of old hurts. You are working your way out of isolation; it will be a while before you are comfortable with your new surroundings. Every social interaction is an opportunity to practice defiance of old abuse-based messages.

7 / There will be times when you feel helpless to change your situation. This is natural, and only a temporary condition. When this happens, remind yourself that you don't have to get it right every time. You don't have to be perfect, only human. Mistakes are acceptable; we can learn from them.

8 / Confrontation (see chapter 18) is a significant means of defying isolation. Whether direct or indirect, physical or psychological, focused on the abuser or the abuse—any form of confrontation indicates that you are no longer going to accept a marginal life.

9 / Isolation can be confused with self-sufficiency. The Hollywood image of the "strong, silent loner" may be romantic, but does he seem to be happy? You can take care of yourself and still maintain a network of friends and allies. In fact, creating a support network is a crucial aspect of self-care.

10 / I have referred to confrontation as a means of ending isolation. Chapter 21 ("Moving On") contains many more examples. When you help another person (or ask for help), join an organization, volunteer for a community project, support a cause you believe in, you are also

performing an act of liberation. This is true whether or not the activity or organization is directly focused on recovery (see chapter 23).

11 / Record each success in your journal, and refer to it when you feel discouraged.

Isolation contributes to making abuse possible, perpetuating it, and inhibiting recovery. Abuse is committed in isolation; recovery takes place in the company of others. There are many forms of isolation, and myriad ways isolation can be confronted and ultimately overcome. Whenever you share your story, join a group, participate in a workshop, attend a party, take a class, have a chat, or even smile at someone, you are healing old wounds. Each time you risk interacting with another person, face-to-face, by phone, letter, or e-mail, you make progress toward ending your isolation. Every bit of social intimacy, however slight, is a victory. And these successes are cumulative, eventually creating a healthy, satisfying, integrated life. Remember your victories. Remind yourself that they are genuine and important. Come out and play. You can do it; you are well on your way.

MOVING ON, HELPING OTHERS

As you move through the various stages of recovery, your feelings about yourself and the world will change. You will feel (and actually be) more in charge of your life. You'll have increased confidence about daily activities and greater energy with which to carry them out. All sorts of new possibilities will be open to you.

For some survivors, this is when they are able to leave the victimization behind and move on with their lives. Although their abusive childhood will never be forgotten, it has been put into perspective. Abuse no longer dominates their every waking moment, draining joy and satisfaction from all their activities. They are able to enjoy a normal, satisfying life—experiencing the full range of pleasure, frustration, joy, sorrow, and upset that comprises a healthy human existence.

For most survivors, there remains one important piece of recovery. It involves engaging in activities that allow positive meaning to emerge from the pain. The essence of this undertaking is using what they learned (in the course of enduring and surviving abuse as well as in recovery) to help other survivors. This type of activity (Dr. Judith Herman refers to it as "altruism") provides the last piece of understanding that many survivors need. Having accomplished it, they are free to go on with their lives.

The exact form of this last activity depends upon the needs, skills, and personality of the individual survivor. What has worked for others might be useful to you, or you may need to come up with your own particular solution. Self-esteem that you regain and develop during recovery enables you to design a method that works for you. The following list includes activities that other survivors found helpful:

1 / **Education.** As you well know, there is not enough reliable information about the sexual abuse of boys and men available to the general public. What exists is often incomplete—or incorrect. Millions of people need to know the facts about sexual child abuse. (Some even *want* to hear the information.) More important, the available information usually concerns the details of abuse, with examples of the ongoing effects. There is not nearly enough about recovery. No one is better able to educate both the public and *mental health professionals* about recovery than someone who has undergone the process. In a word—*you*!

You don't need to be a professional educator; find an outlet that fits your style. If you are comfortable with public speaking, talk at schools, churches, community groups, and other public forums. Talk to parents, children, and/or other survivors. You may be surprised that there are groups of mental health, human service, and medical professionals eager to hear what you have to say. The media may be receptive to your message, and you will find yourself interviewed in newspapers or magazines—or appearing on radio or television public affairs shows. (You are under no obligation to do any of these things, or to do them in any way that isn't right for you. Don't permit yourself to be pressured, bullied, or coerced. That would be a form of revictimization. It would do no one any good.) If you find it easier to work less visibly, write articles, books, or letters to the editor about your experiences. Your writing can be nonfiction or take the form of novels, short stories, plays, or poetry. Express yourself (and spread information) through song, dance, painting, or sculpture.

Don't be stopped by the feeling that nobody would be interested in what you have to say, or that you are too inarticulate or untalented. That's all nonsense, coming from the old misinformation you received about yourself. You are the expert here. No one knows better than you what happened, how it felt, what the effects were—and what you did about it. That's the information that is so helpful to other people. Say it in your own words, at your own pace. Take charge. You will be amazed by how powerful you feel when you stand up to abuse in this way.

2 / **Lobbying and legislation.** Very few states have enacted laws that deal adequately with the realities of child abuse or the needs of adult survivors. In many localities there are groups working to promote legislation that will protect children from sexual abuse and extend or eliminate statutes of limitation on criminal and civil prosecution of perpetrators. Find out what the existing laws in your state are and join (or start) a group to influence legislation in this area. There is tremendous satisfaction in knowing that you had a hand in insuring that our society recognizes and responds adequately to the needs of victims and survivors.

3 / **Advocacy.** Although it is vital that our laws address the needs of survivors, the legal process is often painfully slow. In the meantime, it is important that survivors know what resources are currently available to them and how to make the best use of existing services. A number of citizens' rights organizations advocate for wider dissemination of information and increased support for survivors. Join other survivors in forming a group to pressure government, social service, educational, religious, and other organizations to be more responsive to survivors' needs. A community that is committed to ending the abuse of any of its members improves the quality of life of all its citizens. Your special expertise makes you a valuable part of that process.

4 / **Direct action.** Another form of advocacy is taking direct action to protect someone who is being abused and seeing that she or he receives the right kind of help. This can mean standing up to the abuse of another member of your family; it may involve forcing other family members to face the facts. Or you can work to create a visible, vocal survivor advocacy organization in your community—on the order of rape crisis hotlines, battered women's shelters, and "safe houses." Advocate to make existing agencies take a more active role in abuse and recovery issues, or start an organization whose sole purpose is protection and advocacy for survivors of sexual child abuse. It isn't as intimidating as you might imagine. Take on as much or as little of this task as is right for you. Many large and powerful organizations began with one or two people recognizing a need—and filling it. Maybe it's time for you to do some intimidating of your own—taking a stand that employs your newly recognized power.

5 / **Direct service.** Just as many drug and alcohol counselors are themselves former addicts and alcoholics, some of the most effective counselors and therapists for abuse survivors were sexually abused as children. You can use what you have learned about recovery to help other survivors. Do this as a volunteer (working on a hotline or in a peer counseling setting) or obtain the training required to take a professional role in addressing the needs of survivors. Whether it involves law, medicine, psychotherapy, social work, teaching, politics, the arts, religious or charitable work, there are many ways to add a professional focus to what you learned during recovery. The time you spent in recovery wasn't wasted. *It was not time taken out of your life—it has been (and continues to be) an important part of your life.* All thinking people, in one way or another, must undertake a journey of self-discovery. Don't devalue your process; make use of it. You have developed an important body of knowledge and experience. It is yours to employ in the ways that best serve you. Doing so provides a positive example for other survivors, while consolidating the gains you have made. Everyone wins.

6 / **Combined activities.** Any of the foregoing activities can be undertaken in combination. Some newsletters and Web sites (see "Other Resources," p. 357) offer articles, poetry, drawings, and personal statements by survivors as well as information about resources, research, legislation, and other matters of concern. Your work can be as general or specific as you wish. Work alone or with others, formally or informally. Devote as much or as little time to it as is right for you. Fit into existing structures or create your own. You can always change the focus of your activity to meet your needs. Figuring out how to take care of yourself while you help others is a crucial bit of learning. Remember, doing what is truly best for you is also in the best interest of those around you.

A word of caution about this aspect of recovery: *It doesn't work if you attempt it prematurely.* Many survivors rush to help others before they have done enough work on their own recovery. They do it for a number of reasons. They may be avoiding the pain of dealing with their own abuse. If that is their motivation, then it isn't part of moving on—helping others has become another form of distraction. The survivor is attempting to provide what he needs for himself—with little chance of getting it back. It continues a caretaking pattern that is deeply ingrained in his self-image. He feels he doesn't deserve attention—and the only justification for his existence is what he can do for others. This is a reflection of how abuse damaged his self-esteem. It should not be respected. If you recognize that tendency in yourself, do your best to resist it. There will be plenty of time to assist others in their recovery, once you have taken care of your own. Taking time to build a solid foundation for yourself will allow you to be far more effective in helping other survivors. Resist feelings of urgency. Not only is there no need to hurry this process, it doesn't work. Furthermore, there is no requirement that you undertake this type of altruism at all. It is not obligatory, and it only works well when it is an outgrowth of your own path of recovery. Be patient with yourself. You will be providing other survivors (and the world) with a healthy example of positive growth. Instead of hiding or running, you are "moving on" with your life, helping others as you help yourself.

Part Five

OTHER PEOPLE, OTHER RESOURCES

22

FOR (AND ABOUT) PARTNERS, FAMILY, AND FRIENDS

This chapter is for people in relationships with men who experienced sexual child abuse. I have two reasons for including it in a book that is directed to male survivors. First, it recognizes that there is virtually no information available for spouses, partners, lovers, family, friends—and counselors—of male survivors. I hope to provide helpful information for readers who are in caring relationships with male survivors of sexual child abuse. (See Books, Articles, and Pamphlets, p. 393, for recent books for allies.)

This chapter will examine issues faced by people who care about men in recovery. It offers perspective on the possibilities and limitations of supportive relationships. Unfortunately, one chapter cannot deal adequately with so complex a situation. I hope it will be a starting point of an enormous outpouring of information for (and by) people who are involved with male survivors. In addition to the paucity of information, there is a tremendous lack of services for partners and friends of survivors. It is hard enough to find adequate services for male survivors—there is virtually nothing available for those who are involved with them.

I also hope this chapter will encourage those who care about male survivors—professionally and personally—to think about supporting the supporters. There is great need for literature, workshops, and support groups for partners and friends of survivors. (I'll use the term "friend" generically, to include spouse, lover, significant other, as well as nonromantic involvement.) Al-Anon evolved in response to the needs of people who are involved with alcoholics. In the same way, we must help people who are experiencing the secondary effects of sexual child abuse—friends and partners of survivors.

Another reason for including this chapter is that it is important for the male survivor to understand that he is not the only person affected by the abuse—and the recovery process. I want the survivor to gain perspective on how his feelings and behavior may be perceived by those around him. This chapter suggests what a survivor can and can't realistically expect from people who care about him. It may allow him to give up unrealistic, "frozen" needs and let in the genuine acceptance and love available to him. His partner and friends have a stake in his recovery, and they undergo their own changes in accommodation to his. Realizing that this is so enables the survivor to see recovery as a cooperative, interactive process—one that involves allies helping to bring about changes that benefit everyone involved.

As the consequences of abuse affect the male survivor, they influence the lives of everyone with whom he interacts. The closer and more intimate the relationship, the more deeply felt are the effects. This is true whether or not the friend is aware that the abuse took place. We know that abuse affects the life of a survivor whether or not he has clear memories of the incident(s). It causes him to play out aspects of his childhood unconsciously in his adult relationships. In the same way, his friends may not be aware of the cause of his behavior, but they experience the results on a daily basis. Just as it is difficult for a survivor to maintain emotional (and physical) intimacy in relationships, it isn't easy to sustain a relationship with a survivor.

Even if the friend has worked out a relatively comfortable mode of interaction, when the survivor begins his recovery all bets are off. Intense, powerful, and confusing feelings are stirred up. As the survivor questions every aspect of his life, his relationships cannot fail to feel the pressure. In fact, his interactions with those closest to him are likely to mirror the changes that he is going through; relationships will undergo strain and hard times. In addition to the elation that comes with progress and change, there will be times of great emotional upheaval, confusion, frustration, and misunderstanding. It's quite a ride, and not every relationship is up to it. Despite all the caring and good intentions in the world, recovery is a risky time for relationships. The chance of surviving this process with friendships intact (though perhaps bloodied) increases if both parties have an idea of what they are getting into.

Focus

If You Suspect Abuse

Even if the survivor hasn't told you anything, you suspect that he was abused as a child. He may not have shared the information because of fears of not being believed, being scorned or ridiculed, or seen as undesirable or unmanly. Maybe he hasn't accepted it as abuse, or admitted it to himself. If you suspect that your friend is a survivor, you can raise the subject of sexual abuse on a general level, showing your openness to talking about it; let him know that you are willing to listen to anything he wants to share with you, but you will wait until he is ready for disclosure. Don't be impatient or overly protective. Avoid "leaping into action." Remember that we are talking about his recovery, not yours. Respect his pace. You can't—nor should you—do it for him.

If you know (or have suspicions) that child abuse is currently taking place, be sure to do everything you can to see that it is stopped. You don't have to wait until you have concrete evidence—there isn't enough time. The hurts compound daily. If you have no direct control over the situation, report it to the proper authorities. In most localities child protective/social service agencies will investigate even anonymous reports of sexual child abuse. Insist that appropriate action be taken. Threaten public exposure if necessary. It is important to your friend, to you, and to the world that we create a society where sexual abuse of a child is literally unthinkable. This is everyone's responsibility. Most survivors have known nonprotective adults who ignored abuse or did nothing to interfere with it. They conclude that no one cares—that there is no safety or protection anywhere in the world. Imagine the difference it would have made to their lives if even one adult had believed them and stood up to the abuse.

Among the participants at a workshop for male and female survivors were a sister and brother. She had been sexually abused by their father. Her brother was the person who stood up to the perpetrator and put a stop to the abuse. He came to the workshop to continue to support his sister in her healing. In the process, he was working toward his own recovery from the effects of having been raised in a dysfunctional family. His presence at the workshop was important for everyone there. It was deeply moving for all of us to see visible evidence of someone standing up to abuse. It contradicted feelings of isolation and lack of safety in the world. In the brother's own words, "I'm not such a wonderful person. . . . It had to be done and I did it." To the rest of us, he is a Hero.

It is always the right time to stand up to abuse. We all need to be heroes.

Note to the Survivor: It is important to be as clear as you can in letting people in your life know what is going on. They cannot read your mind. Even if they see that something is up, they can only guess at the complexity of what you're going through. The more fully you share with them, the better they will understand how to support you in a useful way. If you learn to state your needs specifically, you have a better chance of having them met. At the same time, recognize that this recovery process is yours. Your expectations and demands must be realistic. As close and caring as the relationships are, you are separate people. They can't be expected to feel what you are feeling. They have lives of their own, and can't give them up to facilitate your recovery. The more realistic your expectations are of the people who care about you, the less you will feel abandoned when they cannot be there for you all the time.

Weather forecasting is an inexact science. We know that hurricanes cause upheaval, but it is impossible to predict the extent of the devastation. Some storms produce high winds and driving rain. Others cause flooding and damage to life and property. Still others pass harmlessly offshore, dissipating their energies virtually unnoticed. In the same way, we cannot accurately anticipate the exact course of anyone's recovery. Each personality is unique. As a survivor's life experiences are his alone, his recovery will follow a path that differs from anyone else's. But, whatever its form, a hurricane is still a hurricane. There are things we know about the nature of this phenomenon. As with hurricanes—although you cannot know exactly what to expect of any individual recovery process—there are some manifestations for which you can prepare. If they don't occur, you are no worse off. If they do, your preparations will help you ride out the storm.

The fact that you are in a caring relationship with a male survivor means that you have already accomplished something significant. If you read the preceding chapters of this book, you know that trust is an overriding issue for any survivor of abuse. To the extent that you have managed to establish a level of trust with him, you have created a degree of safety. You may be the first (and only) person the survivor feels he can trust. If this is true, you have probably already experienced some negative aspects of the situation. Since the abuse involved violation of a position of trust, the fact that he trusts you brings up his fear of further abuse. The times you are closest and most loving (physically or emotionally) are likely to be the most difficult for the survivor. On the other hand, if he accepts that you are trustworthy and truly care about him, he is likely to view you as his "only" chance for a caring relationship, and cling tightly to you. You feel smothered, crowded, and overwhelmed. There may be jealous demands on your time and energy. He may want you to join him in withdrawing from the rest of society, creating your own "safe" and isolated little world. If this is the case, demands on you increase until they occupy every moment. Any attention to your own needs—or interest in other people—is seen as abandonment. You may be accused of not caring enough, or even of behaving abusively.

If you find that you enjoy this type of jealous, demanding relationship, it may be because it speaks to a frozen childhood need of your own. Healthy relationships exist in the open; healthy lives require variety and interaction. No one can (or should be expected to) meet all of another person's needs. If you are involved in a relationship that is draining you of all energy, free time, and independence, you are well advised to think about what you are getting out of it. This is a good time to explore therapy or counseling for yourself. There are several good books on codependency in relationships. Reading them may help you to understand your situation. Other resources (whether or not you were raised in an alcoholic family) are Al-Anon, ACOA, or CoDA meetings (see "Other Twelve-Step Programs," p. 384). These programs teach people how to detach themselves from the unhealthy aspects of caretaking relationships.

Co-dependent relationships are ultimately unhealthy because they inhibit the growth of both parties. People in healthy relationships respect each other's individuality and support each other from a position of self-respect. Only by beginning with the premise that *you deserve and demand to be treated with respect* can you hope to help someone else achieve the same goal. What is true for the survivor is also true for you: *Meeting your real needs is always in the best interest of those who care about you.* Resist becoming a caretaker. It isn't good for him or for you. By taking charge of your own life (no matter how selfish it feels), you are providing a model of recovery for your friend. If the relationship survives the changes, it will be stronger and healthier. So will both of you.

As difficult as it is to sustain a relationship when the ability to trust has been weakened, many survivors manage to engage in long-lasting friend-ships, marriages, and other intimate relationships. Some of these are strong and loving; others are needy and huddling, immature and shallow, or lonely and isolated; still others depend on actually or symbolically reliving the abuse. (**Note:** It is never helpful to allow yourself to be abused in a rela-tionship, no matter what the rationale. If you cannot stop the abuse your-self, leave. Furthermore, it is never healthy to abuse another person, no matter how great the provocation. Anyone who invites abuse is reliving past hurts; be careful not to reinforce this behavior.)

Whatever the dynamics of these relationships, they can remain stable over relatively long periods as long as there is no serious threat to the mutually accepted (often unstated) rules. But a stable relationship is not necessarily a healthy one. There are dysfunctional and abusive relation-ships that endure for many years. Each party to the relationship knows his or her role and plays it well. There is a certain comfort in knowing that there will be no surprises. But, in order to last, these associations must remain stagnant. Any growth or positive change by either partner threatens the delicate balance that keeps the union intact.

When the survivor begins to work actively on his recovery, all the rules are up for reevaluation. Ripples are felt in every corner of his life. As his insights, feelings, and behaviors change, it is inevitable that all his relationships need to adjust to the transition. You may find that the man you thought you knew so well is behaving like a total stranger. Familiar traits and actions will alter focus. Feelings and reactions are magnified and intensified. There are times when you feel confused or lonely. This is a difficult period, but it is a necessary time of healing. When things are the roughest, try to remember that it won't last forever. *Recovery is a time of crisis; the crisis is temporary.* But be prepared. As I said to survivors in another part of this book, it will feel worse before it gets better. This is equally true for those around them. You are under no obligation to stick it out through the hard times. Staying or leaving is your choice. Not all relationships can stand the strain of the recovery process. Those that manage it are irrevocably altered. We don't know what the precise outcome will be, only that it will be healthier (though not necessarily much easier). It will therefore have to be reassessed as a brand-new relationship, and both partners will have to decide whether it makes sense to continue. If you choose to be there through the recovery process, there will be rewards—the real pleasures of forging a mutually nourishing relationship with another adult. There will still be hard times, but the daily interactions will no longer be in service to past abuses. There is room for joy and celebration.

As much as I'd like to prepare you for all that will happen, it is sure to be a surprise when the changes begin. I can only give you notice of some reactions that you might encounter:

1 / **Withdrawal.** Overwhelmed by the enormity of his feelings, the survivor retreats physically or emotionally. He engages in long periods of silence, is generally uncommunicative, or requires more time alone. At these times he might disappear for long periods or be uninterested in his usual pursuits. When this happens, friends of the survivor feel shut out or rejected. You feel confused and resentful. It is very isolating to have someone close to you "check out." In the absence of communication it is hard to know what is going on, whether you had anything to do with it, and if there is anything you can do to help. It's easy to jump to the worst conclusions. But there are many possible explanations for the withdrawal.

The survivor is experiencing a confusing welter of emotions. He may need time and space to sort them out. He may not know what to say to anyone. He might be attempting to protect you from his pain or to avoid letting his angry feelings explode in your direction. He may also be having some negative thoughts and feelings about you that he doesn't want to express until he can make sense of them. He could be reacting to feelings of hopelessness and self-doubt that have nothing to do with you.

Unless you think that there is danger that he will harm himself (or others), the best course of action is to do little or nothing. Reassure him that you care about him, and will listen if he wants to talk—and then allow him the time and space he needs. You can always do more later if necessary. For now, try to resist intrusion into his solitude by caretaking or expressing resentment at being excluded. It is likely that what is going on inside him has little to do with you. Even if it does, nagging him about it will shut him down even further. He may be working through these issues elsewhere—in individual therapy or a recovery group. If so, it is an appropriate way to deal with them. It is to your advantage to support his process. An active, welcoming patience can pay dividends for both of you. As he opens communication in therapy and group, your communication improves as well. In the meantime, get similar support for yourself—whether in therapy, individual counseling, or participation in a support group. Problems in relationships are rarely one-sided. It will be helpful for you and your friend to discover your part in the unhealthy aspects of the interaction.

2 / **Mood swings.** The course of recovery is never smooth and steady. There are times of rapid, visible progress, periods of apparent inactivity, and occasional lapses into old patterns of behavior and feelings of hopelessness. These shifts of focus evoke powerful emotional reactions. The survivor can be flying high one day, full of confidence in his progress, only to sink into despair the next. A moment's tenderness can quickly explode into anger. Needless to say, these mood swings are difficult and confusing to friends of the survivor. This is particularly true if you have taken on the caretaking role of protecting him from "bad" feelings. Difficult as it may be, you must train yourself to step out of the caretaking role.

The survivor's feelings are his. You did not cause them, nor are you responsible for alleviating them. Furthermore, they are necessary to healing. As hard as it is to see someone you care about in pain, you must allow him room for having—and getting through—his feelings. Celebrate the good times with him. Be there for the hard times if you can (and if you are allowed to), but recognize that he must do his own recovery work. Your support will help ease his recovery.

3 / **Crying jags.** You may find that your survivor friend, once so completely in control of his emotions, seems to be crying all the time. Don't be dismayed. Welcome and celebrate his tears when they come. This is an important facet of the process—"Tears are the lubricant that allows recovery to move forward." If he cries in your presence, try not to be embarrassed or distract him. Don't try to "make him feel better"; crying itself will accomplish that. You can occasionally share an encouraging word or two, but stop talking if it seems to distract him from the emotions. You will see that, with safety and encouragement, he will cry as long as he needs to. Afterward, he will be calmer, clearheaded, and a little tired. Both of you will be less worried that crying indicates being "out of control."

4 / **Irrational anger.** As the survivor begins to accept the unfairness of what was done to him, feelings of anger surface. Expression of anger may be an unfamiliar experience for him. He may come from a family where any angry word or feeling inevitably led to physical violence or other abuse. If this is the case, he will have learned to keep his emotions—particularly angry feelings—rigidly in check. Expressing anger can be terrifying for him and those around him. The tiniest angry display feels like he is raging out of control. Inexperienced in expressing anger, he is likely to vent it inappropriately. The first target for his angry feelings may be the person he feels safest with—you. This isn't a comfortable position in which to find yourself. The slightest area of disagreement can trigger an excessively angry response, and you end up feeling like a target. There doesn't seem to be anything that you can say or do that will prevent these outbursts. This is a tricky situation to nego-

tiate. Remember that if the angry response is completely out of proportion to what is going on at the moment, it probably has little to do with the present situation. Something in the present is restimulating old memories and feelings. The safety of the current situation allows these feelings to be expressed.

This knowledge can help you understand what is going on, but it doesn't do much to help you feel good when someone you care about is yelling at you. Nor should you accept the situation passively. Verbal abuse doesn't benefit anyone. It is perfectly acceptable to validate someone's right to feel angry *without accepting that you have caused his anger.* You never have to be the target of abusive behavior. (It should go without saying that you never need to expose yourself to violence or other physical harm. If you even suspect that an encounter might become violent, leave the situation immediately. You can always straighten it out later.) Assure your friend that you understand that he is angry. Let him know that if the anger has anything to do with something you have done, you are willing to work it out with him. But tell him that if he continues to rail at you, you will leave until he is able to discuss it with you more calmly. Then, if he continues, do just that.

When someone is in the midst of an angry outburst, he will not be amenable to reason, nor will yelling back at him solve anything. Neither of you is really hearing what the other is saying—you're too busy feeling attacked. Later, during a calmer time, the two of you (perhaps with a third party present) can discuss what was going on. Let him know that you care about him but are not willing to allow yourself to be the target of misdirected anger. Ask him for suggestions about how you can respond in a helpful manner without becoming a target. By not accepting anger that doesn't belong to you, you are helping your friend focus it where it belongs. He then learns to use his anger to facilitate his recovery. In this way, anger is transformed from weak, frightened, defensive posturing to the power of righteous indignation—standing up to the abuse.

5 / **Blaming.** Similar to irrational anger is the tendency to cast blame. When the survivor accepts that he was not to blame for what was

done to him—and that he is not to blame for everything that is wrong with the world—he is apt to search for who is. He hasn't been exposed to the idea that not everything that happens is somebody's fault. It is difficult to understand the concept of responsibility without blame. He feels that if it isn't his fault, it must be yours. You find yourself in a situation where you can't seem to do anything right. The correct response to irrational blame is the same as to irrational anger. Don't accept it if it isn't yours. Let your friend know (at the time, if he can hear it; later, if he can't) that you understand that he is upset. Enlist his aid in thinking about the situation. Assure him of your good intentions to work with him to solve whatever problem exists, *without needing to find a villain.* In doing this you are both refusing to fall victim to further effects of the abuse, while allowing any blame to be placed where it belongs.

6 / **Unreasonable demands.** It isn't easy to say no to someone you care about. It becomes even more difficult when the person is obviously having a hard time. You want to step in and make it all better. You want to solve the problems, salve the wounds, relieve the pain and resolve the confusion. As the survivor puts increasing attention and effort into recovery, he may also place greater demands on the time and energy of those around him. If this is allowed to continue unchecked, it can fill all the available space, leaving you little room to lead your own life. Even though you might want to, you can't do it all for him. This is *his* recovery process and *he* has to go through it. The most helpful thing you can do is to decide on how much time is reasonable to offer your friend, and limit yourself to that. Don't buy into protestations that you are abandoning him. This is not selfish or uncaring behavior. It is important that you reserve what you need to keep your own life on an even keel. If you burn yourself out, you are of no use to your friend or yourself. Continue to reassure your friend about the importance of his recovery, and that you are in full support of it, but don't be put upon. He doesn't need a model of martyrdom or self-sacrifice. The best image to offer him is of someone who cares for others without giving up looking after her- or himself. This image of self-respect can only help both of you.

7 / **Sexual behavior.** Since the abuse was acted out sexually, recovery will involve feelings about sex and intimacy. If your relationship with the survivor has a sexual component (or even if it doesn't), expect to encounter difficulties in this area. Among his unreasonable demands may be insistence on more frequent sexual activity than you find comfortable. You may feel pressured to engage in sexual practices that are not acceptable to you. On the other hand, the survivor may lose interest in any form of closeness or touching, including sexual intimacies. You may even find yourself in the position of being with someone who wants sex one minute and is repulsed by the thought of it the next. He may demand sex, yet recoil from being touched. He may be unable to achieve an erection, or seem to be sexually aroused all the time.

This is certainly a confusing situation. The reason you're having such a hard time making sense out of it is that it isn't logical. It is pure feeling, reacting to powerful changes in the survivor's perception of his experience. He is trying to sort out the meanings of abuse, sex, love, caring, and intimacy. He is testing the world and trying to learn about reasonable, nonabusive boundaries between people. The most helpful thing you can do in this instance is be scrupulous about maintaining your own boundaries.

Sexual testing may occur whether or not your relationship was sexual previously. Whether you are friend, therapist, or family member, it is possible that you will be dealing with it. He may have learned that the way to get close to someone is to relate sexually, and this behavior reappears during times of crisis. This is not the time to initiate a sexual relationship. He is too vulnerable. You would both be allowing yourselves to be seduced by an old pattern of distress. Yielding to a sexual pull at this point will severely damage the trust and intimacy you have established.

If you are already sexually involved, do nothing that doesn't make sense to you. Remember that the essence of abuse is taking sexual advantage of a trusting relationship. The survivor needs to know that it is all right to say no and have that refusal respected. At the same time, difficult as it is, you must respect the survivor's need to refrain from sexual activity. Don't interpret it as evidence of lack of love or caring. It probably has nothing to do with you.

He is asserting his right not to be sexual unless it is right for him. If both of you understand and accept this basic right to control over your bodies, it will ultimately lead to more fulfilling intimacies, sexual and otherwise.

8 / **Regression.** As memories of childhood return, they can be accompanied by a tendency to behave in a juvenile (or infantile) manner. Sometimes this takes the form of healthy playfulness. At other times, the survivor may get unusually clingy, needy, silly, whiny, self-centered, inarticulate, incompetent, irresponsible, or childish. He may resort to comforts (or obsessions, compulsions, and addictions) he employed when the abuse was taking place. There's really nothing that you need to do about these regressive behaviors (some may even be enjoyable) unless they are actually dangerous. As people used to say about you when you were a child, "This is just a stage he is going through." In this case it isn't a flippant comment. Abuse robbed the survivor of a normal childhood. Regression may be an attempt to reclaim some portion of what was lost. It is okay to seek comfort from a teddy bear, a pet, or a newly discovered capacity for silliness. You, as a trusted friend, provide a safe environment for regressive behavior.

9 / **Physical abuse.** Genuine recovery *never* requires the survivor to behave abusively or be abused further. Nothing positive is ever gained by allowing yourself to be the victim of physical abuse. Neither is abusing a survivor (or any other person) ever helpful in any way. If feelings of anger and resentment require a release, it is okay to express them by hitting a punching bag with a baseball bat, pounding a pillow, or screaming into a friend's shoulder (it effectively muffles the sound so that neighbors don't call the police). You can engage in wild revenge fantasies with the survivor, sharing what you would like to do to the perpetrator. He can beat up a doll or other representation of the abuser. He can buy a cheap set of dishes and smash them. (Wear goggles and gloves so you won't be hurt.) But anger must be focused in the right direction—toward the hurts of the past. It is not helpful to create another victim. You are not a perpetrator; don't let yourself be treated as one. It is unlikely that someone who was not abusive

in the past will suddenly become brutal, but if he does, get protection. If you feel physically threatened or even intimidated, leave immediately. Discuss it later when things are calmer. Make it clear that people who love each other do not hurt each other. People who have a healthy level of self-respect don't permit themselves to be harmed. Any attempt at physical violence should be seen for what it is—capitulation to the original abusive behavior. Protecting yourself from harm is consistent with recovery. If your friend becomes violent or threatening (or suggests that you abuse him), let him know that you care about him (and yourself) enough to reject the abuse.

10 / **Resentment.** As the survivor becomes aware of what he lost to the abuse—as he accepts that he deserved (and deserves) better treatment—he may feel and express resentment. Resentment may be general, focused on lost time and opportunities. He may resent the loss of childhood, or the time, money, and anguish spent on recovery. These are understandable sentiments, and it is fairly easy to empathize. Empathy is more difficult when the resentment is focused on a specific person (you) because you weren't subjected to the same kind of pain: "It was easy for you, your father didn't . . ." It isn't helpful to argue that you didn't have it so good, or that your having been abused wouldn't have made his life any better. It will be easier on you if you see this expression of resentment for what it is—longing for a normal life. It really has nothing to do with you. Ignore the direction of the attack and respond to the underlying message. *It wasn't fair. It never should have happened. You have a right to feel resentful.* Don't waste time taking on blame or responsibility that isn't yours. Validate his feelings and move on.

11 / **Confusion and preoccupation.** Putting the past into perspective and establishing strategies for the present and future require a tremendous outlay of thought and feeling. Recovery is the central focus of the survivor's energy and the task can seem all-encompassing. This means that he has less attention for other matters, and may appear bewildered and remote. Even a normally well organized, efficient individual can become "spacy" and careless. You might have to speak to him a couple of times before he

hears you. Routine chores are left undone, bills unpaid and phone messages unanswered. Try not to get too upset about this, even if you have to take up some of the slack for a time. This state of mind is usually temporary, lessening as recovery is incorporated into the survivor's life. If this situation is intolerable to you, insist that he pull himself together enough to carry his load—but don't be surprised if he is unable to comply fully. He isn't doing this to upset you. If you have the patience to ride out this storm, he will eventually return to a normal level of responsiveness and responsibility.

12 / **Fear.** As the powerful feelings generated by past hurts are dealt with openly in the present, the survivor will experience frightening emotions. Fear may intimidate him to the extent that he will avoid even people and activities he normally enjoys. This state is also temporary, and should resolve itself once the most difficult part of this process is past. While it is going on, validate the survivor's feelings, reassure him that what was done to him was, indeed, frightening. Offer to sit with him or hold him gently while he shakes, shivers, and/or sobs the fear away. If the avoidance continues for a long time, you might suggest that you will accompany him in visiting some friends or engaging in a pleasurable activity that isn't too threatening. This can provide a healthy refocusing of attention away from pain and fear. Although recovery is a long-term, ongoing process, it doesn't have to occupy his every waking moment. Relaxation restores energy. Laughter is healing. If he is unwilling to participate in these excursions, go without him. Don't become a prisoner of someone else's fear; avoid burnout yourself. You will be a better, more effective ally if you pay attention to your own needs.

13 / **Mistrust.** The survivor in recovery is actively questioning all his previous assumptions. Recognizing that much of what he learned was misinformation and outright lies, he is reevaluating his entire world. He must learn (perhaps for the first time) who and what can be trusted. It is hard to be mistrusted by someone you care about. If the survivor indicates that he doesn't trust you, try not to personalize it. Most likely it is a statement about himself ("I have trouble trusting people") and has very little to do with you. He is

relearning to trust and the first step is recognition that he doesn't trust people. That he can tell you about it is evidence that he feels relatively safe with you. If you are certain that you are a trustworthy friend, you needn't be upset by the survivor's trust difficulties. In time, as recovery continues, his trust of you will deepen.

14 / **Inconsistency of response.** Just as a survivor experiences mood swings, the powerful changes he is going through can translate into unpredictable behavior. Whereas you once knew the range of responses to expect from him, it now seems that nothing is guaranteed. You are left feeling confused, bewildered, and abandoned. Is this the same man you knew and cared about? These rapid, unpredictable changes of behavior are reactions to confusing internal dynamics. Don't be alarmed. In time, things will become more stable and consistent. In the meantime, you can explore the inconsistencies with the survivor. Avoid taking a critical or censuring tone; seek to open communication with your friend to understand what is going on.

The early stages of active recovery are highly intense, trying times. Unusual strains are put on relationships. You may experience all, some, or none of the aforementioned responses. In any case, the configuration will be unique to your relationship. The only reassurance I can offer is that *it does get easier.* You won't be riding the whirlwind forever, and the rewards of recovery are great. In the meantime, keep remembering that you are not the perpetrator, and it does no good to allow yourself to be a target of hostility, ill will, or abuse. Be clear about that. Be alert to any tendency on your part to engage in *survivor's guilt.* (The term "survivor's guilt" most commonly refers to a phenomenon that was identified among combat veterans of the U.S. armed forces in Vietnam. Upon returning to their homeland, they found themselves unable to explain why they had survived the war while their buddies had died. The inexplicable unfairness of their situation produced a reaction of self-blame for not having been able to save their friends, and shame at having survived. This torment is a common component of the form of post-traumatic stress disorder known as *Post-Vietnam Syndrome.*)

You were not to blame for the boyhood abuse of your friend. You were not there and could have done nothing to stop it. Don't let misguided guilt feelings freeze you into helplessness. Not having been abused as a child is nothing to be ashamed of. In fact, because the hurts you experienced were different than his, you may be in a better position to provide him with support, encouragement, perspective, and alternatives to dysfunctional relationships. (See chapter 11 for a discussion of relationships where both partners are survivors.) Don't try to join him in his pain—doing that would create two victims. Instead, provide him with a picture of life beyond abuse. Insist on your right to respectful treatment as you provide a healthy model of self-respect. Trust your caring and include yourself under its umbrella. Good luck.

Frank's Statement

Frank's statement relates some of the supports and resources he discovered and developed during his journey of recovery. He is thirty-four years old.

Since I learned to read I have loved fantasy and science fiction literature. I could escape into a character, travel in strange worlds, find truth, justice, life, and love. I think I understand why now.

Until two years ago I denied my family had any serious problems. When Nancy, the woman I love, started going to Al-Anon adult child meetings, she told me about the program. I was amazed at what it was doing for her and for our relationship. I read the literature, thought about my father's drinking, and called some relatives to check memories. I figured out that my father had a drinking problem. In the next couple of months it became clear to me that while I did not even drink, I had a problem. My parents and I live five hundred miles apart. We interacted only a few times a year. In spite of this I had a large and constant problem in my life, a mark left from my childhood. This was a new way of thinking for me.

I went to my first Twelve-Step meeting. The speaker talked about how he had become very sick over his wife's drinking. I clung to my chair as he described their relationship and his life. It fit like a glove. It was not that either of us drank. We had an alcoholic relationship. What other type of relationship could we have learned in our families? We tried to change, regulate, and control each other instead of ourselves. We did not trust. We avoided intimacy. Seeing this hurt so much I thought my heart would break and at the same time it felt like the relief of having a splinter pulled.

My life took on a new character. I found myself quite magically dealing with one appropriate issue after another. An issue would start with pain and confusion and resolve into just what I needed to learn next. I was being given what I needed to learn, helped step by step toward health. The first Al-Anon meeting I went to is a good example of this. At that meeting I first admitted to myself that the drinking in my family of origin had been very harmful to me. Looking back on it, I can see that I worked up to the moment of insight at the meeting by gathering and puzzling over information about my family and odd bits of my life. Then at the meeting while hearing the man's story, the pieces came together in an extremely painful moment. It was very hard to admit what I saw now in myself. After the realization there was a readjustment period, during which my new understandings made changes in a surprising number of places in my life. It was wonderful to make sense of things that never did before.

I was surprised to find this process repeat itself again and again. The next thing I had to admit to myself was that the driving force behind my wanting to save the world came from these very problems in my own family and myself that I would not heal or even admit. I had used a sense of mission to hide my own need. My own pain had driven me to more and more frantic acts of trying to help others. After years of "sacrificing myself" at home and at work, admitting that was a tough pill to swallow.

Now I admitted I had pain. Now I would simply try to see what was going on when I hurt; before, I tried to hide it. I had hidden my feelings from even myself for most of my life. Each admission seemed worse than the last. I had to admit that I was a people pleaser and that I had a terrible self-image. With each tearful victory came wonderful insights. As I adjusted to my new understanding, I would make wonderful gains in areas like self-confidence, fear of people, and embarrassment about memories from my childhood. I could know with certainty things about my life I did not understand before. I found myself becoming much better at acting on my feelings and integrating them into my decisions and plans. I could know whether I liked someone or not. Before, I would have tried to reason out whether I should like them or not.

I did not discover these issues in a book or from other people. These issues rose inside me out of my own pain. I found that this is the journey of my life. The one I had looked for in fantasy. I have a life and it is mine. I know what it means to me and why. It is exciting. I am going places. It means something in the sweep of history if the abuse and obsession in my family that have been passed on for so many generations stops here with this generation. That goal has more of what is real in it than the goal I had before of trying to feed the hungry and clothe the poor. Not because one goal is better than the other, but because one is the task that is in front of me now. I truly want my freedom. When I did not know myself, I did not know I was not free. My working for someone else's benefit, when I was in terrible need and could not admit it, was denying myself and just acting out. This may explain why my efforts worked out the way they did. I did not achieve the goals I stated, and in fact, when I look back over my actions, I can see they were quite confused and erratic. I am freer now. I am able to understand so many feelings for the first time—like in a fairy tale when a magic door opens and a new world and adventures unfold, allowing the character to grow and learn. My life became like that for me. Instead of hiding my confusion and raging emotions inside and trying to fix others, I am feeling what it is like to be me and I am trying to help myself.

I have enjoyed a great deepening in my ability to be close with people. I learned to see more in other people as I became friends with my own pain. Nancy and I were able to marry. When I look on the communication I had then, it seems so little and shallow compared to now. Making the room in my life to be close with people has had many parts. Finding my feelings is one of them. Some others are: Admitting my family of origin was not there for me allowed me the space and the reason to let others in. Admitting that what had passed for love and closeness before in my life was not adequate allowed me to look for something else. Admitting I needed understanding allowed me to look for it. Being able to understand someone else's story and comment on it draws me into people's lives. I still have trouble organizing my time, so how I spend it reflects what is most important to me. While I no longer work sixty hours a week, I do not yet plan in regular, ongoing time with friends, but see them catch as catch can. I think what is in front of me now has a lot to do with how I organize my time. I need to admit how hard it is for me to schedule what I really choose in a clear plan without becoming overcome with the fear of disappointment or being exposed as a failure. I have a terror of finding out just how much of the time I am involved in obsessive behavior and how often I cannot control. That keeps me from clear planning.

If you work hard on yourself and give yourself a safe space with relaxed time to really look at yourself, the rewards are amazing. On my honeymoon I had such a space. My wife and I had this very special time to look at ourselves, so we read together, as was by now our habit, literature to help us explore ourselves. While reading *On the Way to the Wedding* by Linda Leonard, I came across a part about a woman who had been deeply hurt by the incest between her father and her sister. I had known about the incest between my father and my sister before I moved out of my parents' house. In spite of this, I had never allowed myself to feel what it was like to have my sister abused by my father sexually and in so many other ways. For the first time I named as pain this upswelling of feelings I felt every time I tried to have sex. I saw why I usually came so soon, running from intimacy I was trying to find. The original examples of what maleness was to me were: drunkenness, violence, and sexual abuse. Every time I made love I had to face feeling myself the abuser and the abused. Every time I tried to be intimate, a pain was triggered. I wept for my sister and myself. As I looked at my pain to see what it would tell me, I found something hard to admit to. The first memories I had were only the physical pain and from that an intuition of what happened. Someone had raped me as a child and I knew who, but was so afraid of it my throat closed so I could not speak it. My father.

That was in the beginning of the summer. The weight of what I worked on was heavy. When I was dealing with the pain of being raised in an alcoholic household with the help of Al-Anon, things had moved faster. I would come to a new realization sometimes by having to sink into pain for an hour or two. Afterward I would bounce back deeper and stronger. With incest I would sink into the pain and keep sinking for hours, crying and thrashing till I sought relief in an activity like eating or computer games. These quickly became obsessive. I can remember playing a computer game all night. As the sun came up, tears ran down my cheeks from staring at the screen for so many hours. I then left for work. Going to sleep is particularly hard for me when I am avoiding the pain I am in. Before the incest surfaced, when I was dealing with alcoholic family issues, the time between the beginning of a realization and the feeling of renewed vigor could take up to a week, with something big enough to take a week coming up about monthly. The incest was harder for me. The weight of these dark realizations went on longer. Renewed vigor came later, less often, and for shorter periods. Also I was having trouble finding help. Al-Anon was not for me the forum I needed for my incest work. It helped a lot—I found other survivors at meetings, but it was hard to talk about incest. I had no clear memories; I had grave doubts and questions about how I would face my parents, sisters, and friends with the truth. Sometimes I would pretend there was some other explanation for these memories and feelings. A turning point came when I found such denials depressed me and knew I had only one way I could go.

I looked for groups on incest. It is hard for a man to find

services that help with having been sexually abused. There is not a lot out there. In January I started with a group for male survivors of sexual abuse. The night before the group started, I began getting clear memories of what had happened to me. Just having a place, a forum, allowed them to start coming out. I heard other people's stories in the group. I found it easier to believe or feel for someone else. I could believe them and I could see how they were not to blame, but I could not see it with myself. We were all that way at times. What a relief to find people like me. Many things people explained about themselves were the same in me and I had not seen or understood them before. This was a way of learning about myself that was faster, easier, and a lot less lonely. It is so clear to see that if a child is abused certain ways, certain problems happen. They happened to each differently, but the ways we were so much the same allowed me to see myself, believe myself, and not be ashamed of myself.

Listening to each other's stories and talking about them was how we started. We have covered a lot of ground together. We have struggled painfully through one person after another's description of trouble at work, with their boss or with their customers, till I could tell the parts where incest/dysfunctional family issues were active in those situations. Our work lives were confused by issues like fear of authority, inability to trust, lack of boundaries, the need to buy love or respect, and fear of being found out. As I could see how many of my reactions come from these issues, I changed. Sharing with other people allowed me to see ways I was very strange. How could I have seen them before? I had only known this way of life. I denied I had pain, fear, or anger as a matter of course. My parents had denied their pain, fear, and anger. I had learned from them that if you pretended something was not happening, it was not happening. It is so hard to see that I am living in fear, spending great amounts of energy pretending not to be in pain, never trusting anyone, and expecting always to be betrayed. As we struggled through many topics—work, money, sex, relationships, children, food, friendships, clothing, possessions, and more—I came to see how completely affected my life has been. It is a package deal. It is not likely one's parent would be a child molester and at the same time a very good role model from whom to learn how to balance work and personal life—to relate to a boss or customers, to budget money, to enjoy friendships or sexual relationships, or to eat a well-balanced diet. Our parents had many compulsive behaviors and addictions. These are the people we learned how to live from.

I found a lot of help in ISA (Incest Survivors Anonymous), a twelve-step program. At the meetings we hear and tell about how incest has affected us and how we are overcoming what happened, and we find a way to trust again. I need to ask for spiritual help. It is hard to trust God after what happened. That may be the greatest damage of all. Without that trust I would not be able to accept this amazing process of healing that has been given to me.

I have gained in my understanding of my compulsive behaviors around money by visiting Debtors Anonymous. I have also been helped in my understanding around my sexual compulsions from Sex and Love Addicts Anonymous.

I have gained a lot from individual therapy. An interesting point is that I am often blocked by my inability to trust my therapist when we are alone together. Because of the nature of my abuse, one-on-one work in an unequal relationship is harder than in a small intimate group.

I used to work full-time and more. I now work twenty to thirty hours a week. I go to a meeting or individual therapy three or four times a week. I want to get back to work. I want to have less pain and upheaval in my life. I try to be patient with my progress. I want this to end. An important part of my recovery is learning not to wait for my recovery to end so I can go back to my life. Sometimes I still think, soon this will all be over and I can forget it and live like before. But I have grown too much to go back to many of my old ways. Many of those old ways were terrible. I lived in fear, hiding from myself and everyone. I forget that when I am tired. I just did not have the type of problems where I could simply take a break from the rut, fix a few things, and go back. I will have a different life. I told my parents, sisters, and friends. I have changed so much. Deep stuff like the way I think, feel, work, and how I act around people. I do not know what my new life will be like. When I am feeling strong I believe what Nancy says, we will be embarrassingly happy. I wait for things to settle out. The realizations about myself are still painful and still come about the same pace. They are still hard to admit, figure out and integrate into my life. I still say to myself after I come to understand something, "What else could I have to deal with? It must be over." Then I slam up against the next behavior of mine or remember something horrible or both. I believe God is giving me the pieces I need as I can deal with them. It is my journey and I pray for the strength to hang on to it.

23

OTHER RESOURCES

Breathe. I went back to the basic breathing techniques.
—Serena Williams, after winning the 2002 Wimbledon
Singles Championship

There are many resources available to assist you in your recovery from the effects of sexual child abuse. This book emphasizes counseling/psychotherapy (see chapters 16 and 17) because it is my area of experience and training. I expanded the traditional definition of therapy to include other activities that are useful to survivors in recovery. This chapter contains a variety of other techniques and resources that survivors have told me were helpful. They are not my primary areas of expertise, and some haven't been explored in a systematic way. I cite them here only briefly. Those of you who wish to investigate further can do so. I welcome your comments about what you find helpful in your recovery.

Important: I want to stress that my mentioning other resources is not a recommendation. As with psychotherapy, these are tools that can be used or abused. It is always important to examine potential resources, accepting only those that make sense to you. Anyone who has overeaten knows that even the best food can cause distress when you consume too much of it—so think about how much is right for you. By the same token, good ingredients that are badly prepared produce terrible results. What works in one situation—or for one individual—may not be helpful in another. The quality of the practitioner is even more important than the quality of the practice. So be aware. Take time to find the right person for the job. If you aren't comfortable with the situation, back off. Get all the information you need, and proceed at your own pace. Don't be pressured or steamrollered. This is your recovery, and you have every right to know what you're getting. Finally, remember that there are no "magic cures." Recovery from abuse is a long-term process. Beware of shortcuts or "miracle" programs. Any of the approaches listed in this chapter can be valuable as part of an overall recovery program.

BODYWORK

Many survivors initially recovered memories of abuse while engaging in some sort of physical activity that involved being touched. For some it was during sex or other interpersonal intimacy. For others, casual touch triggered memories of the original abuse. A great number of survivors had abuse memories while undergoing some sort of physical treatment designed to relax, heal, or otherwise treat the body. When you think about it, it makes perfect sense that memories of physical abuse are triggered by physical contact. It also makes sense, since the hurts were inflicted in a physical way, that healing includes a physical component. (**Important:** This does *not* mean that sex should be considered a therapeutic technique. Beware of any so-called healer or therapist who attempts to convince you that she or he can help you recover by teaching you to be "less uptight" about sex. That is not recovery; it is sexual exploitation and only adds to the abuse.)

There is tremendous healing power in loving, nonabusive touch. It can be a very important aspect of recovery, but once again, only if and when it is right for you. For some people receiving a massage is a delightful, relaxing experience. For others (especially survivors) it can so closely resemble the abuse that it becomes an occasion of abject terror. In any case, all the various types of bodywork involve being touched by another person. This brings up feelings. You have the choice of letting yourself feel (even the uncomfortable feelings) or shutting down your emotions. I recommend that you choose the former option, once you have established the safety to do so. It may be more comfortable (and more familiar) to lie there feeling nothing, but it isn't going to help you recover.

If you decide to explore some sort of bodywork, consider the following guidelines:

1 / **Talk to other people who have tried it—preferably other survivors.** Get an idea of what to expect. Ask whether any pain is involved. Ask how you will be touched. Are you clothed during the treatment? Can another person be present if you choose? Get recommendations of competent and sensitive experts.

2 / **Interview the practitioner.** If he is reluctant or unwilling to answer all your questions to your satisfaction, he is not being responsive to your needs. Ask about what will be done to you, and what are the benefits of these treatments. Ask about frequency and duration of treatment. Inquire about any possible risks. Is there any available literature about this practice? Ask about her professional training and other qualifications. If there is a professional organization that approves, licenses, or certifies this treatment, is the practitioner a member? Being touched is likely to bring up feelings. How comfortable is she with the expression of emotions? Will you be allowed to cry, shake, laugh, and show other emotions whenever you need to? Can you have someone else present? (Sometimes just knowing that you have this option is enough to make you feel safer.) Can the procedure be terminated at any point that you want it stopped? Speak with more than one person. There may be a range of ideas and approaches. Select one that feels safest.

3 / **Ask yourself some questions.** Why am I interested in doing this? Do I have enough information? If not, what more do I need and how can I get it? Do I feel that this person is trustworthy? Was I treated with consideration, respect, and professionalism? Did he ask enough questions to get the information he needs to do his job well? Did she avoid intrusive personal questions that have nothing to do with the treatment? Did he seem to respect my concerns? Am I ignoring my own feelings and reservations in order to be a cooperative client? Do I feel safe and powerful enough to get what I need out of it? To cry, if I need to? To tell the practitioner to stop if I don't like what she is doing? What (if anything) do I need to tell this person about myself? About the abuse? Am I ready to go ahead with it?

4 / **Provide information to the practitioner.** If you have thought about why you are interested in this treatment and what you hope to get out of it, provide the practitioner with any information that you think will be useful to her. You must decide whether you want to disclose information about the abuse and, if so, how much. It might be difficult to ask questions about the practitioner's experience working with survivors without explaining why you are asking. But it is likely to be important to know how she feels about abuse and recovery, and what information and experience she has.

5 / **Give yourself permission.** Allow yourself to feel and express the emotions evoked by bodywork. Talk about the memories, thoughts, and feelings with friends and your therapist. Assess the benefits. Give yourself permission to stop if you don't think it's helpful (no matter what the practitioner says). And permit yourself to continue if it's helpful (or just because it feels good—you deserve it).

6 / **Trust your judgment.** Please yourself. You don't need a "legitimate" reason not to do it. None of these treatments is a requirement for recovery. Not wanting to do it is reason enough. Don't "caretake" the practitioner. Practice saying "no" to what isn't right for you, and "yes" to what is.

Types of bodywork that survivors have told me are helpful include:

Cranio-Sacral Therapy

Not as well known as many other types of bodywork, cranio-sacral therapy is an outgrowth of osteopathy. It is an extremely gentle manipulation of the bones of the skull and spine as well as the body's system of connective tissue. It can be performed while the client is clothed. Despite (or perhaps because of) the gentleness of this approach, survivors have found that it can evoke powerful memories and emotions. As with all the techniques I mention, the quality of care will depend upon the skills and sensitivity of the practitioner. Without the right practitioner, even the finest technique will fail to accomplish your aims. Keep looking until you find the person who is right for you. One cranio-sacral practitioner I spoke with (who is himself a survivor) asks clients about their abuse histories. He suggests to survivors that they do the work in conjunction with psychotherapy for dealing with their deep feelings and memories.

Massage/Muscular Therapy

There are, of course, many types of massage. They range from sensual/sexual practices performed by untrained individuals to therapeutic techniques carried out by licensed professionals under the auspices of medical personnel. Some are light and gentle, some active and vigorous, and others may be quite painful. Although they vary in style, intensity, and goal, what they share is that you will be having parts of your body touched by another person. Surrendering sufficient control over your body to allow it to be touched doesn't mean allowing it to be violated. Make sure that you know what to expect. Question massage therapists about their training, certification/licensing, and what type of massage they do. If their answers are vague or evasive, don't proceed with the treatment. They should know what they are doing and find the time and patience to explain it to you properly. Types of therapeutic massage that survivors have reported to me as helpful include Shiatsu and Swedish. Shiatsu (also called acupressure) is the stimulation of acupuncture points by finger pressure. Shiatsu does not employ needles. Swedish is what Westerners most commonly think of as massage. It uses long strokes over large areas of the body.

Related Techniques

Other manipulative healing techniques that don't define themselves as massage but have related components include Polarity Therapy and Reflexology. Polarity is a deep-relaxation therapy that uses massagelike techniques, working with the entire body. Reflexology (also known as zone therapy) is a system of treating the whole body by deeply massaging "reflex points" on the soles of the feet—or sometimes the hands.

Deeper Bodywork

Although I know very little about these practices, I have worked with clients who swear by the benefits of Rolfing, Soma, and Feldenkrais.

Rolfing and Soma are systems for realigning the muscles and bones. They involve deep, sometimes painful muscle work. Feldenkrais is a very gentle, noninvasive system for "reeducating" the body through movement. Once again, I would suggest doing your homework before embarking on a course of treatment, both in terms of the technique and the individual practitioner.

Acupuncture

Acupuncture is a Chinese healing art that has been successfully practiced in the Orient for many centuries. It is now receiving recognition in Western medicine. An acupuncturist I questioned about his work with survivors told me that it can be useful in dealing with chronic physical manifestations of abuse in conjunction with psychotherapy. Remember that acupuncture, which involves the use of small needles, is an invasive procedure that, while virtually painless, can evoke powerful memories of having your body invaded. (This, by the way, is true of any invasive medical examination or treatment procedure. Make certain that any suggested invasive procedure is necessary, and be prepared for heavy feelings.)

Dance, Movement, Exercise, Aerobics, Sports, and Weight Training

Any of these activities can be quite helpful when you are ready for them. Their benefits include improving physical well-being by increasing your strength, stamina, and/or agility. You enhance self-esteem through improving your body image and deriving a sense of what you can accomplish. Regular exercise will make you feel better. (Expect that physical activity will also bring up emotions. If you feel bad about your body, you will have feelings about using it and displaying it. Don't let that discourage you; feel the feelings and keep going. It is the same as other areas of recovery; it provides an opportunity to work through the sad and frightening emotions to the joy that is on the other side.) As with any other activity, these programs are most beneficial when they are done sensibly. Choose a reasonable program; don't take on too much (setting yourself up for injury and failure) or become an "exercise junkie" (engaging in excessive activity to numb feelings or keep you from living a full and varied life). Add a social dimension by selecting activities that are done in the company of others, rather than choosing solitary pursuits. When they are well chosen and kept in perspective, physical activities are of tremendous value in recovery.

Other Bodywork

This list is by no means exhaustive. There are many methods of healing and treating the body, some traditional and others new. I am an expert on none of them. Those I included were selected because survivors recommended them. Please investigate them (and others) carefully. Share the information, both positive and negative, with others. Let me know what you find out.

PRAYER, MEDITATION, AND SPIRITUALITY

This is a tricky area. Like family, religion is considered a private and personal matter. We have institutionalized noninterference with religious beliefs and practices, and passed laws to insure freedom of religious expression. It is not my purpose here to champion or attack religious beliefs. Just as I am not an expert on bodywork, I don't offer expertise on the specifics of any religion or spiritual path. Some people tell me that their religious (or spiritual) beliefs and practices are all that enabled them to survive the abuse. Others relate stories of abusive religious institutions, beliefs, and attitudes that contributed to their hurts and interfered with their recovery. I have no doubt that all of these experiences and perspectives are true. I suggest that you examine your spiritual needs with the same care that you use in other areas of your life. They are certainly as important.

Attitudes and practices vary widely among religious traditions and within specific religions. Religious doctrine is open to a wide range of interpretation. Scriptures can be found and quoted to support virtually any position. It is important to explore the teachings of your faith (or a belief system that you are considering). Find out whether they are protective of children or consider a child to be his or her parents' property. What are the attitudes toward sex and sexuality? Do the teachings encourage positive self-esteem or are they rooted in guilt and shame? Are they rigid or flexible? Are individuals required to submit unquestioningly to the will of an authoritarian leader, or is there room for individual choice and decision making? Is there a sense of warm, caring community? Does it encourage contact outside the group or try to limit social interaction to group members? Is there room for you to be yourself—to grow as an individual? In short, *be wary of any religion or community that resembles your abusive childhood.* Your faith can be a powerful healing force or a means of perpetuating your hurts. One man's salvation may be another's hell.

As difficult as it is to question your basic religious beliefs and practices, it is important to do so. While some of my clients say that their religious or spiritual beliefs are the most important aspect of their survival and recovery, others found it necessary to abandon their childhood religion to leave the abuse behind. Some have adopted other religious traditions and spiritual practices (Eastern as well as Western), created their own belief systems, or chosen a purely secular lifestyle.

I don't advocate any specific religious or secular path. That is a profoundly personal decision. I do, however, believe strongly that no survivor (or anyone else) should spend another minute in an abusive or exploitive situation—including those that cloak themselves in the mantle of religion. There are good, caring people in all religions and good, caring people who adhere to no specific religious beliefs. And there are hurtful, destructive individuals in any environment—religious or secular. It isn't necessary to be "a religious person" in order to recover, but it is vital to be treated with respect and consideration. If your religious system doesn't provide this, question what you are getting out of it. If it does, your religion can be a powerful aspect of your recovery.

Prayer

There are probably as many forms and definitions of prayer as there are religions. Prayers can be highly structured formulas, involving requests, questions, or giving thanks to a specific Supreme Being, or a nonspecific outpouring of thoughts and feelings into the Universe. Prayers can be expressed silently or aloud, alone or in the company of others. There are those who view artistic expression, music, or good deeds as forms of prayer. Some survivors report that prayer provides them with feelings of calm, comfort, and connection with a source of strength beyond themselves—offering a perspective greater than the abuse.

Meditation

Like prayer, there are many forms of meditation, ranging from the deeply religious to the purely secular. Some define it as communication with God or forces of the Universe; others see meditation as a pleasant means of relaxation or self-examination. Some people contend that prayer and meditation are simply different names for the same phenomenon. As is true of prayer, meditation can provide benefits on a physical and emotional level. When one meditates, there is a focusing of attention that results in a measurable "relaxation response." It is possible to slow the pulse and lower blood pressure through meditation. The practice of meditation can be a highly structured, formal undertaking, involving sitting in one position and/or chanting for hours—or as simple as sitting on a riverbank watching the water flow. For those who practice it, meditation is a way of slowing down, "getting in touch with" themselves, and treating themselves kindly.

Ascetic Practices

I urge you to be extremely careful about entering into any program or practice that involves sensory deprivation, punishment, prolonged fasting, pain, shame, or humiliation. Whatever their rationale, they are likely to be based on distress. Confirming the negative self-image of the abused child re-creates an abusive environment. You have had more than enough pain and deprivation in your life. It's time for celebration.

HYPNOSIS

Hypnosis is a powerful tool that, like any tool, is useful when used correctly. Also like any tool, its misuse carries the potential of harm. In hypnosis, you are dealing with areas of the mind that are not usually accessible to direct communication. This part of what is commonly called the "unconscious" operates through imagery and metaphor. Like meditation, prayer, and guided imagery, hypnosis can be employed effectively for relaxation and stress reduction. It has been used successfully as an aid in habit control, dealing with fears and phobias, and control of pain. In my clinical practice I have used hypnosis to help women reduce pain and anxiety associated with childbirth and help clients deal with anxiety attacks, sexual dysfunction, and fear (of dentists, public speaking, interviews, airplanes, and lightning).

The area where I am most reluctant to use hypnosis (particularly with survivors) is in attempting to recover memories of abuse. My thinking is twofold. First, memories are blocked for a reason. They are hidden to enable the individual to survive a traumatic situation. I have found that, when the proper degree of safety and distance from the abuse has been achieved, memories present themselves. I question the benefit of dragging out memories before you are ready to deal with them. Second, I don't think it makes good sense to make your primary goal the recovery of specific abuse memories. Doing this gives the misleading impression that if you recover the memories everything will be all right. If you adopt this mistaken notion, you will be deeply disappointed when you discover that there is still much work to be done after the memories are in place. As I stated earlier, you can do powerful recovery work in the absence of specific childhood memories.

If, however, you choose to do hypnosis work on abuse issues, make sure to find the right person for the job. We are not talking about parlor games here. The hypnotist (or hypnotherapist) should be professionally trained in psychotherapy so that he is prepared to help with whatever issues and feelings are brought up. She should, in addition, have direct experience working with abuse issues. All the considerations I discussed about selecting an individual therapist apply to your choice of hypnotherapist. If you already have an individual therapist, discuss it with him fully, and if you go to someone else for hypnosis, insist that he speak with your therapist directly. Be clear about what you want to accomplish, and remain in charge of your program. If at any point you feel that you wish to end the process, feel free to do so. Remember that you don't have to answer to anyone for the way you structure your recovery. You are doing this for yourself.

EMDR

EMDR has received a great deal of attention recently. Some have hailed it as a huge breakthrough in trauma treatment. Others find it a useful tool for certain tasks. Still others report little success from its use. As I have very little experience with this technique, I am grateful to Thom Harrigan for providing the following description:

"Eye Movement Desensitization and Reprocessing (EMDR) is a technique of therapy for treating simple and complex reactions to negative life experiences and trauma. It was developed by Frances Shapiro, Ph.D., and may be one of the most studied and documented treatment modalities in use today. The idea behind EMDR is that the nervous system 'locks in' the original experience, and then reproduces it in the form of anxiety, intrusive thoughts, flashbacks, nightmares, sleeplessness, etc. The goal of EMDR is to resolve and/or eliminate the complaint. Treatment is, and should only be, provided by trained and certified therapists who are experienced in the area you are seeking help with—preferably your own therapist or someone known to them. As with any technique, the choice of EMDR should be made with care, caution, and attention to your needs."

ORGANIZATIONS

Almost daily new organizations and services for survivors come into being throughout the world. Other groups change their focus or cease operations with similarly dizzying regularity. This fluidity makes the task of writing a helpful chapter on resources rather difficult. I guarantee that if I start the morning writing about resources, by day's end some of it will be obsolete. Fortunately, technology has provided a solution. The following sections differ from the original edition. For additional information I refer you to the more extensive resource section in my other book, *Leaping upon the Mountains,* and the resource lists on my Web site: www.victimsnolonger.org.

On the Web site you will find sporadic updates of books, organizations, and other resources. I assume that nowadays few readers of this book don't have access to the Internet through their home or workplace computers, friends, relatives, neighbors, schools or the public library. Many organizational Web sites, including mine, provide links to other helpful sites. For all its problems, the Internet has been enormously important to survivors, especially those who are isolated geographically and/or in the early, fearful stages of recovery. In the interest of space, and because they change so frequently, I did not include in this section resources that consist only of a Web site (with one exception). You can locate those resources as links on my Web site or in the resource section of *Leaping upon the Mountains.*

(**Warning:** Not all Internet sites are helpful, nor is everyone who uses the Internet safe. When you conduct a search for sites concerned with sexual abuse, incest, and related issues, you will encounter some that offer pornography, or are the institutional sites of abusive groups. This is the price of free speech. You are free to ignore sites that are hurtful and to stay with those that help.)

When I first wrote *Victims No Longer,* there were far fewer resources available, and I felt lucky to find enough to comprise a reasonably helpful section. Now there are so many that I must limit them, leaving out some useful entries. (And there are many others I'm not yet aware of.) Don't confine yourself to my listings; build a list of your own, tailored to your specific needs and interests.

The following lists of organizations, books, and films focus on those specifically directed to male survivors, or that include male survivors as a significant component of their mission. I've chosen groups that are representative samples of different types of resources and geographical areas. I tried to limit the list to resources that are nonprofit, for nonprofessionals, and regional, national, or international in scope. I apologize to those excellent groups I've left out through oversight or overwhelm. I'm happy to add you to my Web site list; just send me the information and be patient.

I have had personal interaction with some of these entries; some were recommended to me; and I have no direct knowledge of others. **Inclusion in this list does *not* constitute my endorsement of any person, program, or service.** No matter how wonderful a program or organization is, it may not be the right one for you now—or ever. Explore this list of resources carefully to determine what sounds useful to you.

Wherever possible I have used or adapted information and descriptive language provided by the organization.

For Male Survivors

FIRE IN ICE
88 Rodney Street, Liverpool, L1 9AR, United Kingdom
Phone: (0151) 708-6339; Helpline: (0151) 707-2614

E-mail: fireinice@freenet.co.uk
Web sites: www.fireinice.co.uk; www.victimsnolonger.org.uk
Manager: Matthew Byrne
Chair: Peter Veste

"Fire in Ice has a clear mission statement: *'Abuse in care and its effects are a reality.' We are committed to encouraging positive change both in the lives of men who have suffered and to the places where children are looked after.* We believe that: Abuse can happen to any boy or man, girl or woman; survivors of abuse may be Black, White, Gay, Straight, or Disabled and our service should always reflect this; the effects of abuse are harmful; with support it is possible to recover from the effects of abuse; people are never to blame for the abuse they have suffered."

PROVIDES

"A free and confidential service consisting of individual support from a fellow survivor; self-help support groups and drop-in services run by men who have experienced child abuse; a support group for the partners or families of men who were abused; a telephone helpline service and visiting non-abusing survivors in prison." They also provide education and training for the public and professionals and have published a self-help book and a diary of feelings.

FIRST STEP

26 Severn Street, Leicester, LE2 0NN, United Kingdom
Phone: (0116) 254-3352; Fax: (0116) 275-5216; Helpline: (0116) 255-8868

"We are able to offer a correspondence service to men in prison. We are sometimes able to provide counselling sessions during the day, but this is limited. Our counsellors are qualified from Advanced Certificate to Master of Arts level. Whilst all our counsellors speak English, we now have counsellors fluent in two Asian languages and Greek. We are members of the British Association for Counselling & Psychotherapy and are aiming for Accreditation status for all our counsellors."

PROVIDES

Support for adult male survivors of childhood sexual abuse or adult rape, and their supporters. Services include individual and group counselling, time-limited advocacy, training, information, and consultancy for organisations. Hours: Mondays 7 P.M.–9 P.M. (Helpline and counselling: all calls returned), and Thursdays 7 P.M.–9 P.M. (counselling only).

MALESURVIVOR: COMMITTED TO ELIMINATING SEXUAL VICTIMIZATION OF BOYS AND MEN (formerly NOMSV, The National Organization on Male Sexual Victimizatiom)

PMB 103, 5505 Connecticut Avenue, NW, Washington, DC 20015-2601, USA

Phone: (800) 738-4181

Web site: www.malesurvivor.org/

President (2002–2004): Richard B. Gartner, Ph.D.; President-Elect: Fred Tolson

"Virtually all-volunteer nonprofit organization of male survivors, professionals, professionals who are themselves survivors, loved ones, and other interested parties. Dedicated to a safe world, we are an organization of diverse individuals, committed through research, education, advocacy and activism to the prevention, treatment and elimination of all forms of sexual victimization of boys and men."

PROVIDES

Newsletter; Web site with articles, bibliographies, and bookstore related to male sexual victimization, professional resource directory, live chat room, and discussion forum; biannual conferences with healing workshops, research presentations, professional development and training; healing retreats for survivors.

MALE SURVIVORS OF SEXUAL ABUSE TRUST (MSSAT)

2nd Floor, 141 Hereford Street, PO Box 22-363, Christchurch 8001, New Zealand

Phone/Fax: (03) 377-6747

E-mail: mssat@survivor.org.nz

"A support agency for male victims of sexual abuse. The purpose of the Trust is to empower male survivors of sexual abuse in their recovery process, and to work towards changing the way the community views sexual abuse, the effects, the victims, and the perpetrators."

RAINBOW MALE SURVIVORS NETWORK (RAINBOW NETWORK)

PO Box 2186, Richmond South, Victoria, 3121, Australia

Phone: 61-3-9513-7937 (messagebank—local Melbourne calls only)

E-mail: care@rainbownetwork.org.au

Web site: www.rainbownetwork.org.au

Contact: Allan

"... an independent support network for gay and bisexual male survivors of sexual abuse."

PROVIDES

Referral service throughout Victoria and Australia, support for gay and bisexual male survivors, information concerning sexual abuse of gay and bisexual men for support agencies, and advocacy services for male survivors. Does not provide telephone counselling.

SEXUALLY ABUSED MALES SURVIVING (SAMS)
47 Campbell Road, Kentville, NS B4N 1Y1, Canada
Phone: (902) 678-2913
E-mail: jerry.h@ns.sympatico.ca
Web site: www.nsnet.org/sams/
Contact: Jerry

"SAMS is a self-help support group for men who have suffered childhood sexual abuse, or any other type of sexual abuse. Founded by survivors for survivors."

SURVIVORS (SHEFFIELD)
PO Box 142, Sheffield, S1 3HG, United Kingdom
Phone: (0114) 279-6333
Web site: www.fstinfo.com/Sheffield/pages/ServiceDetailResults.PHP
?ContactID=131&SearchStrategy=SearchName
Contact: Ian Warwick

"Counselling service for sexually abused men and male partners of victims of abuse or rape. If you need to talk to someone, our counsellors are here to listen and believe. You will not be judged, condemned or told what to do. We offer a safe and supportive environment. The service is confidential and free."

PROVIDES

Phone help line, face-to-face counselling, support groups, counselling for male partners, trainings for volunteers and professional organisations.

SURVIVORS SWINDON
c/o Focus on Carers & Self Help
25 Morley Street, Swindon, SN1 1SG, United Kingdom
Phone: (01793) 87-83-16 Wed: 7 P.M.–9 P.M.; 24-hour answerphone

E-mail: survivorsswindon@hotmail.com

Web site: www.survivorsswindon.com/

"We offer a unique experience, providing weekly group therapy sessions, run by male Survivors for male Survivors, in a safe supportive environment in which to overcome the traumas of your abusive past. Survivors Swindon is a regionally based and nationally recognised agency, offering a confidential telephone helpline and specialised training to NHS Trusts, Social Services, Victim Support and related agencies. Web site covers all aspects of sexual abuse, but primarily focuses upon the immense strength and courage all Survivors possess, proving it is possible to become true Survivors, leaving the past where it belongs! The choice is yours to take."

SURVIVORS UK: FOR MALE VICTIMS OF SEXUAL ABUSE

PO Box 2470, London SW9 6WQ, United Kingdom

Phone: (020) 7357-6222 (office); (0845) 1221201 (helpline)

E-mail: info@survivorsuk.org.uk

Web site: www.survivorsuk.co.uk

"A national support and information service for any adult male survivor of sexual violence."

PROVIDES

Telephone Helpline Tuesday evenings 7 P.M.–10 P.M., facilitated therapeutic groups, individual counselling, public, professional and media education, especially on issues of male rape.

For All Survivors

ACCURACY ABOUT ABUSE

PO Box 3125, London, NW35 QB, United Kingdom

Phone: (0171) 431-5339; Fax: (0171) 431-3101

E-mail: orr@aastar.demon.co.uk

Contact: Marjorie Orr

"Aims to get an accurate picture of abuse across to the public."

PROVIDES

Newsletter, research, information, and networking support for survivors, professionals, and activists working in the field of child abuse, incest, and ritual abuse.

ADVOCATES FOR SURVIVORS OF CHILD ABUSE (ASCA)

PO Box 361, Cessnock. NSW 2325, Australia

Phone: 02-4990-9030 or 1300-657-380; Fax: 02-4990-8941; Information: 1300-657-380

E-mail: asca@hunterlink.net.au

Web site: www.asca.org.au

". . . an Australian national organisation, for men and women, dedicated to serving the needs of adult survivors of child abuse . . . ASCA's goal is to break the silence, so that healing becomes available for all and so end the cycle of abuse for the benefit of the next generation."

PROVIDES

Advocacy, education, support meetings for survivors and friends, and monthly newsletter. "Assisting survivors of child abuse with self-help groups throughout Australia and New Zealand. Also with Mayumarri, a five-day healing retreat, set in the Hunter Valley, NSW."

GIFT FROM WITHIN

16 Cobb Hill Road, Camden, ME 04843, USA

Phone: (207) 236-8858; Fax: (207) 236-2818

E-mail: JoyceB3955@aol.com

Web site: www.giftfromwithin.org/

Executive Director: Joyce Boas

"An international organization for survivors of trauma and victimization, is a private, nonprofit organization dedicated to those who suffer post-traumatic stress disorder (PTSD), those at risk for PTSD, and those who care for traumatized individuals."

PROVIDES

Develops and disseminates educational material, including videotapes, articles, books, and a resource catalog; maintains a roster of survivors who are willing to participate in an international network of peer support.

INCEST RESOURCES, INC.

46 Pleasant St., Cambridge, MA 02139, USA

PROVIDES

Several groups in Boston, Massachusetts, area; educational and resource materials for female and male survivors of childhood abuse, and the professionals who work with them; international listing of survivor self-help groups, and manual for starting survivor groups. For complete information send self-addressed envelope with two first-class stamps.

INNERMOTION, INC.

E-mail: innermot@ix.netcom.com

Web site: www.innermotion.org

"A nonprofit organization located in Ft. Lauderdale, Florida, Innermotion performs across the country, telling the story of childhood sexual abuse and healing through interpretive dance and theater . . . also uses other art forms to heal the individual and the community from childhood sexual abuse."

PROVIDES

Twelve-week movement groups and all-day movement workshops for adult survivors of childhood sexual abuse. Open to both men and women at no charge.

ISRAEL CENTER FOR THE TREATMENT OF PSYCHOTRAUMA

PO Box 35300, Jerusalem, 91352, Israel

Phone: 02-623-0576; Fax: 02-623-0564

E-mail: dbrom@netvision.net.il

Web site: www.herzoghospital.org/

Director: Danny Brom, Ph.D.

THE MORRIS CENTER

PO Box 14477, San Francisco, CA 94114, USA

Phone: (415) 928-4576; Fax: (415) 452-6253

E-mail: tmc_asca@dnai.com

Web site: www.ascasupport.org

"The Morris Center for healing from child abuse is a nonprofit, 501(c)(3) tax-exempt service organization. . . . Our mission is to provide adult survivors of physical, sexual, or emotional child abuse with economical and effective opportunities to recover from their child abuse and to revive their identities as thrivers. . . ."

PROVIDES

Meetings, Adult Survivors of Child Abuse (ASCA) guided self-help recovery program, manual, art and poetry events, and workshops.

NATIONAL COALITION AGAINST SEXUAL ASSAULT (NCASA)

125 N. Enola Drive, Enola, PA 17025, USA
Phone: (717) 728-9764; Fax: (717) 728-9781
E-mail: ncasa@redrose.net
Web site: www.dreamingdesigns.com/other/indexncasa.html

"The National Coalition Against Sexual Assault is a feminist organization which provides leadership to the movement to end sexual violence through advocacy, education and public policy. Our vision is to eliminate sexual assault and all forms of oppression. We work to attain quality services for victims/survivors and we challenge the nation to commit to a rape-free culture."

NATIONAL ORGANIZATION FOR VICTIM ASSISTANCE (NOVA)

1730 Park Road NW, Washington, DC 20010, USA
Phone: (800) try-nova or (202) 232-6682
Web site: www.try-nova.org/index.html

"The National Organization for Victim Assistance is a private, non-profit, 501(c)(3) organization of victim and witness assistance programs and practitioners, criminal justice agencies and professionals, mental health professionals, researchers, former victims and survivors, and others committed to the recognition and implementation of victim rights and services."

ONE VOICE: THE NATIONAL ALLIANCE FOR ABUSE AWARENESS AND AMERICAN COALITION FOR ABUSE AWARENESS (ACAA)

PO Box 27958, Washington, DC 20038-7958, USA
Phone: (202) 462-4688; Fax: (202) 462-4689
E-mail: acaadc@aol.com or 0voicedc@aol.com
President and Counsel: Sherry Quirk, Esq.

". . . a national nonpartisan coalition founded in 1993 by adult survivors and child advocates, mental health/legal professionals, and non-offending parents to advocate for the rights of child victims and adult survivors of sexual abuse to appropriate treatment and redress through the courts. The ACAA is working toward a broad-based alliance of individuals and organizations to promote the enactment of legislation establishing the rights of children to be free of sexual victimization and exploitation."

PROVIDES

Legislative activity, newsletter, informational packets, judicial education, amicus curiae briefs, testimony, speakers and conferences.

RAPE INTERVENTION PROGRAM/CRIME VICTIM ASSESSMENT PROJECT

St. Luke's—Roosevelt Hospital Center
411 W. 114th Street #6D, New York, NY 10025, USA
Phone: (212) 523-4728
Contact: Louise Kindley or Tony Sidoti

"For over fifteen years, we have been providing individual and group treatment to survivors of violence. Our groups are specifically designed to reduce isolation and provide a safe, healing environment for people who have been traumatized. . . ."

PROVIDES

Free and confidential short-term groups for survivors of violent crimes, including groups for male survivors of childhood sexual abuse.

THE SAFER SOCIETY FOUNDATION

PO Box 340, Brandon, VT 05733-0340, USA
Phone: (802) 247-3132; Referral Line: (802) 247-5141
E-mail: Direct from their Web site
Web site: www.safersociety.org/

". . . a nonprofit agency, is a national research, advocacy, and referral center on the prevention and treatment of sexual abuse. . . . The Safer Society Press . . . publishes relevant research, studies, video- and audiotapes, and books that contribute to the development of sexual abuse treatment, sexual abuse prevention, emerging topics, and developments in the field."

PROVIDES

Computerized program network, sex offender treatment referrals, training and consultation, resource/research library, resource lists, publications, and media advocacy.

SEXUAL ASSAULT TREATMENT CENTER

Sinai Samaritan Medical Center
945 North 12th Street, Milwaukee, WI 53233, USA

Phone: (414) 219-5555
Web site: www.coperesources.net/iris/fxOilyos.htm

Among the increasing number of sexual assault treatment centers committed to understanding and support of male survivor issues.

PROVIDES

Counseling, referrals, information, and a midsummer training institute for professionals.

THE SIDRAN INSTITUTE FOR TRAUMATIC STRESS EDUCATION & ADVOCACY

200 East Joppa Road, Suite 207, Baltimore, MD 21286, USA
Phone: (410) 825-8888; Fax: (410) 337-0747
E-mail: sidran@sidran.org for general information; help@sidran.org for resource and referrals
Web site: www.sidran.org
President: Esther Giller

"Sidran is a nonprofit organization devoted to promoting understanding about the long-term effects of traumatic experiences. All of Sidran's educational and advocacy programming models our relational philosophy of healing."

PROVIDES

Programs for survivors, significant others and health professionals including training, peer support, information and referral, curriculum development and publications.

SURVIVORS AND VICTIMS EMPOWERED (SAVE)

PO Box 3030, Lancaster, PA 17604-3030, USA
Phone: (717) 291-1940; Fax: (717) 219-5977
E-mail: treatabuse@aol.com
Web site: www.s-a-v-e.org/
Executive Director: Jim Hughes

"A national, nonprofit organization created to help prevent the criminal neglect, physical, emotional, and sexual abuse of children and to help adult survivors of childhood traumas. . . ."

PROVIDES

Survivors and Victims Resource Database (SVRD), child protection guide and programs for abused children.

DABS (DIRECTORY AND BOOK SERVICES)
4 New Hill, Conisbrough, Doncaster, DN12 3HA, United Kingdom
Phone/Fax: (01709) 860023
Web site: www.dabsbooks.co.uk

A specialist book and information service for people who have been abused and those who live or work with them.

PROVIDES

DABS Resource Packs for survivors, including help sheets and details of the specialist counselors and organizations in your area (£4.50); DABS National Resource Directory for workers, listing over 500 specialist organizations in the UK and Ireland, and updated quarterly for maximum accuracy (£10.00); a confidential mail-order book service on childhood abuse, sexual abuse and related issues. Phone for a free annotated book catalogue or for further information.

VOICES IN ACTION, INC.
PO Box 13, Newtonsville, OH 45158, USA
Phone: (800) 7-VOICE-8 or (513) 625-1300; Fax: (513) 625-1194
E-mail: voicesinaction@aol.com
Web site: www.voices-action.org
President: Holly Broach-Sowels

"Victims of Incest Can Emerge Survivors . . . an international organization to provide assistance to victims of incest and child sexual abuse in becoming survivors and to generate public awareness of the prevalence of incest."

PROVIDES

Newsletter, Special Interest Groups (mail support groups), national and regional conferences, publications and audiotapes, sixty-page informational "Survival Kit," and referral network.

WINGS FOUNDATION, INC.
8725 West 14th Avenue, Suite 150, Lakewood, CO 80215, USA
Phone: (303) 238-8660; Toll-free: (800) 373-8671
E-mail: wings@vs2000.org
Web site: www.wingsfound.org

"... a private, nonprofit organization ... has established a solid reputation as a powerful resource for survivors of childhood sexual abuse. WINGS assists survivors as they work to reduce the trauma of childhood sexual abuse, improve their quality of life, and break the cycle of childhood sexual abuse."

PROVIDES

Facilitated peer support groups, referrals to therapists, research library on childhood sexual abuse, educational workshops, advocacy, speakers bureau, handbook, and information and referral services.

Twelve-Step Programs for Survivors

INCEST SURVIVORS ANONYMOUS (ISA)

PO Box 17245, Long Beach, CA 90807-7245, USA

Phone: (562) 428-5599

E-mail: isa@lafn.org

Web site: www.lafn.org/medical/isa/home.html

"An international self-help, mutual-help recovery program for men, women and teens ... run for and by survivors and their personal prosurvivors. No perpetrators or satanist individuals permitted. No professionals as professionals—only as survivors. No students as students—only as survivors."

PROVIDES

Assistance in starting ISA groups. When writing for meeting information and literature, state if you are a survivor or other status, and include a self-addressed stamped envelope.

SEXUAL ABUSE ANONYMOUS (SAA)

PO Box 9665, Berkeley, CA 94709, USA

SEXUAL ASSAULT RECOVERY ANONYMOUS SOCIETY (SARA)

PO Box 16, Surrey, BC V3T, Canada

Phone: (604) 584-2626; Fax: (604) 584-2888

"National. Thirty-three groups. Education and support for adults and teens who were sexually abused as children."

PROVIDES

Group development guidelines and assistance for starting groups, literature on behavioral modification, newsletter.

SURVIVORS OF INCEST ANONYMOUS (SIA)
World Service Office
PO Box 190, Benson, MD 21018-9998, USA
Phone: (410) 893-3322
Web site: www.siawso.org/

"A self-help group of men and women, eighteen years or older, who have been victims of child sexual abuse. SIA, a nonprofit organization with no dues or fees . . . works to help victims realize that they are not responsible for what happened, and they are not alone. Members use a set of twelve suggested steps. Meetings are confidential. Members are encouraged to seek professional therapy." Groups in many countries.

PROVIDES

Newsletter, literature, assistance in starting groups, volunteer information and referral line, speakers bureau. Send self-addressed stamped envelope when writing.

For Native American/Indian Survivors

INA MAKA FAMILY PROGRAM
United Indians of All Tribes Foundation
1945 Yale Place East, Seattle, WA 98102, USA
Phone: (206) 325-0070
Web site: www.unitedindians.com/fondprograms.html
Contact: Arlene Red Elk or Jack Spotted Eagle

". . . providing a traditional based approach to recovery for Native American Families."

PROVIDES

Counseling, foster care, sexual abuse counseling for primary and secondary victims, crime victims advocacy, education, talking circles, and sweat lodges.

For Clergy Abuse Survivors

THE CENTER FOR THE PREVENTION OF SEXUAL AND DOMESTIC VIOLENCE
2400 North 45th Street, #10, Seattle, WA 98103, USA
Phone: (206) 634-1903; Fax: (206) 634-0115
E-mail: cpsdv@cpsdv.seanet.com
Web site: www.cpsdv.org/
Executive Director: Rev. Dr. Marie M. Fortune
"... is an interreligious educational program designed to equip religious leaders in addressing violence in the family, sexual assault and abuse by clergy."
PROVIDES
Videos, written materials, workshops, and leadership training.

THE INTERFAITH SEXUAL TRAUMA INSTITUTE (ISTI)
Saint John's Abbey and University, Collegeville, MN 56321-2000, USA
Phone: (320) 363-3931; Fax: (320) 363-2115
E-mail: isti@csbsju.edu
Web site: www.csbsju.edu:80/isti/index.html
Executive Director: Fr. Roman Paur, OSB
"... facilitates the building of healthy, safe, and trustworthy communities of faith."
PROVIDES
Internet Web site, newsletter, books, audiocassettes, bibliography, and workshops.

THE LINKUP
1412 W. Argyle #2, Chicago, IL 60640, USA
Phone: (773) 334-2296; Fax: (773) 334-0274
E-mail: ilinkup@aol.com or tobeau@creative-net.net
Web site: www.thelinkup.com
President: Sue Archibald; Vice President: Fr. Gary Hayes
National organization of survivors of clergy abuse.

PROVIDES

Newsletter (Missing Link, PO Box 40676, Albuquerque, NM 87196; Phone: 505-254-4634), conference, and symposia dealing with sexual abuse, clergy sexual abuse, alcoholism & drug abuse, and awareness & prevention for professional/corporate America, the ecumenical community, and parents and educators.

SURVIVOR CONNECTIONS, INC.—THE TRUE MEMORY FOUNDATION®
52 Lyndon Road, Cranston, RI 02905-1121, USA
Phone: (401) 941-2548; Fax: (401) 941-2335
E-mail: scsitemail@cox.net
Web site: www.angelfire.com/ri/survivorconnections/
Contact: Frank & Sara Fitzpatrick

Advocacy for activism by incest and sexual assault survivors.

"Survivor Connections is an activist center for survivors of sexual assault, incest, and child molestation. A nonprofit, all-volunteer operation 'for survivors of sexual assault and their supportive, nonoffender relations.'"

PROVIDES

Quarterly newsletter (*The Survivor Activist*), database of information on False Memory Syndrome Foundation (FMSF) members, conferences, peer support groups, merchandise.

SURVIVORS NETWORK OF THOSE ABUSED BY PRIESTS (SNAP)
PO Box 6416, Chicago, IL 60680-6416, USA
Phone: (312) 409-2720
Web site: www.survivorsnetwork.org/

". . . a self-help organization of men and women who were sexually abused by spiritual elders (Catholic priests, brothers, nuns, ministers, teachers, etc.). Members find healing and empowerment by joining with other survivors. We are an all-volunteer group with local chapters scattered throughout the United States and Canada."

PROVIDES

Extensive phone network, online e-mail support group with members from throughout the world, newsletter, advocacy, conferences, information and referrals, advocacy, support group meetings, assistance in starting new groups.

For Jewish Survivors

THE AWARENESS CENTER
PO Box 65273, Baltimore, MD 21209, USA
Phone: (443) 857-5560
E-mail: VickiPolin@TheAwarenessCenter.org or
NaamaYehuda@TheAwarenessCenter.org
Web site: www.TheAwarenessCenter.org

"Dedicated to addressing sexual abuse in Jewish communities around the globe.... The Jewish Survivors Resource Pages are dedicated to Jewish survivors of child abuse, domestic violence, and violent crimes. The purpose of these pages is to remind survivors of violence that they are not alone. The hope is that our communities will familiarize themselves with the issues surrounding sexual abuse and other domestic violence, and will help stop the cycle of violence . . . we are especially looking for rabbis who are sensitive to victimization issues, as well as self-help groups geared toward Jewish Survivors of childhood trauma."

Other Survivor Organizations

RESPOND
3rd Floor, 24-32 Stephenson Way, London NW1 2HD, United Kingdom
Phone: (020) 7383-0700; Fax: (020) 7387-1222
Toll-free helpline: (0808) 808-0700 Mon–Fri 1:30 P.M.–5:00 P.M.
E-mail: feedback@respond.org.uk
Web site: www.respond.org.uk/
Contact: Richard Curen; richardcuren@hotmail.com

"Respond is an organisation that helps people with learning disabilities who have been sexually abused or have suffered trauma."

PROVIDES

Psychotherapy to help people recover and move forward positively in their lives, telephone service for carers and professionals who are supporting people with learning disabilities who have been sexually abused, consultancy, referrals to psychotherapy and risk-assessment services.

SESAME (STOP EDUCATOR SEXUAL ABUSE, MISCONDUCT, EXPLOITATION)
PO Box 94601, Las Vegas, NV 89193-4601, USA
Phone: (702) 371-1290
E-mail: Babe4Justice@aol.com
Web site: www.sesamenet.org

"National network. Founded 1993. Support and information network for families of children (K–12) who have been sexually abused by a school staff member. Aims to raise public awareness."

PROVIDES
Information and referrals, phone support, literature, advocacy, newsletter.

Partners of Survivors

PARTNERS OF ADULTS SEXUALLY ABUSED AS CHILDREN (PASAC)
E-mail: support@pasac.net
Web site: www.PASAC.net

New and growing. This Web site, started by the partner of a male survivor, provides support and information to other partners.

Other Twelve-Step Programs

There are many peer support programs based to some degree on the model of Alcoholics Anonymous. Millions who participate in these organizations consider them an invaluable part of their recovery from some form of addiction or trauma. Many other people have decided that these programs are not what they need. It is important to remember that not all meetings/groups within a program are alike. Some may meet your needs better than others; some may be safer than others. There is no guarantee, for example, that there will not be abusers attending a meeting. Not all of these organizations understand the role of sexual child abuse in addictive behaviors, or what is necessary for recovery from the effects of sexual abuse.

If you think that a twelve-step program might be useful to you, it is a good idea to attend several different meetings at a number of locations. I urge you to follow your own judgment, accepting what makes sense to you and rejecting the rest. Nothing in recovery is mandatory except taking the best possible care of yourself. The twelve-step organizations included in the following list are all based in North America. This list is not exhaustive; you may be able to get more local information and locate groups outside North America from your telephone directory or on the Internet.

The following descriptions of organizations are taken from their literature. I cannot guarantee their accuracy or whether the information is up-to-date.

ALCOHOLICS ANONYMOUS (AA)
475 Riverside Drive, 11th Floor, New York, NY 10115, USA
Phone: (212) 870-3400; Fax: (212) 870-3003; TDD: (212) 870-3199
Web site: www.alcoholics-anonymous.org/

". . . an international fellowship of men and women who share their experiences with each other, so that they may solve their common problem and help others to recover from alcoholism. The only requirement is a desire to stop drinking. There are no dues or fees for AA membership; the organization is self-supporting through member contributions. AA is not allied with any sect, denomination, politics, organization, or institution; does not want to engage in any controversy, and neither endorses nor opposes any causes. The primary purpose of members is to stay sober and help other alcoholics to achieve sobriety. AA was founded in 1935 and currently has over 2 million members."

AL-ANON FAMILY GROUP HEADQUARTERS (AL-ANON/ALATEEN)
1600 Corporate Landing Parkway, Virginia Beach, VA 23454-5617, USA
Phone: For free literature and information: (800) 356-9996
E-mail: WSO@al-anon.org
Web site: www.al-anon.alateen.org/

". . . Al-Anon was an adjunct of Alcoholics Anonymous until 1954, when it was incorporated as a separate, unaffiliated organization. Al-Anon is a self-help fellowship of men, women, and children whose lives have been affected by the compulsive drinking of a family member or friend. Alateen, a part of Al-Anon Family Groups, helps teenage sons and daughters of alcoholics to cope with problems in their homes. These groups provide direct services to individuals by giving comfort, hope, and friendship to the family and friends of alcoholics, by providing information on alcoholism and sharing experience in coping with the disease, and by providing the opportunity to learn to grow spiritually. . . ."

CO-DEPENDENTS ANONYMOUS (CoDA)
Co-Dependents Anonymous World Service, Inc.
PO Box 7051, Thomaston, GA 30286-0025, USA
Phone: (706) 648-6868; Fax: (706) 647-1755
E-mail: coda.usa.nsc.outreach@usa.net or wscoda@alltel.net
Web site: www.codependents.org/ or www.codaws.org

". . . established in 1986 as a self-help recovery program for individuals coping with co-dependency. Co-dependency is a compulsive, self-destructive behavior, usually caused by dysfunctional family systems. The disorder is characterized by an inability to maintain functional relationships, and may include a history of addiction. CoDA is a nonprofessional organization, and is not allied with any sect, denomination, politics, organization or institution. Its group activities are patterned after twelve-step recovery programs. Group meetings have been established in forty-nine states and ten countries, and an International Service Conference is held annually in Phoenix."

FAMILIES ANONYMOUS (FA)
PO Box 3475, Culver City, CA 90231-3475, USA
Phone: (800) 736-9805 or (310) 313-5800; Fax: (310) 313-6841
Web site: www.familiesanonymous.org/

". . . founded in 1971 as a mutual support group for families of people involved in drug abuse and related behavioral problems. Group meetings and discussions are modeled on the Twelve Steps of Alcoholics Anonymous and focus on providing emotional support for the member rather than changing the behavior of the substance abuser. There are no fees or dues for group membership. Assistance is offered to people forming new FA groups."

GAMBLERS ANONYMOUS

Information Services Offices

PO Box 17173, Los Angeles, CA 90017, USA

Phone: (213) 386-8789

E-mail: isomain@gamblersanonymous.org

Web site: www.gamblersanonymous.org/

"Gamblers Anonymous, formed in 1957, is a fellowship of men and women who share their experiences, strengths, and hopes with each other in order to solve their common problem and to help others recover from a compulsive gambling problem. The Twelve Steps used in Alcoholics Anonymous are modified for use in this self-help fellowship. A booklet presenting the basic program is available, and requesters will be referred to the local group nearest them."

NARCOTICS ANONYMOUS (NA)

Public Information Coordinator, World Services Office, Inc.

PO Box 9999, Van Nuys, CA 91409, USA

Phone: (818) 773-9999; Fax: (818) 700-0700

E-mail: info@na.org

Web site: www.na.org/

". . . a nonprofit, international organization founded in 1953; it was created to help people of all ages, races, religious perspectives, occupations, and lifestyles stop using drugs. There are twenty-two thousand NA groups in over fifty countries . . . and more than two thousand meetings are held in correctional and treatment facilities . . . provides and distributes complimentary group starter kits and NA literature upon request . . . NA approaches the twelve-step recovery program by focusing on the disease of addiction itself, and not a particular drug. There are no dues or fees for NA services."

OVEREATERS ANONYMOUS (OA)

World Service Office

PO Box 44020, Rio Rancho, NM 87174-4020, USA

Web site: www.onlinerecovery.org/ed/oa/

". . . founded in 1960, is a self-help group of compulsive overeaters, which promotes a lifetime program of action to relieve the obsession of eating compulsively. Compulsive overeating is viewed as a progressive disease, which can be controlled by a twelve-step recovery program adapted from Alcoholics Anonymous. OA provides pamphlets on its program and holds regular local group meetings worldwide, which are open to all compulsive overeaters."

PARENTS ANONYMOUS® INC.
675 W. Foothill Blvd., Suite 220, Claremont, CA 91711, USA
Phone: (909) 621-6184; Fax: (909) 625-6304
E-mail: parentsanonymous@parentsanonymous.org
Web site: www.parentsanonymous.org/index.htm

SECULAR ORGANIZATIONS FOR SOBRIETY (SOS)
SOS Clearinghouse, 4773 Hollywood Blvd., Hollywood, CA 90027, USA
Phone: (323) 666-4295
E-mail: SOS@CFIWest.org
Web site: www.secularsobriety.org/
"Also known as Save Our Selves. Dedicated to providing a path to sobriety, an alternative to those paths depending upon supernatural or religious beliefs. We respect diversity, welcome healthy skepticism, and encourage rational thinking as well as the expression of feelings. We choose to make our Sobriety a separate issue from our religion. We are not against popular twelve-step programs which work well for many people, but we find that they do not work for us. Research has shown that both approaches are equally effective. SOS is a network of independent local meetings in the USA and in many countries of Europe. Their work is coordinated by the SOS Clearinghouse, which publishes a quarterly Newsletter."

SEX AND LOVE ADDICTS ANONYMOUS (SLAA)
The Augustine Fellowship, PO Box 338, Norwood, MA, 02062-0338, USA
Phone: (781) 255-8825
E-mail: General-Questions@slaafws.org or slaaoffice@slaafws.org
Web site: www.slaafws.org/
"Please leave a message on our machine or send us an e-mail and we will respond within two to four days. We apologize for any inconvenience this may cause, but we will do what we can to assist as soon as possible."

Mental Health Consumers

NATIONAL MENTAL HEALTH CONSUMERS' SELF-HELP CLEARINGHOUSE
1211 Chestnut Street, Suite 1207, Philadelphia, PA 19107, USA
Phone: (800) 553-4539; Fax: (215) 636-6312
E-mail: info@mhselfhelp.org
Web site: www.mhselfhelp.org

"The Clearinghouse is committed to helping mental health consumers improve their lives through self-help and advocacy. With our publications, library materials, and personal consultations, we help people establish and develop self-help groups and projects, advocate for mental health systems change, and fight the stigma that society places on mental illness."

Other Organizations

KIRKRIDGE RETREAT & STUDY CENTER
2495 Fox Gap Road, Bangor, PA 18013, USA
Phone: (610) 588-1793; Fax: (610) 588-8510
E-mail: kirkridge@fast.net
Web site: www.kirkridge.org/
Director: Rev. Cynthia Crowner

"... has welcomed seekers of personal and social transformation since 1942." A retreat and study center in a beautiful forested ridgetop location, with a supportive, respectful staff.

PROVIDES

Workshops and retreats on a variety of topics, many with a nondenominational spiritual focus, individual retreats and other events. (For many years we have held our annual male survivor recovery weekend at Kirkridge.)

MEN'S RESOURCE CENTER OF WESTERN MASSACHUSETTS (MRC)
236 No. Pleasant Street, Amherst, MA 01002, USA
Phone: (413) 253-9887; Fax: (413) 253-4801
E-mail: mrc@mensresourcecenter.org
Web site: www.mensresourcecenter.org
Executive Director: Steven Botkin; Associate Director: Rob Okun

"The mission of the Men's Resource Center of Western Massachusetts is to support men, challenge men's violence, and develop men's leadership in ending oppression to ourselves, our families, and our communities. Our programs support men to overcome the damaging effects of rigid and stereotyped masculinity, and simultaneously confront men's patterns of personal and societal violence and abuse toward women, children, and other men."

PROVIDES

Support group programs and weekly drop-in support groups, including a group for male survivors of childhood abuse and neglect, workshops and trainings, *Voice Mail* magazine, Web site links to other men's resources. (**Note:** Men's Resource Centers and similar organizations exist in other states, including California, Florida, Maine, Minnesota, New Mexico, North Carolina, Ohio, Oregon, Vermont, and Washington. The MRC of Western Massachusetts is one of the finest examples of these organizations. You can locate others through links on their Web site or by conducting an Internet search.)

NATIONAL ASSOCIATION FOR CHILDREN OF ALCOHOLICS (NACoA)

11426 Rockville Pike, Suite 100, Rockville, Maryland 20852, USA
Phone: (888) 55-4COAS or (301) 468-0985; Fax: (301) 468-0987
E-mail: NACoA@nacoa.org
Web site: www.nacoa.org/

"NACoA is the national nonprofit membership organization working on behalf of children of alcohol- and drug-dependent parents. Our mission is to advocate for all children and families affected by alcoholism and other drug dependencies. In a word, we help kids hurt by parental alcohol and drug use. We work to raise public awareness, provide leadership in public policy at the national, state, and local levels, advocate for appropriate, effective and accessible education and prevention services, and facilitate and advance professional knowledge and understanding—affiliate organizations throughout the country and Great Britain."

PROVIDES

Bimonthly newsletter, videos, booklets, posters, and other educational materials, Web site, information packets sent to all who ask, and a toll-free phone available to all.

THE NATIONAL CLEARINGHOUSE FOR ALCOHOL & DRUG INFORMATION (NCADI)

PO Box 2345, Rockville, MD 20847-2345, USA

Phone: (800) 729-6686 or (301) 468-2600; Hablamos Español: (877) 767-8432; TDD: (800) 487-4889; Fax: (301) 468-6433

E-mail: info@health.org

Web site: www.health.org/

"The world's largest resource for current information and materials concerning substance abuse."

PROVIDES

An information services staff (English, Spanish, TDD capability) equipped to respond to the public's alcohol, tobacco, and drug (ATD) inquiries; free or low-cost ATD materials, including fact sheets, brochures, pamphlets, monographs, posters, and videotapes from an inventory of over one thousand items; culturally diverse prevention, intervention, and treatment resources tailored for use by parents, teachers, youth, communities and prevention/treatment professionals; customized searches in the form of annotated bibliographies from alcohol and drug databases; access to the Prevention Materials Database (PMD) including over eight thousand prevention-related materials and the Treatment Resources Database, available to the public in electronic form; and rapid dissemination of federal grant announcements for ATD prevention, treatment, and research funding opportunities.

NATIONAL COUNCIL ON SEXUAL ADDICTION AND COMPULSIVITY (NCSAC)

National Office, PO Box 725544, Atlanta, GA 31139, USA

Phone: (770) 541-9912

E-mail: ncsac@mindspring.com

Web site: www.ncsac.org/

"NCSAC is a private, nonprofit organization dedicated to the promotion of public and professional recognition, awareness and understanding of Sexual Addiction, Sexual Compulsivity, and Sexual Offending."

PROVIDES

Access to education, information and referral resources encouraging wellness for all those we serve.

THE NATIONAL MEN'S RESOURCE CENTER
PO Box 1080, Brookings, OR 97415-0024, USA
E-mail: Menstuff@aol.com
Web site: www.menstuff.org
Executive Director: Gordon Clay
      "Working since 1982 to end men's isolation."

BOOKS, ARTICLES, AND PAMPHLETS

This partially annotated bibliography lists writings of interest and help to adult male survivors. I have included works written for male survivors, and some for female survivors (these are seldom foreign to the concerns of the men). Also included are a few books not specifically concerned with sexual child abuse, but which have been helpful to many survivors in their recovery. I have not included much research-oriented, academic, or professional material, as this book is primarily for nonprofessionals. Readers who wish to investigate the professional literature may refer to my longer, more extensive bibliography, which includes both professional and mass-market books. It is posted on my Web site and updated periodically: **www.victimsnolonger.org.**

On the Topic of Sexual Child Abuse

Adams, Kenneth M. *Silently Seduced: When Parents Make Their Children Partners—Understanding Covert Incest.* Deerfield Beach, FL: Health Communications, 1991.

Bass, Ellen, and Laura Davis. *The Courage to Heal.* New York: HarperCollins Publishers, 1988. The original "bible" for women survivors; it also provided help and guidance to many men.

Bear, Euan, with Peter T. Dimock. *Adults Molested as Children.* Orwell, VT: Safer Society, 1988. A simple, straightforward manual written by a female survivor to help other survivors understand "what they are going through now as a result of what they went through then."

Berry, Jason. *Lead Us Not into Temptation: Catholic Priests and the Sexual Abuse of Children.* New York: Doubleday, 1992.

Cassese, James (ed.). *Gay Men and Childhood Sexual Trauma: Integrating the Shattered Self.* Binghamton, NY: Harrington Park Press, 2000.

Creswell, Mark. *Male Survivors: A Self-Help Pack.* Sheffield, U.K.: Survivors Sheffield, 1996. Revised June 2000 by Ian Warwick and Andy Bateman. Available from PO Box 142, Sheffield, S1 3HG, United Kingdom.

Davis, Laura. *Allies in Healing.* New York: HarperCollins Publishers, 1991. Very helpful to caring partners, family, and friends of survivors.

————. *The Courage to Heal Workbook.* New York: HarperCollins, 1990. Combining checklists and open-ended questions, this innovative and in-depth workbook is designed for use by women and men, individually or as a basis for work in therapy or groups.

Fredrickson, Renee. *Repressed Memories: A Journey to Recovery from Sexual Abuse.* New York: Simon & Schuster, 1992. An influential work that continues to be attacked by many who deny the validity of survivors' memories.

Gil, Eliana. *United We Stand: A Book for People with Multiple Personalities.* Walnut Creek, CA: Launch, 1990.

————. *Outgrowing the Pain.* Walnut Creek, CA: Launch, 1983. A simple, easy-to-read book about recovering from all types of abuse.

Graber, Ken. *Ghosts in the Bedroom: A Guide for Partners of Incest Survivors.* Deerfield Beach, FL: Health Communications, 1991. Many survivors and their partners find this book a great help to their relationship.

Henton, Darcy, with David McCann. *Boys Don't Cry.* Toronto: McClelland & Stewart, 1995.

Herman, Judith Lewis. *Trauma and Recovery.* New York: Basic Books, 1992. Required reading for professionals who work with survivors.

Hunter, Mic. *Abused Boys.* Lexington, MA: Lexington Books, 1989. In this and other books, Mic Hunter educates professionals about male victimization.

Investigative Staff of *The Boston Globe. Betrayal: The Crisis in the Catholic Church.* Boston: Little, Brown, 2002. "... a terrible, horrible, awful book. Thank God for it."   Fr. Andrew M. Greeley.

Love, Patricia, with J. Robinson. *The Emotional Incest Syndrome.* New York: Bantam, 1990.

Lew, Mike. *Leaping upon the Mountains: Men Proclaiming Victory over Sexual Child Abuse.* Boston: Small Wonder Books, and Berkeley, CA: North Atlantic Books, 1999. Male survivors themselves identify what was most important during various stages of their recovery. Contains contributions from hundreds of men of all ages and backgrounds throughout the United States and forty-five other countries.

Maltz, Wendy. *The Sexual Healing Journey.* New York: HarperCollins Publishers, 1991. A very accessible, nuts-and-bolts book about repairing sexuality damaged by sexual abuse.

Mathews, Frederick. *The Invisible Boy: Revisioning the Victimization of Male Children & Teens.* Online book, 1996: www.aest.org.uk/survivors/male/ibc.html

Merseyside Survivors. *2000 Fire in Ice: A Self-Help Pack.* A clear, intelligent, and beautifully designed booklet written by male survivors for male survivors. For more information, see Fire in Ice listing in Organizations section.

Miletski, Hani. *Mother-Son Incest: The Unthinkable Broken Taboo.* Brandon, VT: Safer Society Press, 1995.

Miller, Alice. **Note:** Dr. Miller has long been one of the original and finest champions of survivors. *Breaking Down the Walls of Silence: To Join the Waiting Child.* London: Virago Press, 1991.

―――. *Banished Knowledge: Facing Childhood Injuries.* New York: Anchor, 1991.

―――. *Thou Shalt Not Be Aware.* New York: New American Library, 1984. Reassessment of Freud's Oedipal Theory emphasizing the reality of sexual child abuse.

————. *For Your Own Good.* New York: Farrar, Straus, 1983.

————. *The Drama of the Gifted Child.* New York: Basic Books, 1981. Originally published as *Prisoners of Childhood.*

Mura, David. *A Male Grief: Notes on Pornography and Addiction.* Minneapolis: Milkweed Editions (PO Box 3226, Minneapolis, MN 55403), 1987. An important, insightful, and moving essay connecting sexual child abuse with adult addiction to pornography. Currently out of print, but worth the effort to locate an old copy.

Sanders, Timothy. *Male Survivors: 12-Step Recovery Program for the Survivors of Childhood Sexual Abuse.* Watsonville, CA: The Crossing Press, 1991. Personal experience integrating twelve-step principles and practice with recovery from sexual child abuse.

Spiegel, Josef. *Sexual Abuse of Males.* New York: Taylor & Francis Books, 2003. This highly technical book was written for professionals, but it is so well researched that I had to include it on this list.

Thomas, T. *Closer to Free.* Tucson, AZ: Timothy Fleming, 1996.

————. *Surviving with Serenity.* Deerfield Beach, FL: Health Communications, 1990.

————. *Men Surviving Incest.* Walnut Creek, CA: Launch, 1989.

Vachss, Andrew. *Another Chance to Get It Right: A Children's Book for Adults.* Milwaukie, OR: Dark Horse Publishing, 1993. This book may be the easiest introduction to the extraordinary, often painful works of Andrew Vachss. I advise you not to read them when you are feeling shaky or isolated.

Vermilyea, Elizabeth G. *Growing Beyond Survival: A Traumatic Stress Toolbox.* Lutherville, MD: The Sidran Press, 2000.

Related Topics of Interest to Survivors

Adams, Kathleen. *The Way of the Journal.* Lutherville, MD: The Sidran Press, 1998.

Black, Claudia. *Double Duty: Dual Dynamics Within the Chemically Dependent Home.* New York: Ballantine, 1990. Claudia Black has written many excellent books for adult children of dysfunctional families.

———. *"It Will Never Happen to Me!"* New York: Ballantine, 1981. Helpful insight for adult children of alcoholics and other dysfunctional families.

Bradshaw, John. *Healing the Shame That Binds You.* Pompano Beach, FL: Health Communications, 1988.

Burns, David. *Feeling Good.* New York: New American Library, 1980. In a practical, down-to-earth style, Burns presents a program for overcoming depression and other life problems.

Carnes, Patrick. *Don't Call It Love: Recovery from Sexual Addiction.* New York: Bantam, 1991.

Fossum, Merle. *Facing Shame: Families in Recovery.* New York: W. W. Norton, 1986.

Glenmullen, Joseph. *The Pornographer's Grief and Other Tales of Human Sexuality.* New York: Harper Perennial, 1993.

Saint-Exupéry, Antoine de. *The Little Prince.* (Translation of *Le Petit Prince*). New York: Harcourt Brace Jovanovich, 1943. The original "inner child" story. If you've read it before, try reading it again in the light of your current understanding. If you haven't read it, you're in for a treat. **Note:** Try to find an old copy. The newest translation robs the book of much of its poetry.

Stoltenberg, John. *The End of Manhood: A Book for Men of Conscience.* New York: Dutton, 1993. "Bingo! He hits it right on the head!" —a male survivor.

Wolfe, Daniel. *Men Like Us: The GMHC Complete Guide to Gay Men's Sexual, Physical and Emotional Well-being.* New York: Ballantine, 2000.

Memoirs and Statements by Male Survivors

Male survivors are telling their stories; more and more are being published. Shining through all of them are courage, strength, resilience, and humanity. Here are some excellent examples. Read them for yourself. Perhaps they will inspire you to tell (or write) your own story.

Note: The two John Andrewses cited below are different individuals, one Australian and the other Canadian.

Andrews, John. *Beyond Closed Doors: Growing Beyond an Abused Childhood.* Melbourne, Australia: David Lovell, 1994.

Andrews, John. *Not Like Dad: One Man's Story of Recovery from Incest.* Toronto: Macmillan Canada, 1994. A courageous personal history by a Canadian survivor.

Baker, Janet, and Trish Berry. *It Happened to Us: Men Talk About Child Sexual Abuse.* Melbourne, Australia: Victorian Government Department of Health & Community Services, 1995.

Berendzen, Richard, and L. Palmer. *Come Here: A Man Overcomes the Tragic Aftermath of Childhood Sexual Abuse.* New York: Villard Books, 1993.

de Milly, Walter. *In My Father's Arms: A True Story of Father-Son Incest.* Madison: University of Wisconsin Press, 1999.

D'Haene, Donald. *Father's Touch: A Survivor's Memoir of Sexual Abuse & Faith.* Salt Lake City: American Book Publishing, 2002.

Fahey, John. *How Bluegrass Music Destroyed My Life.* Chicago: Drag City Incorporated, 2000. The cover copy says that these stories by the renowned guitarist are fictional. You be the judge.

Hoffman, Richard. *Half the House: A Memoir.* New York: Harcourt, Brace, 1995. Every survivor, male and female, will benefit from reading this extraordinary work, as will anyone who cares about truth, honesty, the struggle for healing, reconciliation, and the ultimate triumph of right over wrong. For more of Richard's writings, see his Web site at www.abbington.com/hoffman/index.html.

Jones, Syl. *Rescuing Little Roundhead.* Minneapolis: Milkweed Editions, 1996. A moving memoir by an African-American survivor.

King, Neal. *Speaking Our Truth: Voices of Courage and Healing for Male Survivors of Childhood Sexual Abuse.* New York: HarperCollins Publishers, 1995. Further evidence of the courage and creativity of male survivors.

Krasnow, Michael. *My Life as a Male Anorexic.* New York: Haworth Press, 1996.

Kuhn, Jill A. (ed.). *In Cabin Six: An Anthology of Poetry by Male Survivors of Sexual Abuse.* Big Bear City, CA: Impact Publishing (PO Box 1648, Big Bear City, CA 92314), 2000. A powerful volume.

Mura, David. *Where the Body Meets Memory: An Odyssey of Race, Sexuality and Identity.* New York: Anchor, 1995.

Richeson, John W. *Without Fear: My Story,* 1999. (Self-published: PO Box 17589, San Diego, CA 92117.)

About Resources

There are many techniques and resources available to aid you in your recovery. It is important that each of us explores possibilities and chooses the combination that works best. Any activity has the potential to be helpful or harmful, healthful or abusive, liberating or addictive. Nobody has all the answers; no method is perfect. A central part of recovery is learning to trust your own judgment while respecting your ability (and your right) to seek out your own best allies and the most helpful solutions. Many others have walked this path before you. You don't have to go it alone, and you don't need to reinvent the wheel. But you do have to exercise judgment and care. Whether we are talking about therapy, religion, bodywork, sports, social activity, hobbies, career, community, family, friends, recovery programs, books, films, local or national organizations, tailor the available resources to your particular needs. It may be more difficult than accepting someone else's package, but the results will be far more satisfying.

A FINAL WORD

This section is very brief and contains nothing new. I've said it all in other parts of the book—but some things bear repeating.

I want to send you a personal message. I want you to complete this book hearing reassurance, encouragement, admiration, and love. You have embarked on a voyage across troubled waters to the other side of your hurt. Your pain will end and you will heal. Recovery is real.

You once had to do it alone, but things are different now. Every day more men and women join you as friends, helpers, and allies. Support, resources, and hope for the future are genuine; they are available to you. Take full advantage of them. You, in the full richness of your humanity, deserve all the abundance that life has to offer. Continue to cherish yourself.

As you, and your brother and sister survivors, continue to heal the wounds of the past, as you maintain your progress toward full recovery of your power and humanity, and as you confront your own abuse history and stand up against abuse everywhere—you are changing the world. I wish you every success.

My love to you.

INDEX

Thom Harrigan

About the Author

MIKE LEW, M.ED., a psychotherapist, trained cultural anthropologist, and group leader, is codirector of The Next Step Counseling and Training Center in Brookline, Massachusetts. A leading expert on recovery from sexual child abuse, particularly issues surrounding adult male survivors, he frequently lectures and provides professional training and workshops for survivors worldwide.